Learn the secrets of great bartending!

From Aalborg Sours to Zooms, from tropical punch to delicious low-calorie drinks, from the classic martini to the
consummate margarita, this is the one guide to keep bar-
side for mixing fabulous drinks that will get the festivities
started.

For parties large or small, reach for

THE COMPLETE
BARTENDER

The only guide you'll need!

THE
COMPLETE
BARTENDER

THE
COMPLETE
BARTENDER

REVISED EDITION

Robyn M. Feller with Laura Lifshitz

Produced by the Philip Lief Group, Inc.

BERKLEY BOOKS, NEW YORK

BERKLEY

An imprint of Penguin Random House LLC
375 Hudson Street, New York, New York 10014

THE COMPLETE BARTENDER

A Berkley Book / published by arrangement with the Philip Lief Group

ISBN: 978-0-425-27972-4

PUBLISHING HISTORY
First Berkley mass-market edition / December 1990
Berkley trade paperback edition / May 2003
Revised Berkley mass-market edition / May 2015

PRINTED IN THE UNITED STATES OF AMERICA

10 9 8 7 6 5 4 3 2 1

Cover photograph: Mojito image © Photographer's Choice/Getty Images.
Cover design by George Long.

Penguin
Random
House

CONTENTS

Introduction 1

Stocking Your Bar 3

Barware and Glassware 8

Measure for Measure 12

Garnishes 15

Bartenders' Secrets 18

On Being a Responsible Bartender 23

Party Planning 26

Theme Parties 30

Holiday Celebrations 36

Frozen Blender Drinks 38

The Perfect Punch 43

Low-Calorie Drinks 46

Beer 48

Wine 56

Aperitifs 67

After-Dinner Drinks 70

Drink Recipes 75

Nonalcoholic Drink Recipes 449

Index by Ingredients 465
Index by Type 000
Index of Low-Calorie Drinks 000
Glossary 521

THE
COMPLETE
BARTENDER

INTRODUCTION

B EING a skinny, blond lightweight, the first time I went to a bar, I had to sneak in illegally. It was a bar in the West Village, and I felt so cool—as if I had pulled a prank on the entire universe. I got kicked out for making out loudly with a patron rather than being an utter drunk, so I guess I get a bonus point for being a flirt and not an alcoholic.

My intimate relationship with liquor began in the city, despite the fact that I was raised in the Garden State. I got to know some of the newest and best drinks by hanging in the *bright lights, big city*, but it wasn't until my stint at bartending school that I really learned the basics of the art heretofore known as mixology. As an actress and stand-up comic, I figured bartending would be a great way to make money at night and maybe even pick up a hot guy or two. My Jewish dad lovingly handed me the bread to pay for the class, but once I realized I might attract more loons behind the bar than I already did in front of the bar, I decided to keep my love for liquor a "nonoccupational" pursuit. Needless to say, my father was not too happy that his precious money had been squandered. To this day he still says, "Remember when you took that bartending course? You never even worked a day behind the bar."

Thanks, Pops.

During the class, I applied my perky overachieving attitude to mixing drinks, just like I do with everything else in life.

"The drink has to be perfect. How do I know exactly how

much to use?" I asked my instructor, a handsome dark-skinned hipster who wasn't even trying to be a hipster.

He pushed his dark Buddy Holly glasses back up his nose and said, "There are no concrete rules in love . . . or alcohol. Just play around until it tastes right. Put your Type-A attitude aside."

I was skeptical of his laissez-faire outlook, but I went with it, and so far, no one's been hurt. And that's just the point of this book. Except, perhaps, for hard-core bartending jobs at pricey restaurants, mixology is at best an inexact science. If it had to be precise, very few people would drink, and the world would be a miserable place (and perhaps less populated). There are always going to be differences in the way two people mix the same drink. Some go heavy on the alcohol, some go light. Some change the ingredients, some change the proportions. Lots of ice versus one or two cubes. You say old-fashioned, I say lowball. The goal is to make a drink that tastes good to you—and to your guests.

Get intimate with your liquor supply. Experiment with what you have using the recipes in this book, or try something new. The recipes—some new, some old, some adapted for today's tastes—are mere guidelines. The step-by-step instructions are intended to make mixing a drink as easy as possible for you.

Because all drink and no play makes for a very unintelligible and dull boy or girl, I've filled this book with party-planning tips and ideas for creating the perfect home bar: the drinks, the ambience, and the attitude that will enable you to be a master mixologist and the perfect host.

And don't forget: Try not to overindulge. While I love a good party as much as the next gal, I'm more concerned about your health, your personal welfare, and the well-being of your friends. Don't let your friends drink and drive. And if health is your main concern when it comes to libations, never fear. In the age of Zumba and the juice cleanse, plenty of folks are drinking more moderately in the interest of fitness. This book offers plenty of ideas for lighter and nonalcoholic drinks that won't make you regain the freshman fifteen.

Bartending can be lots of fun if you follow your instincts, do what you like, and provide your guests with a safe good time. Relax and enjoy yourself, and you'll always be the life of the party.

Cheers!

STOCKING YOUR BAR

THE home bar should reflect your personal taste and reveal a little about what makes you you. Not everyone needs to stock every exotic liquor on the market just to impress a few visitors. If all you and your friends ever drink is beer, wine and straight vodka, well then, there's your shopping list, my friend. But home bars can grow. Maybe you'll start out with three items and gradually add a few different liquors and a flavorful liqueur or two. Then one day you'll be browsing in a liquor store and you'll pick up a small bottle of whatever it is you've been meaning to try—and so grows your home bar.

Your initial purchases, then, should be based on what you'll use most and what you and your friends and family like. If you know what you want, you're better off buying in large quantities, since larger bottles are generally less expensive per unit than smaller bottles. But there's no need to go overboard when making your initial purchases; buy reasonable amounts, unless, of course, you are sure that you like something in particular. Then, by all means buy as much as you want, especially if you find it for a good price.

While every bar will be slightly different, here are some basic guidelines. Outlined below is a suggested shopping list for a starter bar. Make any adjustments you like.

The Basic Home Bar Checklist

LIQUORS

1 bottle bourbon (750 ml)

1 bottle brandy (750 ml)

1 bottle Canadian whiskey (750 ml)

1 bottle dry gin (1¾ liters)

1 bottle rum (1¾ liters)

1 bottle Scotch whiskey (750 ml)

1 bottle tequila (1¾ liters)

1 bottle vodka (1¾ liters)

Rocks

(Tall) Collins

LIQUEURS

small bottles of the following:

triple sec	amaretto
crème de menthe	Drambuie
crème de cacao	Bénédictine
Kahlúa	Cointreau

Mixing Pitcher

WINE AND BEER

1 bottle dry vermouth (small)

1 bottle sweet vermouth (small)

2 six-packs beer (1 regular, 1 light)

2 bottles white wine

2 bottles red wine

1 bottle rosé wine (optional)

1 bottle champagne or sparkling wine

Long Bar Spoon

Goblet

The Home Bar of Champions

If the basic stocking suggestions don't appeal to you, perhaps you're looking for liquors that make a bolder statement. Well, take a look below. The spirits mentioned here are more daring—they go beyond the ordinary bartender's collection, allowing you to be a mixologist's mixologist. But you needn't invest in the entire list right off the bat. Go slowly. Find out what you like by tasting, whether at friends' homes or when you go out for a drink.

And if you like a drink you taste when you're out, ask the friendly bartender for his or her number—for the drink recipe, I mean.

LIQUOR

1 bottle brandy

1 bottle V.S.O.P. cognac

1 bottle dry English gin

Rocks (Stemmed)

1 bottle Irish whiskey

1 bottle dark rum (Jamaican)

1 bottle gold rum

1 bottle light rum

1 bottle blended Scotch whiskey

1 bottle Tennessee whiskey

Covered Cocktail Shaker

1 bottle gold tequila

1 bottle white tequila

1 or 2 bottles premium vodka (Russian or Scandinavian; store in your freezer)

LIQUEURS

small bottles of the following:

framboise, kirschwasser, plum brandy (slivovitz) or other flavored brandies of your choice crème de cassis, sambuca, Galliano, Frangelico, Kahlúa, peppermint schnapps, peach schnapps or any other of your favorite liqueurs, approximately five bottles in all

WINE

3 aperitif wines, such as Dubonnet, Lillet, Campari

1 bottle cream sherry

1 bottle port

1 bottle madeira

several bottles of your favorite white wines, including at least one table wine and one dessert wine

several bottles of your favorite red wines, ranging from dry to sweet

2 or 3 bottles champagne and/or sparkling wine

Mixers

Whether you stock a basic bar or one with all the extras, you will need to keep on hand a supply of the following:

Bloody Mary mix

club soda

coffee

cola

cranberry juice cocktail

cream (heavy and light)

cream of coconut

Falernum

ginger ale

grapefruit juice

grenadine

lemon juice

lime juice (Rose's is the most popular—it is not a substitute for fresh lime juice, however, since it contains a sugary syrup)

orange juice

orgeat (almond syrup)

passion fruit juice (or nectar)

piña colada mix

pineapple juice

seltzer

lemon-lime soda (such as Sprite or 7-Up)

sour mix

tomato juice

tonic water

water (distilled or spring)

Seltzer Bottle

Odds and Ends

No bar would be complete without the miscellaneous ingredients and garnishes that make mixed drinks truly special. Don't hesitate to include the following in your bar:

bitters (Angostura, orange)

cherries (maraschino)

cinnamon sticks

ice (three types: cubes, cracked and crushed)

lemons

limes

nutmeg

olives

onions (pickled pearl)

oranges

salt

sugar

Tabasco

Worcestershire sauce

Red Wine

Martini Pitcher

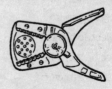

Lemon Squeezer

BARWARE AND GLASSWARE

KEEPING the right tools on hand can make bartending a lot easier. And as anyone who works with their hands can tell you, the right equipment can make the difference between a hassle and a pleasure. The lists below suggest some of the utensils and serving ware that will help make your bartending experience a success.

EQUIPMENT

bar spoon (long)

can/bottle opener

champagne bucket

cocktail napkins

corkscrew (winged version or waiter's)

covered cocktail shaker

cutting board

electric blender

ice bucket and tongs

juice extractor

lemon/lime squeezer

martini pitcher

Waiter's Corkscrew

Strainer

Juice Extractor

Wing Type Corkscrew

Can/Bottle Opener

measures/shot glasses (these vary in size—a jigger is 1½ ounces)

measuring cup

measuring spoons

mixing pitcher

muddler (wooden)

paring knife/bar knife

Bar Knife

picks (for garnishes)

punch bowl and glasses

saucers for salt and sugar (if you need to frost the rim of a glass)

seltzer bottle

shaker set: shaker (mixing) glass and metal tumbler

speed pourers (optional)

strainer

straws

Wooden Muddler

swizzle sticks

towels

Glassware

The trend these days is toward multipurpose glassware, so if you choose to have only one or two types, large wineglasses, rocks glasses and highball glasses are good choices. A description of the various types of glassware follows.

balloon (large wineglass) Ranges in size from 9 to 14 ounces.

beer goblet A stemmed balloon-type glass that holds about 12 ounces.

beer mug 12 to 16 ounces.

brandy snifter Best to choose those that hold 3, 6 or 12 ounces. They do come larger, though. For straight brandy.

champagne flute For champagne, champagne drinks or wine. Holds 4 to 6 ounces.

champagne saucer Also for champagne, but this type allows bubbles to escape more readily than the fluted or tulip type. Holds about 4 ounces.

champagne tulip For champagne, champagne drinks or wine. Holds 4 to 6 ounces.

cocktail This is your basic glass for drinks "straight up." Ranges in size from 3 ounces to 6 ounces. The large ones can be used for frozen drinks. The 4½-ounce size can be used for martinis, Manhattans and stingers. Sturdy, solid stems are best since you can hold on to the stem without warming the drink.

Collins Ranges in size from 10 to 14 ounces. Used for Collins drinks, fizzes, exotic drinks like Mai Tais, Singapore Slings, relatives of Long Island Ice Teas and other mixed drinks that require a bit more room than a highball. Some Collins glasses are frosted for effect.

double rocks Holds 14 to 16 ounces. For larger drinks "on the rocks." A gaining trend on the glassware scene.

goblet Approximately 12 ounces. Great for tropical drinks, blended drinks, frozen drinks. The 22-ounce hurricane glass can also be used for really mammoth drinks.

highball Ranges in size from 8 to 12 ounces. Good for most standard mixed drinks. Similar to a Collins glass, but shorter and wider.

martini Similar to a cocktail glass, but with a distinctive V shape. Nothing beats a martini in an actual martini glass. About 4 ounces.

hot drink mug 10 to 12 ounces. Used for hot drinks, hot coffee drinks, cappuccinos, Irish coffee, etc.

parfait A specialty glass, approximately 7½ ounces; can be used for drinks containing ice cream and/or fruit.

pilsner 10 to 16 ounces. Used for beer.

pony (cordial) Up to 2 ounces. Can be used for liqueurs, brandy and small pousse-cafés.

pousse-café A specialty glass for drinks that are "floated," such as Rainbow Pousse-Café or Traffic Light.

red wine Holds 6 to 11 ounces. Is more rounded than a white wine glass, in order to direct the bouquet of red wine to the drinker's nose.

rocks (stemmed or not stemmed) Ranges in size from 6 to 8 ounces. Also called "lowball" or "old-fashioned." Used for drinks served "on the rocks." If you don't own shot glasses, you can use these to serve straight shots of liquor or liqueur.

sherry Holds about 3 ounces. Used for cordials and liqueurs. You can substitute the popular Spanish *copita*.

shot Ranges from a fraction of an ounce to 2 ounces (long shot). The standard shot measure these days is 1½ ounces (also called a jigger). Can hold one liquor or can be used for mixed shooters. It also comes in a two-sided metal measuring version, where one side holds 1 ounce and the other side holds 1½ ounces.

sour Also called a delmonico glass or a whiskey sour glass. Holds 5 or 6 ounces. Known for its use with sours of all kinds.

white wine Can also hold from 6 to 11 ounces, although generally a bit smaller than red wine glasses.

MEASURE FOR
MEASURE

S OMEHOW, the ways alcoholic beverages are measured, in both the bottle and the mixing glass, have always managed to confuse most people. Just what *is* a fifth? Which holds more—a pony or a jigger? The charts below should help clear things up.

Bottle Sizes

Remember when you rolled your eyes in math class, wondering why you should bother learning the metric system? Well, your teachers must have known something, because on December 31, 1979, the sizing of liquor bottles in America was converted to metrics. I always knew I should have been nicer to my math teacher!

Spirits

OLD NAME	OLD SIZE (fl. oz.)	NEW SIZE (fl. oz.)	NEW SIZE (metric)
miniature	1.6	1.7	50 ml

OLD NAME	OLD SIZE (fl. oz.)	NEW SIZE (fl. oz.)	NEW SIZE (metric)
half pint	8.0	6.8	200 ml
pint	16.0	16.9	500 ml
fifth	25.6	25.4	750 ml
quart	32.0	33.8	1 liter
half gallon	64.0	59.2	1.75 l

Wines

OLD NAME	NEW SIZE (fl. oz.)	NEW SIZE (metric)
split	6.3	187 ml
tenth	12.7	375 ml
fifth	25.4	750 ml
quart	33.8	1 liter
magnum	50.7	1.5 l
double magnum	101.4	3 l

Standard Bar Measurements

No, bar measurements don't have anything to do with metrics, but they are confusing enough nonetheless. Keep this chart handy, though, and you'll do all right.

1 teaspoon (barspoon) . . . . ⅛ ounce
1 tablespoon . . . . ⅜ ounce
1 pony . . . . .1 ounce
1 jigger. . . . . 1½ ounces
1 wineglass . . . . 4 ounces

1 split . . . . 6 ounces
1 cup . . . . 8 ounces
1 dash . . . . $\frac{1}{32}$ ounces

Measuring Spoons

Measure/Shot Glass

Shot

GARNISHES

GARNISHES can add flavor or flair to any drink. Here are the garnishes you'll encounter most often, plus a few special ones.

Types of Garnishes

bitters The leading name in bitters is Angostura, but orange bitters are sometimes called for instead.

celery A Bloody Mary would be incomplete without celery. And, hey, it makes the drink healthy—right?

cherries Maraschino cherries are most often used. They usually are red, but green ones exist, too. Maraschino cherries make great garnishes for tropical drinks and many sours, as well as the standard Manhattan.

cinnamon sticks You'll get the most use out of extra-long cinnamon sticks. They can be used to stir and flavor certain hot drinks.

cucumber Cucumber slices are popular garnishes for drinks with Pimm's in them.

lemons Lemons, one of the most essential garnishes, can be cut into wedges, slices or wheels, and the rinds can be used to make twists. Lemons are especially popular for drinks with club soda in them. Twists are becoming more and more popular as garnishes for martinis.

limes Limes, too, can be cut into wedges, slices, wheels or twists. Limes are especially popular for drinks with tonic water in them.

mint leaves An absolute must for mint juleps.

nutmeg A nice alternative to cinnamon, nutmeg can be sprinkled on hot drinks or certain cream drinks, especially Alexanders.

olives The most popular olives for drinks are small green pitted olives, although other types may be used. This is the quintessential martini garnish. Store in the refrigerator, tightly covered.

onions Pearl onions are used in Gibsons (martinis with pearl onion garnish).

oranges Orange slices are not only decorative but provide a nice flavor to tropical or exotic drinks, sours or even vodka on the rocks.

pineapples Spears, slices or chunks—pineapple can add excitement to many tropical drinks, such as the famous piña colada.

salt Salt is an essential part of a Margarita or a Salty Dog. It also adds zip to Bloody Mary mix. (Salt substitutes may be used for those who are concerned with their salt intake.) A coarse salt works best for frosting glasses.

sugar Superfine granulated sugar is good for making simple sugar syrup, as well as for frosting glasses.

Cutting and Preparing Garnishes

There are several different ways to cut basic fruit garnishes—wedges, slices, wheels and twists. (*Note:* To cut fruit, use a good paring knife and a cutting board.)

To cut lemon or lime wedges, cut off the ends of the fruit

and discard. Slice the fruit lengthwise. Take one of the lemon or lime halves and cut that lengthwise as well. Holding the two sections together, cut crosswise so that each cut produces two wedges. Repeat with the other half.

To cut lemon, lime or orange slices, cut off the ends of the fruit and discard. Slice the fruit lengthwise. Take one of the fruit halves and cut across so that each cut produces one slice. Repeat with other half of lemon or lime.

To make fruit "wheels" that can be fitted onto the rim of a glass, take a lemon, lime or orange and cut off the ends. Make a cut approximately ¼ inch deep along the length of the fruit. Slice the fruit perpendicular to the original cut. These "wheels" can be arranged on the rim of the glass, which will fit inside the small cut in the garnish.

An easy method of making fruit peel twists is to stand the fruit on its end (after cutting off the ends) and cut from top to bottom, staying close to the meat of the fruit. Each cut can be approximately ½ inch wide. When you have finished, you may cut each of those slices into ¼-inch strips.

Olives and pearl onion garnishes may either be placed at the bottom of the drink "solo" or you can spear one to three olives or onions on a toothpick and place in the cocktail glass.

With cherry and orange garnishes, you can spear the cherry with a toothpick and then push the toothpick through the rind of the orange slice. Place on top of the drink.

Serving Garnishes

For the most part, lemons are used as garnishes when the mixer is club soda. Limes are used when the mixer is tonic water. Limes are also popular with drinks containing cranberry juice (and no other juice) and one liquor, such as a Cape Codder.

A "twist" usually refers to lemon peel only, but recently other fruit twists have become popular. To use a twist, actually twist the peel over the drink to release the essence of the fruit, rub it around the rim of the glass, then drop it into the drink.

BARTENDERS' SECRETS

TO CHOOSE GLASSWARE:
- Most bartenders these days use multipurpose glassware. The recipes in this book offer suggestions for the traditional types of glassware to use, but feel free to use whatever you have on hand, provided the drink fits inside. A large wineglass is your best bet if you can afford to buy only one type of glassware. Don't be too concerned if a drink doesn't completely fill the glass, either.

TO FROST A GLASS, THERE ARE TWO METHODS:
- With ice: Dip in water, place in freezer for a half hour. It will get a frosted white look. When removing, hold by the handle or stem so as not to melt the ice with your hand. With salt or sugar (for frosting the rim of a glass only): Moisten the rim of a chilled glass with a lemon or lime wedge. Dip rim into salt or sugar.

TO CHILL A GLASS:
- Refrigerate at least one hour before pouring a drink into it, or
- Fill glass with ice and cold water and let sit while you are preparing the drink. When you are ready to pour the drink, dump out the ice and water.

TO MAKE TWISTS AND FLAVOR RIMS:

- When a recipe calls for a fruit twist as a garnish, twist the peel above the drink and then drop into the drink.

- When using a fruit garnish, rub the rim of the glass with the fruit to leave the flavor on the glass.

TO MAKE DRINKS CALLING FOR ICE:

- Although many mixed-drink recipes instruct the bartender to fill a shaker glass with ice, you may use just ¼ cup, or 4 to 5 ice cubes if you prefer.

- Fresh ice is the key to a great drink. It's a good idea to use a fresh bag of ice when mixing drinks, since freezer odors can ruin the flavor of a drink.

TO MAKE DRINKS CALLING FOR SODA:

- To prevent soda from "exploding," especially if it is on the warm side, turn the cap very slowly—just a tiny bit at a time. Do this over or near a sink in case any soda sprays out.

TO MAKE DRINKS CALLING FOR WATER:

- Always use distilled water or springwater in drinks calling for water. Tap water can make a drink look clouded—and it doesn't taste as good.

TO MAKE DRINKS CALLING FOR PREMIUM VODKA:

- A great vodka will taste even better if it's exceptionally cold. Keep a bottle of the good stuff in your freezer.

TO MAKE DRINKS CALLING FOR EGG WHITES:

- For drink recipes calling for half an egg white, you might be better off doubling the recipe and making two drinks, since an egg white is very difficult to divide.

TO SHAKE A DRINK:

- Drinks containing numerous or difficult-to-mix ingredients are usually shaken. A shaker set is made up of a mixing glass and a metal tumbler. The mixing glass is sometimes referred to as a shaker glass.

- When using a shaker set, put any ice in the mixing glass, add the other ingredients, fit the metal container snugly over the glass and shake several times. Tip the set so the liquid ends up in the metal tumbler. Use a metal strainer, which fits into the top of the metal tumbler, to strain the liquid into a drink glass.

- Sometimes a *short shaker* can be used. This is a smaller metal cup that fits directly over the glass from which you will drink. If you don't have a shaker set, a glass with a cover that fits on top or the jug portion of an electric blender will do.

TO STIR A DRINK:
- Mixed drinks are usually stirred if they do not contain cream or sour mix, or if only one or two different ingredients are involved.

- Either half of the shaker set can be used as a mixing cup for drinks that require stirring rather than shaking.

- Don't overstir drinks made with sparkling beverages such as sodas or champagne. You don't want to spoil the fizz.

TO POUR A DRINK:
- If you're making a pitcherful of a mixed drink, set up all the glasses and pour a little into each glass, repeating the process until all are filled the same amount.

- To pour hot drinks into glasses, put a metal spoon in the glass before pouring. This absorbs the heat so the glass won't break.

TO POUR A POUSSE-CAFÉ:
- To float liqueurs or liquors, always put the heaviest one on the bottom of the glass, and float them in order of density and thickness. To do this, hold a bar spoon facedown in the glass and pour the liqueur over the back of the spoon—very slowly.

- If you have more time, pour the liqueurs into the glass and refrigerate for about an hour. In that time, the liqueurs will find their own place according to their weight, forming the layers you desire.

TO FLAME LIQUEURS:
- If it is possible to avoid this process, please do, because it can be dangerous. But if you insist, pre-warm the glass over a low flame, add most of the spirit and warm a teaspoon. Preheat just one teaspoonful of liquor over the flame and then set afire. Pour the flaming liquid into the glass with the remaining liquor—CAREFULLY!

TO OPEN A BOTTLE OF WINE:
- Using a sharp knife, remove the seal around the neck of the bottle. Peel the seal off so that the cork is exposed. Insert the tip of the corkscrew into the center of the cork and twist until it is as far down into the cork as possible. Slowly and steadily pull the cork out. It is common etiquette for the server to taste the wine before serving his or her guests.

TO OPEN A BOTTLE OF CHAMPAGNE OR SPARKLING WINE:
- Wrap a towel around a well-chilled bottle. With the mouth of the bottle pointed away from people and breakable objects, carefully remove the foil and undo the wire over the cork. Holding the cork in one hand and the rest of the bottle in the other, slowly turn the bottle until you feel the cork loosen. *Slowly* wiggle the cork out. When opening a bottle of sparkling wine or champagne, try for as little sound as possible. While the sound of a cork popping is festive, it allows precious bubbles to escape.

TO CLEAN GLASSWARE:
- No matter what type of glassware you use, make sure it's always sparkling clean. When you wash your glassware, air-dry it with the rim down on a towel to avoid spotting.

- You can also dry with one towel and polish with another.

- Wash glassware immediately after use.

- If you can't wash up right away, soak the glasses in warm, sudsy water so that the drink residues don't stick.

- Don't stack glasses one on top of the other; they might stick together. If they do get stuck together, put the bottom glass in very warm water and fill the top glass with cold water. The bottom glass will expand and the top one will contract until the difference frees them up.

SOUR MIX

12 oz. lemon juice (juice of approximately 6 lemons)
18 oz. distilled water
¼ cup refined sugar
1 egg white

1. Blend in a blender or shake in a large jar.
2. Refrigerate (it will keep for no more than 7 to 10 days).
3. Always blend or shake before use.

SUGAR SYRUP (SIMPLE SYRUP)

2 cups sugar
1 cup water

1. Dissolve sugar in water in a saucepan.
2. Simmer for approximately 10 minutes, stirring.
3. Cover and refrigerate until needed.

ON BEING A RESPONSIBLE BARTENDER

W E'VE all heard news stories about drinking and driving, and we've all read cautionary tales about the dangers of drinking to excess. Drinking and hosting parties are basic social activities, both time-honored and fun, but the very real fact remains that people get drunk from too much alcohol.

When you serve drinks to your guests, you are responsible for the amount of alcohol consumed under your supervision. In some states, in fact, hosts are considered legally liable for whatever may occur as a result of their guests' alcohol consumption. You owe it to your friends to make sure drinking remains a safe and enjoyable experience in your home.

Here are some basic tips to keep in mind so you and your guests can relax and have fun while drinking:

- Always keep a generous supply of nonalcoholic beverages available for guests who either are driving or choose not to drink alcohol. These can include soft drinks, mineral water, fruit and vegetable juices, alcohol-free punches, alcohol-free beers, tea or coffee. "Virgin" drinks are a festive option, especially if you are serving frozen blender drinks. See the chapter on nonalcoholic drinks for recipes you can use to make delicious alcohol-free concoctions.

- Don't make your drinks overly strong. Guests will down strong drinks just as quickly as normal-strength ones, but they will become intoxicated more quickly. Moderation is the key to an enjoyable drinking experience.

- Keep tabs on how much your guests have consumed. If someone seems to have had one too many, there is no shame in cutting him or her off. The only shame is in letting someone drink too much at the expense of his or her safety, the safety of others or a congenial atmosphere. If a guest does get drunk, make sure he or she does not drive home.

- If a guest requests a drink that is light on the booze, do oblige. You will not do him or her a favor by loading a drink with alcohol. Never pressure someone into having just one more. There's nothing that ruins the mood more quickly than a pushy bartender.

- Always serve food along with alcohol. Alcohol is absorbed into the bloodstream directly from the stomach, and good food provides a balance for drinkers, slowing the rate at which they drink and absorb alcohol. Serving food also adds to the air of hospitality, allowing everyone to have an even better time. Sandwiches, dairy products, meats and fish are good bets.

- Mixers can affect the rate of absorption of alcohol into the system, so take them into account when planning and hosting any get-together. Water dilutes alcohol and slows absorption; carbonated beverages tend to speed it up.

- Don't throw parties whose sole purpose is drinking. If your guests have something else to do, they are less likely to get drunk. Food, conversation, games, videos and business are possible diversions.

- If you have young children and keep a supply of liquor in your home, make sure it is always locked safely away.

- Be aware that as few as one or two drinks can affect the average adult's coordination and ability to think. Alcohol is an anesthetic which could prevent the drinker from realizing he or she is impaired.

Drinking and Driving

Of course, the safest rule for drinking and driving is: DON'T
DO IT. Encourage your guests to use designated drivers, who
don't drink at your party and who make sure everyone else gets
home safely. For any number of reasons, though, some of your
guests may be unable to use the designated driver system from
time to time. When you know this is the case, bear in mind the
following general guidelines for how long it takes people of
different sizes to metabolize the drinks they consume.

BODY WEIGHT	NUMBER OF DRINKS					
(IN POUNDS)	1	2	3	4	5	6
100–119	0 hours	3	6	10	13	16
120–139	0	2	5	8	10	12
140–159	0	2	4	6	8	10
160–179	0	1	3	5	7	9
180–199	0	0	2	4	6	7
200–219	0	0	2	3	5	6
Over 220	0	0	1	3	4	6

These figures will vary from individual to individual, but they
provide valuable insight into just how long it can take for someone to recover from the effects of drinking. If a guest has had a
few drinks, encourage him or her to wait before getting behind
the wheel. When in doubt, try an app for your smartphone to
help you and your guests track how much you've been drinking
and decide if you're safe to drive. Good options include Last
Call, DrinkTracker and AlcoDroid Alcohol Tracker. You could
save a life.

Highball   Double Rocks

PARTY PLANNING

WHEN planning your next bash, be it an intimate cocktail party, dinner for six or a full-fledged extravaganza, your first rule of thumb should be that the drinks you serve should reflect the tastes of your guests. If you'll be entertaining a room full of beer drinkers, then your planning will be no more complex than making sure you have enough to go around. If, on the other hand, your crowd has a penchant for exotic mixed drinks or interesting cocktails like a Rhubarb Fix (recipe page 350), you should make sure you have all the necessary ingredients on hand in large enough quantities.

Your guests will not expect you to have a bar as complete as the most upscale establishment in town, but they will expect you to keep up with demand. Too much instead of too little will help ensure the success of your party. Count on each of your guests consuming about three or four drinks over the course of a four-hour party. Have plenty of glassware on hand—at least two glasses per guest, although if it's possible to keep more handy you'll be even better off.

While all the recipes in this book call for a particular type of glass, there's really no need for you to run out and buy every type of glass there is, unless you're a bartending geek, in which case, buy them all. A basic highball glass and a rocks glass should serve nearly all your needs. Also, large wine-glasses can be used for virtually any type of drink. If you're looking for versatility, that's the one to keep around.

There's no way to overemphasize the great importance of

fresh ice for your party. Approximately 1½ to 2 pounds per guest should be adequate. Buy your ice in bags to ensure freshness. Who knows what is lurking in the depths of your home freezer? Freezer odors can spoil the taste of your drink masterpieces. Do you really want a Chocolate Martini (recipe p. 145) to taste like your leftover ziti dish? I think not.

Make sure to serve foods that will not spoil during the course of your party. Otherwise you'll have lots of leftovers and drunk, hungry guests. Remember, too, that the amount of liquor and the type of drinks you'll be serving will vary, depending on the time of day as well as the type of party. Daytime parties usually warrant a smaller liquor supply.

What to serve? Punch is inappropriate at cocktail parties, but it is perfect for a holiday party or other special occasion, such as an anniversary or bridal shower. Dinner parties are good times for trying out wines. Brunches are perfect for champagne drinks, such as Mimosas, Kir Royales or a Poinsettia. Also nice to serve are highball drinks with juice mixers. Cocktail parties are your chance to get a bit more creative. If your guests don't fall into a particular pattern of drinking (such as all vodka drinkers or all gin drinkers), then experiment with your newfound knowledge of mixing drinks.

Here's a list of basic supplies to help you plan a successful party. The good news is that even if you have leftovers, these liquors will store well in your bar and you'll be even better prepared the next time around. This list assumes that an average bottle (750 ml) of liquor will provide twenty drinks of 1½ ounces each (1½ ounces is the size of the average shot). When selecting your liquors, get the best you can afford. Premium brands make a party an even more special occasion, and your guests will enjoy them.

Cocktail Party Shopping List

LIQUOR, BEER AND WINE
> 2 bottles vodka (*Note:* This is conservative considering vodka's popularity. Absolut is the favorite brand, but any of the other premium vodkas will serve your purposes just as well)

1 bottle dry gin

1 bottle scotch

1 bottle American whiskey

1 bottle rum

1 bottle tequila

1 small bottle dry vermouth

1 small bottle sweet vermouth

2 bottles white wine

2 bottles red wine

1 or 2 cases of beer (it's nice to have a mix of regular beer and light beer)

3 or 4 bottles of your favorite liqueurs (Kahlúa, amaretto and crème de cacao are ingredients in many popular drinks)

MIXERS

5 or 6 bottles club soda

5 or 6 bottles tonic water

4 or 5 bottles cola

2 or 3 bottles diet soda

2 to 3 bottles 7-Up

3 bottles orange juice

2 bottles tomato juice

2 bottles grapefruit juice

Ice Bucket & Tongs

2 bottles pineapple juice

3 to 4 bottles cranberry juice cocktail

4 quarts sour mix (see recipe, p. 22)

1 bottle Rose's (or other brand) lime juice

4 bottles fresh springwater

GARNISHES
- 1 jar olives
- 1 jar maraschino cherries
- limes
- lemons
- oranges

SUPPLIES
- cocktail napkins
- straws
- stirrers/swizzle sticks

Cocktail Shaker Set

EQUIPMENT
- blender
- shaker set

THEME PARTIES

LOOKING to host a party with some real kick? Spiking the punch is one approach, but it's a lot more fun when you also add a dash of imagination. Instead of inviting everyone over for just another night of a few drinks, come up with a clever theme for your bash.

Sporting events, news events, television shows and popular movies; historical themes, nostalgia and international motifs— each can be incorporated into a great party. With a little planning, the right ambience and the appropriate beverage, you can celebrate almost any occasion in style. Here are a few suggestions to get you started.

A Kentucky Derby Party

Turn on the TV for the pre-race show, then cheer on your favorite horse while you and your guests enjoy pitchers of Mint Juleps (recipe p. 288). For authenticity, serve the drinks in silver tumblers, and offer your guests some Derby Pie.

Red roses, wall decorations modeled after the competitors' racing silks and broad-brimmed hats like those worn by Kentucky belles add festive touches. If you like, each guest can pick a horse and lay an informal bet to win a small prize— perhaps a bottle of fine Kentucky bourbon.

A Mexican Fiesta

Pull up some mariachi music on iTunes, put on a sombrero and serve up some margaritas (on the rocks, p. 278, or frozen, p. 195), Mexican beer (such as Tecate or Corona) with lime squeezed in for extra zip, tequila shots (Cuervo Gold is recommended) or Tequila Poppers (recipe p. 398).

When downing a shot of tequila, put some salt on the skin at the base of your thumb and forefinger, lick the salt off, do the shot, and finish off by sucking the juice of a wedge of lime.

It's not a fiesta without the food, so break out your appetites. Some food suggestions include nachos, chips and salsa or guacamole, and do-it-yourself tacos. Make it community style: Have your guests bring the various ingredients for tacos and set up a buffet. That will make prepping for the party easier on both you and your wallet.

Bachelorette Party

Did someone say, "Here comes the bride"? If your favorite gal pal is about to say "I do," you better be sure that the cocktails are numerous and the atmosphere is right. Before heading out for a night of dancing and debauchery, mix some cocktails at the maid of honor's place. Try a Shotgun Wedding Cocktail to stir the spirit of impulse love (recipe p. 373). If you're looking for a cocktail to remember, serve her a California Stripper (recipe p. 135). With cocktails like these, who needs the groom?

Dress to impress, and let all the ladies know that there's no time for FaceTiming boyfriends. Get on your slinkiest dresses and evening wear, and prepare to devour a Cosmopolitan (recipe p. 154).

James Bond Party

If the numbers 007 get your blood pumping, break out the tuxes and fancy dresses for a party of adventure and fine liquor. Keep the music dramatic or drop it to a soft classical piano as you swirl a White Russian (recipe p. 435) or a 007 if you like your drinks extra sweet (recipe p. 168).

Where's the party? James Bond wouldn't be seen in some dive bar, so rent out a boat if money's no object, or deck out your home in a casino theme. Turn your cell phones off and pretend you're in some exotic country and that one of you could be armed. Make sure to keep the drinks smooth: Bond was never bumpy with his small talk and he never spilled a drink—or lost his woman.

A Spanish *Tapas* Party

Get some pitchers of sangria (red or white, p. 361) flowing, and your guests will be doing the flamenco all evening. Flamenco music is, in fact, a great backdrop for a party. YouTube salsa and flamenco dance instruction, or even hire an on-site teacher.

Alongside the sangria, serve a variety of the Spanish finger foods known as *tapas*. These can range from simple olives to marinated seafood. You might also want to offer your guests a paella (made with rice, chicken and seafood), a Spanish omelette (egg, onion and potatoes) or any other typically Spanish food you enjoy.

Dorm Party Revisited

Do you miss your college days? Do you long for the easy fun and rowdiness of no-hassle dorm parties? Well, why not host your own grown-up dorm party? All you need is a keg of beer in the bathtub and a punch made with fruit juice, club soda, vodka, gin and rum (see the chapter on punch for ideas), served up by the bucket, of course. Decorations? Don't bother.

Snacks can include nuts, pretzels, potato chips and onion dip. And as for music, download Pandora or Spotify and make a playlist of all your favorites—whatever you were listening to and dancing to at your alma mater.

A Super Bowl Party

Whether your team's made it to post-season play or not—whether you even follow football or not—you can have a blast watching the most spectacular sporting event of the year. Put on your favorite team colors and invite your favorite couch potatoes over for a lazy afternoon of camaraderie.

Cases of beer are a must at any Super Bowl gathering, but old standards like rum and coke (Cuba Libre, recipe p. 158) and screwdrivers (recipe p. 367) add much-appreciated variety. To go with the drinks, hearty food like chili, cheese dogs and pizza hit the spot.

A Night in the Tropics

You can throw a tropical theme party any time of year, but during the dead of winter it's especially nice to host a little getaway, even if your wallet can't fund a real vacation. Tropical favorites such as Mai Tais (recipe p. 274), Zombies (recipe p. 447) and Piña Coladas (recipe p. 323) are always big hits. You can also try something a little different. Prepare Fogcutters (recipe p. 187), Blue Hawaiians (recipe p. 117) or Wombat shooters (recipe p. 439) for your guests and leave them with an evening they'll never forget.

Set out bowls and platters of fresh tropical fruits, as well as food on a Polynesian or Caribbean theme, anything from jerk chicken to roast pork. Reggae, hula or calypso music—or just your favorite party music—will add to the fun. If your friends are up for it, ask them to come dressed in beachwear, whether it's bikinis or Hawaiian shirts. Find some exotic flowers at your florist and decorate in an island motif to make your party a smash.

Royal Wedding

If your friends cried over the last royal wedding or fantasize about being called "Your Majesty," skip the Facebook invites and text message announcements and opt for monogrammed invitations instead. This party is for royalty! Dress in your best Anglophile wedding gear—fancy hats and morning suits preferred.

A bit of classical music will have you and your guests feeling educated, refined and perhaps even a bit snooty. There are several great cocktails you can serve, such as the Queen Elizabeth Wine Cocktail for strong and cutthroat individuals (recipe p. 342) or the Absolut Royalty (recipe p. 78). If a cocktail isn't your speed, a little bubbly champagne certainly won't hurt. When it comes to feeding the royalty, grab a good cook and make a modified version of a Thanksgiving duck, turkey or goose, and whipped potatoes. It doesn't have to be British food but it does have to be exquisite. Leave the finger foods for another party. Tonight it's sophistication city.

The *Godfather* Party

Lots of people dream of being Marlon Brando or Al Pacino, but very few have the acting chops. No one needs to be a great actor to attend this party, but everyone should come in costume and be prepared to talk fast and loud at this party. Guys can dress in either a sharp suit or a T-shirt and a gold chain with a cigar, and the women can break out the fake nails and the Aqua Net for big, full hair. For the soundtrack, turn up the Frank Sinatra and Dean Martin.

In order to get people "talking," you'll have to supply some serious pasta—penne vodka and manicotti are sure to please even the vegetarians. No *Godfather* party would be quite right without a few nice bottles of wine, but when it comes to the hard stuff, try the Italian Assassin (recipe p. 238) or the Mafia's Kiss (recipe p. 272).

These are only a few of the countless theme possibilities you can use to create fantastic parties. From Halloween to Mardi

Gras, from *Gone With the Wind* to *Star Wars,* themes can suit all your moods and entertain all your guests.

Cocktail   Parfait   White Wine

HOLIDAY CELEBRATIONS

WE all know that eggnog is served at Christmas parties and champagne flows freely on New Year's Eve, but why stop there? There are plenty of other drinks that can add a festive touch to any holiday. If you look beyond the traditional winter holiday season, there are many overlooked holidays during the year that deserve something special, too.

Almost any holiday offers a good excuse to get creative in the bar. Here are some suggestions for drinks that can make your holiday parties occasions to be remembered. Check the recipe section for instructions on how to make each of them.

New Year's Day: Poinsettia; Bellini Punch; Mimosa

Washington's Birthday: Cherry Daiquiri (frozen); Washington

Mardi Gras: Ramos Gin Fizz; Daiquiris of any sort; Hurricane; Sazerac

Valentine's Day: Love; Big Blue Sky; Cupid's Kiss; Raspberry Chocolate Martini

Leap Year (February 29): Leap Year

Groundhog Day: Mudslide

Saint Patrick's Day: Leprechaun's Libation; St. Patrick's Day Mocha Java; Irish Car Bomb

Tax Day (April 15): Income Tax

Easter: Easter Egg Hatch (nonalcoholic); Easter Egg Cocktail; April Shower

Memorial Day/Flag Day: Big Blue Sky; Summer Share; Betsy Ross

Mother's Day: Blushing Lady; Goose in Spring; Teatini; In & Out Lemontini; Rosy Rum Cosmo

Midsummer's Eve: shots of aquavit (akvavit); shots of Swedish Punsch (see Glossary); Fjord; May Blossom Fizz; Midnight Sun; Strawberry Shortcake

Canada Day: Canada Cocktail; The Caesar; Hotel Georgia

Independence Day: Stars and Stripes; Rainbow Sherbet Punch (nonalcoholic; made with red, white and blue sherbet); Vanilla Creamsicle; Sweet Independence

Halloween: Cat's Eye; Zombie (made in a punch bowl); Black Witch; Black Martini; Bloody Rum Punch; Devil's Handshake

Thanksgiving: Turkey Shooter; Cranberry-Vodka Punch; Cranberry Spice Cocktail; Pumpkin Pie Martini; Pomegranate Fizz

Hanukkah: Spicy Hot Cocoa; Lamplighter; Jelly Donut Martini

Christmas: Eggnog; Sherry Eggnog; Cold Weather Punch; Fish House Punch; Cranberry Pineapple Vodka Punch

New Year's Eve: White Grape, Tangerine and Sparkling Wine Punch; Champagne Cocktail; Champagne-Maraschino Punch; Midori Melon Ball Drop

Champagne Tulip

Champagne Saucer

Champagne Flute

FROZEN BLENDER DRINKS

I T doesn't take fancy tools or a bartending degree to make mixology magic—just open your pantry and break out your blender (drink umbrellas optional). The best part? Blender drinks are so easy, even a toddler can do it . . . well, maybe not. Suitable for whipping up rich, creamy concoctions, fun and refreshing tropical drinks or low-calorie, nonalcoholic treats for the nondrinker or the designated driver in your life, the blender can be your most prized piece of bar equipment.

The blended drink makes a glorious sight at any party. Guests are sure to be impressed with a fabulous frozen margarita (which is quickly becoming the nation's most popular drink). Or you can dazzle them with the incredible sensation of a frozen mango daiquiri, the likes of which they'd never dreamed possible. For a glimpse of the full range of blender drinks you can make, see Index by Type at the back of this book.

If you don't already have one, buy a good sturdy blender for your bar. All you really need is two speeds—high and low—so don't worry about finding a blender with twenty-four settings or any fancy functions. Clean it carefully before using it, then go wild. Once you've gotten used to your blender, experiment with your favorite drink recipes. You never know what you'll discover. For instance, many of the recipes in this book call for a shaker to mix drinks. Try using a blender instead—you might be surprised with the results. Add some fruit here, some cream there. The possibilities are truly infinite.

As a general rule, drinks containing ingredients that don't readily mix—such as cream, sour mix, eggs, ice cream or syrupy ingredients like grenadine or heavy liqueurs—need to be shaken vigorously at least, but blending yields superior smoothness.

After-Dinner Drinks

Just say no to dessert this time and instead, try out a sweet drink that will satiate your taste buds and keep the party flowing. If you're ready for a post-dinner drink that will keep you awake enough in case the conversation gets dull, try a Coffee Frappe (recipe p. 150). Starbucks has nothing on this one. If you're not in the mood for coffee, why not try a Sweet Tart Cocktail (recipe p. 393)? Warning: If your taste buds don't fancy sour, you may not be up for this icy adult version of a childhood candy favorite.

Brunch Drinks

If you're hosting a brunch in the dog days of summer, you might want to ditch the classic mimosa and go with a frosty alternative, like a frozen Bellini (recipe p. 106). For something a little more creative, try a Honeydew Margarita (recipe p. 223)—you'll be cooling off and getting your daily serving of fruit all at the same time.

Tropical Drinks

Tropical drinks mix particularly well with the blender. Whip up a Piña Colada (recipe p. 323), make a batch of virgin Strawberry Daiquiris for designated drivers and younger guests (recipe p. 388) or get back to your childhood roots with a frozen Pink Lemonade (recipe p. 327). Top your drinks with an exotic flower and you'll be mentally adrift in the pool in no time.

Drinks for a Diet

Dieting got you down? Indulge in a Blended Raspberry Cocktail (recipe p. 113) for a sweet, alcoholic treat with just 115 calories. Or a Mojito Smoothie (recipe p. 290) that's sure to please both your taste buds and your nutritionist. If citrus sounds appealing to you, sip on a Tropical Grapefruit Splash (recipe p. 409) guilt free!

Here are some basic tips for a great blending experience.

Rules of Thumb

- Always use twice as much ice as your ingredients.

- Use small ice cubes—oversized cubes will destroy your blender.

- Avoid canned fruit. Fresh or frozen are both better options.

For blending cream drinks

Fill blending cup one-quarter full of ice

Measure liqueurs first

Add cream

Blend at medium speed for 5–10 seconds or until smooth

For blending sours

Fill blending cup one-quarter full of ice

Measure liqueurs first

Measure other alcohols next

Add sour mix

Add any other ingredients

Blend at medium speed for 5–10 seconds or until smooth

For blending tropical drinks

Fill blending cup one-quarter full of ice

Add fresh fruit (if any)

Measure liqueurs

Measure other alcohols next

Add sour mix (if any)

Add any other ingredients

Blend at medium speed for 10–15 seconds or until smooth

Average blending times are mentioned above, but use your discretion. You will be able to tell if a drink is ready. When the drink is completely blended, you should not hear the rattle of ice cubes.

And now a few words about your blender:

- Before you use a new blender for the first time, fill it with warm water, and with the lid on, turn the machine on for about 25 seconds. This will remove any dirt or residues in the blender.

- Be certain the machine is turned off before you plug it in.

- Always remove foreign objects such as bar spoons or bar strainers from the blender before you use the machine. Do not insert utensils into the blender cup while the machine is operating.

- Always make sure the blade assembly is attached securely to the bottom of the blender cup. You don't want any leaks!

- Do not pour boiling water into the blender container. It might cause the cup to crack.

- Don't fill the container beyond its capacity, since the efficiency of the machine will be reduced.

- Make sure the lid is on tight before you turn the machine on.

- Don't remove the lid of the blender while the machine is running.

- Never reach into the blender while it is in use. Make sure hair or loose clothing does not get caught.

- Make sure the blades have ceased to spin before removing the container from the base of the machine.

- Always be sure the switch is turned to the OFF position when you are finished.

- To clean your blender after use, fill the mixing container with warm water, put the lid on, and turn the machine on for about 25 seconds. This will loosen any particles stuck to the inside of the container. Then remove and rinse the blender cup in warm water.

- Always wash the container immediately after use. Don't let residues sit for too long, or they will be more difficult to remove.

- When washing the inside of the blender, take care not to cut yourself on the metal blades.

If you keep these common-sense safety tips in mind, you'll find out how much fun it is to create a great blender drink. Enjoy!

Electric Blender

THE PERFECT PUNCH

PUNCH, a sometimes bizarre mixture of ingredients that complement and set each other off, is a great way to entertain the masses. It's cheaper and easier to make one large concoction than it is to handle your guests one drink at a time. The punch tradition, which dates back to the eighteenth and nineteenth centuries, when rum was all the rage, has made a resurgence. Today, however, the main ingredient can be any liquor, depending on what you and your guests like, or on the occasion and the season. But, of course, rum is still a favorite component of punch, since it lends itself to mixing well with other ingredients.

For traditional punches, the rum-based varieties are probably your best bet. As for choosing which rum (or other liquor, for that matter) to purchase, a cheaper variety will usually work well, since some of the nuances will be camouflaged. The assortment of juices, sugars, fruits and sodas, or the milk, cream or eggs that the liquor mingles with in the punch bowl can disguise a less expensive rum. But there is no substitute for fine quality, and some discerning palates may notice the difference. So if it is within your means to go for the more expensive brands, you should do it.

In cold weather substantial punches, milk-based punches and hot punches are particular favorites. The traditional Cold Weather Punch, Fish House Punch (first made at the Fish House Club near Philadelphia to cheer our nation's founders),

Hot Rum and, of course, Eggnog (for Christmas parties) are favorites.

Punch Bowl & Cups

A champagne-based punch, such as the Bellini Punch, a peach and champagne blend, are great for New Year's celebrations, weddings, bridal showers, or engagement parties.

While punches are not appropriate fare for a typical cocktail party (which, of course, calls for cocktails), they are certainly right for special-occasion parties, especially holiday gettogethers or birthday and anniversary parties.

The greatest advantage to serving a punch is that once the punch is made, you can just relax and enjoy the party while your guests help themselves. And since the majority of punches contain just a fraction of alcohol, you'll save money on liquor. Do make sure, however, that you have enough of the mixture reserved so that you can refill the punch bowl when it runs low, but don't mix fresh punch with whatever remains in the bowl. Empty the bowl and prepare the punch with new ice. Otherwise, the taste will be weakened.

Nonalcoholic punches are great for parties where there will be nondrinkers or children. For the kids, a Rainbow Sherbet Punch is always lots of fun.

Sangrias and other wine-based punches, and punches with loads of fruit and exotic juices, are also popular. Especially when the weather starts getting warmer, guests call for something refreshing and lighter. A Polynesian Punch is an extra-special refresher. Juleps or coolers can be made in large quantities simply by multiplying your ingredients. And milk punches are a rich and smooth treat.

Ice cubes are not recommended for preserving your punch's chill. The preferred method of keeping your punch cool is a block of ice placed in the punch bowl. Ingredients in cold punches are usually best if chilled ahead of time (see individual recipes). Generally, for cold punches, a two-quart block of ice is recommended for every gallon of punch. Another tip: Sodas and carbonated beverages do their best if added to the punch just before you're ready to serve it.

Try some of the single-serving punch recipes in this book. They're great for experimenting with new tastes before you venture to serve a crowd.

LOW-CALORIE DRINKS

I N this age of health and fitness, almost everyone watches
what and how much they eat and drink. Alcoholic beverages
have gotten a bad rap as a source of empty calories, but there are
plenty of options open to the weight-conscious bartender. The
first step toward having fun without putting on the pounds is to
know the facts about the caloric content of the drinks you serve.
The following charts should give you an idea of how many calories are in your favorite drinks. (Numbers are approximate.)

Spirits

80-proof liquors (1½ fluid ounces) . . . . 97 calories
86-proof liquors (1½ fl. oz.) . . . . 105 calories
90-proof liquors (1½ fl. oz.) . . . . 110 calories
94-proof liquors (1½ fl. oz.) . . . . 116 calories
100-proof liquors (1½ fl. oz.) . . . . 124 calories
Aromatic bitters (1 tsp.) . . . . 13 calories
Beer (lager type, 12 fl. oz.) . . . . 151 calories
Beer (light, 12 fl. oz.) . . . . 98 calories
Champagne (25 proof, 3½ fl. oz.) . . . . 91 calories
Liqueurs (1 fl. oz.) . . . . 66–106 calories
    (e.g., 1 fl. oz. crème de
    menthe = 100 calories;
    1 fl. oz. sloe gin = 68 calories;
    1 fl. oz. amaretto = 82 calories)

Vermouth, dry (1 fl. oz.) . . . . 33 calories
Vermouth, sweet (1 fl. oz.) . . . . 44 calories
Wine, dry (3½ fl. oz.) . . . . 87 calories
Wine, sweet, dessert or aperitif (2 fl. oz.) . . . . 80 calories
Wine, sherry (2 fl. oz.) . . . . 80 calories

Mixers

Club soda . . . . 0 calories
Cola (12 fl. oz. can) . . . . 144 calories
Cranberry juice cocktail (2 fl. oz.) . . . . 37 calories
Diet cola (12 fl. oz. can) . . . . 0 calories
Fresh lemon juice (1 tbsp.) . . . . 4 calories
Fresh lime juice (1 tbsp.) . . . . 4 calories
Fresh orange juice (2 fl. oz.) . . . . 28 calories
Ginger ale (12 fl. oz. can) . . . . 113 calories
Heavy cream (1 tablespoon) . . . . 53 calories
Pineapple juice, unsweetened (2 fl. oz.) . . . . 34 calories
Tomato juice (2 fl. oz.) . . . . 12 calories
Tonic water (12 fl. oz. can) . . . . 113 calories

Many of the drinks in this book are relatively low in calories, and you can lower the calorie counts of many simply by using less alcohol. For instance, if a recipe calls for 1½ ounces of vodka, limit it to one ounce and you've already cut out 32 calories if you're using 80-proof vodka. See the index of low-calorie drinks for a representative sampling of drinks that contain approximately 110 calories or less. Refer to the recipe section for instructions on how to make them.

BEER

I T used to be synonymous with fraternity parties and base-ball games, but beer has really come into its own in the last decade. What used to be considered a cheap, basic drink for the masses has turned into a complex and varied option that can appeal to everyone from the patrons of a local dive bar to sophisticated young urbanites. Beer appreciation has truly become an American passion, not to mention an international affair. Whether it's a light beer for dieters, craft beers for urban hipsters or imported beer for the more experimental, the quality of beer available to consumers has been consistently on the rise since the early 2000s. And there is some especially good news about beer: Despite what you may believe, it has fewer calories than many other spirits. An average bottle contains just 150 calories, and light beers have even less.

Beer is made by cooking and fermenting grain, including malt, barley, rice, corn and others. It is then flavored with hops, which give it its bitter flavor. The brewing process varies from beer to beer depending on what ingredients are used, and on fermenting techniques and temperatures.

Here's a basic summary of how beer is made:

1. Malting: The grains are put through a process of heating, drying out and cracking in order to activate the enzymes needed for brewing.

2. Mashing: The grains are steeped in hot water for about an hour. This "mashing" process causes grains to break down and release all their sugars. Afterwards, the water is drained from the mash, and what is left is a sweet liquid called wort.

3. Boiling: The wort is boiled for about an hour, then hops and any other spices are added to the mixture.

4. Fermentation: Once the wort is cooled and filtered post-boil, it's time to add the yeast. Brewers put the wort in what is called a fermenting vessel, and the beer sits and ferments for a period of time determined by the type of beer.

5. Bottling: After the fermentation is done, the beer is flat and uncarbonated. Brewers either artificially carbonate the beer or allow it to carbonate on its own with yeast. The beer is bottled, then brewers let it sit for anywhere from a couple of weeks to months before it's shipped out to stores.

An astounding array of brews results from this process, as the following list of beer types shows.

Types of Beer

Ale a brew made with top-fermenting yeast; has a distinctive fruitiness; sharper and stronger than lager.

Amber ale a Belgian ale. With excess malt, this ale is sweeter and dark in color.

Barley wine actually a type of ale, barley wine can be amber colored or black. It usually has a strong, fruity flavor and a high alcohol content.

Beer includes all beer, lager, porter and stout.

Bitter a well-hopped ale, usually on draft; typically acidic, with a color that varies from bronze to deep copper.

Bock the German term for a strong beer.

Cold-filtered beer that is not pasteurized like other bottled and canned beers, giving it the fresh taste of draft beer.

"Dark beer" usually refers to a dark brew of the Munich type; heavier, deeper flavor.

Dry beer cold filtered and dry brewed for a beer that leaves no aftertaste.

IPA IPA stands for India Pale Ale. A hoppy pale ale, usually with a bitter taste.

Lager any beer made by bottom fermentation; in Britain, typically golden; in continental Europe, can be dark; in Germany and the Netherlands, indicates everyday beer.

Light beer lager-type beers that have a lower alcohol and calorie content.

Märzen a pale lager, this full-bodied beer of Bavarian origins is malty in taste. In Germany, Märzen beer goes from pale to dark colored, and in Austria it's typically pale.

Nonalcoholic brew, or near beer a beer that has no alcohol in it.

Pilsner a golden-colored, dry, bottom-fermenting beer; flowery aroma, dry finish.

Porter an ale with a rich, heavy foam; sweeter than ale.

Sake although often considered a wine, sake is actually a beer, since it is a refermented rice brew; has a high alcohol content.

Steam beer a term coined by the San Francisco company that produces Anchor Steam; has elements of both ale and lager.

Stout extra-dark, top-fermenting brew; can sometimes be sweetish and has a very strong taste.

Wheat beer an ale that's brewed with barley and large amounts of wheat malt. Light in color and sometimes flavored with coriander or orange.

Craft beer can come in all of these styles, and is kind of an independent businessman of the beer world. According to the Brewers Association, a craft brewer is defined as:

- Small: Brewery distributes no more than six million barrels of beer annually.

- Independent: Less than 25 percent of the brewery is owned by a non-craft beer brewery.

- Traditional: Beers' flavor derives from traditional or innovative brewing ingredients and their fermentation.

With all these beers available, you have plenty of possibilities to choose from. Do you prefer light-bodied, light-tasting, low-calorie beer, or a fuller-tasting brew? Does the familiar taste of Budweiser or Miller do it for you, or does a Mexican style—such as Corona or Sol—or a heavy, rich Irish style like Guinness Stout wet your whistle? Wherever your tastes take you, exploring the options can be lots of fun.

The quality of American beers is going up, and some of the best domestic beers available today come from regional breweries and microbreweries throughout the country. These smaller operations have experienced a resurgence in the past decade or so, delivering beers of exceptional quality to local or regional markets. The development offers a real advantage for beer drinkers, and not only because they now have more to choose from. Because many of these independent breweries supply relatively small amounts of product to limited geographic areas, their beer does not have to travel far and therefore offers greater freshness and better flavor to the consumer. Among the beers currently available:

Anchor Steam, brewed by Anchor Brewing Company in San Francisco, has a strong malt flavor, creamy head and somewhat sweet taste. Their Anchor Liberty Ale is golden but somewhat cloudy, and has a sweet aroma of hops and an exotic, perfumy flavor.

Coors, the beer of the West, is produced in Golden, Colorado. It is light and easy to drink, and is now available nationwide.

Dixie Beer from New Orleans offers lots of flavor in a crisp, clean brew.

Lone Star Beer, from Texas, of course, is dry with a pleasant malt taste.

New Amsterdam Amber Beer comes from New York City's Old New York Beer Company. It's full-bodied, aromatic and a real crowd-pleaser in the metropolitan area.

Rolling Rock Premium Beer, widely available on the East Coast, has become the preferred drink of hip young urbanites.

Redhook Extra Special Bitter Ale, from the Redhook Ale Brewery in Seattle, is spicy, bitter and dark amber.

Sierra Nevada Pale Ale is amber colored with a light, lemony flavor. It is produced by Sierra Nevada Brewing Company in Chico, California.

Samuel Adams Boston Stock Ale, from the Boston Beer Company, is clear, light amber and fruity. Their Samuel Adams Boston Lager is also good; it is clear, and light amber, has a fruity scent and delivers clean, sweet taste.

Light beers are extremely popular in this nation of fitness buffs. Some of the offerings out there include:

Amstel Light (95 calories) from Holland; the leader of the lights

Budweiser Light Beer (108 calories)

Bud Select (99 calories)

Coors Light (110 calories)

Kirin Light (105 calories) from Japan

Michelob Light (134 calories)

Miller Lite (96 calories)

Stroh Light (115 calories)

For draft beer lovers whose home bar does not include the equipment to tap a keg, cold-filtered beer is an excellent alternative. Choose from the following:

Busch Light Draft

Miller Genuine Draft

Sapporo, one of Japan's finest exports

A wide variety of imports, from almost any country you can think of, are available on the market today. No bar is complete without at least one imported selection, but you should have no trouble finding something you like among the hundreds of foreign beers offered for sale in America. Here are just a few of the many excellent imports:

Australia—Foster's Lager

Austria—Gosser Export Beer

Belgium—Westmalle "Triple" Abbey Trappist Beer; St. Sixtus Belgium Abbey Ale

Canada—Carling Black Horse Ale; Labatt's 50 Ale; Labatt's Crystal Lager Beer; Labatt's Pilsner Blue; Molson's Ale; Moosehead Canadian Beer

China—Tsing Tao

Czech Republic—Pilsner Urquell

Denmark—Carlsberg Royal Lager Beer

France—Kronenbourg 1664 Imported Beer; "33" Export Brew

Germany—Beck's Beer and Beck's Dark; Lowenbrau; St. Pauli Girl Beer

Great Britain—Bass Pale Ale I.P.A.; Newcastle Brown Ale; Watney's Red Barrel

Holland—Heineken Lager Beer; Grolsch Natural Holland Beer

Ireland—Guinness Extra Stout; Guinness Gold Lager; Harp Lager

Jamaica—Red Stripe

Japan—Kirin Beer; Sapporo Lager Beer

Mexico—Dos Equis XX Beer; Corona; Tecate Cerveza; Sol; Chihuahua

Norway—Aas Bok Beer; Rignes Special Beer

Switzerland—Cardinal Lager Beer

An increasing number of surprisingly good nonalcoholic brews are making their way into stores nationwide. The better choices include:

Beck's Non-Alcoholic

Kaliber, produced by the Guinness Brewing Company

Moussy

O'Doul's (Premium or Amber)

St. Pauli N.A.

Wartech Nonalcoholic Brew

Once you've decided which beers to include in your home bar, storing and serving them correctly is a snap. Store beer upright in your refrigerator and away from the light. Keep in mind that it's not a good idea to re-chill beer once it has been removed from refrigeration.

Beers should be served cold, but not *too* cold, or they lose some of their flavor. As a general guideline, most American light-bodied beers are good at about 42 degrees F, typical imported beers are best at 47–50 degrees and full-bodied ales offer peak flavor at 55 degrees.

Beer can be served in mugs, goblets or pilsner glasses, depending on the occasion. If you like, frost the glasses by placing them in your freezer at least an hour before serving. To serve beer—whether from a bottle, can or tap—pour it slowly into a glass tilted at a forty-five-degree angle so the stream of beer flows down its side. This prevents excessive head from forming. When the glass is about two-thirds full, straighten the glass and pour the beer into the center until full, leaving a head of about three-fourths of an inch. If you prefer your beer without a head, keep the glass tilted until full.

Beer Tasting Tips

If you're visiting a brewery or just want to assess your happy hour beer with an expert's eye, consider these characteristics:

- Head: Is the head (the foam on top) of the beer thick or thin? What's the color? White? Medium brown?

- Translucence/Color: Is the beer color cloudy or clear? Is it amber, golden or dark brown?

- Scent: Paler-shaded beers will smell more like hops, whereas darker options tend to have a malt aroma, possibly with hints of coffee or chocolate.

- Texture: Some beers are thick, others silky, and others more fizzy. How does your favorite beer compare?

- Aftertaste: Does your beer end on a malty sweet note, or is it more of a bitter end?

Beer is a perfect accompaniment to a casual gathering of friends. Pour a few, raise your glass and savor the unique joys of this cool and frothy refreshment.

Beer Mug   Pilsner Glass   Beer Goblet

WINE

MODERN wine drinkers have eschewed the hard-and-fast rules that have long dictated the drinking of wine. Now we all can enjoy the wine that we like with the foods we like— anytime we like. Those unfamiliar with the many subtleties of wine, and those who are simply not experts, have been scared away in the past. The good news is that there's no longer a stigma attached to simply finding a wine you enjoy and then sticking with it. But, of course, experimentation is bound to lead to some wonderful new discoveries.

Those on the cutting edge, then, are drinking whatever tastes right to them. The basic guideline, however, is that lighter wines best complement lighter foods, and fuller-bodied wines go with heavier foods.

As for serving wine, it is a common misconception that white wine should be served ice cold and red wine rather warm. Actually, both should be served at approximately the same temperature (red wine, usually 60 degrees F; white wine at about 55 degrees). An exception to the red wine rule is Beaujolais wines, which are usually better if chilled slightly, since these wines lack a high acid balance and chilling helps to compensate for the low acidity. Also, the better the quality of your wine, the less you should chill it, since chilling masks the flavor.

What about the old rule that you should let a bottle of red wine "breathe" before serving? When wine is exposed to the air, it "ages" and mellows. Breathing can thus enhance the flavor of any wine that is too astringent or tannic. Simply removing the cork from the bottle and letting it stand for a while will accomplish nothing, since only a very small portion of the wine makes contact with the air. Pour the wine into a glass or a decanter, allowing it to mix with the air, and let it stand for a while. The exposure to air will soften the flavor.

The most popular wines are produced in France, the United States (especially California, but also in Oregon, Washington and New York), Italy, Germany, Australia, Spain, Portugal, Argentina and Chile. The following list names the most popular categories of wine, the grapes they are made from, the general characteristics of those wines, and some suggestions for what sort of foods taste good with them. The descriptions are meant to give only a basic impression of each wine; any number of good books on wine can give you much more detailed information. What reminds one person of cedar, for instance, might evoke a pine forest for someone else. It's a good idea when tasting a new wine to keep a notebook and jot down anything memorable about the wine, so that you'll be able to recall later on what it tasted and smelled like to you.

French Wines

These are named for the region they are grown in. For example, if you pick up two bottles of white Burgundy, one might say Meursault and one might be a Macon-Villages. They are both made from the Chardonnay grape, but they come from different areas in Burgundy. Here are the general categories of wine produced in France.

Red Wines

1. Red Bordeaux: Made from a mix of three grapes, usually Cabernet Sauvignon, Merlot and Cabernet Franc. Their general flavor characteristics are cassis and cherry, sometimes eucalyptus, woody or cedarlike; some have a tobacco flavor. Commonly served with simply roasted meats or fowl. Good with mushrooms, cheese dishes and other medium to full-flavored dishes.

2. Red Burgundy: Made from the Pinot Noir grape. Characteristically less tannic, softer and fruitier than Bordeaux, emphasizing fruit flavors such as strawberries and boysenberries; jammy, plummy and woody are other possible descriptions. Good with roasted meats and lighter dishes such as fish. Also good with cheeses and other earthy foods.

3. Rhone Wines: Made from a mix of many different grapes, depending on the region. The most common is the Syrah grape. Some Rhone wines contain up to twenty different kinds of grapes. They are typically bigger, heavier, full-bodied wines; tannic with a higher alcohol content. Other characteristics are pepperiness, cherry flavor, spiciness, jamminess and fruitiness. Go well with heavily spiced, full-flavored foods, such as barbecue, spicy pasta dishes, sausages and stews.

4. Beaujolais: Made from the Gamay grape. There are two types of Beaujolais. One, Beaujolais Nouveau, receives a lot of attention each November when it's released. It is shipped almost immediately after bottling and is very light, fresh and fruity and contains very little acidity. It's an easy wine for beginning wine drinkers to like. The other, referred to simply as Beaujolais, or "Cru Beaujolais," has a bit more body, acid and concentration of flavor, although it is also considered a light, fruity wine. Both have a grapeyness and are berry flavored and jammy. They are often best if served a bit chilled and are good paired with light, simple summer fare. A great picnic wine.

White Wines

1. White Burgundy: Made from Chardonnay grapes. These are oaky and buttery, with hints of lemon, spice and flowers. There's a great range in style among white burgundies, from fuller, heavier bodied to lighter wines. They go well with fish dishes, especially salmon, and cream sauces, as well as light pastas and various kinds of lightly prepared meats, such as veal.

2. White Bordeaux: Made primarily from the Sauvignon Blanc grape. It is lighter, crisper, more acidic. Often described as herbaceous, grassy, appley and lemony. Goes best with lighter, simpler foods.

   A subcategory of White Bordeaux is Sauterne, which is a dessert wine made primarily from the Semillon grape. It is sweet, honeyed and syrupy, and is excellent with desserts, especially fresh fruit or custards, or as an aperitif.

3. Loire: Made from the Chenin Blanc or Sauvignon Blanc grape. They are light, crisp, acidic wines, known for their flintiness or smokiness, as well as grassy or herbaceous characters. These benefit from being served a little colder and are drunk fairly young, usually three to four years from the date on the bottle. They tend to go well with seafood, especially oysters, clams, crabs and scallops and other light fish or salad dishes. Also great with vegetable soup.

4. Alsatian: This is a huge category of wine, but the two most famous types are made from the Riesling grape and the Gewurztraminer grape. These wines are much like the German-style whites—steely, highly acidic and crisp, with a spiciness and fruitiness. These wines go well with Chinese food and Indian food, as well as pork, quiche or German cuisine.

   (*Note:* Many mistake "fruitiness" to mean sweetness, particularly in Alsatian and German wines. Typically, in fact, these wines are very dry on the tongue, with very little sugar.)

Champagne

This is the sparkling wine made in the Champagne region of France, from a mix of grapes—predominantly Chardonnay and Pinot Noir. There are two types, vintage and nonvintage. Vintage means that the wine was made predominantly from grapes of a particularly excellent year. While vintage champagnes are more expensive, the difference in quality between vintage and nonvintage (a blend of grapes and wines from different years to conform to a house style) is small, so average drinkers gain little from the extra cost of vintage champagne. Champagne varies from light, crisp and acidy to heavy, toasty and yeasty. Try different brands of champagne to learn which is to your liking.

Champagne goes with just about everything, except perhaps Mexican and other very spicy foods. It also makes a wonderful aperitif. Like other wines, champagne is also best served not too cold. And even though the loud pop associated with opening a champagne bottle is a festive tradition, the quieter the event, the better. The louder the sound, the more gases and bubbles escape, ruining champagne's wonderful effervescent quality. Slip the cork out as gently and as slowly as possible.

American Wines

In the United States, the primary identifier of wines is the type of grape. The most popular are from California, which in some cases now equals and even surpasses France in the quality of wine produced. Many other states, particularly in the Northwest, also produce very good wines.

Red Wines

1. Cabernet Sauvignon: This is made from the same grape as the primary grape in French red Bordeaux, and it has the same basic characteristics—cassis, cherry, sometimes eucalyptus, woody, cedarlike. It goes with the same foods.

2. Pinot Noir: This is the American version of a red burgundy. Recently, Oregon has gained acclaim for the quality of its pinot noirs.

3. Zinfandel: This wine is indigenous to America but similar to the Rhone wines of France—big, full-bodied, peppery and heavy. It goes well with heavy foods, such as barbecue, chili and garlicky foods.

White Wine

1. Chardonnay-based wines: Made from the same grape used to produce French white Burgundy. One of the most popular wines in America, it has a unique complexity and clarity. This wine emphasizes the more oaky and fruity aspects, while these qualities of the French version are more balanced by acidity. It complements the same foods.

2. Sauvignon blanc–based wines: Made from the same grapes used in French white Bordeaux. There's more acid and fruitiness and less wood in these wines than in the French white Bordeaux, but they complement the same foods.

Sparkling Wines

Made in the champagne style, American sparkling wines cannot legally call themselves champagne. Nonetheless, these wines can be quite excellent—much a match for their French counterparts. The same serving guidelines apply.

Other U.S. Wines

1. White Zinfandel: This wine is still very popular. It is light, crisp and easy to drink, and goes well with any light fare.

2. Rosé: A light pink wine made from red grapes. The skins are removed before fermentation begins, so only some of their color remains in the wine. Rosé is light, crisp and not necessarily sweet.

3. Blush: A mixture of white and red wine, with white the predominant ingredient. The wine has all the characteristics of the white used as its base.

Italian Wines

There are no hard-and-fast rules for wine labeling in Italy, but wines are usually named for the town near where the grapes come from. The name may also refer to the grape variety used. Italian wines go very well with most Italian foods, but they can be served as an accompaniment to any type of meal, depending on the individual characteristics of the wine.

Red Wines

1. Barolo: Made from the nebbiolo grape. It is full, warm, robust; has a slightly greater alcohol content than its very close relative, Barbaresco. This wine must be aged for a minimum of three years before it is bottled. It goes with full-bodied, spicy foods, such as tomato sauces, lasagna, roasted meats and pizza.

2. Barbaresco: Also made from the nebbiolo grape. It has many of the same qualities as Barolo but is a bit lighter, not as tannic and more fruity. Aged for a minimum of two years, it goes with the same foods as Barolo.

3. Chianti: The best known of Italian red wines, it is a simple red wine, not very tannic and lighter bodied. The predominant grape variety is Sangiovese. It is best with basic Italian foods such as pizza.

4. Valpolicella: A relatively light and fruity wine, it nevertheless has some substance. Age improves this wine only up to a point; it should be drunk five to eight years after the date on the bottle. The more basic Corvina and Molinara grapes are its ingredients. It goes well with simple Italian foods.

White Wines

In general, Italian whites are crisp, light, fruity and not very woody. They tend to be clean and acidy, almost lemony. Their flavors stand up well to vinaigrettes and seafood dishes.

1. Pinot Grigio: A fine, full-bodied wine that ranges in color from pale straw to copper. This is a very simple wine made from the pinot gris grape. It complements deep-fried seafood dishes and other simple foods.

2. Orvieto: Made from the Trebbiano grape, this is a medium-bodied dry wine. It goes well with seafood.

3. Frascati: Also made from the Trebbiano grape, with the malvasia. A medium-bodied, dry wine, it goes with lighter Italian foods, particularly seafood.

4. Soave: A crisp, fruity wine made from the garganega and Trebbiano grapes. Light and simple, it goes well with the same light fare.

German Wines

Riesling is the most popular German wine, made from the riesling grape. It ranges from very dry to very sweet and is similar to the Alsatian wines of France. A rating system of six categories delineates the sweetness of each riesling, with the first (*Kabinett*) being the driest and the sixth (*Eiswein*) being the sweetest. This information is given on the bottle, so you can choose accordingly. The wine should be served a bit colder than others. Depending on its sweetness, it can be served with anything from desserts (sweeter) to Indian and Chinese food (drier).

Australian Wines

There is no formal labeling system for Australian wines, because wine making is a fairly recent development there and the country is so large. Most Australian wines are classified by grape variety. In red wine, look for Cabernet Sauvignon, Shiraz (the equivalent of the syrah in the Rhone wines of France) or one that combines Cabernet Sauvignon with Shiraz. Australian Shiraz is rich, complex and smoky or spicy—truly one of the most enjoyable reds available today.

In white wine, some of the best are Chardonnay or wines

that combine Sauvignon Blanc with Semillon. The results are not as sweet in Australia as in France, but the wine is heavily wooded, oaky and fuller flavored.

Spanish Wines

Spain is known mostly for its red wines. The most popular table wine from Spain is Rioja, a full-bodied and often very woody wine. The predominant grape is the Tempranillo, but some varieties of Rioja also contain Graciano, Mazuelo and Garnacho.

Fortified Wine

Fortified wine contains brandy or other spirits, added in order to increase alcohol content or to stop the fermentation process. These wines are typically sweet, although some are dry. The drier ones are sometimes used as aperitifs as well as dessert wines or after-dinner drinks. More and more, fortified wines can be found not only on their own but mixed in cocktails, such as the Madeira Cocktail, the Prince of Wales, the Tuxedo, the Affinity Cocktail, the Adonis, the Soviet Cocktail and the Sherry Twist. Madeira, marsala, port and sherry fall into the fortified wine category.

Madeira

Named for the island on which they are produced, these wines are fortified with brandy made from madeira wine. They can range in taste from light and dry to heavy and sweet. The types are:

Sercial ("rainwater") light, dry

Verdelho light, dry; rare

Bual golden, sweet

Malmsey deep gold, very sweet

Marsala

Developed in the 1800s, these wines come from Marsala on Sicily, Italy. The wines are warm golden yellow in hue and have a caramel aroma. For the most part they are used for cooking. The important types are:

Fine must have at least 17 percent alcohol and be aged for a minimum of four months

Superiore sweet and dry; must have at least 18 percent alcohol and be aged for a minimum of two years

Vergine extremely dry; must have at least 18 percent alcohol and be aged for a minimum of five years

Speciale made with eggs and other flavorings; must have at least 18 percent alcohol and be aged for at least six months

Port

Originally from Portugal and now associated with England, most ports are red; all are sweet. The types are:

Pony Glass

Vintage bottled two years in wood after the vintage and aged for decades; this is a fortified wine of the most excellent quality

Ruby young and fruity; bright in color

Tawny paler, less sweet and softer than ruby port

White made from white grapes; similar in taste to ruby

Sherry

Authentic sherry is made in Spain; sherry-like wines are made, however, in a variety of places, including Australia, Cyprus and California. The types range from pale and dry to deeply rich and sweet. They are:

Manzanilla very pale and dry; serve chilled

Fino pale and dry; serve chilled

Amontillado pale gold and not as dry as fino; fuller in body; serve at room temperature straight or on the rocks

Oloroso golden, full-bodied, can be dry but is usually sweet; cream sherry is the most common variety; sweeter olorosos should be served at room temperature, drier ones on the rocks

Vermouth

Although vermouth is technically a wine, it is usually considered an aperitif. See the section on aperitifs for discussion.

APERITIFS

THE term "aperitif" may sound fancy, but it actually refers to nothing more than any drink taken before a meal—a drink intended to "open up the appetite." Light spirits such as wine, champagne or fortified wine make superb openings to a meal. But there are many other exciting aperitifs on the market, including vermouths and bitters. Aperitifs can be enjoyed on their own, chilled, on the rocks or as ingredients in a large variety of mixed drinks.

Chilled vermouth offers an enjoyable way to ease yourself into a meal. A processed wine-based beverage, vermouth also contains sugar additives, herbal and plant flavorings and extra alcohol. At one time, dry vermouth was produced by the French and sweet vermouth by the Italians. Today the lines are less clear-cut, and both countries produce both varieties. Vermouth can be enjoyed on its own and is especially good on the rocks or with soda. Dry vermouth is a main ingredient in martinis; sweet vermouth is a main ingredient in Manhattans. Two of the more popular vermouths are Martini & Rossi and Cinzano, both from Italy. They come in dry and sweet varieties.

Other favorite aperitifs include Lillet Aperitif from France, which comes in white and red types. This wine-based drink with an orange flavoring has a rather delicate flavor. Dubonnet Aperitif Wine is manufactured both in France and in the

United States. Its red (rouge) version is sweet, its white (blanc) dry.

Bitters might also appeal to you. Most bitters have, as one would assume, a bitter note to them, and many, although not all, have some alcohol content. They are generally derived from formulas that include some combination of aromatic plants, such as barks, seeds, roots, flowers, herbs, fruits and, many times, quinine. Many bitters have medicinal uses. In fact, a glass of club soda with some Angostura bitters is a great way to relieve an upset stomach. Bright red Campari, which comes from Italy, is one of the leading bitters aperitifs. It is very appealing to the eye, but watch out—it has a 96 proof alcohol base. It tastes bitter but is aromatic and has a very slight hint of underlying sweetness.

Another to try is Amer Picon, a French product based on orange, quinine and gentian roots. England offers orange bitters and peach bitters; Italy produces Punt e Mes bitters, which are wine-based with quinine and have a sweet and bitter taste. Angostura bitters from Trinidad are a popular component of many mixed drink recipes, but some adventurous drinkers take them straight. In the same vein are Peychaud's bitters from Louisiana, which are slightly more pungent than Angostura.

Anise-flavored Pernod (90 proof, so watch out) from France is the best known of its type. It is best taken five parts water to one part liquor, and it turns cloudy when mixed. Ouzo is another favorite among fans of anise and is sometimes served with three coffee beans floating on top.

Those looking for a truly great aperitif might try mixing up a Campari and Soda, an Americano, a Negroni or a Vermouth Cassis. Some others to try are the Knockout, the Addington, the Punt e Mes Negroni, the Cat's Eye, the Bitter Bikini, the Via Veneto, the Dubonnet Cocktail, the Dubonnet Negroni, the Depth Charge and the Kiss Me Quick. Kir and Kir Royale are two more ways to whet your palate. Check the Index by Ingredients for various spirits to find additional recipes.

Remember, too, that as the rules are no longer formal,

aperitifs can be consumed before, during or after a meal—or just by themselves. Drink what you want when you want.

Sour Glass   Martini Glass   Sherry Glass

AFTER-DINNER DRINKS

COFFEE drinks, pousse-cafés, pony glasses filled with your favorite liqueur or snifters of brandy or cognac make the perfect conclusion to a meal. As this partial list of options shows, after-dinner drinks are typically liqueur based. Their soothing quality induces a sense of relaxation and well-being after the evening meal, promoting good digestion. While it is acceptable today to drink these drinks anytime, after dinner is still the preferred time for most. A fine after-dinner drink can inspire friendly conversation or simply wipe away the cares of the day.

Coffee, which makes a superb ending to a great meal, offers the perfect complement to many liqueurs. Try a Spanish Coffee, Mexican Coffee or any other coffee drink (see coffee drink index, p. 476) to top off your dining experience. Mixed liqueur drinks, such as a B & B or Jelly Bean, Dirty Mother or Sicilian Kiss, are adventurous alternatives for those seeking something a little different. And if you like pousse-cafés, why not try a Rainbow Pousse-Café or a Traffic Light? The recipe section of this book contains many possibilities to choose from. For those who prefer the simplicity of just one liqueur, however, cordials running the gamut from amaretto to Drambuie to Frangelico, and from Grand Marnier to Chambord to Tia Maria make for some sweet evening thoughts.

If a mellower, more complex flavor is more to your liking, brandy, the leading category of after-dinner drinks, offers a wide range of tastes. The term brandy comes from the Dutch word *brandewijn,* meaning "burned wine," which refers to the heating of wine for distillation into spirits. The results of this process are liqueurs with an aroma as rewarding as their flavor, so brandies should always be served in a snifter.

While brandies come from a variety of regions, such as Spain, Italy and California, it is France that most people think of as the finest source, thanks largely to that nation's production of two very special forms of brandy. Subtle, sophisticated cognac and pungent, smooth armagnac are distilled under the strictest regulations, aged in oak barrels and carefully blended to perfection. Both have an alcohol content of 40 to 43 percent, but they differ in that cognac is distilled twice and armagnac just once. Armagnac thus has a larger, and often sweeter, flavor. It is also distinguished from cognac by vintaging—it can be vintaged, while cognac cannot.

Among the better-known brands of cognac are Courvoisier, Hennessey, Rémy-Martin and Martell. But despite cognac's enduring appeal, armagnac has recently overtaken it in popularity, with such brands as Sempé attracting a great deal of attention.

Reading the labels on bottles of these fine spirits is somewhat overwhelming to the untrained eye, but this simple key should unravel the mystery:

V.S. = Very Special or Very Superior, equivalent to the three stars designation; the least expensive blend, aged at least 2½ years (most brandies are aged from 3 to 5 years)

V.O. = Very Old, aged at least 4½ years

V.S.O.P. = Very Superior Old Pale, aged at least 4½ years but generally for 7 to 10 years

Vieille Réserve = a finer grade of brandy, aged as long as V.S.O.P.

Extra or Napoleon = designates the very finest brandies, 6½ years or older

Aside from cognac and armagnac, other brandies include those made from apples, such as Calvados, from Normandy, and applejack, a less refined version from the United States. A strong, woody-tasting brandy known as *marc* in France is called *grappa* in Italy, while Spain produces a brandy that is a sweeter and heavier alternative to cognac and armagnac.

Another type of brandy is true fruit brandy, known as *eau-de-vie* or *alcools blanc*. These are not the same as the colored, sweet brandies more familiar to Americans. Instead, true fruit brandies are unsweetened and usually clear. Aged in the bottle, they deliver a purer and more sophisticated flavor to the palate than their syrupy cousins. Cherry, plum, pear, raspberry and strawberry types are some of the best known and widely used true fruit brandies. Unlike cognac and armagnac, these fruit brandies should be served slightly chilled.

Cordials and liqueurs are another group of after-dinner drinks most everyone can enjoy. These alcoholic beverages are particularly sweet and are flavored with any of a number of herbs, seeds, fruits, nuts and other special flavorings. Cream liqueurs, such as Baileys Original Irish Cream, add cream to the spirits as a stabilizer. Another distinct category is crèmes such as crème de noyaux, crème de cassis and crème de cacao. These liqueurs have an exceptionally high sugar content, which results in a consistency quite similar to cream.

Some other popular liqueurs are aquavit (akvavit), distilled from rye and caraway; Bénédictine, made from a secret formula of herbs; Galliano, a piquant herb-based liqueur; peppermint schnapps, a refreshing eye-opener; crème de fraises, derived from strawberries; crème de banana, formulated from bananas; a Danish cherry drink called Cherry Heering; Cointreau, distilled from orange peels; coffee-flavored Kahlúa; and Southern Comfort, a whiskey-based drink with peaches added.

Liqueurs are traditionally served in pony glasses after a meal, but today, more and more liqueurs can be found in exciting mixed drinks. From the famed Grasshopper, made with crème de menthe, to the Sombrero's Kahlúa and cream; from the Good and Plenty, a combination of ouzo and anisette, to the Jelly Bean, mixed from anisette and blackberry brandy: Liqueurs add a delicious dimension to mixed drinks.

Whatever your pleasure in after-dinner drinks, a sip of spirits following the evening meal is indeed a pleasure.

Hot Drink Mug

Brandy Snifter

Pousse-Café

DRINK
RECIPES

AALBORG SOUR

2 oz. Aalborg akvavit (or
   substitute any
   Scandinavian akvavit/
   aquavit)
1 oz. sour mix

1. Fill mixing glass with ice
2. Add akvavit and sour mix
3. Shake
4. Strain into a cocktail glass
5. Add ice (optional)

ABBEY COCKTAIL (1)

1½ oz. gin
¾ oz. orange juice
1 or 2 dashes orange
   bitters

1. Fill mixing glass with ice
2. Add gin, orange juice and
   orange bitters
3. Shake
4. Strain into a chilled cocktail
   glass
5. Garnish with a cherry or an
   orange peel

ABBEY COCKTAIL (2)

1½ oz. gin
¾ oz. orange juice
¼ oz. sweet vermouth

1. Fill mixing glass with ice
2. Add gin, orange juice, sweet
   vermouth and bitters

1 or 2 dashes Angostura bitters	3. Shake
	4. Strain into a chilled cocktail glass
	5. Add ice
	6. Garnish with a cherry

ABSOLUT ROYALTY COCKTAIL

1 oz. amaretto	1. Mix ingredients in shaker with ice
2 oz. cranberry juice	
1 oz. peach schnapps	2. Shake
1 oz. vodka	3. Strain into shot glasses
2 oz. Chambord	

ABSOLUT SANTO*

3 oz. Absolut vodka	1. Fill mixing glass with ice
dash Chambord	2. Add Absolut vodka and Chambord
	3. Shake
	4. Strain into a chilled martini glass

ACAPULCO

1¾ oz. rum	1. Fill mixing glass with ice
¼ oz. triple sec	2. Add rum, triple sec, egg white, lime juice and sugar
1 egg white	
½ oz. lime juice	3. Shake
¼ tsp. sugar	4. Strain into a rocks glass
mint leaves	5. Add ice
	6. Garnish with 2 or 3 torn mint leaves

---

* Courtesy of Sign of the Dove, New York City.

ADDINGTON

1½ oz. sweet vermouth	1. Fill a highball glass with ice
1½ oz. dry vermouth	2. Add sweet vermouth and dry
4 oz. club soda	vermouth
	3. Fill with club soda
	4. Stir
	5. Garnish with a lemon twist

ADMIRAL COCKTAIL

1 oz. bourbon	1. Fill mixing glass with ice
1½ oz. dry vermouth	2. Add bourbon, dry vermouth and
½ oz. lemon juice	lemon juice
	3. Shake
	4. Strain into a chilled cocktail
	glass
	5. Garnish with a lemon twist

ADONIS

1½ oz. dry sherry	1. Fill mixing glass with ice
¾ oz. sweet vermouth	2. Add sherry, sweet vermouth and
dash orange bitters	orange bitters
	3. Stir
	4. Strain into a chilled cocktail
	glass
	5. Garnish with an orange peel

ADRIENNE'S DREAM

2 oz. brandy	1. Fill mixing glass with ice
½ oz. peppermint schnapps	2. Add brandy, peppermint
½ oz. white crème de cacao	schnapps, white crème de
½ oz. lemon juice	cacao, lemon juice and sugar

½ tsp. sugar
1 oz. club soda

3. Shake
4. Strain into a Collins glass
5. Add ice
6. Top with club soda
7. Garnish with a mint sprig

ADULT HOT CHOCOLATE

1½ oz. peppermint
  schnapps
1 cup hot chocolate
whipped cream

1. Pour peppermint schnapps into
   a mug
2. Add hot chocolate
3. Top with a dollop of whipped
   cream, if desired

AFFAIR

----

2 oz. strawberry schnapps
2 oz. cranberry juice
  cocktail
2 oz. orange juice
1 oz. club soda (optional)

1. Fill a highball glass with ice
2. Add strawberry schnapps,
   cranberry juice cocktail and
   orange juice
3. Stir
4. Top with club soda, if desired

AFFINITY COCKTAIL

----

1 oz. scotch whiskey
1 oz. dry sherry
1 oz. port
2 dashes Angostura bitters

1. Fill mixing glass with ice
2. Add scotch, sherry, port and
   bitters
3. Stir
4. Strain into a chilled cocktail
   glass
5. Garnish with a lemon twist and
   a cherry

AFTER DINNER

1½ oz. apricot brandy 1½ oz. curaçao 2 oz. lime juice	1. Fill mixing glass with ice 2. Add apricot brandy, curaçao and lime juice 3. Shake 4. Strain into a rocks glass with ice 5. Garnish with lime

AFTER EIGHT (SHOOTER)

⅓ oz. Kahlúa ⅓ oz. Baileys Original Irish Cream ⅓ oz. white crème de menthe	Layer Kahlúa, Baileys and white crème de menthe in a rocks glass without ice

AFTER FIVE (SHOOTER)

⅓ oz. Kahlúa ⅓ oz. peppermint schnapps ⅓ oz. Baileys Original Irish Cream	Layer Kahlúa, peppermint schnapps and Baileys in a rocks glass without ice

A.J.

1½ oz. applejack (apple brandy) 1½ oz. grapefruit juice 3 or 4 dashes grenadine	1. Fill mixing glass with ice 2. Add applejack, grapefruit juice and grenadine 3. Shake 4. Strain into a chilled cocktail glass

ALABAMA

1 oz. brandy	1. Fill mixing glass with ice
1 oz. curaçao	2. Add brandy, curaçao, lime juice
½ oz. lime juice	and sugar syrup
½ tsp. sugar syrup	3. Shake
	4. Strain into chilled cocktail glass
	5. Garnish with orange peel

ALABAMA SLAMMER

½ oz. sloe gin	1. Fill mixing glass with ice
½ oz. Southern Comfort	2. Add all ingredients
½ oz. triple sec	3. Shake
½ oz. Galliano	4. Strain into a highball glass
2-3 oz. orange juice	5. Add ice
	6. Garnish with a cherry and an
	orange slice

ALABAMA SLAMMER (SHOOTER)

1½ oz. sloe gin	1. Fill mixing glass with ice
1½ oz. amaretto	2. Add sloe gin, amaretto,
1½ oz. Southern Comfort	Southern Comfort and
1½ oz. orange juice	orange juice
	3. Shake
(MAKES ABOUT 4 SHOTS)	4. Strain into shot glasses

ALABAZAM

2 oz. cognac	1. Fill mixing glass with ice
1 tbsp. curaçao	2. Add cognac, curaçao, lemon
1 tsp. lemon juice	juice, sugar syrup and orange
2 tsp. sugar syrup	bitters
2 dashes orange bitters	3. Shake

82

4. Strain into a rocks glass filled
   with ice

ALASKA

1½ oz. gin
1 oz. yellow Chartreuse

1. Fill mixing glass with ice
2. Add gin and yellow Chartreuse
3. Shake
4. Strain into a chilled cocktail
   glass
5. Garnish with a lemon wedge

ALBERMARLE

----

2 oz. gin
½ tbsp. powdered sugar
dash raspberry syrup
1½ tbsp. lemon juice
club soda

1. Fill mixing glass with ice
2. Add gin, sugar, raspberry syrup
   and lemon juice
3. Strain into a rocks glass filled
   with ice
4. Fill with club soda

ALEXANDER

----

1 oz. white crème de cacao
1 oz. gin
1 oz. heavy cream

1. Fill mixing glass with crushed
   ice
2. Add crème de cacao, gin and
   cream
3. Shake
4. Strain into a chilled cocktail
   glass
5. Sprinkle with nutmeg (optional)

ALEXANDER'S SISTER'S COCKTAIL

1 oz. green crème de menthe 1 oz. gin 1 oz. heavy cream	1. Fill mixing glass with crushed ice 2. Add crème de menthe, gin and cream 3. Shake 4. Strain into a chilled cocktail glass 5. Sprinkle with nutmeg (optional)

ALFREDO

1½ oz. gin 1½ oz. Campari	1. Fill mixing glass with ice 2. Add gin and Campari 3. Shake 4. Strain into a rocks glass filled with ice

ALGONQUIN

1½ oz. whiskey 1 oz. dry vermouth 1 oz. pineapple juice	1. Fill mixing glass with ice 2. Add whiskey, dry vermouth and pineapple juice 3. Shake 4. Strain into a chilled cocktail glass

ALLEGHENY

1 oz. bourbon 1 oz. dry vermouth 1½ tsp. blackberry brandy 1½ tsp. lemon juice	1. Fill mixing glass with ice 2. Add bourbon, dry vermouth, blackberry brandy and lemon juice

3. Shake
4. Strain into a chilled cocktail glass
5. Garnish with a twist of lemon

ALLIANCE

1 oz. gin
1 oz. dry vermouth
2 dashes aquavit (akvavit)

1. In a mixing glass, combine gin, dry vermouth and aquavit with several ice cubes
2. Shake
3. Strain into a rocks glass containing a couple of ice cubes

ALMOND COCKTAIL

2 oz. gin
1 oz. dry vermouth
½ oz. amaretto

1. Fill mixing glass with ice
2. Add gin, dry vermouth and amaretto
3. Stir
4. Strain into a rocks glass filled with ice

ALMOND JOY

1 oz. cream of coconut
1 oz. amaretto
1 oz. dark crème de cacao
2 oz. cream

1. Fill mixing glass with ice
2. Add cream of coconut, amaretto, dark crème de cacao and cream
3. Shake
4. Strain into a highball glass filled with ice

ALTO PARLARLE

1 oz. orange sherbet
½ oz. Cointreau
chilled dry Italian sparkling
   wine
dash grenadine
	1. In a chilled 8-oz. wineglass,
	   combine orange sherbet and
	   Cointreau
	2. Blend together
	3. Top with chilled dry Italian
	   sparkling wine
	4. Add dash of grenadine to top

AMARETTO AND CREAM

1½ oz. amaretto 1½ oz. cream	1. Fill mixing glass with cracked ice 2. Add amaretto and cream 3. Shake 4. Strain into chilled cocktail glass

AMARETTO COFFEE (ITALIAN COFFEE)

1½ oz. amaretto hot coffee whipped cream	1. Pour amaretto into a mug 2. Fill with hot coffee 3. Add whipped cream to top

AMARETTO MIST

1½ oz. amaretto	1. Add crushed ice to a rocks glass 2. Pour in amaretto 3. Garnish with a lemon twist

AMARETTO SOUR

1½ oz. amaretto 3 oz. sour mix	1. Fill mixing glass with ice 2. Add amaretto and sour mix

3. Stir
4. Strain into a sour glass filled with ice
5. Garnish with a cherry and orange slice

AMERICANA

1 tsp. bourbon
dash orange bitters
½ tsp. superfine sugar
dry sparkling wine
1 slice brandied peach

1. Combine bourbon, bitters and sugar in a mixing glass
2. Pour into a chilled champagne glass
3. Top with sparkling wine
4. Do NOT stir
5. Garnish with 1 slice brandied peach

AMERICAN BEAUTY

¾ oz. brandy
¾ oz. dry vermouth
½ oz. grenadine
¾ oz. orange juice
½ oz. crème de menthe

1. Fill mixing glass with ice
2. Add brandy, dry vermouth, grenadine, orange juice and crème de menthe
3. Shake
4. Strain into a chilled cocktail glass

AMERICANO

1 oz. Campari
1 oz. sweet vermouth
3 oz. club soda

1. Fill a highball glass with ice
2. Add Campari, sweet vermouth and club soda
3. Stir

AMER PICON COCKTAIL

1½ oz. Amer Picon
1 tsp. grenadine
½ oz. fresh lime juice

1. Fill mixing glass with ice
2. Add Amer Picon, grenadine and lime juice
3. Shake
4. Strain into a chilled cocktail glass

ANDALUSIA

1½ oz. dry sherry
½ oz. brandy
½ oz. light rum

1. Fill mixing glass with ice
2. Add sherry, brandy and rum
3. Stir
4. Strain into a chilled cocktail glass

ANGEL FACE

1 oz. gin
½ oz. apricot brandy
½ oz. apple brandy

1. Fill mixing glass with ice
2. Add gin, apricot brandy and apple brandy
3. Shake
4. Strain into a chilled cocktail glass

ANGEL'S KISS

1 oz. dark crème de cacao
1 oz. cream

1. Pour dark crème de cacao into 2 oz. pony glass
2. Float cream on top by slowly pouring the cream over the back of a long-handled bar spoon (the liquids should not mix)

(*Note:* See further instructions under pousse-cafés.)

ANGEL'S TIT

1 oz. dark crème de cacao
1 oz. cream

1. Pour dark crème de cacao into 2 oz. pony glass
2. Float cream on top by slowly pouring the cream over the back of a long-handled bar spoon (the liquids should not mix)
3. Garnish with a cherry on a toothpick centered across the top

(*Note:* See further instructions under pousse-cafés.)

ANNA'S BANANA

1½ oz. vodka
1 oz. lime juice
½ small banana, peeled and sliced
1 tsp. honey

1. Fill blender with 4 oz. ice
2. Add vodka, lime juice, banana slices and honey
3. Blend at medium speed for about 15 seconds, until smooth
4. Pour into a chilled goblet or large wineglass
5. Garnish with a lime slice

ANTE

1 oz. apple brandy
½ oz. triple sec
1 oz. Dubonnet

1. Fill mixing glass with ice
2. Add apple brandy, triple sec and Dubonnet
3. Stir
4. Strain into a chilled cocktail glass

ANTI-FREEZE (SHOOTER)

½ oz. green crème de
   menthe
½ oz. vodka

1. Fill mixing glass with ice
2. Add green crème de menthe and
   vodka
3. Shake
4. Strain into a rocks glass

APERITIVO COCKTAIL

1½ oz. gin
1 oz. sambuca
3 dashes orange bitters

1. Fill mixing glass with ice
2. Add gin, sambuca and orange
   bitters
3. Shake
4. Strain into a chilled cocktail
   glass

APPLECAR

1 oz. applejack (apple
   brandy)
1 oz. triple sec
1 oz. lemon juice

1. Fill mixing glass with ice
2. Add applejack, triple sec and
   lemon juice
3. Shake
4. Strain into a chilled cocktail
   glass

APPLE DAIQUIRI

½ oz. apple juice
½ oz. lime juice
1½ oz. light rum
½ tsp. superfine sugar

1. Fill mixing glass with 4 oz.
   shaved ice
2. Add apple juice, lime juice,
   light rum and sugar
3. Shake
4. Strain into a chilled cocktail
   glass

APPLE EDEN

1½ oz. vodka
3 oz. apple juice

1. Pour vodka and apple juice over ice cubes in a rocks glass
2. Stir
3. Garnish with an orange twist

APPLE GINGER PUNCH

18 oz. apple brandy
2 oz. cherry liqueur
2 oz. kirsch
1 qt. pineapple-grapefruit juice
24 oz. green ginger wine
1 qt. plus 1 pt. ginger ale
2 red apples
2 yellow apples

1. Chill all ingredients
2. Pour apple brandy, cherry liqueur, kirsch, juice and wine over a block of ice in a large punch bowl
3. Stir
4. Refrigerate for one hour
5. Cut apples into wedges and hold on side
6. When ready to serve, pour in ginger ale
7. Float apple slice on top of punch

APPLE GROG

1½ oz. applejack (apple brandy)
1 tbsp. brown sugar
4 oz. water
2 whole allspice
1 piece cinnamon stick
½ oz. 151-proof rum

1. Pour applejack, sugar and water into a small saucepan
2. Add allspice and cinnamon
3. Bring to boiling point, but do not boil
4. Pour into a heat-resistant mug
5. Float 151-proof rum on top
6. Garnish with a twist of lemon

APPLE JACQUES

1½ oz. Lillet
1½ oz. apple brandy

1. Fill mixing glass with ice
2. Add Lillet and apple brandy
3. Shake
4. Strain into a cocktail glass

APPLE PIE

1½ oz. light rum
¾ oz. sweet vermouth
½ oz. apple brandy
1 tsp. lemon juice
dash grenadine
dash apricot brandy

1. Fill mixing glass with ice
2. Add light rum, sweet vermouth, apple brandy, lemon juice, grenadine and apricot brandy
3. Shake
4. Strain into a cocktail glass

APRÈS SKI

1 oz. peppermint schnapps
1 oz. Kahlúa
1 oz. white crème de cacao

1. Fill mixing glass with ice
2. Add peppermint schnapps, Kahlúa and white crème de cacao
3. Shake
4. Put approximately 1 oz. of crushed ice into a cocktail glass
5. Strain drink into the glass

APRICOT

1½ oz. apricot brandy
¾ oz. orange juice
¾ oz. lemon juice
dash gin

1. Fill mixing glass with ice
2. Add apricot brandy, orange juice, lemon juice and gin
3. Shake
4. Strain into a chilled cocktail glass

APRICOT FIZZ

1½ oz. apricot brandy
3 oz. sour mix
1 oz. club soda

1. Fill mixing glass with ice
2. Add apricot brandy and sour mix
3. Shake
4. Strain into a Collins glass
5. Add club soda
6. Add ice
7. Garnish with a cherry and an orange slice

APRICOT SOUR

1 oz. lemon juice
½ tsp. superfine sugar
2 oz. apricot brandy

1. Pour lemon juice and sugar into mixing glass
2. Stir to dissolve sugar
3. Add apricot brandy and ice cubes
4. Shake
5. Strain into a chilled cocktail glass
6. Garnish with a cherry and an orange slice (or a lemon twist)

APRIL SHOWER

1 oz. brandy
¼ oz. yellow Chartreuse
1 oz. orange juice

1. Pour the ingredients into a cocktail shaker with ice
2. Shake well
3. Strain into a chilled cocktail glass

ARAWAK PUNCH

1½ oz. gold Jamaican rum
½ oz. pineapple juice
½ oz. cranberry juice
½ oz. lime juice
1 tsp. almond-flavored syrup

1. Fill mixing glass with ice
2. Add all ingredients
3. Shake
4. Pour into a rocks glass
5. Add ice

(*Note:* Recipe may be multiplied by number of servings desired and prepared in a punch bowl.)

AROUND THE WORLD

1½ oz. gin
1½ oz. green crème de menthe
1½ oz. pineapple juice

1. Fill mixing glass with ice
2. Add gin, crème de menthe and pineapple juice
3. Shake
4. Strain into a rocks glass filled with ice

ARTILLERY

2 oz. dry gin
1 oz. sweet vermouth

1. Fill mixing glass with ice
2. Add gin and sweet vermouth
3. Shake
4. Strain into a chilled cocktail glass

ARTILLERY PUNCH

1 qt. bourbon
1 qt. red wine
1 qt. black tea
1 pt. dark rum
1 pt. orange juice

1. Combine all ingredients and allow to chill in refrigerator
2. When ready to serve, pour over ice in a large punch bowl

1 cup brandy
1 cup gin
1 cup lemon juice
sugar syrup (to taste)

(MAKES APPROXIMATELY 40
SERVINGS)

3. Adjust sweetness and garnish
with lemon twists

ASSASSINO

2 oz. whiskey
1 oz. dry vermouth
1 oz. pineapple juice
1 oz. club soda
2–3 dashes Sambuca
Romana

1. Fill mixing glass with ice
2. Add whiskey, dry vermouth and
pineapple juice
3. Shake
4. Strain into a Collins glass
5. Top with club soda
6. Add ice
7. Add a few dashes Sambuca to
top of drink

ASTRONAUT

1½ oz. Jamaican rum
1½ oz. vodka
1½ tsp. lemon juice
1½ tsp. passion fruit juice

1. Fill mixing glass with ice
2. Add rum, vodka, lemon juice
and passion fruit juice
3. Shake
4. Strain into a Collins glass
5. Add ice
6. Garnish with a lemon twist

ATLANTIC BREEZE

1 oz. light rum
½ oz. apricot brandy
4 oz. pineapple juice
1 oz. lemon juice

1. Fill mixing glass with ice
2. Add light rum, apricot brandy,
pineapple juice, lemon juice and
grenadine

dash grenadine
½ oz. Galliano

3. Shake
4. Strain into a Collins glass half-filled with ice
5. Top with Galliano
6. Garnish with a cherry and an orange slice

AUBADE

2½ oz. light rum
1 oz. lime juice
½ oz. grenadine
2–3 oz. tonic

1. Fill a highball glass with ice
2. Add rum, lime juice and grenadine
3. Stir
4. Add tonic
5. Stir gently

AUNT AGATHA

2 oz. light rum
4 oz. orange juice
2–3 drops Angostura bitters

1. Fill a rocks glass with ice
2. Add rum and orange juice
3. Stir
4. Float bitters on top
5. Garnish with an orange slice

AUNT JEMIMA

½ oz. brandy
½ oz. white crème de cacao
½ oz. Bénédictine

Layer ingredients into a pony glass, beginning with the brandy.

AVIATION

1½ oz. gin
½ tsp. apricot brandy
½ tsp. cherry brandy
½ oz. lemon juice

1. Fill mixing glass with ice
2. Add gin, apricot brandy, cherry brandy and lemon juice
3. Shake
4. Strain into a chilled cocktail glass

AZTECA

1½ oz. light rum (tequila may be substituted)
1 oz. Kahlúa
1 oz. white crème de cacao
1–2 dashes curaçao

1. Fill mixing glass with ice
2. Add rum (or tequila), Kahlúa, white crème de cacao and curaçao
3. Shake
4. Strain into a chilled cocktail glass

B

B-52

1 oz. Baileys Original Irish Cream 1 oz. Kahlúa 1 oz. Grand Marnier	1. Fill mixing glass with ice 2. Add Baileys, Kahlúa and Grand Marnier 3. Shake 4. Strain into a rocks glass filled with ice

B-53 (SHOOTER)

½ oz. Kahlúa ½ oz. Baileys Original Irish Cream ½ oz. Grand Marnier ½ oz. Stolichnaya	Layer Kahlúa, Baileys, Grand Marnier and Stolichnaya in a shot glass

B & B

½ oz. Bénédictine ½ oz. brandy	1. Pour the Bénédictine into a cordial glass 2. Float the brandy on top

BABY RUTH (SHOOTER)

½ oz. Frangelico	1. Layer Frangelico and vodka in a shot glass
½ oz. vodka	2. Add peanuts
2 or 3 peanuts	

BACARDI

1½ oz. Bacardi light or gold rum	1. Fill mixing glass with ice
½ oz. lime juice	2. Add Bacardi, lime juice and grenadine
3 dashes grenadine	3. Shake
	4. Strain into a chilled cocktail glass

BAHAMA MAMA

1½ oz. light rum	1. Put a dash of grenadine in the bottom of a Collins glass or a hurricane glass
1½ oz. gold rum	2. Fill a mixing glass with ice
1½ oz. dark rum	3. Pour in light rum, gold rum, dark rum, sour mix, pineapple juice and orange juice
2 oz. sour mix	4. Shake
2 oz. pineapple juice	5. Pour into the Collins or hurricane glass
2½ oz. orange juice	6. Garnish with a cherry and an orange slice
dash grenadine	

BAILEYS AND COFFEE

1½ oz. Baileys Original Irish Cream	1. Pour Baileys into a mug
hot coffee	2. Fill with hot coffee
whipped cream	3. Add whipped cream to top

BAMBOO COCKTAIL

1½ oz. dry sherry
¾ oz. dry vermouth
dash orange bitters

1. Fill mixing glass with ice
2. Add dry sherry, dry vermouth and orange bitters
3. Stir
4. Strain into a chilled cocktail glass

BANANA BANSHEE

1 oz. white crème de cacao
1 oz. banana liqueur
1 oz. cream

1. Fill mixing glass with ice
2. Add crème de cacao, banana liqueur and cream
3. Shake
4. Strain into a chilled cocktail glass

BANANA BOAT

1½ oz. tequila
½ oz. banana liqueur
1 oz. lime juice

1. In a blender, combine tequila, banana liqueur, lime juice and 2 oz. crushed ice
2. Blend at medium speed for approximately 15 seconds, or until smooth
3. Pour into a sour glass

BANANA DAIQUIRI (FROZEN)

1½ oz. light rum
½ oz. lime juice
1 oz. banana liqueur
¼ banana, sliced

1. In a blender, put ½ cup crushed ice
2. Add rum, lime juice, banana liqueur, banana, sugar and cream

1 tsp. sugar or honey
(optional)
½ oz. cream

3. Whip at low speed until smooth
4. Pour into an oversized
   wineglass, sour glass or chilled
   champagne glass
5. Garnish with a lime slice

BANANA MAMA

1½ oz. light rum
½ oz. dark rum
1 oz. banana liqueur
1 oz. cream of coconut
1 oz. fresh or frozen
   strawberries
2 oz. pineapple juice

1. In blender, combine light rum,
   dark rum, banana liqueur,
   cream of coconut, strawberries
   and pineapple juice with 3 oz.
   crushed ice
2. Blend until smooth
3. Pour into a goblet

BANANA MOO

1½ oz. banana liqueur
1½ oz. cream

1. Fill mixing glass with ice
2. Add banana liqueur and cream
3. Shake
4. Strain into a rocks glass filled
   with ice

BANANA SPLIT

1½ oz. banana liqueur
¾ oz. white crème de cacao
¾ oz. crème de noyaux
dash milk
several dashes cherry
   brandy

1. In blender, combine banana
   liqueur, white crème de cacao,
   crème de noyaux and milk with
   3 oz. ice
2. Blend until smooth
3. Pour into a pilsner glass
4. Top with cherry brandy
5. Garnish with a cherry

BANANA TREE

1 oz. banana liqueur
½ oz. white crème de cacao
½ oz. Galliano
½ banana, peeled and
   sliced
5 oz. vanilla ice cream
4 drops vanilla extract

1. Fill blender with banana liqueur, white crème de cacao, Galliano, banana slices, vanilla ice cream and vanilla extract (Add ¼ cup crushed ice to make it thicker, if desired)
2. Blend until smooth
3. Pour into a large goblet or wineglass
4. Garnish with a slice of banana, with skin

BARBADOS BOWL

8 ripe bananas
8 oz. lime juice
1 cup sugar
12 oz. light rum
12 oz. dark rum
1 qt. plus 12 oz. pineapple
   juice
12 oz. mango nectar
2 limes, sliced

1. Chill all ingredients, except bananas
2. Thinly slice 6 bananas
3. Place banana slices, lime juice and sugar in a blender
4. Blend for a few seconds, until mixture is smooth
5. Pour over a block of ice in a large punch bowl
6. Pour in light rum, dark rum, pineapple juice and mango nectar
7. Stir
8. Refrigerate one hour before serving
9. Cut the remaining bananas into thin slices
10. Cut limes into thin slices
11. Float fruit on top of punch

BARBARELLA

2 oz. Cointreau
1 oz. sambuca

1. Fill mixing glass with ice
2. Add Cointreau and sambuca
3. Shake
4. Strain into a rocks glass filled with ice

BARBARY COAST

¾ oz. light rum
¾ oz. scotch
¾ oz. gin
¾ oz. crème de cacao
¾ oz. light cream

1. Fill mixing glass with ice
2. Add all ingredients
3. Shake
4. Strain into a large cocktail glass filled with ice

BARN DOOR

1½ oz. scotch
1 oz. triple sec
2 dashes orange bitters

1. Fill mixing glass with ice
2. Add scotch, triple sec and orange bitters
3. Shake
4. Strain into a rocks glass

BARNUM

1 oz. gin
½ oz. apricot brandy
2 dashes bitters
dash lemon juice

1. Fill mixing glass with ice
2. Add gin, apricot brandy, bitters and lemon juice
3. Shake
4. Strain into a rocks glass filled with ice

BATIDO MANGO

2 oz. Cachace
4 oz. fresh mango, chopped
2 tsp. granulated sugar
1 cup crushed ice

1. In a blender, combine all the ingredients
2. Blend well
3. Pour into a wineglass

BAY BREEZE

1½ oz. vodka
4 oz. pineapple juice
1 oz. cranberry juice

1. Fill a highball glass with ice
2. Add vodka, pineapple juice and cranberry juice
3. Stir

BEADLESTONE COCKTAIL

1½ oz. scotch
1½ oz. dry vermouth

1. Fill mixing glass with ice
2. Add scotch and dry vermouth
3. Stir
4. Strain into a chilled cocktail glass

BEAM ME UP, SCOTTY (SHOOTER)

⅓ oz. Kahlúa
⅓ oz. Baileys Original Irish Cream
⅓ oz. banana liqueur

Layer Kahlúa, Baileys and banana liqueur in a shot glass

BEAUTY SPOT COCKTAIL

1 oz. gin
½ oz. dry vermouth
½ oz. sweet vermouth

1. Put a dash of grenadine in a chilled cocktail glass
2. Fill mixing glass with ice

1 tsp. orange juice
dash grenadine

3. Add gin, dry vermouth, sweet vermouth and orange juice
4. Shake
5. Strain into glass

BEER BUSTER

1 oz. chilled vodka
2 dashes Tabasco sauce
draft beer

1. Combine chilled vodka, Tabasco and cold beer (usually draft beer) in a chilled beer mug
2. Stir

BEE'S KNEES

1½ oz. light rum
1 tsp. honey
1 tsp. fresh lemon juice

1. Fill mixing glass with ice
2. Add light rum, honey and fresh lemon juice
3. Shake
4. Strain into a chilled cocktail glass

BEE-STUNG LIPS

2 oz. light rum
1 tsp. honey
1 tsp. heavy cream

1. Fill mixing glass with ice
2. Add rum, honey and cream
3. Shake
4. Strain into a chilled cocktail glass

BELLINI

1 fresh peach
brut champagne

1. Puree a peach in a blender
2. Pour into a champagne glass
3. Add ice-cold champagne

BELLINI, FROZEN

2½ oz. sparkling wine
1 oz. triple sec
1 oz. peach puree (blend a
    ripe peach)
1 oz. simple syrup (dissolve
    one part sugar in one part
    boiling water; let cool)
a squeeze of lemon

1. Blend all ingredients with ice
2. Garnish with a peach wedge

BELLINI PUNCH

fresh peaches
iced brut champagne
1 tbsp. lemon juice
sugar

1. In a blender, puree enough
   peaches to fill the bottom of
   punch bowl
2. Pour mixture into bowl
3. Add approximately 3 times as
   much champagne
4. Add lemon juice and sugar
   (to taste)
5. Stir thoroughly

BELMONT

1½ oz. gin
¾ oz. raspberry syrup
½ oz. cream

1. Fill mixing glass with ice
2. Add gin, raspberry syrup and
   cream
3. Stir well
4. Strain into a chilled cocktail
   glass

BELMONT BREEZE

1½ oz. whiskey	1. Fill mixing glass with ice
¾ oz. Harvey's Bristol Cream Sherry	2. Add whiskey, Harvey's Bristol Cream Sherry, lemon juice, sugar syrup, orange juice and cranberry juice
½ oz. fresh lemon juice	
1 oz. sugar syrup	3. Shake
1½ oz. fresh orange juice	4. Strain into a highball glass
1½ oz. cranberry juice	5. Top half with 7–Up and half with club soda
approx. 1 oz. 7-Up	
approx. 1 oz. club soda	6. Garnish with fresh strawberry, mint sprig and lemon wedge

BENNETT

1½ oz. gin	1. Fill mixing glass with ice
½ oz. fresh lime juice	2. Add gin, lime juice, bitters and powdered sugar
1–2 dashes Angostura bitters	
1 tsp. powdered sugar	3. Shake
	4. Strain into a chilled cocktail glass

BENTLEY

1½ oz. apple brandy	1. Fill mixing glass with ice
1½ oz. Dubonnet	2. Add apple brandy and Dubonnet
	3. Stir
	4. Strain into a chilled cocktail glass

BENT NAIL

1½ oz. Canadian whiskey
½ oz. Drambuie
1 tsp. kirsch

1. Fill mixing glass with ice
2. Add whiskey, Drambuie and kirsch
3. Shake
4. Strain into a cocktail glass

BERMUDA HIGHBALL

1 oz. gin
1 oz. brandy
½ oz. dry vermouth
ginger ale or club soda

1. Fill a highball glass with ice
2. Add gin, brandy and dry vermouth
3. Fill with ginger ale or club soda
4. Stir

BETSY ROSS

1½ oz. brandy
1½ oz. port
2 dashes Angostura bitters
2 drops blue curaçao

1. Fill mixing glass with ice
2. Add brandy, port, bitters and blue curaçao
3. Stir
4. Strain into a brandy snifter

BETWEEN THE SHEETS

¾ oz. brandy
¾ oz. triple sec
¾ oz. light rum
¾ oz. sour mix

1. Fill mixing glass with ice
2. Add brandy, triple sec, rum and sour mix
3. Shake
4. Strain into a rocks glass filled with ice

BIBLE BELT*

2 oz. Jack Daniel's
2 oz. Rose's lime juice
2 oz. sour mix
1 oz. triple sec

1. Fill mixing glass with ice
2. Add Jack Daniel's, Rose's lime juice, sour mix and triple sec
3. Shake
4. Frost the rim of a highball glass with sugar
5. Strain mixture into the glass
6. Add ice if necessary

BIG BLUE SKY

½ oz. light rum
½ oz. blue curaçao
½ oz. cream of coconut
2 oz. pineapple juice

1. Fill blender with light rum, blue curaçao, cream of coconut, pineapple juice and 3 oz. crushed ice
2. Blend until smooth
3. Pour into a goblet

BITTER BIKINI

1½ oz. Campari
1 oz. dry vermouth
½ oz. triple sec

1. Fill mixing glass with ice
2. Add Campari, dry vermouth and triple sec
3. Shake
4. Strain into a rocks glass filled with ice (preferably crushed ice)

BLACKBERRY DEMITASSE

1 oz. blackberry brandy
½ oz. brandy
1 tbsp. blackberry jelly
½ oz. water

1. Heat blackberry brandy, brandy, blackberry jelly, water and lemon juice in a small saucepan (do NOT bring to a boil)

---

* Courtesy of The Cowgirl Hall of Fame, New York City.

½ tsp. lemon juice

2. Stir well (jelly should be dissolved)
3. Pour into a demitasse cup
4. Garnish with a slice of lemon

BLACK-CHERRY RUM PUNCH

24 oz. light rum
4 oz. dark rum
2 oz. 151-proof rum
2 cans (17 oz. each) pitted black cherries in heavy syrup
4 oz. Peter Heering
4 oz. crème de cassis
4 oz. orange juice
8 oz. sour mix
2 limes
1 qt. chilled club soda

1. In a large punch bowl add light rum, dark rum, 151-proof rum, cherries, Peter Heering, crème de cassis, orange juice and sour mix
2. Slice limes into thin slices and add to mixture
3. Add a block of ice
4. Stir well
5. Refrigerate for about one hour
6. When ready to serve, pour in club soda
7. Stir gently

BLACK-EYED SUSAN

2 oz. Grand Marnier
½ oz. white crème de menthe
½ oz. brandy

1. Fill mixing glass with ice
2. Add Grand Marnier, white crème de menthe and brandy
3. Shake
4. Strain into a chilled cocktail glass

BLACK HAWK

1½ oz. blended whiskey
1½ oz. sloe gin

1. Fill mixing glass with ice
2. Add blended whiskey and sloe gin
3. Stir

4. Strain into a chilled cocktail glass
5. Garnish with a cherry

BLACK LADY

2 oz. Grand Marnier
½ oz. Kahlúa
1 tbsp. brandy

1. Fill mixing glass with ice
2. Add Grand Marnier, Kahlúa and brandy
3. Shake
4. Strain into a chilled cocktail glass

BLACK LICORICE

½ oz. sambuca
½ oz. Kahlúa

Pour sambuca and Kahlúa into a brandy snifter or a pony glass

BLACK MAGIC

1½ oz. vodka
¾ oz. Kahlúa
1–2 dashes lemon juice

1. Fill a rocks glass with ice
2. Add vodka, Kahlúa and lemon juice
3. Garnish with a lemon twist

BLACK MANHATTAN

1½ oz. Old Bushmills Black Bush Irish whiskey
¼ oz. sweet vermouth

1. Fill mixing glass with ice
2. Add Old Bushmills Black Bush Irish whiskey and sweet vermouth
3. Stir
4. Strain into a chilled martini glass or rocks glass filled with ice
5. Garnish with a cherry

BLACK MARBLE

| 4 oz. Stolichnaya vodka (or other Russian or Polish vodka) | 1. Fill a rocks glass with ice
2. Pour in Stolichnaya
3. Garnish with a black olive and an orange slice |

BLACK MARTINI

| 3 oz. gin or vodka
½ oz. blackberry brandy or black raspberry liqueur | 1. Pour the ingredients into a cocktail shaker with ice
2. Shake well
3. Strain into a chilled cocktail glass or serve on the rocks in an old-fashioned glass
4. Garnish with a lemon twist |

BLACK RUSSIAN

| 2 oz. vodka
1 oz. Kahlúa | 1. Fill rocks glass with ice
2. Add vodka and Kahlúa
3. Stir |

BLACKTHORN

| 1½ oz. sloe gin
1½ oz. sweet vermouth | 1. Fill mixing glass with ice
2. Add sloe gin and sweet vermouth
3. Stir
4. Strain into a chilled cocktail glass |

BLACK VELVET

Guinness Stout champagne	1. Combine equal amounts of Guinness (preferably on draft) and champagne in a chilled Collins glass 2. Stir

BLACK WITCH

1½ oz. gold rum ¼ oz. dark rum ¼ oz. apricot brandy ½ oz. pineapple juice	1. Fill mixing glass with ice 2. Add gold rum, dark rum, apricot brandy and pineapple juice 3. Shake 4. Strain into a chilled cocktail glass

BLANCHE

1 oz. Cointreau 1 oz. curaçao 1 oz. anisette	1. Fill mixing glass with ice 2. Add Cointreau, curaçao and anisette 3. Stir 4. Strain into a chilled cocktail glass

BLENDED RASPBERRY COCKTAIL

½ cup ice or several ice cubes 8 oz. Minute Maid Light Raspberry with Tea 1½ oz. vodka	1. Combine ingredients in a blender 2. Garnish with several fresh raspberries

BLIND MELON

1 oz. vodka
1 oz. Southern Comfort
1 oz. amaretto
1 oz. Midori melon liqueur
cranberry juice

1. Fill a highball glass with ice
2. Combine vodka, Southern Comfort, amaretto, Midori and cranberry juice to fill
3. Stir

BLINKER

1½ oz. blended whiskey
3 oz. grapefruit juice
½ oz. grenadine

1. Fill mixing glass with ice
2. Add whiskey, grapefruit juice and grenadine
3. Strain into a rocks glass filled with ice

BLIZZARD

3 oz. bourbon
1 oz. cranberry juice
1 tbsp. lemon juice
2 tbsp. sugar syrup
3 oz. crushed ice

1. Pour all ingredients into a blender
2. Blend at low speed for about 15 seconds (until smooth)
3. Pour into a large wineglass or a highball glass

BLOOD AND SAND

1 oz. scotch
¾ oz. cherry brandy
¾ oz. sweet vermouth
¾ oz. orange juice

1. Fill mixing glass with ice
2. Add scotch, cherry brandy, sweet vermouth and orange juice
3. Stir
4. Strain into a chilled cocktail glass

BLOODY MARIA

1½ oz. tequila
3 oz. tomato juice
½ oz. lemon juice
3 drops Tabasco sauce
3 drops Worcestershire
   sauce
pinch celery salt
pinch pepper
dab horseradish (squeeze
   out liquid)

1. Combine tequila, tomato juice, lemon juice and seasonings (to taste) in a well-chilled mixing glass
2. Shake
3. Pour into an oversized wineglass or a chilled Collins glass
4. Garnish with a lime slice or a celery stalk

(*Note:* A Bloody Maria may also be served on the rocks and stirred in the glass, or it may be shaken with ice and strained into the glass.)

BLOODY MARY

1½ oz. vodka
3 oz. tomato juice
½ oz. lemon juice
3 drops Tabasco sauce
3 drops Worcestershire
   sauce
pinch celery salt
pinch pepper
dab horseradish (squeeze
   out liquid)

1. Combine vodka, tomato juice, lemon juice and seasonings (to taste) in a well-chilled mixing glass
2. Shake
3. Pour into an oversized wineglass or a chilled Collins glass
4. Garnish with a lime slice or a celery stalk

(*Note:* A Bloody Mary may also be served on the rocks and stirred in the glass, or it may be shaken with ice and strained into the glass.)

BLOODY RUM PUNCH

1 bottle rum (750 ml)
½ bottle red wine
6 oz. fresh lime juice
6 oz. triple sec
6 oz. simple syrup
2 limes sliced in thin wheels
2 red oranges sliced in thin
   wheels

1. Add all ingredients into a large
   punch bowl and place in the
   refrigerator for at least two
   hours before serving
2. Serve over ice in a punch glass

BLOW JOB (SHOOTER)

½ oz. vodka
½ oz. coffee-flavored brandy
½ oz. Kahlúa
whipped cream

1. Fill mixing glass with ice
2. Add vodka, coffee-flavored
   brandy and Kahlúa
3. Shake well
4. Strain into a shot glass
5. Top with whipped cream

BLUE BAYOU

1 cup ice
1½ oz. vodka
½ oz. blue curaçao
½ cup fresh or canned
   pineapple
2 oz. grapefruit juice

1. Pour the ingredients into a
   blender
2. Blend until smooth
3. Pour into a chilled margarita
   glass
4. Garnish with a chunk of
   pineapple

BLUE CARNATION

½ oz. white crème de cacao
½ oz. blue curaçao
2 oz. cream

1. Fill mixing glass with ice
2. Add white crème de cacao, blue
   curaçao and cream

3. Shake
4. Strain into a chilled cocktail glass

BLUE DENIM

½ oz. dry vermouth
½ oz. bourbon
2 dashes Angostura bitters
dash blue curaçao

1. Fill mixing glass with ice
2. Add dry vermouth, bourbon, Angostura bitters and blue curaçao
3. Shake
4. Strain into a rocks glass filled with ice
5. Garnish with a twist of lemon

BLUE HAWAIIAN

1 oz. light rum
2 oz. pineapple juice
1 oz. blue curaçao
1 oz. cream of coconut

1. Fill blender with 3 oz. crushed ice
2. Pour in rum, pineapple juice, blue curaçao and cream of coconut
3. Blend at low speed for about 15 seconds (until smooth)
4. Pour into a goblet
5. Garnish with a cherry and an orange slice

BLUE MARGARITA

2 oz. tequila
¾ oz. blue curaçao
2 oz. sour mix
½ oz. lime juice
salt for glass (optional)

1. Rub the rim of a margarita or large cocktail glass with the lemon or lime wedge (if you are going to salt the rim)
2. Turn the rim of the glass in a bed of salt (if desired)

lemon or lime wedge (if you use salt)

3. Fill a mixing glass with ice
4. Add tequila, blue curaçao, sour mix and lime juice
5. Shake
6. Strain into the glass
7. Add ice cubes (if desired)
8. Garnish with a cherry or a lime wedge

BLUE MARTINI

1½ oz. gin
½ oz. dry vermouth
½ oz. blue curaçao

1. Fill mixing glass with ice
2. Add gin, dry vermouth and blue curaçao
3. Shake
4. Strain into a martini glass
5. Garnish with a lime twist

BLUE MOON

1½ oz. gin
½ oz. dry vermouth
1 tsp. blue curaçao
dash Angostura bitters

1. Fill mixing glass with ice
2. Add gin, dry vermouth, blue curaçao and bitters
3. Shake
4. Strain into a chilled cocktail glass

BLUE SHARK

1 oz. white tequila
1 oz. vodka
¾ oz. blue curaçao

1. Fill mixing glass with ice
2. Add tequila, vodka and blue curaçao
3. Shake
4. Strain into a chilled cocktail glass

BLUSHING LADY

2 oz. vodka
1 oz. PAMA pomegranate liqueur
1 oz. pink grapefruit juice

1. Rub a wedge of lemon around the rim of a cocktail glass and dip the glass into a plate of coarse sugar
2. Set the glass aside
3. Pour the ingredients into a cocktail shaker with ice
4. Shake and strain into the prepared glass
5. Garnish with a lemon wedge

BOARDWALK BREEZER

1½ oz. dark rum
½ oz. banana liqueur
½ oz. lime juice
4 oz. pineapple juice
dash grenadine

1. Fill mixing glass with ice
2. Add dark rum, banana liqueur, lime juice and pineapple juice
3. Shake
4. Strain into a Collins glass
5. Add ice
6. Top with a dash of grenadine
7. Garnish with a cherry and an orange slice

BOBBY BURNS

1 oz. scotch
1 oz. dry vermouth
1 oz. sweet vermouth
dash Bénédictine

1. Fill mixing glass with ice
2. Add scotch, dry vermouth, sweet vermouth and Bénédictine
3. Stir
4. Strain into a chilled cocktail glass

BOCCI BALL

1½ oz. amaretto
6 oz. orange juice
club soda (if desired)

1. Fill a highball glass with ice
2. Add amaretto and orange juice
3. Stir
4. Splash club soda on top (optional)

BOILERMAKER

2 oz. whiskey
1 glass of beer

1. Drink a straight shot of whiskey
2. Chase it down with a glass of your favorite beer

(*Note:* If you prefer, mix the whiskey and beer in a highball glass and drink them together.)

BOLERO

1½ oz. light rum
¾ oz. apple brandy
¼ tsp. sweet vermouth

1. Fill mixing glass with ice
2. Add light rum, apple brandy and sweet vermouth
3. Stir
4. Strain into a chilled cocktail glass

BOMBAY

1 oz. brandy
1 oz. dry vermouth
½ oz. sweet vermouth
½ tsp. curaçao
dash of Pernod

1. Fill mixing glass with ice
2. Add brandy, dry vermouth, sweet vermouth, curaçao and Pernod
3. Shake
4. Strain into a chilled rocks glass filled with ice

BOOSTER

2 oz. brandy ½ oz. curaçao 1 egg white	1. Fill mixing glass with ice 2. Add brandy, curaçao and egg white 3. Shake 4. Strain into a chilled cocktail glass

BOOTLEG

¾ oz. Jack Daniel's ¾ oz. sambuca ¾ oz. Southern Comfort	1. Fill a rocks glass with ice 2. Add whiskey, sambuca and Southern Comfort 3. Stir

BOSTON RUM PUNCH

2 oz. Smith & Cross Traditional Jamaica Rum lemonade	1. Fill a shaker with finely cracked ice 2. Add the rum and fill with lemonade 3. Shake briefly and pour (unstrained) into a pint glass 4. Add a straw and garnish with either freshly grated nutmeg or half a strawberry and an orange slice

THE BOTTOM LINE

1½ oz. vodka ½ oz. lime juice 4 oz. tonic	1. Fill a highball glass with ice 2. Add vodka and lime juice 3. Fill with tonic 4. Garnish with a lime slice

BOURBON DAISY

1½ oz. bourbon
½ oz. Southern Comfort
½ oz. lemon juice
½ oz. grenadine
1 oz. club soda

1. Fill mixing glass with ice
2. Add bourbon, Southern Comfort, lemon juice and grenadine
3. Shake
4. Strain into a Collins glass
5. Add ice
6. Top with club soda
7. Garnish with a pineapple spear or a cherry and an orange slice

BOURBON OLD-FASHIONED

1 tsp. sugar
2 dashes bitters
1 tsp. water
3 oz. bourbon

1. Put sugar, bitters and water in rocks glass
2. Muddle to dissolve sugar
3. Add 1 or 2 ice cubes to glass
4. Pour in the bourbon
5. Add more ice (if desired)
6. Twist a lemon peel over the drink and add as garnish
7. If desired, may also garnish with a cherry and an orange slice

BOURBON SOUR

1½ oz. bourbon
3 oz. sour mix

1. Fill mixing glass with ice
2. Add bourbon and sour mix
3. Shake
4. Strain into a sour glass
5. Add ice
6. Garnish with a cherry and an orange slice

BOURBON STREET

2 fresh strawberries, hulled and quartered

½ oz. honey syrup (1 to 1 honey dissolved in water)

2 oz. bourbon

¾ oz. ginger syrup (use a commercial version like B.G. Reynolds' or make one with equal parts fresh ginger juice and granulated sugar)

¾ oz. fresh lemon juice

2 dashes rhubarb bitters

club soda

1. In the base of a shaker, muddle strawberries with honey syrup
2. Add remaining ingredients, except club soda, and shake with ice
3. Strain into an ice-filled highball glass
4. Top with soda
5. Garnish with a fresh strawberry slice and a mint sprig

BRAIN

1 oz. Kahlúa

1 oz. peach schnapps

1 oz. Baileys Original Irish Cream

Layer Kahlúa, peach schnapps and Baileys in a rocks glass filled with ice

BRAIN ERASER

1 oz. vodka

½ oz. Kahlúa

½ oz. amaretto

club soda

1. Fill a rocks glass with ice
2. Add vodka, Kahlúa and amaretto
3. Top with club soda
4. Drink it in one shot through a straw

BRAIN TUMOR

2 oz. Baileys Original Irish Cream 6 drops strawberry liqueur	1. Fill a rocks glass with ice 2. Pour in Baileys 3. Drop in strawberry liqueur 4. Do NOT stir (Drink is supposed to resemble an unhealthy brain.)

BRANDY ALEXANDER

½ oz. white crème de cacao ½ oz. brandy ½ oz. heavy cream nutmeg or cinnamon	1. Fill mixing glass with ice 2. Add crème de cacao, brandy and cream 3. Shake 4. Strain into a chilled cocktail glass 5. Sprinkle nutmeg or cinnamon on top

BRANDY COBBLER

2½ oz. brandy 1 tsp. peach liqueur (curaçao may be substituted) 2 tsp. lemon juice 1 tsp. sugar syrup (to taste)	1. Fill a chilled highball glass or goblet with cracked ice 2. Add brandy, peach liqueur, lemon juice and sugar syrup 3. Stir (the glass should frost) 4. Garnish with a cherry and an orange slice

BRANDY EGGNOG

2½ oz. brandy 1 cup milk 2 tbsp. powdered sugar	1. Combine all ingredients with ice 2. Shake well 3. Strain into a mug

| 1 egg | 4. Garnish with a sprinkle of nutmeg |

BRANDY GUMP

½ oz. brandy	1. Fill mixing glass with ice
½ oz. fresh lemon juice	2. Add brandy and lemon juice
2–3 drops grenadine	3. Shake
	4. Strain into a chilled cocktail glass
	5. Add a couple of drops of grenadine

BRANDY ICE

1½ oz. brandy	1. Combine all ingredients in a blender
½ oz. white crème de cacao	2. Blend until smooth
2 scoops French vanilla ice cream	3. Pour into a large brandy snifter
2 oz. shaved ice	4. Garnish with shaved sweet chocolate

BRANDY MANHATTAN

2 oz. brandy	1. Fill mixing glass with some ice
½ oz. sweet vermouth	2. Add brandy, sweet vermouth and bitters
dash Angostura bitters	3. Stir gently
	4. Strain into chilled martini glass
	5. Garnish with a cherry

BRANDY MILK PUNCH

2 oz. brandy
5 oz. cold milk
pinch sugar

1. Add a few ice cubes to a highball glass
2. Add brandy, milk and generous pinch of sugar
3. Stir
4. Sprinkle with nutmeg or cinnamon

BRANDY OLD-FASHIONED

2½ oz. brandy
1 cube sugar
1–2 dashes Angostura bitters

1. In a rocks glass, combine bitters and sugar cube
2. Pour in the brandy
3. Stir until sugar cube is dissolved
4. Add ice

BRASS MONKEY

½ oz. vodka
½ oz. light rum
orange juice

1. Fill a highball glass with ice
2. Add vodka, rum and orange juice
3. Stir

BRASSY BLONDE

1½ oz. whiskey
1½ oz. grapefruit juice
1 tsp. strawberry liqueur
1 oz. club soda

1. Fill a Collins glass with ice
2. Add whiskey, grapefruit juice and strawberry liqueur
3. Stir
4. Top with club soda
5. Stir again

BRAVE BULL

1½ oz. tequila
1 oz. Kahlúa

1. Fill a rocks glass with ice
2. Add tequila and Kahlúa
3. Stir

BREAKFAST EGGNOG

1 egg
1 oz. brandy
½ oz. curaçao
4 oz. cold milk

1. Fill mixing glass with ice
2. Add egg, brandy, curaçao and cold milk
3. Shake well
4. Strain into a chilled highball glass

BRONX CHEER

2 oz. apricot brandy
6 oz. raspberry soda

1. Fill a Collins glass with ice
2. Add apricot brandy and raspberry soda
3. Stir
4. Garnish with an orange slice

BROWN

1¼ oz. bourbon
1¼ oz. dry vermouth
2 dashes orange bitters

1. Fill mixing glass with ice
2. Add bourbon, dry vermouth and bitters
3. Shake
4. Strain into a rocks glass filled with ice

BROWN BOMBER

½ oz. peanut liqueur
½ oz. white crème de cacao
2 oz. cream

1. Fill mixing glass with ice
2. Add peanut liqueur, white crème de cacao and cream
3. Shake
4. Strain into a chilled cocktail glass

BUBBLE GUM (SHOOTER)

1½ oz. vodka
1½ oz. banana liqueur
1½ oz. peach schnapps
1½ oz. orange juice

(MAKES ABOUT 4 SHOTS)

1. Fill mixing glass with ice
2. Add vodka, banana liqueur, peach schnapps and orange juice
3. Shake
4. Strain into shot glasses

BUCKS FIZZ

1½ oz. gin
½ tsp. sugar
2 oz. orange juice
1 oz. sour mix
1 oz. club soda

1. Fill mixing glass with ice
2. Add gin, sugar, orange juice and sour mix
3. Shake
4. Strain into a Collins glass
5. Add club soda
6. Fill with ice
7. Garnish with a cherry and an orange slice

BUFFALO SWEAT (SHOOTER)

1½ oz. bourbon
dash of Tabasco sauce

1. Pour bourbon into a shot glass
2. Add a dash of Tabasco

BULLDOG

1 oz. gin	1. Fill mixing glass with ice
4 oz. orange juice	2. Add gin and orange juice
ginger ale	3. Shake
	4. Strain into a rocks glass filled with ice
	5. Top off with ginger ale

BULL FROG

1½ oz. vodka	1. Fill a highball glass with ice
limeade	2. Add vodka and limeade
	3. Stir
	4. Garnish with a slice of lime

BULL SHOT

1½ oz. vodka	1. Fill a rocks glass with ice
1 tsp. lemon juice	2. Add vodka, lemon juice, Worcestershire and Tabasco
3–4 drops Worcestershire sauce	3. Fill with bouillon
dash Tabasco sauce	4. Stir
beef bouillon, chilled	

BUTTERSCOTCH COLLINS

1 tsp. sugar	1. Dissolve sugar in water
water	2. Pour over ice in a Collins glass
1½ oz. scotch	3. Add scotch, Drambuie and lemon juice
½ oz. Drambuie	4. Stir
½ oz. lemon juice	5. Top with club soda
1 oz. club soda	6. Garnish with a cherry and an orange slice

BUTTERY NIPPLE (SHOOTER)

½ oz. butterscotch schnapps ½ oz. Baileys Original Irish Cream	Layer butterscotch schnapps and Baileys in a shot glass

B.V.D.

1½ oz. gin ¾ oz. light rum ¾ oz. dry vermouth	1. Fill mixing glass with ice 2. Add gin, light rum and dry vermouth 3. Stir 4. Strain into a chilled cocktail glass

CABLEGRAM

2 oz. blended whiskey 1 tsp. sugar syrup ½ oz. lemon juice ginger ale	1. Fill mixing glass with cracked ice 2. Add whiskey, sugar syrup and lemon juice 3. Shake 4. Pour into a highball glass 5. Fill with ginger ale

CADIZ

¾ oz. blackberry brandy ¾ oz. dry sherry ½ oz. triple sec ¼ oz. cream	1. Fill mixing glass with ice 2. Add blackberry brandy, dry sherry, triple sec and cream 3. Shake 4. Strain into a rocks glass filled with ice

THE CAESAR

lime wedge celery salt 2 oz. vodka	1. Wet the rim of your glass with the lime wedge and dip the wetted glass in some celery salt

5 oz. Mott's Clamato juice
2 dashes of Worcestershire sauce
2 dashes of Tabasco

2. Combine vodka and Clamato juice
3. Add dashes of Worcestershire and Tabasco
4. Squeeze in the juice from your lime wedge
5. Add ice
6. Garnish with a celery heart stalk

CAFÉ BONAPARTE

1½ oz. brandy
cappuccino (espresso and steamed milk)

1. Pour brandy into a hot drink glass
2. Fill with cappuccino

CAFÉ FOSTER*

1 oz. Bacardi Black Label rum
½ oz. crème de banana
hot coffee
vanilla-flavored whipped cream

1. Pour Bacardi and crème de banana into a coffee mug or glass
2. Fill with hot coffee
3. Top with whipped cream

CAFÉ MARNIER

1½ oz. Grand Marnier
strong coffee or espresso

1. Pour Grand Marnier into a coffee mug
2. Add hot coffee so that mug is three-fourths full
3. Stir
4. Add whipped cream, if desired

---

* Courtesy of Café L'Europe, Sarasota, Florida.

CAFÉ THEATRE

½ oz. Baileys Original Irish
    Cream
½ oz. white crème de cacao
hot coffee
dash Frangelico (amaretto
    may be substituted)
dash dark crème de cacao

1. Pour Baileys and white
   crème de cacao into a
   coffee mug
2. Add enough coffee so that the
   cup is almost filled
3. Add a dash each of Frangelico
   and dark crème de cacao
4. Top with whipped cream
5. Garnish with a cinnamon
   stick

CAFÉ ZURICH

1½ oz. anisette
1½ oz. cognac
½ oz. amaretto
hot coffee
1 tsp. honey
whipped cream

1. Pour anisette, cognac and
   amaretto into a coffee mug
2. Add hot coffee so that mug is
   three-fourths filled
3. Allow honey to float on top of
   drink
4. Stir
5. Add whipped cream,
   if desired

CAIPIRINHA

2 or 3 lime wedges
dash sugar
3 oz. Brazilian rum
½ oz. sour mix

1. Mash the lime wedges with
   sugar in a mixing glass
2. Add ice, rum and sour mix
3. Shake
4. Pour into a highball glass
5. Garnish with lime slice

CAJUN BLOODY MARY

1 oz. Absolut Peppar vodka
(or other pepper-flavored
vodka)
Bloody Mary mix (see recipe
for Bloody Mary or Virgin
Mary)

1. Fill a highball glass
   with ice
2. Add Absolut Peppar
   vodka
3. Fill with Bloody Mary mix
4. Stir
5. Garnish with a celery stalk or
   lime or a hot pepper (if you
   dare)

(*Note:* For an extra spicy experience,
rub hot spices along the rim of the
glass.)

CALIFORNIA DRIVER

1 oz. vodka
3 oz. orange juice
3 oz. grapefruit juice

1. Fill a highball glass
   with ice
2. Add vodka, orange juice
   and grapefruit juice
3. Stir

CALIFORNIA ICE TEA

½ oz. vodka
½ oz. gin
½ oz. light rum
½ oz. triple sec
½ oz. white tequila
½ oz. sour mix
1 oz. orange juice
1 oz. pineapple juice

1. Fill mixing glass with ice
2. Add all ingredients
3. Shake
4. Strain into a Collins glass
5. Add ice
6. Garnish with a lemon slice

CALIFORNIA LEMONADE

½ oz. vodka
½ oz. gin
½ oz. brandy
2 oz. sour mix
2 oz. orange juice
¼ oz. grenadine

1. Fill mixing glass with ice
2. Add all ingredients
3. Shake
4. Strain into a Collins glass
5. Add ice

CALIFORNIA ROOT BEER

1 oz. Galliano
1 oz. Kahlúa
2 oz. club soda
1 oz. cola
splash beer (optional)

1. Fill a rocks glass with ice
2. Pour in Galliano and Kahlúa
3. Add club soda and cola
4. Stir
5. Splash beer on top (if desired)

CALIFORNIA STRIPPER

1 oz. half-and-half
2 oz. raspberry schnapps

1. Mix ingredients together with crushed ice in a glass
2. Garnish with mint leaves

CALYPSO (ALSO CALLED JAMAICAN COFFEE)

¾ oz. Tia Maria
¾ oz. Jamaican rum
hot coffee

1. Pour Tia Maria and rum into a coffee mug
2. Add hot coffee
3. Top with whipped cream (if desired)

CAMPARI AND SODA

2 oz. Campari
2 oz. club soda

1. Fill a highball glass with ice
2. Add Campari and club soda
3. Stir
4. Garnish with an orange peel (twist)

CAMPOBELLO

1½ oz. gin
1 oz. sweet vermouth
1 oz. Campari

1. Fill mixing glass with ice
2. Add gin, sweet vermouth and Campari
3. Shake
4. Strain into a cocktail glass

CANADA COCKTAIL

1½ oz. Canadian whiskey
½ oz. triple sec
2 dashes Angostura bitters
1 tsp. sugar

1. Fill mixing glass with ice
2. Add Canadian whiskey, triple sec, bitters and sugar
3. Shake
4. Strain into a chilled cocktail glass

CANDY BAR (SHOOTER)

½ oz. Frangelica
½ oz. vodka

1. Fill mixing glass with ice
2. Add Frangelica and vodka
3. Strain into a rocks glass with ice or a shot glass

CAPE COD

1½ oz. vodka
6 oz. cranberry juice

1. Fill a highball glass with ice
2. Add vodka and cranberry juice
3. Stir
4. Garnish with a wedge of lime

CAPE GRAPE

1½ oz. vodka
4 oz. grapefruit juice
1 oz. cranberry liqueur

1. Fill a highball glass half full of ice
2. Add vodka, grapefruit juice and cranberry liqueur
3. Stir slowly
4. Garnish with a twist of grapefruit peel

CAPPUCCINO MOCHA

hot espresso
¾ oz. Kahlúa
¾ oz. crème de cacao
steamed milk

1. Fill coffee mug with hot espresso (about half full)
2. Add Kahlúa and crème de cacao
3. Top with steamed milk
4. Dust with cinnamon or chocolate

CAPRI

¾ oz. white crème de cacao
¾ oz. banana liqueur
¾ oz. cream

1. Fill mixing glass with ice
2. Add white crème de cacao, banana liqueur and cream
3. Shake
4. Strain into a rocks glass filled with ice

CARAMEL NUT

1 oz. white crème de cacao 1 oz. caramel liqueur 5 oz. vanilla ice cream, soft	1. In blender, combine white crème de càcao, caramel liqueur and ice cream 2. Blend at medium speed until smooth 3. Pour into a large goblet or wineglass 4. Garnish with whipped cream 5. Top with chopped nuts, if desired

CARROLL COCKTAIL

1½ oz. brandy ¾ oz. sweet vermouth	1. Fill mixing glass with ice 2. Add brandy and sweet vermouth 3. Stir 4. Strain into a chilled cocktail glass 5. Garnish with a cherry

CARUSO

½ oz. gin ½ oz. dry vermouth ½ oz. crème de menthe	1. Fill mixing glass with ice 2. Add gin, dry vermouth and crème de menthe 3. Stir 4. Strain into a chilled cocktail glass

CASABLANCA

2 oz. light rum 1½ tsp. triple sec 1½ tsp. lime juice	1. Fill mixing glass with ice 2. Add rum, triple sec, lime juice and cherry liqueur

1½ tsp. cherry liqueur

3. Shake
4. Strain into a chilled cocktail glass

CAT'S EYE

2 oz. dry vermouth
½ oz. yellow Chartreuse
2 dashes orange bitters

1. Fill mixing glass with ice
2. Add dry vermouth, yellow Chartreuse and orange bitters
3. Shake
4. Strain into a chilled cocktail glass

CEREBRAL HEMORRHAGE

1 oz. Kahlúa
1 oz. peach schnapps
1 oz. Baileys Original Irish Cream
⅛ oz. grenadine

1. Layer Kahlúa, peach schnapps and Baileys in a rocks glass filled with ice
2. Add several drops of grenadine

CHABLIS COOLER

1 oz. vodka
1 tsp. grenadine
½ oz. lemon juice
dash vanilla extract
3 oz. California chablis
club soda

1. Put 4 ice cubes in a wineglass
2. Add vodka, grenadine, lemon juice and vanilla extract
3. Pour in chablis
4. Stir gently
5. Top with club soda

CHAMBORD DAIQUIRI

¾ oz. Chambord
¾ oz. light rum
juice of ½ lime
1 tsp. powdered sugar
3 or 4 black raspberries
(optional)

1. In a blender, combine 1 cup crushed ice with Chambord, light rum, lime juice and powdered sugar
2. Throw in raspberries (optional)
3. Blend for approximately 30 seconds or until smooth
4. Pour into a champagne glass

CHAMBORD ROYALE SPRITZER

1½ oz. Chambord
chilled champagne
club soda

1. Pour Chambord into wineglass
2. Add a splash of champagne
3. Top with club soda

CHAMPAGNE COCKTAIL

1 cube sugar
dash bitters
twist of lemon
chilled champagne

1. Put sugar cube, bitters and lemon twist in the bottom of a champagne glass
2. Fill glass with chilled champagne

CHAMPAGNE-MARASCHINO PUNCH

6 oz. maraschino liqueur
6 oz. brandy
1 tsp. orange bitters
2 oranges
1 lemon
4 fifths iced brut champagne

1. Slice oranges and lemon into thin slices
2. Place sliced fruit, maraschino liqueur, brandy and orange bitters in punch bowl
3. Refrigerate for one hour
4. When ready to serve, add a large chunk of ice to the punch bowl and pour mixture over it

5. Pour in the champagne
6. Stir gently

CHAMPAGNE PUNCH

16 oz. triple sec
1 bottle (500 ml) rum
8 oz. maraschino liqueur
3 cups chilled pineapple
   juice, unsweetened
8 oz. club soda
8 oz. ginger ale
4 bottles (750 ml each)
   champagne (or sparkling
   wine)

1. In a punch bowl, combine triple sec, rum, maraschino liqueur and pineapple juice
2. Stir
3. Refrigerate for one hour
4. Add a block of ice
5. Add club soda, ginger ale and champagne or sparkling wine
6. Stir again

CHAMPAGNE SHERBET PUNCH

2 bottles dry champagne or
   sparkling wine (750 ml
   each)
1 bottle chilled white wine
1 qt. orange or raspberry
   sherbet

1. In a punch bowl, combine champagne or sparkling wine and white wine
2. Add a block of ice
3. Add scoops of sherbet

CHARRO

1 oz. tequila
1⅓ oz. evaporated milk
⅔ oz. strong coffee

1. Fill mixing glass with 4 oz. crushed ice
2. Add tequila, evaporated milk and coffee
3. Shake
4. Strain into a rocks glass half filled with ice

CHEAP MAN'S PIÑA COLADA

1½ oz. Malibu
3 oz. pineapple juice
dash milk

1. In blender, combine Malibu, pineapple juice and milk with 3 oz. crushed ice
2. Blend until smooth
3. Pour into a goblet
4. Garnish with a pineapple spear or an orange slice

CHERRY BOMB (ALSO CALLED FIREWORKS)

½ oz. vodka
½ oz. light rum
½ oz. tequila
3 oz. pineapple juice
1 oz. cream of coconut
2 tsp. milk
1 drop grenadine

1. Fill mixing glass with ice
2. Add vodka, light rum, tequila, pineapple juice, cream of coconut, milk and grenadine
3. Shake well
4. Strain into a Collins glass half filled with ice
5. Garnish with a cherry

CHERRY COLA

2 oz. dark rum
½ oz. cherry brandy
2 oz. cola

1. Fill a rocks glass with ice
2. Add rum, cherry brandy and cola
3. Stir
4. Garnish with a lemon twist

CHERRY DAIQUIRI (FROZEN)

1½ oz. light rum
½ oz. cherry brandy
½ oz. lime juice
2–3 dashes kirsch

1. Put 4 oz. ice in blender
2. Add light rum, cherry brandy, lime juice and kirsch
3. Blend at medium speed for about 15 seconds, until smooth

4. Pour into a goblet or large wineglass
5. Garnish with a lime slice

CHICAGO

1½ oz. brandy
1 dash curaçao
1 dash Angostura bitters
cold brut champagne
lemon wedge
superfine granulated sugar

1. Rub rim of a goblet or large wineglass with lemon wedge
2. Roll rim of glass in a dish of the sugar so that the rim is evenly frosted
3. Fill mixing glass with cracked ice
4. Add brandy, curaçao and bitters
5. Shake
6. Strain into prepared glass
7. Fill with champagne

CHI-CHI

1½ oz. light rum
½ oz. blackberry brandy
5 oz. pineapple juice

1. Fill mixing glass with ice
2. Add rum, blackberry brandy and pineapple juice
3. Shake
4. Strain into a highball glass filled with ice
5. Garnish with a spear of pineapple

CHINESE COCKTAIL

1½ oz. Jamaican rum
1 tbsp. grenadine
1 tbsp. maraschino liqueur
1 tbsp. triple sec
1 dash Angostura bitters

1. Fill mixing glass with ice
2. Add all ingredients
3. Shake
4. Strain into a cocktail glass

CHIQUITA COCKTAIL

½ oz. banana liqueur
½ oz. Cointreau
½ oz. light cream

1. Fill mixing glass with ice
2. Add banana liqueur, Cointreau and light cream
3. Shake
4. Fill a sour glass halfway with crushed ice
5. Strain drink into the sour glass

CHOCOLATE BANANA BANSHEE

¾ oz. banana liqueur
¾ oz. white crème de cacao
¾ oz. Kahlúa
1 oz. cream (milk may be substituted)

1. Fill mixing glass with ice
2. Add banana liqueur, crème de cacao, Kahlúa and cream
3. Shake
4. Strain into a highball glass
5. Add ice

CHOCOLATE BLACK RUSSIAN

1½ oz. Kahlúa
¾ oz. vodka
5 oz. chocolate ice cream

1. In blender, combine Kahlúa, vodka and ice cream
2. Blend at medium speed until smooth
3. Pour into a large goblet or wineglass

CHOCOLATE-COVERED CHERRY (SHOOTER)

½ oz. Kahlúa
½ oz. amaretto
½ oz. white crème de cacao
drop grenadine

1. Fill mixing glass with ice
2. Add Kahlúa, amaretto and white crème de cacao
3. Shake
4. Strain into a shot glass

5. Put a drop of grenadine through the center

CHOCOLATE MARTINI

1½ oz. vodka
¾ oz. white crème de cacao

1. Fill mixing glass with ice
2. Add vodka and white crème de cacao
3. Shake
4. Cocoa powder the rim of a chilled martini glass
5. Strain into a chilled martini glass
6. Place a Hershey Kiss point up in the bottom of the glass

CHOCOLATE RUM

1 oz. white rum
2 tsp. white crème de cacao
2 tsp. white crème de menthe
2 tsp. heavy cream
1 tsp. rum (151 proof)

1. Fill mixing glass with ice
2. Add white rum, crème de cacao, crème de menthe and heavy cream
3. Shake
4. Strain into a rocks glass filled with ice
5. Top with 151-proof rum

CINZANO

3 oz. Cinzano dry vermouth
3 dashes orange bitters
3 dashes Angostura bitters

1. Fill mixing glass with ice
2. Add Cinzano dry vermouth, orange bitters and Angostura bitters
3. Stir

4. Strain into a chilled cocktail glass
5. Garnish with a twist of orange peel

CITY SLICKER

2 oz. brandy 1 oz. curaçao dash Pernod	1. Fill mixing glass with ice 2. Add brandy, curaçao and Pernod 3. Shake 4. Strain into a chilled cocktail glass

CLAMDIGGER

1½ oz. vodka 3 oz. clam juice 3 oz. tomato juice dash Tabasco sauce dash Worcestershire sauce salt and pepper (to taste)	1. Fill a highball glass with ice 2. Pour in all ingredients 3. Stir 4. Garnish with a lime slice

CLARET CUP

2 tbsp. sugar ¼ cup water 2 bottles red wine, chilled (750 ml each) 4 oz. Cointreau 4 oz. crème de cassis 2½ oz. port 2½ oz. lemon juice 1 liter club soda, chilled	1. In a small saucepan, combine the sugar and water 2. Bring to a boil 3. Simmer for 5 minutes 4. Allow mixture to cool completely 5. In a large punch bowl, combine red wine, Cointreau, crème de cassis, port, lemon juice and the sugar mixture

6. Cover and refrigerate until cold
7. When ready to serve, pour in club soda
8. Garnish with slices of lemon and orange

CLARIDGE

1 oz. gin 1 oz. dry vermouth ½ oz. apricot brandy ½ oz. Cointreau	1. Fill mixing glass with ice 2. Add gin, dry vermouth, apricot brandy and Cointreau 3. Shake 4. Strain into a chilled cocktail glass

CLASSIC

1½ oz. brandy ¼ oz. Cointreau ¼ oz. maraschino liqueur 1 tsp. lemon juice	1. Fill mixing glass with ice 2. Add brandy, Cointreau, maraschino liqueur and lemon juice 3. Shake 4. Strain into a chilled cocktail glass

CLIMAX

½ oz. white crème de cacao ½ oz. amaretto ½ oz. triple sec ½ oz. vodka ½ oz. banana liqueur 1 oz. cream	1. Fill mixing glass with ice 2. Add white crème de cacao, amaretto, triple sec, vodka, banana liqueur and cream 3. Shake 4. Strain into a chilled cocktail glass

CLUB MED

1½ oz. vodka
¾ oz. Chambord
½ oz. lemon juice
3 oz. pineapple juice

1. Fill mixing glass with ice
2. Add vodka, Chambord, lemon juice and pineapple juice
3. Shake
4. Strain into a Collins glass
5. Add ice

COCOA-COLADA*

1½ oz. Myers's rum
1 oz. Kahlúa
2 oz. pineapple juice
1 oz. coconut cream

1. In blender, combine rum, Kahlúa, pineapple juice and coconut cream with 1 scoop ice
2. Blend until smooth
3. Pour into a 16-oz. soda glass
4. Garnish with a slice of orange

COCO-LOCO

----

1 whole coconut, in shell
1 oz. tequila
1 oz. rum
1 oz. gin
½ oz. grenadine

1. Cut a 3-inch hole in top of coconut
2. With juice of coconut still inside, pour in tequila, rum, gin and grenadine
3. Add several ice cubes and stir
4. Garnish with a slice of lemon or lime (squeeze in juice and then throw in)
5. Drink with a long straw

----

* Courtesy of Sugar Reef, New York City.

(If you prefer to serve this drink in a glass, drill two holes in coconut and drain liquid into a mixing glass over several ice cubes, add liquors and grenadine and stir well. Then, pour into a goblet or highball glass, add lemon or lime.)

COCONUT COLA

1½ oz. Malibu rum liqueur cola	1. Fill a highball glass with ice 2. Add Malibu 3. Fill with cola 4. Garnish with a wedge of lime

COCO-TOASTIE

1 oz. light rum ½ oz. Malibu 3 oz. vanilla ice cream 2 tbsp. whipping cream	1. In blender, combine light rum, Malibu, vanilla ice cream and whipping cream 2. Blend until smooth 3. Pour into a chilled cocktail glass 4. Garnish with toasted shredded coconut

COFFEE ALEXANDER

1 oz. Kahlúa 1 oz. dark crème de cacao 1 oz. cream	1. Fill mixing glass with ice 2. Add Kahlúa, dark crème de cacao and cream 3. Shake 4. Strain into a chilled cocktail glass

COFFEE COOLER

1½ oz. vodka
1 oz. Kahlúa
1 oz. heavy cream
4 oz. iced coffee
½ tsp. sugar syrup (optional)
1 scoop coffee ice cream

1. Fill mixing glass with ice
2. Add vodka, Kahlúa, heavy cream, iced coffee and sugar syrup
3. Shake
4. Strain into a rocks glass
5. Add some ice and the coffee ice cream

COFFEE KEOKEE

¾ oz. brandy
¾ oz. Kahlúa
hot coffee

1. Pour brandy and Kahlúa into a coffee mug
2. Add hot coffee
3. Top with whipped cream (if desired)

COFFEE FRAPPE*

1½ cups cold water
1½ tsp. instant coffee
2 tsp. sugar
½ to 1 shot ouzo
milk

1. Blend briefly 5 tbsp. of the water with the coffee and the sugar
2. Pour into a glass
3. Add ouzo, milk, ice and the remaining water
4. Top with vanilla ice cream, chocolate syrup and mint

(*Note:* The amounts of ice cream, chocolate syrup and mint can be adjusted to suit personal taste.)

---

* Courtesy of *Food and Wine* magazine.

COLD DECK

1½ oz. brandy
¾ oz. sweet vermouth
¾ oz. peppermint schnapps

1. Fill mixing glass with ice
2. Add brandy, sweet vermouth and peppermint schnapps
3. Shake
4. Strain into a chilled cocktail glass

COLD WEATHER PUNCH

2 medium-sized lemons
½ cup sugar
1 tsp. ground ginger
1 bottle (750 ml) dark rum
1 bottle (750 ml) brandy
8 oz. sherry
3 pints boiling water

1. In a small earthenware bowl, combine the rinds of the lemons (save the rest of the lemon) with the sugar
2. Soften the lemon rinds using a muddler or the back of a spoon
3. Add the juice of the two lemons and the ginger
4. Mix well
5. Switch mixture to a larger earthenware bowl
6. Add, in order, rum, brandy, sherry and boiling water
7. Mix and let sit for approximately 20 minutes
8. Garnish with grated nutmeg
9. Serve immediately

COLORADO BULLDOG

1½ oz. vodka
¾ oz. Kahlúa
3 oz. cola

1. Fill a highball glass with ice
2. Add vodka, Kahlúa and cola
3. Stir

COLUMBIA COCKTAIL

1½ oz. light rum
¾ oz. raspberry syrup
½ oz. lemon juice

1. Fill mixing glass with ice
2. Add light rum, raspberry syrup and lemon juice
3. Shake
4. Strain into a chilled cocktail glass

COMBIER MARGARITA

¾ oz. lime juice
1 oz. Combier Liqueur d'Orange or any triple sec
1½ oz. silver tequila

1. Fill a cocktail shaker with ice
2. Add the lime juice, triple sec and tequila
3. Shake and strain into an ice-filled glass
4. Garnish with citrus wheels (1 lime and 1 orange) and serve

CONCHITA

1 oz. tequila
1 oz. grapefruit juice
2–3 drops lemon juice

1. Fill a rocks glass with ice
2. Add tequila, grapefruit juice and lemon juice
3. Stir

CONCORDE

2 oz. cognac
2 oz. chilled pineapple juice
champagne

1. Combine cognac and chilled pineapple juice in a mixing glass
2. Stir
3. Strain into a champagne glass filled with cracked ice
4. Fill rest of glass with champagne

CONTINENTAL

4 oz. rye
½ oz. Jamaican rum
1½ oz. sweet cream
1½ oz. lemon juice

1. Fill mixing glass with ice
2. Add rye, rum, sweet cream and lemon juice
3. Shake
4. Strain into a Collins glass
5. Add ice

COOL BREEZE

1½ oz. vodka
3 oz. unsweetened pineapple juice
3 oz. cranberry juice cocktail
1 oz. ginger ale

1. Fill a highball glass with ice
2. Add vodka, pineapple juice and cranberry juice
3. Stir
4. Top with ginger ale

COOLER BY THE LAKE*

3 oz. white wine
2 oz. cranberry juice cocktail
¼ oz. peach schnapps
¼ oz. sugar syrup
¼ oz. sour mix
club soda

1. Fill a 10-oz. glass with ice
2. Add white wine, cranberry juice cocktail, peach schnapps, sugar syrup and sour mix
3. Stir well
4. Fill with club soda
5. Stir again, gently
6. Garnish with a slice of fresh peach

_____

* Courtesy of the Ritz-Carlton Hotel, Chicago, Illinois.

CORONADO

1½ oz. gin
½ oz. curaçao
2 oz. unsweetened
   pineapple juice
3 dashes kirsch

1. Fill mixing glass with ice
2. Add gin, curaçao, pineapple juice and kirsch
3. Shake
4. Strain into a rocks glass filled with ice

COSMOPOLITAN

2 oz. vodka (preferably
   lemon-flavored)
1 oz. triple sec
1 oz. cranberry juice
½ oz. lime juice

1. Fill mixing glass with ice
2. Add vodka, triple sec, cranberry juice and lime juice
3. Shake
4. Strain into a chilled martini glass
5. Garnish with a lime slice

COSTA DEL SOL

2 oz. gin
1 oz. apricot brandy
1 oz. Grand Marnier

1. Fill mixing glass with ice
2. Add gin, apricot brandy and Grand Marnier
3. Shake
4. Strain into a rocks glass

COUNTRY CLUB COOLER

4 oz. Lillet blanc (dry
   vermouth may be
   substituted)
1 tsp. grenadine
club soda

1. Pour Lillet and grenadine into a Collins glass
2. Add several ice cubes
3. Stir
4. Top with club soda
5. Garnish with a lemon twist

CRANBERRY PINEAPPLE VODKA PUNCH

2 qts. chilled cranberry juice
  cocktail
1 qt. 14 oz. chilled
  pineapple juice
  (unsweetened)
8 oz. vodka
16 oz. chilled ginger ale
16 oz. chilled club soda
several fresh pineapple
  spears

(MAKES APPROXIMATELY 20
  SERVINGS)

1. In a punch bowl, combine
   cranberry juice cocktail,
   pineapple juice, vodka, ginger
   ale and club soda
2. Add a block of ice
3. Garnish with pineapple spears

CRANBERRY SPICE COCKTAIL

1 orange wedge
13 cranberries
3 1-inch pieces crystallized
  ginger (2 minced and 1
  whole for garnish)
2 oz. Aperol
1 oz. Lillet blanc
4 dashes bitters
4 oz. hard cider

1. In a cocktail shaker, muddle the
   orange wedge with 10 of the
   cranberries and the minced ginger
2. Add the Aperol, Lillet Blanc,
   bitters and ice
3. Shake well
4. Double strain the drink into an
   ice-filled Collins glass and top
   off with the hard cider
5. Garnish with the 3 remaining
   cranberries and the slice of ginger skewered on a toothpick

CRANBERRY SPLASH

4 oz. vodka
cranberry juice cocktail

1. Pour vodka into a rocks glass
   filled with ice
2. Add a splash of cranberry juice
3. Garnish with a slice of lime
   (optional)

CRANBERRY VODKA

premium vodka
fresh cranberries

1. Fill a large, clean jar with fresh cranberries
2. Add a premium vodka
3. Cover and let stand for 3 days, turning the jar several times daily
4. Remove most of the fruit and refrigerate
5. Serve the vodka over ice in a wineglass or rocks glass

CRANBERRY-VODKA PUNCH

2 qts. chilled cranberry juice cocktail
1 bottle (750 ml) vodka
2 cups chilled ginger ale
2 cups chilled club soda

1. In a large punch bowl, combine cranberry juice cocktail and vodka
2. Stir
3. Add a block of ice
4. Pour in ginger ale and club soda
5. Garnish with slices of fresh fruit

CREAM SODA

1½ oz. amaretto
club soda

1. Fill a highball glass with ice
2. Add amaretto
3. Fill with club soda
4. Stir

CREAM SUPREME

1 oz. triple sec
1 oz. white crème de cacao

1. Fill mixing glass with ice
2. Add triple sec, crème de cacao and cream

1 oz. cream (milk may be substituted)	3. Shake
	4. Strain into a highball glass
	5. Add ice
	6. Garnish with an orange slice

CREAMY MIMI

1 oz. vodka	1. Fill mixing glass with 3 oz. crushed ice
1 oz. sweet vermouth	2. Add all ingredients
2 tsp. triple sec	3. Shake
2 tsp. white crème de cacao	4. Strain into a rocks glass
	5. Add ice (if desired)

CRICKET

1 oz. white crème de cacao	1. Fill mixing glass with ice
1 oz. green crème de menthe	2. Add white crème de cacao, green crème de menthe, cream and brandy
1 oz. cream	3. Shake
dash brandy	4. Strain into a chilled champagne glass

CRUISE CONTROL

1 oz. light rum	1. Fill mixing glass with ice
½ oz. apricot brandy	2. Add rum, apricot brandy, Cointreau and lemon juice
½ oz. Cointreau	3. Shake
½ oz. lemon juice	4. Strain into a highball glass half filled with ice
1 oz. club soda	5. Top with club soda

CUBA LIBRE (COMMONLY CALLED RUM AND COKE)

1½ oz. light rum
6 oz. cola

1. Fill a highball glass with ice
2. Add rum and cola
3. Stir
4. Garnish with a lime wedge or slice

CUBAN COOLER

2 oz. light rum
ginger ale

1. Fill a highball glass with ice
2. Add rum
3. Fill glass with ginger ale
4. Garnish with a lemon twist

CUPID'S KISS*

½ oz. crème de noyaux
¼ oz. white crème de cacao
1 oz. cream
1 strawberry

1. Fill mixing glass with ice
2. Add crème de noyaux, white crème de cacao and cream
3. Shake
4. Pour into a tulip glass
5. Garnish with a strawberry

CZAR

1 oz. vodka
1 oz. Grand Marnier
½ oz. lime juice
dash orange bitters
3 oz. dry sparkling white wine

1. Fill mixing glass with ice
2. Add vodka, Grand Marnier, lime juice and orange bitters
3. Shake
4. Strain into a large wineglass
5. Top with sparkling wine

---

* Courtesy of Timbers Charhouse, Highland Park, Illinois.

CZARINA

½ oz. vodka
¼ oz. dry vermouth
¼ oz. apricot brandy
dash Angostura bitters

1. Fill mixing glass with ice
2. Add vodka, dry vermouth, apricot brandy and bitters
3. Shake
4. Strain into a chilled cocktail glass

DAIQUIRI

2 oz. light rum
1 oz. lime juice
1 tsp. sugar

1. Fill mixing glass with ice
2. Add rum, lime juice and sugar
3. Shake
4. Strain into a cocktail glass
5. Garnish with a lime slice

DAISY

2 oz. tequila
1 oz. lemon juice
2 tsp. grenadine
splash club soda

1. Fill mixing glass with ice
2. Add tequila, lemon juice and grenadine
3. Shake
4. Strain into a rocks glass
5. Add ice
6. Top off with a splash of club soda

DAMN-THE-WEATHER

1 oz. gin
¼ oz. triple sec
½ oz. sweet vermouth

1. Fill mixing glass with ice
2. Add gin, triple sec, sweet vermouth and orange juice

½ oz. orange juice

3. Shake
4. Strain into a cocktail glass
5. Add ice
6. Garnish with a cherry

DANDY

1½ oz. Canadian or rye whiskey	1. Fill mixing glass with ice
1½ oz. Dubonnet	2. Add whiskey, Dubonnet, Cointreau and bitters
3 dashes Cointreau	3. Stir
dash Angostura bitters	4. Strain into a chilled cocktail glass

DANISH MARY

1 oz. aquavit (akvavit)	1. Fill a highball glass with ice
Bloody Mary mix	2. Add aquavit and Bloody Mary mix (see Bloody Mary recipe, p. 115)
	3. Stir
	4. Garnish with a celery stalk or a lime slice

DARB

1 oz. gin	1. Fill mixing glass with ice
1 oz. dry vermouth	2. Add gin, dry vermouth, apricot brandy, lemon juice and sugar
1 oz. apricot brandy	3. Shake
½ oz. lemon juice	4. Strain into a cocktail glass
1 tsp. sugar	

DARK EYES

1½ oz. vodka ¼ oz. blackberry brandy 2 tsp. lime juice	1. Fill mixing glass with ice 2. Add vodka, blackberry brandy and lime juice 3. Shake 4. Strain into a brandy snifter

DAVIS

1½ oz. light rum 1½ oz. dry vermouth 1 oz. lime juice 2 dashes raspberry syrup	1. Fill mixing glass with ice 2. Add rum, dry vermouth, lime juice and raspberry syrup 3. Shake 4. Strain into a rocks glass 5. Add ice

DEATH BY CHOCOLATE

1 oz. Baileys Original Irish Cream ½ oz. brown crème de cacao ½ oz. vodka 1 scoop chocolate ice cream 1 cup crushed ice	1. In a blender, add Baileys, brown crème de cacao, vodka, chocolate ice cream and ice 2. Blend until smooth 3. Pour into a parfait glass 4. Garnish with whipped cream and chocolate curls

DEATH IN THE AFTERNOON

1½ oz. Pernod chilled champagne	1. Pour Pernod into a chilled champagne glass 2. Fill the glass with champagne

DEAUVILLE COCKTAIL

½ oz. lemon juice
½ oz. brandy
½ oz. apple brandy
½ oz. triple sec

1. Fill mixing glass with ice
2. Add lemon juice, brandy, apple brandy and triple sec
3. Shake
4. Strain into a chilled cocktail glass

DEEP THROAT (SHOOTER)

½ oz. Kahlúa
½ oz. vodka
whipped cream

1. Pour Kahlúa and vodka into a shot glass
2. Top with whipped cream

DELMONICO

¾ oz. gin
½ oz. dry vermouth
½ oz. sweet vermouth
½ oz. brandy

1. Fill mixing glass with ice
2. Add gin, dry vermouth, sweet vermouth and brandy
3. Stir
4. Strain into a cocktail glass
5. Garnish with a lemon twist

DEMPSEY

1½ oz. gin
1 oz. apple brandy
2 dashes grenadine
2 dashes Angostura bitters

1. Fill mixing glass with ice
2. Add gin, apple brandy, grenadine and bitters
3. Shake
4. Strain into a rocks glass filled with ice

DEPTH BOMB

1½ oz. apple brandy
1½ oz. brandy
¼ tsp. grenadine
¼ tsp. lemon juice

1. Fill mixing glass with ice
2. Add apple brandy, brandy, grenadine and lemon juice
3. Shake
4. Strain into a chilled cocktail glass

DEPTH CHARGE

1½ oz. gin
1½ oz. Lillet
2 dashes Pernod

1. Fill mixing glass with ice
2. Add gin, Lillet and Pernod
3. Shake
4. Strain into a chilled cocktail glass

DERBY SPECIAL

1½ oz. light rum
½ oz. Cointreau
1 oz. orange juice
½ oz. lime juice

1. Add approximately 4 oz. cracked ice to a blender
2. Pour in light rum, Cointreau, orange juice and lime juice
3. Blend at medium speed until smooth
4. Pour into a highball glass

DE RIGUEUR

1½ oz. whiskey
¾ oz. grapefruit juice
1 tsp. honey

1. Fill mixing glass with ice
2. Add whiskey, grapefruit juice and honey
3. Shake
4. Strain into a chilled cocktail glass

DEVIL'S HANDSHAKE

1½ oz. tequila
¾ oz. lime juice
½ oz. simple syrup
1 oz. pineapple juice
1 tsp. sweet ginger puree*
¼ part egg white

1. Dry shake all ingredients vigorously
2. Add ice and shake again
3. Strain over fresh ice in a highball glass
4. Garnish with a lime wedge

DIAMOND FIZZ

1½ oz. gin
juice of ½ lemon
1 tsp. powdered sugar
chilled champagne

1. Fill mixing glass with ice
2. Add gin, lemon juice and sugar
3. Shake
4. Strain into a large wineglass
5. Add a few ice cubes
6. Fill with champagne

DIAMOND HEAD

1½ oz. gin
½ oz. curaçao
2 oz. pineapple juice (unsweetened)
1 tsp. sweet vermouth

1. Fill mixing glass with cracked ice
2. Add gin, curaçao, pineapple juice and sweet vermouth
3. Shake
4. Strain into a chilled cocktail glass

DIANA

3 oz. white crème de menthe
1 oz. brandy

1. Fill a rocks glass with ice
2. Add white crème de menthe and brandy
3. Stir

DINAH COCKTAIL

1½ oz. blended whiskey
1 oz. sour mix
½ tsp. powdered sugar

1. Fill mixing glass with ice
2. Add whiskey, sour mix and sugar
3. Shake
4. Strain into a cocktail glass
5. Garnish with a mint leaf

DIPLOMAT

2 oz. dry vermouth
1 oz. sweet vermouth
2 dashes maraschino liqueur

1. Fill mixing glass with ice
2. Add dry vermouth, sweet vermouth and maraschino liqueur
3. Stir
4. Strain into a chilled cocktail glass
5. Garnish with a twist of orange peel

DIRTY MARTINI

2½ oz. gin
splash olive juice

1. Fill mixing glass with ice
2. Add gin and olive juice
3. Shake
4. Strain into a martini glass
5. Garnish with 3 olives

DIRTY MOTHER (ALSO CALLED A SEPARATOR)

1½ oz. brandy
¾ oz. Kahlúa

1. Fill a rocks glass with ice
2. Add brandy and Kahlúa
3. Stir

DIRTY WHITE MOTHER

1½ oz. brandy
½ oz. Kahlúa
1 oz. cream

1. Fill a rocks glass with ice
2. Add brandy and Kahlúa
3. Float cream on top

DOCTOR

1½ oz. Swedish Punsch
2 oz. lime juice

1. Fill mixing glass with ice
2. Add Swedish Punsch and lime juice
3. Shake
4. Strain into a rocks glass
5. Add ice

DR. PEPPER

½ oz. amaretto
½ oz. 151-proof rum
cold beer

1. Pour amaretto and 151-proof rum into a beer glass or mug
2. Fill with beer

DODGE SPECIAL

1½ oz. dry gin
1½ oz. Cointreau
dash grape juice

1. Fill mixing glass with ice
2. Add gin, Cointreau and grape juice
3. Stir
4. Strain into a cocktail glass

DOMINICAN COCO LOCO

1½ oz. light rum
½ oz. amaretto
1 tsp. grenadine

1. In blender, combine all ingredients with 3 oz. crushed ice
2. Blend until smooth

½ oz. pineapple juice
(unsweetened)
1 oz. coconut cream
several dashes milk

3. Pour into a goblet or large
wineglass
4. Garnish with a pineapple slice

(*Note:* This drink can also be served
in a pineapple.)

DORADO

2 oz. tequila
1½ oz. lemon juice
1 tbsp. honey

1. Fill mixing glass with ice
2. Add tequila, lemon juice and
honey
3. Shake
4. Strain into a highball glass
filled with ice

007 COCKTAIL

1 part lemon-lime soda
1 part orange juice
1 part orange vodka

1. Mix ingredients in a tall glass
full of ice

DOUGLAS

2 oz. English gin
1 oz. dry vermouth

1. Fill a rocks glass with ice
2. Add English gin and dry
vermouth
3. Stir
4. Garnish with a lemon twist

DOWN THE HATCH

2 oz. whiskey
3 dashes blackberry brandy
2 dashes orange bitters

1. Fill mixing glass with ice
2. Add whiskey, blackberry
brandy and orange bitters

3. Shake
4. Strain into a cocktail glass

DOWN UNDER SNOWBALL

1 oz. light rum
1 oz. peach schnapps
½ oz. grenadine
3 oz. orange juice

1. Fill mixing glass with ice
2. Add light rum, peach schnapps, grenadine and orange juice
3. Shake
4. Strain into a highball glass

DRAWBRIDGE

5 oz. dry white wine
club soda
splash of blue curaçao

1. Fill a wineglass with ice
2. Pour in white wine
3. Top with club soda
4. Add a splash of blue curaçao
5. Garnish with a lemon twist

DREAM

2 oz. brandy
¾ oz. curaçao
¼ oz. Pernod

1. Fill mixing glass with ice
2. Add brandy, curaçao and Pernod
3. Shake
4. Strain into a cocktail glass

DREAM COCKTAIL

1½ oz. brandy
½ oz. Cointreau
½ tsp. anisette

1. Fill mixing glass with ice
2. Add brandy, Cointreau and anisette
3. Stir
4. Strain into a chilled cocktail glass over 2 or 3 ice cubes

DUBONNET COCKTAIL

1 oz. gin (or vodka)
1 oz. Dubonnet (red)

1. Fill mixing glass with ice
2. Add gin or vodka and Dubonnet
3. Stir
4. Strain into a chilled cocktail glass or a rocks glass filled with ice

DUBONNET FIZZ

1½ oz. gin
1½ oz. Dubonnet
½ oz. cherry brandy
½ oz. lemon juice
club soda

1. Fill a highball glass with ice
2. Add gin, Dubonnet, cherry brandy and lemon juice
3. Stir
4. Top with club soda
5. Stir again
6. Garnish with a cherry

DUBONNET MANHATTAN

1 oz. Dubonnet
1 oz. whiskey

1. Fill mixing glass with ice
2. Add Dubonnet and whiskey
3. Shake
4. Strain into a cocktail glass
5. Garnish with a cherry

DUBONNET NEGRONI

1½ oz. Dubonnet
1½ oz. gin
1½ oz. Campari

1. Fill mixing glass with ice
2. Add Dubonnet, gin and Campari
3. Stir
4. Strain into a wineglass
5. Garnish with a lemon twist

DUCHESS

¾ oz. Pernod
¾ oz. dry vermouth
¾ oz. sweet vermouth

1. Fill mixing glass with ice
2. Add Pernod, dry vermouth and sweet vermouth
3. Shake
4. Strain into a rocks glass
5. Add ice
6. Garnish with a cherry

DUNDEE

1½ oz. gin
2 tbsp. scotch
2 tsp. Drambuie
1 tsp. lemon juice

1. Fill mixing glass with ice
2. Add gin, scotch, Drambuie and lemon juice
3. Shake
4. Strain into a rocks glass and add ice
5. Garnish with a cherry and a lemon twist

DUNLOP

3 oz. light rum
1½ oz. sherry
2 dashes Angostura bitters

1. Fill mixing glass with ice
2. Add rum, sherry and bitters
3. Shake
4. Strain into a rocks glass filled with ice

DUTCH COFFEE

1½ oz. Vandermint liqueur
hot coffee

1. Pour Vandermint liqueur into a coffee mug
2. Add hot coffee
3. Top with whipped cream

DUTCH VELVET

½ oz. chocolate mint liqueur
½ oz. banana liqueur
2 oz. cream

1. Fill mixing glass with ice
2. Add chocolate mint liqueur, banana liqueur and cream
3. Shake
4. Strain into a chilled cocktail glass
5. Garnish with 1 tsp. shaved chocolate, if desired

E

EARTHQUAKE

1½ oz. rye whiskey
1½ oz. gin
1½ oz. Pernod

1. Fill mixing glass with ice
2. Add rye, gin and Pernod
3. Shake
4. Strain into a chilled cocktail glass

EASTER EGG COCKTAIL

1 oz. blue curaçao
1 oz. white crème de cacao
half-and-half

1. Pour the blue curaçao and crème de cacao over ice cubes in an old-fashioned glass
2. Float the half-and-half on top to taste

EAST INDIA COCKTAIL

1½ oz. brandy
1 tsp. light rum
½ tsp. triple sec
½ tsp. pineapple juice (unsweetened)
dash bitters

1. Fill mixing glass with ice
2. Add brandy, rum, triple sec, pineapple juice and bitters
3. Shake
4. Strain into a chilled cocktail glass
5. Garnish with a lemon twist

ECLIPSE (1)

1½ oz. sloe gin
1 oz. gin
3–4 dashes grenadine
1 maraschino cherry

1. Put a cherry in a rocks glass
2. Cover cherry with grenadine
3. In a separate glass, shake sloe gin and gin with ice
4. Strain the gins into the rocks glass (they should float on the grenadine, not mix with it)

ECLIPSE (2)

1½ oz. Old Bushmills Black Bush Irish whiskey
seltzer

1. Fill a highball glass with ice
2. Add Old Bushmills Black Bush Irish whiskey
3. Top with seltzer
4. Stir
5. Garnish with a slice of orange

EGGHEAD

1½ oz. vodka
4 oz. orange juice
1 egg

1. In blender, add vodka, orange juice, egg and 3 or 4 ice cubes
2. Blend at medium speed for about 15 seconds
3. Pour over 4 or 5 ice cubes in a rocks glass

EGGNOG (STANDARD RECIPE)

1 dozen eggs
2 cups superfine granulated sugar
1 pt. Jamaican rum
1 pt. cognac
3 pts. milk
1 pt. cream

1. Separate eggs
2. Beat yolks and sugar until thick
3. Add rum, cognac, milk and cream
4. Stir mixture
5. Set aside and chill in refrigerator

nutmeg or cinnamon

(MAKES APPROXIMATELY
28–30 SERVINGS)

6. When ready to serve, put this mixture into a punch bowl
7. Do NOT add ice cubes
8. Beat egg whites (until they are stiff) and fold into egg mixture
9. Do NOT beat or stir
10. Sprinkle top with nutmeg

EL CID

1½ oz. tequila
1 oz. lime juice
½ oz. almond-flavored syrup
tonic water
dash of grenadine

1. Pour tequila, lime juice and almond syrup into a Collins glass
2. Stir well
3. Fill with tonic water
4. Add a dash of grenadine to top
5. Garnish with a lime slice

EL DIABLO

1½ oz. tequila
½ oz. crème de cassis
1½ tsp. lime juice
1 oz. ginger ale

1. Fill a Collins glass with ice
2. Add tequila, crème de cassis and lime juice
3. Fill with ginger ale
4. Stir

ELECTRIC KOOL-AID

½ oz. amaretto
½ oz. Midori melon liqueur
½ oz. cherry brandy
½ oz. Southern Comfort
½ oz. triple sec
½ oz. sour mix
½ oz. cranberry juice
dash grenadine

1. Fill mixing glass with ice
2. Add all ingredients
3. Shake
4. Strain into a chilled cocktail glass

EL PRESIDENTE EDUARDO

1½ oz. gold rum
½ oz. curaçao
1 oz. dry vermouth
dash grenadine

1. Fill mixing glass with ice
2. Add rum, curaçao, dry vermouth and grenadine
3. Shake
4. Strain into a chilled cocktail glass

EL SALVADOR

1½ oz. light rum
¾ oz. Frangelico
½ oz. lime juice
1 tsp. grenadine

1. Fill mixing glass with ice
2. Add light rum, Frangelico, lime juice and grenadine
3. Shake
4. Strain into a chilled cocktail glass

EMERALD ISLE COOLER

3 scoops vanilla ice cream
1 oz. green crème de menthe
1 oz. Irish whiskey
1 oz. club soda

1. In blender, combine vanilla ice cream, green crème de menthe and Irish whiskey
2. Blend until smooth
3. Pour into a chilled highball glass
4. Add club soda
5. Stir gently

EMPIRE

1½ oz. gin
½ oz. apple brandy
¾ oz. apricot brandy

1. Fill mixing glass with ice
2. Add gin, apple brandy and apricot brandy
3. Stir
4. Strain into a chilled cocktail glass

ENGLISH ROSE

2 oz. gin
1 oz. dry vermouth
1 oz. apricot brandy
½ oz. lemon juice
1 tsp. grenadine

1. Pour the ingredients into a cocktail shaker with ice cubes
2. Shake well
3. Strain into a chilled cocktail glass
4. Garnish with a maraschino cherry

E.T. (SHOOTER)

¾ oz. Midori melon liqueur
¾ oz. vodka
¾ oz. Baileys Original Irish Cream

Layer Midori, vodka and Baileys in a shot glass

EVE

½ tsp. Pernod
1 tbsp. cognac
2 tsp. sugar
2 tsp. curaçao
chilled pink sparkling wine

1. Pour Pernod into a large wineglass
2. Turn glass so that Pernod coats the sides
3. Add cognac
4. In a small bowl, combine sugar and curaçao, allowing sugar to dissolve
5. Add to wineglass
6. Stir
7. Add 3 or 4 ice cubes
8. Fill with chilled pink sparkling wine

EVERGLADES SPECIAL

1 oz. light rum 1 oz. white crème de cacao 1 oz. light cream 2 tsp. Kahlúa (or other coffee liqueur)	1. Fill mixing glass with ice 2. Add rum, white crème de cacao, light cream and Kahlúa 3. Shake 4. Strain into a chilled cocktail glass 5. Add ice

EVERYTHING BUT

1 oz. whiskey 1 oz. gin 1 oz. lemon juice 1 oz. orange juice 1 egg 1 tsp. apricot brandy ½ tsp. powdered sugar	1. Fill mixing glass with ice 2. Add all ingredients 3. Shake 4. Strain into a sour glass 5. Add ice (if desired)

EXPRESS*

1½ oz. Grand Marnier ½ oz. Absolut vodka	1. Fill mixing glass with ice 2. Add Grand Marnier and Absolut vodka 3. Shake 4. Strain into a chilled martini glass

EYE-OPENER

1½ oz. light rum 1 tsp. triple sec	1. Fill mixing glass with ice 2. Add all ingredients

---

* Courtesy of Sign of the Dove, New York City.

1 tsp. white crème de cacao

3 dashes anise-flavored liqueur

1 tsp. Falernum syrup (or sugar syrup)

1 egg yolk

3. Shake
4. Strain into a rocks glass
5. Add ice

FAIR AND WARMER

1½ oz. light rum
1 tbsp. sweet vermouth
2 dashes curaçao

1. Fill mixing glass with ice
2. Add light rum, sweet vermouth and curaçao
3. Shake
4. Strain into a rocks glass filled with ice
5. Garnish with a lemon twist

FAIRBANKS

1 oz. gin
1 oz. dry vermouth
1 oz. apricot brandy
dash grenadine
dash lemon juice

1. Fill mixing glass with ice
2. Add gin, dry vermouth, apricot brandy, grenadine and lemon juice
3. Shake
4. Strain into a cocktail glass
5. Garnish with a cherry

FALLEN ANGEL

2½ oz. gin
2½ oz. lemon juice
2 dashes crème de menthe
dash Angostura bitters

1. Fill mixing glass with ice
2. Add gin, lemon juice, crème de menthe and bitters
3. Shake
4. Strain into a rocks glass filled with ice

FANS

2 oz. scotch
1 oz. Cointreau
1 oz. grapefruit juice
   (unsweetened)

1. Fill mixing glass with ice
2. Add scotch, Cointreau and grapefruit juice
3. Shake
4. Strain into a rocks glass filled with ice

FANTASIO

1½ oz. brandy
¾ oz. dry vermouth
1 tsp. white crème de cacao
1 tsp. maraschino liqueur

1. Fill mixing glass with ice
2. Add brandy, dry vermouth, white crème de cacao and maraschino liqueur
3. Shake
4. Strain into a rocks glass filled with ice

FARE-THEE-WELL

1½ oz. gin
1½ oz. dry vermouth
2 dashes sweet vermouth
6 dashes curaçao

1. Fill mixing glass with ice
2. Add gin, dry vermouth, sweet vermouth and curaçao
3. Shake
4. Strain into a cocktail glass

FATHER SHERMAN

1½ oz. brandy
½ oz. apricot brandy
2 tbsp. orange juice

1. Fill mixing glass with ice
2. Add brandy, apricot brandy and orange juice
3. Shake
4. Strain into a chilled cocktail glass

FAVORITE

¾ oz. gin
¾ oz. dry vermouth
¾ oz. apricot brandy
¼ tsp. lemon juice

1. Fill mixing glass with ice
2. Add gin, dry vermouth, apricot brandy and lemon juice
3. Shake
4. Strain into a rocks glass filled with ice

FERN GULLY

1 oz. light rum
1 oz. dark rum
½ oz. cream of coconut
1 oz. orange juice
2 tsp. lime juice
½ oz. crème de noyaux (any almond-flavored liqueur may be substituted)

1. Fill mixing glass with ice
2. Add light rum, dark rum, cream of coconut, orange juice, lime juice and crème de noyaux
3. Shake
4. Strain into a goblet or large wineglass
5. Add ice

FERRARI

2 oz. dry vermouth
1 oz. amaretto

1. Fill a rocks glass with ice
2. Add dry vermouth and amaretto
3. Stir
4. Garnish with a lemon twist

FESTIVAL

¾ oz. dark crème de cacao
1 tbsp. apricot brandy
1 tsp. grenadine
¾ oz. heavy cream

1. Fill mixing glass with ice
2. Add dark crème de cacao, apricot brandy, grenadine and heavy cream
3. Shake
4. Strain into a rocks glass filled with ice

FIFTY-FIFTY

1½ oz. gin
1½ oz. dry vermouth

1. Fill mixing glass with cracked ice
2. Add gin and dry vermouth
3. Stir
4. Strain into a chilled cocktail glass
5. Garnish with an olive

'57 CHEVY WITH A WHITE LICENSE PLATE

1 oz. white crème de cacao
1 oz. vodka

1. Fill a rocks glass with ice
2. Add white crème de cacao and vodka
3. Stir

FIJI FIZZ

1½ oz. dark rum
½ oz. bourbon
1 tsp. cherry brandy
3 dashes orange bitters
4 oz. cola

1. Fill mixing glass with ice
2. Add dark rum, bourbon, cherry brandy and orange bitters
3. Shake
4. Strain into a Collins glass
5. Add a few ice cubes
6. Fill with cola
7. Garnish with a lime slice

FILBY

2 oz. gin	1. Fill mixing glass with ice
¾ oz. amaretto	2. Add gin, amaretto, dry
½ oz. dry vermouth	vermouth and Campari
½ oz. Campari	3. Stir
	4. Strain into a cocktail glass
	5. Garnish with an orange peel

FINE AND DANDY

1½ oz. gin	1. Fill mixing glass with ice
¾ oz. Cointreau	2. Add gin, Cointreau, lemon juice
¾ oz. lemon juice	and bitters
dash Angostura bitters	3. Shake
	4. Strain into a rocks glass filled
	with ice
	5. Garnish with a cherry

FINO

1½ oz. fino sherry	1. Fill mixing glass with ice
1½ oz. sweet vermouth	2. Add fino sherry and sweet
	vermouth
	3. Shake
	4. Strain into a rocks glass filled
	with ice
	5. Garnish with a slice of lemon

FISH HOUSE PUNCH*

2 cups lemon juice
6 oz. superfine granulated sugar
2 bottles Jamaican rum (750 ml each)
1 bottle brandy or cognac (750 ml)
1 cup peach brandy or ½ cup peach liqueur
8 oz. club soda, chilled

1. One day in advance, combine sugar and lemon juice in a bowl
2. Stir until sugar is dissolved
3. In a container with a cover, combine the sugar-lemon mixture, rum, brandy and peach brandy (or liqueur)
4. Stir
5. Cover and refrigerate
6. When ready to serve, place a block of ice in a punch bowl
7. Add club soda
8. Stir gently

FJORD

1 oz. brandy
½ oz. aquavit
1 oz. orange juice
½ oz. lime juice
1 tsp. grenadine

1. Fill mixing glass with ice
2. Add brandy, aquavit, orange juice, lime juice and grenadine
3. Shake
4. Strain into a chilled cocktail glass

FLAMINGO (1)

2 oz. gin
¾ oz. apricot brandy
¾ oz. lime juice
dash of grenadine

1. Fill mixing glass with ice
2. Add gin, apricot brandy, lime juice and grenadine
3. Shake
4. Strain into a cocktail glass

---

* This recipe has been around since 1732. It originated at The Fish House, a men's club in Schuylkill, Pennsylvania. It packs a mean punch—even George Washington knew that!

FLAMINGO (2)*

- 1¾ oz. añejo (aged) rum
- juice of ½ lime
- 2 oz. pineapple juice
- ½ oz. grenadine

1. Fill a mixing glass with ice
2. Add rum, lime juice, pineapple juice and grenadine
3. Shake vigorously
4. Strain into a stemmed cocktail glass

FLIM FLAM

- 1½ oz. light rum
- ¾ oz. triple sec
- ½ oz. lemon juice
- ½ oz. orange juice

1. Fill mixing glass with ice
2. Add light rum, triple sec, lemon juice and orange juice
3. Shake
4. Strain into a chilled cocktail glass

FLORIDA

- ½ oz. gin
- 3 oz. orange juice
- 1 tsp. kirschwasser
- 1 tsp. triple sec
- 1 tsp. lemon juice

1. Fill mixing glass with ice
2. Add gin, orange juice, kirschwasser, triple sec and lemon juice
3. Shake
4. Strain into a Collins glass
5. Add ice
6. Garnish with an orange slice

---

* This is a recipe that originated at La Floridita Bar in Havana in the 1920s. It was resurrected by Dale DeGraff at the Rainbow Room in New York City.

FLORIDA PUNCH

1½ oz. Myers's dark rum
½ oz. brandy
1 oz. grapefruit juice
1 oz. orange juice

1. Fill mixing glass with ice
2. Add Myers's rum, brandy, grapefruit juice and orange juice
3. Shake
4. Strain into a highball glass filled with crushed ice
5. Garnish with an orange slice

FLYING GRASSHOPPER

1½ oz. vodka
½ oz. green crème de menthe
½ oz. white crème de menthe

1. Fill mixing glass with ice
2. Add vodka, green crème de menthe and white crème de menthe
3. Shake
4. Strain into a rocks glass
5. Add ice, if desired

FLYING SCOT

1 oz. scotch
1 oz. sweet vermouth
2–3 dashes sugar syrup
2–3 dashes Angostura bitters

1. Fill mixing glass with ice
2. Add scotch, sweet vermouth, sugar syrup and bitters
3. Shake
4. Strain into a rocks glass filled with ice

FOGCUTTER

½ oz. brandy
½ oz. rum
½ oz. gin

1. Fill mixing glass with ice
2. Add brandy, rum, gin, pineapple juice and sour mix

3 oz. pineapple juice
1 oz. sour mix

3. Shake
4. Strain into a Collins glass filled with ice
5. Garnish with a lemon twist

FOGGY DAY

1½ oz. gin
1 oz. Pernod

1. Fill mixing glass with ice
2. Add gin and Pernod
3. Shake
4. Strain into a rocks glass
5. Add ice
6. Garnish with a lemon twist

FOG HORN

2½ oz. gin
ginger ale

1. Fill a highball glass with ice
2. Add gin
3. Fill with ginger ale
4. Garnish with a lemon slice

FORESTER

----

1 oz. bourbon
¾ oz. cherry liqueur
1 tsp. lemon juice

1. Fill mixing glass with ice
2. Add bourbon, cherry liqueur and lemon juice
3. Shake
4. Strain into a rocks glass filled with ice
5. Garnish with a cherry

FOXHOUND

- 1½ oz. brandy
- ½ oz. cranberry juice cocktail
- 1 tsp. kümmel
- 1 tsp. lemon juice

1. Fill mixing glass with ice
2. Add brandy, cranberry juice, kümmel and lemon juice
3. Shake
4. Strain into a rocks glass filled with ice
5. Garnish with a lemon slice

FOX RIVER

- 1½ oz. rye whiskey
- ½ oz. dark crème de cacao
- 2 dashes orange bitters

1. Fill mixing glass with ice
2. Add rye, dark crème de cacao and bitters
3. Shake
4. Strain into a rocks glass filled with ice
5. Garnish with a lemon twist

FOXTAIL

- beer

1. Fill a beer stein or a Collins glass with ice
2. Fill with beer
3. Garnish with a twist of lemon

FOX TROT

- 1½ oz. light rum
- ½ oz. lemon juice (or lime juice)
- 2 dashes curaçao

1. Fill mixing glass with ice
2. Add rum, lemon juice and curaçao
3. Shake
4. Strain into a chilled cocktail glass

FOXY LADY

½ oz. amaretto
½ oz. dark crème de cacao
2 oz. cream

1. Fill mixing glass with ice
2. Add amaretto, dark crème de cacao and cream
3. Shake
4. Strain into a chilled cocktail glass

FRANKENJACK COCKTAIL

1 oz. gin
½ oz. dry vermouth
½ oz. apricot brandy
½ oz. triple sec

1. Fill mixing glass with ice
2. Add gin, dry vermouth, apricot brandy and triple sec
3. Shake
4. Strain into a rocks glass filled with ice

FRAPPES

Use any liqueur

Pour 1½ oz. of that liqueur over crushed ice

FREDDY FUDPUCKER

1 oz. tequila
½ oz. Galliano
orange juice

1. Fill a Collins glass with ice
2. Add tequila
3. Fill with orange juice
4. Stir
5. Top with Galliano
6. Stir again

FRENCH CONNECTION

2 oz. brandy 1 oz. amaretto	1. Fill a rocks glass with ice 2. Add brandy and amaretto 3. Stir

FRENCH GREEN DRAGON

1½ oz. cognac 1½ oz. green Chartreuse	1. Fill mixing glass with ice 2. Add cognac and green Chartreuse 3. Shake 4. Strain into a rocks glass filled with ice

FRENCH LIFT

3 oz. dry sparkling wine, chilled ½ oz. grenadine 2 oz. Perrier water 3 or 4 fresh blueberries	1. Half fill a chilled champagne glass with sparkling wine 2. Add grenadine 3. Fill with Perrier 4. Drop blueberries into drink

FRENCH ROSE

1 oz. gin ½ oz. cherry-flavored brandy ½ oz. cherry liqueur	1. Fill mixing glass with ice 2. Add gin, cherry brandy and cherry liqueur 3. Shake 4. Strain into a chilled cocktail glass

FRENCH 75

1½ oz. cognac ½ oz. sugar syrup	1. Fill mixing glass with cracked ice

juice of ½ lemon
brut champagne

2. Add cognac, sugar syrup and
   lemon juice
3. Shake
4. Pour into a highball glass
5. Fill with cold champagne
6. Garnish with a lemon twist

THE FRENCH SUMMER

¾ oz. Chambord
3 oz. sparkling water (or
   club soda)
a few drops fresh lemon
   juice

1. Fill a wineglass with ice
2. Add Chambord
3. Add sparkling water and lemon
   juice
4. Garnish with a slice of lemon
   and a slice of orange

FRIAR TUCK

2 oz. Frangelico
2 oz. lemon juice
1 tsp. grenadine

1. Fill mixing glass with ice
2. Add Frangelico, lemon juice
   and grenadine
3. Shake
4. Strain into a rocks glass half
   filled with ice
5. Garnish with an orange slice

FRISCO SOUR

1½ oz. blended whiskey
¾ oz. Bénédictine
1 tsp. lime juice
1 tsp. lemon juice

1. Fill mixing glass with ice
2. Add blended whiskey, Bénédictine, lime juice and lemon juice
3. Shake
4. Strain into a sour glass
5. Garnish with an orange slice

FROBISHER

2 oz. gin
3 dashes Angostura bitters
chilled champagne

1. Fill a highball glass with ice
2. Add gin and bitters
3. Stir
4. Fill with champagne
5. Add more ice, if desired
6. Garnish with a lemon twist

FROOT LOOP

1 oz. apple brandy
½ oz. cherry brandy
½ oz. vodka
splash orange juice

1. Fill mixing glass with ice
2. Add apple brandy, cherry brandy, vodka and orange juice
3. Shake
4. Strain into a cocktail glass

FROSTBITE

1½ oz. tequila (white)
½ oz. white crème de cacao
2-3 dashes blue curaçao (optional)
2 oz. cream

1. Fill mixing glass with ice
2. Add tequila, white crème de cacao, blue curaçao (if desired) and cream
3. Shake
4. Strain into a frosted sour glass
5. Add ice

FROTH BLOWER

1½ oz. gin
1 tsp. grenadine
½ egg white

1. Fill mixing glass with ice
2. Add gin, grenadine and egg white
3. Shake
4. Strain into a chilled cocktail glass

FROUPE

1½ oz. brandy
1½ oz. sweet vermouth
1 tsp. Bénédictine

1. Fill mixing glass with ice
2. Add brandy, sweet vermouth and Bénédictine
3. Stir
4. Strain into a chilled cocktail glass

FROZEN BIKINI*

2 oz. vodka
1 oz. peach schnapps
3 oz. peach nectar
2 oz. orange juice
splash fresh lemon juice
1 oz. chilled champagne

1. In blender, combine all ingredients (except champagne) with 4 oz. crushed ice
2. Blend until smooth
3. Pour into a 12–16 oz. goblet
4. Top with champagne

FROZEN DAIQUIRI

2 oz. light rum
1½ oz. lime juice
1 tsp. sugar

1. Fill blender with approximately 4 oz. crushed ice
2. Add rum, lime juice and sugar
3. Blend at low speed for several seconds, until snowy in texture
4. Pour into a champagne saucer

FROZEN FRUIT DAIQUIRI

1½ oz. light rum
½ oz. sour mix
1 oz. appropriate fruit liqueur

1. Fill blender with about 4 oz. of ice
2. Add all ingredients

---

* Courtesy of the Winter Garden Cafe in the World Financial Center, New York City.

        1 oz. honey if fruit is
          unsweetened
        ½ oz. cream
        lots of fresh fruit

3. Blend at medium speed for
   approximately 15 seconds, or
   until smooth
4. Pour into a large goblet or large
   wineglass

FROZEN FRUIT MARGARITA

        1½ oz. tequila
        ½ oz. triple sec
        ½ oz. sour mix
        fresh fruit to taste
        1 oz. appropriate fruit
          liqueur
        dash Rose's lime juice

1. Fill blender with about 4 oz. of
   ice
2. Add all ingredients
3. Blend at medium speed for
   approximately 15 seconds, or
   until smooth
4. Pour into a large goblet or large
   wineglass
5. Garnish with a lime slice

FROZEN MARGARITA

        1½ oz. tequila
        ½ oz. triple sec
        1 oz. sour mix
        dash Rose's lime juice

1. Fill blender with about 4 oz. of
   ice
2. Add tequila, triple sec, sour mix
   and lime juice
3. Blend at medium speed for
   approximately 15 seconds, or
   until smooth
4. Pour into a large goblet or large
   wineglass
5. Garnish with a lime slice

FROZEN MATADOR

----

        1 oz. tequila
        2 oz. pineapple juice

1. Fill blender with about 3 oz.
   crushed ice

2 tsp. lime juice

2. Add tequila, pineapple juice and lime juice
3. Blend at medium speed for approximately 15 seconds
4. Pour into a large goblet or large wineglass
5. Garnish with a pineapple slice

FROZEN MINT DAIQUIRI

2½ oz. light rum
2 tsp. lime juice
1 tsp. sugar
6 mint leaves

1. Fill blender with about 6 oz. of ice
2. Add light rum, lime juice, sugar and mint leaves
3. Blend at medium speed for approximately 15 seconds, or until smooth
4. Pour into a large goblet or large wineglass

FROZEN MINT JULEP

2 oz. bourbon
1 oz. lemon juice
1 oz. sugar syrup
5 or 6 small mint leaves

1. Muddle bourbon, lemon juice, sugar syrup and mint leaves in a glass
2. Pour mixture into a blender
3. Add 6 oz. crushed ice
4. Blend at high speed for 15 or 20 seconds
5. Pour into a chilled highball glass
6. Garnish with a mint sprig

FUZZY FRUIT

1½ oz. peach schnapps
5 oz. grapefruit juice
  (unsweetened)

1. Fill a highball glass with ice
2. Add peach schnapps and grapefruit juice
3. Stir

FUZZY MARTINI

2 oz. vanilla-flavored vodka
½ oz. coffee-flavored vodka
1 tsp. peach schnapps

1. Fill mixing glass with ice
2. Add vanilla-flavored vodka,
   coffee-flavored vodka and
   peach schnapps
3. Shake
4. Strain into a martini glass
5. Garnish with a peach slice

FUZZY MOTHER

1½ oz. gold tequila
151-proof rum

1. Pour tequila into a pony glass
2. Top with 151-proof rum
3. Ignite

FUZZY NAVEL

1½ oz. peach schnapps
6 oz. orange juice

1. Fill a highball glass with ice
2. Add peach schnapps and orange
   juice
3. Stir

G

GASPER

1½ oz. dry gin 1½ oz. apricot brandy	1. Fill mixing glass with ice 2. Add gin and apricot brandy 3. Shake 4. Strain into a chilled cocktail glass

GAUGIN

2 oz. light rum 1 tbsp. passion fruit syrup 1 tbsp. lime juice 1 tbsp. lemon juice	1. In blender, combine light rum, passion fruit syrup, lime juice and lemon juice with 3 oz. crushed ice 2. Blend at medium speed until smooth 3. Pour into a rocks glass 4. Garnish with a twist of lime

GAZETTE

1½ oz. brandy 1 oz. sweet vermouth 1 tsp. lemon juice	1. Fill mixing glass with ice 2. Add brandy, sweet vermouth, lemon juice and sugar syrup

1 tsp. sugar syrup

3. Shake
4. Strain into a chilled cocktail glass

GEISHA

2 oz. bourbon
1 oz. sake
2 tsp. sugar syrup
1½ tsp. lemon juice

1. Fill mixing glass with ice
2. Add bourbon, sake, lemon juice and sugar syrup
3. Shake
4. Strain into a sour glass

GENOA

1½ oz. vodka
¾ oz. Campari
2 oz. orange juice

1. Fill mixing glass with ice
2. Add vodka, Campari and orange juice
3. Shake
4. Strain into a rocks glass filled with ice

GENTLE BULL

1½ oz. tequila
¾ oz. Kahlúa
1 tbsp. heavy cream

1. Fill mixing glass with ice
2. Add tequila, Kahlúa and cream
3. Shake
4. Strain into a rocks glass filled with ice

GEORGIA PEACH FIZZ

1½ oz. brandy
½ oz. peach brandy
½ oz. lemon juice
1 tsp. banana liqueur

1. Fill mixing glass with ice
2. Add brandy, peach brandy, lemon juice, banana liqueur and sugar syrup

1 tsp. sugar syrup
club soda

3. Shake
4. Strain into a Collins glass
5. Add ice
6. Top with club soda
7. Garnish with a fresh peach slice

GIBSON

2 oz. gin
½ oz. dry vermouth

1. Fill mixing glass with ice
2. Add gin and dry vermouth
3. Stir
4. Strain into a martini glass or a rocks glass filled with ice
5. Garnish with a pearl onion

(*Note:* A Gibson is a martini with a pearl onion garnish instead of an olive. Like a martini, the drier the Gibson, the less vermouth is used in proportion to the gin.)

GIMLET

2 oz. gin
¼ oz. Rose's lime juice (½ oz. fresh lime juice may be substituted)

1. Fill mixing glass with ice
2. Add gin and lime juice
3. Shake
4. Strain into a chilled rocks glass
5. Add ice
6. Garnish with a lime slice

GIN ALEXANDER

½ oz. gin
½ oz. dark crème de cacao
½ oz. heavy cream

1. Fill mixing glass with ice
2. Add gin, dark crème de cacao and cream

nutmeg or cinnamon

3. Shake
4. Strain into a chilled cocktail glass
5. Sprinkle nutmeg or cinnamon on top

GIN AND SODA

1½ oz. gin
6 oz. club soda

1. Fill a highball glass with ice
2. Add gin and club soda
3. Stir
4. Garnish with a lemon twist

GIN AND TONIC

2 oz. gin
tonic water

1. Fill a highball glass with ice
2. Add gin
3. Fill with tonic water
4. Stir
5. Garnish with a wedge of lime

GIN CASSIS

1½ oz. gin
½ oz. crème de cassis
½ oz. lemon juice

1. Fill shaker glass with ice
2. Add gin, crème de cassis and lemon juice
3. Shake
4. Strain into a rocks glass filled with ice

GIN DAIQUIRI

1½ oz. gin
½ oz. light rum
2 tsp. lime juice

1. Fill mixing glass with ice
2. Add gin, light rum, lime juice and sugar

1 tsp. sugar

3. Shake
4. Strain into a rocks glass filled with ice
5. Garnish with a lime slice

GIN DAISY

1½ oz. gin
½ tsp. sugar
juice of ½ lemon
1 tsp. grenadine
club soda

1. Fill mixing glass with ice
2. Add gin, sugar, lemon juice and grenadine
3. Shake
4. Strain into a highball glass over ice
5. Top with club soda
6. Garnish with a wedge of lemon

GIN FIZZ

1½ oz. dry gin
1 tbsp. powdered sugar
3 oz. sour mix
1 oz. club soda

1. Fill mixing glass with ice
2. Add gin, sugar and sour mix
3. Shake
4. Pour into a Collins glass over ice
5. Add club soda
6. Garnish with a cherry and an orange slice

GINGER BREEZE

1½ oz. light rum
1 tsp. cherry brandy
4 oz. orange juice
1 oz. ginger ale

1. Fill mixing glass with ice
2. Add rum, cherry brandy and orange juice
3. Shake
4. Strain into a highball glass
5. Add ice
6. Top with ginger ale

GINGER SHANDIES

3 bottles (11.2 oz.) chilled
    Hoegaarden beer
1 bottle (12 oz.) chilled
    ginger beer
1 thinly sliced lemon
mint sprigs

1. In a large pitcher, combine the Hoegaarden with the ginger beer
2. Stir in most of the lemon slices and the mint sprigs
3. Fill rocks glasses with ice
4. Add remaining lemon slices to glasses and pour in the shandy
5. Garnish with the remaining mint sprigs

GIN RICKEY

1½ oz. gin
juice of ½ lime
club soda

1. Fill a highball glass with ice
2. Add gin and lime juice
3. Fill with club soda

GIN SOUR

1½ oz. gin
4 oz. sour mix

1. Fill mixing glass with ice
2. Add gin and sour mix
3. Shake
4. Strain into a sour glass
5. Add ice
6. Garnish with a cherry and an orange slice

GIRL SCOUT COOKIE

1½ oz. Kahlúa
1½ oz. cream
½ oz. peppermint schnapps

1. Fill mixing glass with ice
2. Add Kahlúa, cream and peppermint schnapps
3. Shake
4. Strain into a rocks glass filled with ice

GLAD EYES

1½ oz. Pernod
½ oz. peppermint schnapps

1. Fill mixing glass with ice
2. Add Pernod and peppermint schnapps
3. Shake
4. Strain into a chilled cocktail glass

GLAMOUR GIRL MARTINI

3 oz. Folonari Pink Pinot Grigio
1 oz. peach schnapps
splash of cranberry juice

1. Pour the ingredients into a cocktail shaker filled with ice
2. Shake well
3. Strain into a chilled cocktail glass
4. Drop a maraschino cherry in the drink for a garnish

GLASGOW

1½ oz. scotch
1 tsp. dry vermouth
1 tbsp. lemon juice
1 tsp. almond extract

1. Fill mixing glass with ice
2. Add scotch, dry vermouth, lemon juice and almond extract
3. Shake
4. Strain into a rocks glass filled with ice

GLOOM CHASER

1 oz. Grand Marnier
1 oz. curaçao
½ oz. lemon juice
1 tsp. grenadine

1. Fill mixing glass with ice
2. Add Grand Marnier, curaçao, lemon juice and grenadine
3. Shake
4. Strain into a chilled cocktail glass

GLOOM LIFTER

2 oz. blended whiskey
½ oz. lemon juice
¼ oz. sugar syrup
½ egg white

1. Fill mixing glass with ice
2. Add blended whiskey, lemon juice, sugar syrup and egg white
3. Shake
4. Strain into a chilled cocktail glass

GLÜHWEIN

6 oz. dry red wine
1 tsp. honey
2 whole cloves
1 cinnamon stick, broken into pieces
pinch ground nutmeg

1. Combine ingredients in a small saucepan
2. Heat without boiling
3. Stir until honey is dissolved
4. Pour into a warm mug

GODCHILD

¾ oz. vodka
¾ oz. amaretto
¾ oz. heavy cream

1. Fill mixing glass with ice
2. Add vodka, amaretto and heavy cream
3. Shake
4. Strain into a champagne glass

GODFATHER

1½ oz. scotch
¾ oz. amaretto

1. Fill a rocks glass with ice
2. Add scotch and amaretto
3. Stir

GODMOTHER

1½ oz. vodka	1. Fill a rocks glass with ice
¾ oz. Kahlúa	2. Add vodka and Kahlúa
	3. Stir

GO-GO JUICE

½ oz. vodka	1. Fill mixing glass with ice
½ oz. gin	2. Add all ingredients, except
½ oz. light rum	7-Up
½ oz. blue curaçao	3. Shake
½ oz. white tequila	4. Strain into a Collins glass
½ oz. orange juice	5. Add ice
1 oz. sour mix	6. Top with 7-Up
7-Up	7. Garnish with a lemon slice

GOLDEN CADILLAC

2 oz. Galliano	1. Fill mixing glass with ice
1 oz. white crème de cacao	2. Add Galliano, crème de cacao
1 oz. cream	and cream
	3. Shake
	4. Pour into a chilled highball glass
	5. Add ice

GOLDEN DAWN

1½ oz. gin	1. Fill mixing glass with ice
½ oz. orange juice	2. Add gin, orange juice and
2 tsp. apricot brandy	apricot brandy
	3. Shake
	4. Strain into a chilled cocktail glass

GOLDEN DAZE

1½ oz. gin
½ oz. apricot brandy
1 oz. orange juice

1. Fill mixing glass with ice
2. Add gin, apricot brandy and orange juice
3. Shake
4. Strain into a chilled cocktail glass

GOLDEN DREAM

2 oz. Galliano
1 oz. white crème de cacao
1 oz. cream
½ oz. orange juice
dash triple sec

1. Fill mixing glass with ice
2. Add Galliano, crème de cacao, cream, orange juice and triple sec
3. Shake
4. Pour into a chilled highball glass
5. Add ice

GOLDEN FIZZ

1 oz. gin
2 oz. sour mix
1 egg yolk
1 oz. club soda

1. Fill mixing glass with ice
2. Add gin, sour mix and egg yolk
3. Shake
4. Strain into a Collins glass filled with ice
5. Top with club soda

GOLDEN GATE

¾ oz. light rum
¾ oz. gin
½ oz. lemon juice
½ oz. white crème de cacao
1 tsp. 151-proof rum

1. Fill mixing glass with ice
2. Add light rum, gin, lemon juice, white crème de cacao, 151-proof rum and Falernum
3. Shake

dash Falernum

4. Strain into a rocks glass filled with ice
5. Garnish with an orange slice

GOLDEN LEMONADE

½ cup sugar
1 cup fresh lemon juice
2 cups gold tequila

1. In a small saucepan, combine sugar with ½ cup water
2. Bring to a boil (over medium flame), stirring so that sugar is dissolved
3. Boil for one minute
4. Remove from heat
5. Add ½ cup cold water to mixture
6. Cool to room temperature
7. Stir in lemon juice
8. Combine lemon syrup and tequila in a pitcher
9. Stir well
10. Add ice
11. Serve in Collins glasses filled with ice

GOLDEN MARGARITA

2 oz. gold tequila
1 oz. curaçao
¾ oz. lime juice

1. Fill mixing glass with 2 oz. crushed ice, gold tequila, curaçao and lime juice
2. Shake
3. Pour into a rocks glass (rim may be frosted with salt, if desired, before pouring drink into glass)
4. Garnish with a slice of lime

GOLDEN SCREW

1½ oz. vodka
dash Angostura bitters
orange juice

1. Fill a highball glass with ice
2. Add vodka and bitters
3. Fill with orange juice
4. Stir

GOLDEN SLIPPER

1 oz. apricot brandy
1 oz. yellow Chartreuse
1 egg yolk

1. Fill mixing glass with ice
2. Add apricot brandy,
   yellow Chartreuse and the
   egg yolk
3. Shake well
4. Strain into a chilled cocktail
   glass

GOLF

2 oz. gin
1 oz. dry vermouth
2 dashes Angostura bitters

1. Fill mixing glass with ice
2. Add gin, dry vermouth and
   bitters
3. Stir
4. Strain into a chilled cocktail
   glass
5. Garnish with an olive

GOOD AND PLENTY

¾ oz. ouzo
¾ oz. anisette

Pour ouzo and anisette into a
brandy snifter or a liqueur
glass

GOOSE IN SPRING

2 raspberries
2 oz. lavender-infused Grey
  Goose vodka
¾ oz. St-Germain
  elderflower liqueur
¼ oz. fresh lemon juice
lavender
lemon peel

1. Muddle the raspberries in a cocktail shaker
2. Add the spirits and lemon juice
3. Shake well
4. Double strain into a chilled, lavender-rubbed cocktail glass
5. Express the lemon peel by squeezing it over the drink to release the oils, wipe the glass rim with the peel, then drop it into the glass

(*Note*: For lavender-infused vodka use two sprigs of lavender, allowing to infuse for 6 days, then double strain to remove all of the herb.)

GORILLA PUNCH

1 oz. vodka
½ oz. blue curaçao
2 oz. orange juice
2 oz. pineapple juice

1. Fill mixing glass with ice
2. Add vodka, blue curaçao, orange juice and pineapple juice
3. Shake
4. Strain into a Collins glass filled with ice
5. Garnish with a cherry

GRADEAL SPECIAL

1½ oz. light rum
¾ oz. apricot brandy
¾ oz. gin
1 tsp. sugar syrup

1. Fill mixing glass with ice
2. Add light rum, apricot brandy, gin and sugar syrup
3. Shake
4. Strain into a chilled cocktail glass

GRAND APPLE

1 oz. apple brandy
½ oz. cognac
½ oz. Grand Marnier

1. Fill mixing glass with ice
2. Add apple brandy, cognac and Grand Marnier
3. Stir
4. Strain into a rocks glass
5. Garnish with a lemon twist

GRAND OCCASION

1½ oz. light rum
½ oz. Grand Marnier
½ oz. white crème de cacao
1 tbsp. lemon juice

1. Fill mixing glass with ice
2. Add light rum, Grand Marnier, white crème de cacao and lemon juice
3. Shake well
4. Strain into a chilled cocktail glass

GRAND PASSION

2 oz. gin
1 oz. passion fruit nectar
2 dashes Angostura bitters

1. Fill mixing glass with ice
2. Add gin, passion fruit nectar and bitters
3. Shake well
4. Strain into a chilled cocktail glass

GRAND SLAM

1½ oz. Swedish Punsch
¾ oz. dry vermouth
¾ oz. sweet vermouth

1. Fill mixing glass with ice
2. Add Swedish Punsch, dry vermouth and sweet vermouth
3. Stir
4. Strain into a chilled cocktail glass

GRAPE CRUSH

1 oz. vodka
½ oz. Chambord
2 oz. sour mix
1 oz. cranberry juice cocktail
7-Up

1. Fill mixing glass with ice
2. Add vodka, Chambord, sour mix and cranberry juice
3. Shake
4. Strain into a highball glass filled with ice
5. Top with 7-Up

GRAPEFRUIT HIGHBALL

1½ oz. light rum
6 oz. grapefruit juice

1. Fill a highball glass with ice
2. Add light rum and grapefruit juice
3. Stir

GRAPESHOT

1½ oz. tequila
½ oz. curaçao
1 oz. grape juice

1. Fill mixing glass with ice
2. Add tequila, curaçao and grape juice
3. Shake
4. Strain into a chilled cocktail glass

GRAPE VINE

1½ oz. gin
2 oz. grape juice
1 oz. lemon juice
dash grenadine

1. Fill a rocks glass with ice
2. Add gin, grape juice, lemon juice and grenadine
3. Stir well

GRASSHOPPER

1 oz. green crème de menthe	1. Fill mixing glass with ice
1 oz. white crème de cacao	2. Add green crème de menthe, white crème de cacao and cream
1 oz. light cream	3. Shake
	4. Strain into a chilled cocktail glass

GRASS IS GREENER

1½ oz. light rum	1. Fill mixing glass with ice
¾ oz. green crème de menthe	2. Add light rum, green crème de menthe and lemon juice
¾ oz. lemon juice	3. Shake
	4. Strain into a chilled champagne glass

GRATEFUL DEAD

¼ oz. vodka	1. Fill mixing glass with ice
¼ oz. rum	2. Add all ingredients
¼ oz. tequila	3. Shake
¼ oz. triple sec	4. Strain into a rocks glass filled with ice
¼ oz. Chambord	
cola (to taste)	

GREAT DANE

1 oz. aquavit	1. Fill mixing glass with ice
½ oz. Peter Heering (or other cherry brandy)	2. Add aquavit, Peter Heering (cherry brandy), cranberry juice and orange bitters
½ oz. cranberry juice cocktail	3. Shake
1 dash orange bitters	4. Strain into a chilled cocktail glass

GREAT SECRET

2 oz. gin	1. Fill mixing glass with ice
½ oz. Lillet	2. Add gin, Lillet and bitters
dash Angostura bitters	3. Shake
	4. Strain into a chilled cocktail glass
	5. Garnish with an orange slice

GREEN DRAGON

2 oz. Russian vodka	1. Fill mixing glass with ice
1 oz. green Chartreuse	2. Add vodka and green Chartreuse
	3. Shake
	4. Strain into a chilled cocktail glass

GREEN EYE-OPENER*

1½ oz. vodka	1. Fill mixing glass with ice
dash Rose's lime juice	2. Add vodka, Rose's lime juice, orange juice, blue curaçao and triple sec
2 oz. orange juice	
dash blue curaçao	3. Shake
dash triple sec	4. Pour into a highball glass
	5. Garnish with a celery stalk, including the leafy part

GREEN FIRE

1½ oz. gin	1. Fill mixing glass with ice
2 tsp. green crème de menthe	2. Add gin, green crème de menthe and kümmel

---

* Courtesy of Sign of the Dove, New York City.

2 tsp. kümmel	3. Shake
	4. Strain into a highball glass
	5. Add ice

GREEN HORNET

1½ oz. brandy	1. Fill a rocks glass with ice
½ oz. green crème de menthe	2. Add brandy and crème de menthe
	3. Stir

GREEN LIZARD (SHOOTER)

| 1 oz. green Chartreuse | 1. Combine in a mixing glass filled with ice |
| ½ oz. 151-proof rum | 2. Strain into a shot glass |

GREEN ROOM

1 oz. brandy	1. Fill mixing glass with ice
1½ oz. dry vermouth	2. Add brandy, dry vermouth and curaçao
2 dashes of curaçao	3. Shake
	4. Strain into a chilled cocktail glass

GRENADIER

2 oz. brandy	1. Fill mixing glass with ice
1 oz. ginger brandy	2. Add brandy, ginger brandy, ginger and sugar syrup
dash ground ginger	3. Stir
1 tsp. sugar syrup	4. Strain into a chilled cocktail glass

GREYHOUND

1½ oz. vodka
6 oz. grapefruit juice

1. Fill a highball glass with ice
2. Add vodka and grapefruit juice
3. Stir

GROG

----

2 oz. Jamaican rum
1 sugar cube
1 tbsp. lemon juice
3 cloves
1 cinnamon stick

1. Combine all ingredients in a large mug
2. Add boiling water
3. Stir drink so that the sugar dissolves
4. Garnish with a lemon twist

GROUND ZERO

¾ oz. peppermint schnapps
¾ oz. bourbon
¾ oz. vodka
½ oz. Kahlúa

1. Fill mixing glass with ice
2. Add peppermint schnapps, bourbon, vodka and Kahlúa
3. Shake
4. Strain into a sour glass
5. Add ice

GYPSY

----

2 oz. vodka
½ oz. Bénédictine
1 tsp. lemon juice
1 tsp. orange juice

1. Fill mixing glass with ice
2. Add vodka, Bénédictine, lemon juice and orange juice
3. Shake
4. Strain into a rocks glass filled with ice

H

HABANERO MARTINI

2 oz. reposado tequila
1 oz. dry vermouth

1. Pour the tequila and dry vermouth into a cocktail shaker filled with ice
2. Shake well
3. Strain into a chilled cocktail glass
4. Garnish with a small whole habanero pepper

HAIRY NAVEL

¾ oz. peach schnapps
¾ oz. vodka
6 oz. orange juice

1. Fill a highball glass with ice
2. Add peach schnapps, vodka and orange juice
3. Stir

HALLEY'S COMFORT

1½ oz. Southern Comfort
1½ oz. peach schnapps
club soda

1. Fill a rocks glass with ice
2. Add Southern Comfort and peach schnapps
3. Stir
4. Fill with club soda

HAMMERHEAD

1 oz. gold rum
1 oz. amaretto
1 oz. curaçao
1 or 2 dashes Southern
   Comfort

1. Fill mixing glass with ice
2. Add rum, amaretto, curaçao
   and Southern Comfort
3. Shake
4. Strain into a chilled cocktail
   glass

THE HAPPY FELLER (SHOOTER)

3 oz. Finlandia or Absolut
   vodka
1 oz. Framboise
1 oz. Cointreau
dash Rose's lime juice

(MAKES APPROXIMATELY
   3 SHOTS)

1. Fill mixing glass with ice
2. Add vodka, Framboise,
   Cointreau and lime juice
3. Stir
4. Strain into shot glasses

HARBOR LIGHT

¾ oz. Metaxa
¾ oz. Galliano

Pour Metaxa and Galliano into a
brandy snifter or a liqueur glass

HARLEM COCKTAIL

1½ oz. gin
1 oz. pineapple juice
½ tsp. maraschino liqueur

1. Fill mixing glass with ice
2. Add gin, pineapple juice and
   maraschino liqueur
3. Shake
4. Strain into a chilled cocktail glass
5. Garnish with 2 pineapple
   chunks (skewer on a toothpick
   and balance across the rim of
   the glass)

HARPER'S FERRY

1½ oz. dry vermouth 1 tbsp. Southern Comfort 1 tbsp. light rum 1 tbsp. curaçao	1. Fill mixing glass with ice 2. Add dry vermouth, Southern Comfort, light rum and curaçao 3. Shake 4. Strain into a chilled cocktail glass

HARVARD

1 oz. brandy 1 oz. sweet vermouth ¼ oz. lemon juice dash sugar syrup 2 dashes Angostura bitters	1. Fill mixing glass with ice 2. Add brandy, sweet vermouth, lemon juice, sugar syrup and bitters 3. Shake 4. Strain into a chilled cocktail glass

HARVEY WALLBANGER

1½ oz. vodka 4 oz. orange juice ½ oz. Galliano	1. Fill a Collins glass with ice 2. Add vodka and orange juice 3. Stir well 4. Float Galliano on top

HAVANA CLUB

1½ oz. light rum 1 tbsp. dry vermouth	1. Fill mixing glass with ice 2. Add rum and dry vermouth 3. Shake 4. Strain into a chilled cocktail glass

HAWAIIAN COCKTAIL

2 oz. gin
½ oz. triple sec
1 tbsp. pineapple juice

1. Fill mixing glass with ice
2. Add gin, triple sec and pineapple juice
3. Shake
4. Strain into a chilled cocktail glass

HAWAIIAN EYE

1½ oz. bourbon
1 oz. Kahlúa
1 oz. heavy cream
½ oz. vodka
½ oz. banana liqueur
1 tsp. Pernod
1 egg white

1. In a blender, combine 3 oz. cracked ice with all ingredients
2. Blend at high speed for 15 seconds
3. Pour straight into a chilled highball glass
4. Garnish with a cherry and a pineapple slice

HAWAIIAN ORANGE BLOSSOM

1½ oz. gin
1 oz. curaçao
2 oz. orange juice
1 oz. pineapple juice

1. Fill mixing glass with ice
2. Add gin, curaçao, orange juice and pineapple juice
3. Shake
4. Strain into a sour glass
5. Garnish with an orange slice

HAWAIIAN PUNCH (SHOOTER)

¼ oz. crème de almond
¼ oz. Southern Comfort
¼ oz. Smirnoff 100-proof vodka
¼ oz. pineapple juice

1. Fill mixing glass with ice
2. Add crème de almond, Southern Comfort, Smirnoff vodka and pineapple juice
3. Shake
4. Strain into a rocks glass

HENNESSEY MARTINI

1¾ oz. Hennessey
splash lemon juice

1. Fill mixing glass with ice
2. Add Hennessey and lemon juice
3. Shake
4. Strain into a chilled martini glass
5. Garnish with a lemon twist

HENRY MORGAN'S GROG

1½ oz. blended whiskey
1 oz. Pernod
½ oz. dark rum
1 oz. heavy cream
ground nutmeg

1. Half fill mixing glass with cracked ice
2. Add whiskey, Pernod, dark rum and heavy cream
3. Shake
4. Pour into a chilled rocks glass
5. Sprinkle top with ground nutmeg

HIGH JAMAICAN WIND

1½ oz. Myers's dark rum
½ oz. Kahlúa
cream

1. Fill a rocks glass with ice
2. Add Myers's dark rum and Kahlúa
3. Float cream on top

HIGHLAND FLING

1½ oz. scotch
½ oz. sweet vermouth
2–3 dashes orange bitters

1. Fill mixing glass with ice
2. Add scotch, sweet vermouth and orange bitters
3. Shake
4. Strain into a chilled cocktail glass
5. Garnish with an olive

HIGH ROLLER

1½ oz. vodka
¾ oz. Grand Marnier
4 oz. orange juice
a few drops grenadine

1. Fill mixing glass with ice
2. Add vodka, Grand Marnier and orange juice
3. Shake
4. Strain into a rocks glass
5. Add ice
6. Add a few drops of grenadine to top

HOFFMAN HOUSE

1½ oz. gin
½ oz. dry vermouth
2 dashes orange bitters

1. Fill mixing glass with ice
2. Add gin, dry vermouth and orange bitters
3. Shake
4. Strain into a chilled cocktail glass
5. Garnish with an olive

HOLLYWOOD TEA

½ oz. vodka
½ oz. gin
½ oz. rum
½ oz. tequila
½ oz. triple sec
1 oz. sour mix
7-Up

1. Fill mixing glass with ice
2. Add vodka, gin, rum, tequila, triple sec and sour mix
3. Shake
4. Strain into a rocks glass filled with ice
5. Top with 7-Up

HOMECOMING

1½ oz. amaretto
1½ oz. Baileys Original Irish Cream

1. Fill mixing glass with ice
2. Add amaretto and Baileys
3. Shake
4. Strain into a chilled cocktail glass

HONEY BEE

½ oz. honey
2½ oz. dark rum
½ oz. lemon juice

1. Fill mixing glass with ice
2. Add honey, dark rum and lemon juice
3. Shake
4. Strain into a chilled cocktail glass

HONEYDEW MARGARITA

1 oz. honeydew melon puree (puree fresh melon in a blender)
1½ oz. tequila
1 oz. triple sec
¾ oz. fresh lime juice
½ oz. simple syrup

1. Shake all ingredients together with ice
2. Pour into a glass, and garnish with melon balls

(*Note*: Salt on the rim is optional.)

HONEYMOON

¾ oz. apple brandy
¾ oz. Bénédictine
1 oz. lemon juice
2 dashes triple sec

1. Fill mixing glass with ice
2. Add apple brandy, Bénédictine, lemon juice and triple sec
3. Shake
4. Strain into a chilled cocktail glass

HONOLULU LULU

1 oz. gin
1 oz. Bénédictine
1 oz. maraschino liqueur

1. Fill mixing glass with ice
2. Add gin, Bénédictine and maraschino liqueur
3. Stir
4. Strain into a chilled cocktail glass

HOOPLA

¾ oz. brandy
¾ oz. Cointreau
¾ oz. Lillet
¾ oz. lemon juice

1. Fill mixing glass with ice
2. Add brandy, Cointreau, Lillet and lemon juice
3. Shake
4. Strain into a chilled cocktail glass

HOOT MON

1½ oz. scotch
¾ oz. sweet vermouth
1 tsp. Bénédictine

1. Fill mixing glass with ice
2. Add scotch, sweet vermouth and Bénédictine
3. Stir
4. Strain into a chilled cocktail glass
5. Garnish with a twist of lemon

HOP TOAD

1 oz. light rum
1 oz. apricot brandy
1 oz. lime juice

1. Fill mixing glass with ice
2. Add light rum, apricot brandy and lime juice
3. Shake
4. Strain into a chilled cocktail glass

HORSE'S NECK

2 oz. blended whiskey
ginger ale
1 lemon, peeled

1. Peel lemon in one strip, creating a spiral effect
2. Set peel aside
3. Pour blended whiskey into a Collins glass

4. Add ice
5. Drop in the lemon peel as a garnish
6. Top with ginger ale
7. Add a few drops of the fresh lemon juice

HOT APPLE PIE

1½ oz. Tuaca liqueur
hot apple cider

1. Pour Tuaca into a mug
2. Fill with hot apple cider

HOT BRICK

⅓ oz. whiskey
pinch cinnamon
pinch sugar
⅓ oz. hot water
small pat butter

1. Fill mug with whiskey, cinnamon and sugar
2. Add hot water
3. Float butter on top to melt

HOT BUTTERED RUM

----

8 oz. apple cider
6 whole cloves
1 cinnamon stick
½ oz. lemon juice
2 oz. dark rum
1 tsp. butter

1. Pour apple cider, cloves, cinnamon stick and lemon juice into a small saucepan
2. Bring to a boil
3. Pour into a mug
4. Add rum
5. Top with butter

HOT COCONUT COFFEE

----

1 oz. Malibu liqueur
hot coffee

1. Pour Malibu into a coffee mug
2. Fill with hot coffee

3. Top with whipped cream, if desired

HOTEL GEORGIA

2 parts gin
1 part orgeat
½ part lemon juice
10 drops orange flower
water
1 egg white

1. Combine ingredients and shake well
2. Add ice to chill and strain into a cocktail glass

HOT PANTS

1½ oz. tequila
¾ oz. peppermint schnapps
1 tbsp. grapefruit juice
½ tsp. grenadine

1. Fill mixing glass with ice
2. Add tequila, peppermint schnapps, grapefruit juice and grenadine
3. Shake
4. Pour into a rocks glass

(*Note:* You may frost the rim of the rocks glass with salt before pouring the drink in, if desired.)

HOT PEPPERMINT PATTY

1 oz. peppermint schnapps
½ oz. dark crème de cacao
1 packet instant hot
chocolate mix
hot water
whipped cream

1. Pour peppermint schnapps and crème de cacao into a coffee mug
2. Add hot chocolate mix
3. Stir until dissolved
4. Fill almost to the top with boiling water

| 1 tsp. green crème de menthe | 5. Stir |
| | 6. Top with whipped cream and crème de menthe |

HOT RUM

| 2 sugar cubes
4 oz. light rum
1½ tsp. lemon juice
hot water | 1. In a mug, dissolve the sugar cubes in a small amount of hot water
2. Add rum and lemon juice
3. Fill with hot water
4. Stir
5. Sprinkle cinnamon on top |

HOT RUM TODDY

| 1½ oz. Jamaican dark rum
1 tsp. sugar
3 cloves
dash cinnamon
1 lemon slice
hot water
dash ground nutmeg | 1. Add rum, sugar, cloves, cinnamon and lemon slice to a large mug
2. Fill with hot water
3. Sprinkle top with nutmeg |

HOT SHOTS (SHOOTER)

| ½ oz. vodka
½ oz. peppermint schnapps
few drops Tabasco sauce | 1. Pour vodka and peppermint schnapps into a shot glass
2. Top with a few drops of Tabasco sauce |

HOT TODDY

1 oz. bourbon
4 oz. boiling water
1 tsp. sugar
3 whole cloves
1 cinnamon stick
1 lemon slice, thinly sliced

1. Put sugar, cloves, cinnamon stick and lemon slice into a heat-resistant mug
2. Add 1 oz. boiling water
3. Stir
4. Let stand for 5 minutes
5. Add bourbon and 3 oz. boiling water
6. Stir well
7. Sprinkle with ground nutmeg

HOUSTON HURRICANE

1 oz. blended whiskey
1 oz. gin
1 oz. white crème de menthe
3 tbsp. lemon juice

1. Fill mixing glass with ice
2. Add blended whiskey, gin, white crème de menthe and lemon juice
3. Shake
4. Strain into a chilled cocktail glass

HUDSON BAY

1 oz. gin
½ oz. cherry brandy
1 tbsp. orange juice
1½ tsp. lime juice
1½ tsp. 151-proof rum

1. Fill mixing glass with ice
2. Add gin, cherry brandy, orange juice and lime juice and 151-proof rum
3. Shake
4. Strain into a chilled cocktail glass

HULA-HULA

2 oz. gin
1 oz. orange juice
dash curaçao

1. Fill a rocks glass with ice
2. Add gin, orange juice and curaçao
3. Stir

HUNDRED PERCENT

1½ oz. Swedish Punsch
1 tsp. lemon juice
1 tsp. orange juice
dash of grenadine

1. Fill mixing glass with ice
2. Add Swedish Punsch, lemon juice, orange juice and grenadine
3. Shake
4. Strain into a sour glass
5. Add ice

HUNTER'S COCKTAIL

1½ oz. rye whiskey
½ oz. cherry brandy

1. Fill a rocks glass with ice
2. Add rye and cherry brandy
3. Stir
4. Garnish with a cherry

HUNTINGTON SPECIAL

1½ oz. gin
½ oz. lemon juice
1 tsp. grenadine

1. Fill mixing glass with ice
2. Add gin, lemon juice and grenadine
3. Shake
4. Strain into a rocks glass filled with ice

HUNTRESS COCKTAIL

¾ oz. bourbon
¾ oz. cherry liqueur
1 tsp. triple sec
1 oz. cream

1. Fill mixing glass with ice
2. Add bourbon, cherry liqueur, triple sec and cream
3. Shake
4. Strain into a chilled cocktail glass

HURRICANE

1 oz. light rum
1 oz. gold rum
½ oz. passion fruit syrup
½ oz. fresh lime juice

1. Fill mixing glass with ice
2. Add light rum, gold rum, passion fruit syrup and lime juice
3. Shake
4. Strain into a chilled cocktail glass

ICEBALL

1½ oz. gin
¾ oz. white crème de
  menthe
¾ oz. sambuca
2–3 tsp. cream

1. In a blender, add 3 oz. crushed
   ice, gin, white crème de
   menthe, sambuca and cream
2. Blend at medium speed for
   about 15 seconds, until smooth
3. Pour into a goblet or a
   wineglass

THE ICEBERG

2 oz. vodka
1 tsp. Pernod

1. Fill mixing glass with ice
2. Add vodka and Pernod
3. Shake
4. Strain into a chilled cocktail
   glass

ICE PALACE

1 oz. light rum
½ oz. Galliano
½ oz. apricot brandy
2 oz. pineapple juice

1. Fill mixing glass with ice
2. Add light rum, Galliano, apricot
   brandy, pineapple juice and
   lemon juice

¼ oz. lemon juice

3. Shake
4. Strain into a Collins glass
5. Add ice
6. Garnish with a cherry and an orange slice

ICHBIEN

2 oz. apple brandy
1 oz. curaçao
1 egg yolk
2 oz. milk or cream

1. Fill mixing glass with ice
2. Add apple brandy, curaçao, egg yolk and cream
3. Shake
4. Strain into a chilled sour glass

IDEAL

2 oz. gin
½ oz. sweet vermouth
1 tbsp. grapefruit juice
3 dashes maraschino liqueur

1. Fill mixing glass with ice
2. Add gin, sweet vermouth, grapefruit juice and maraschino liqueur
3. Shake
4. Strain into a chilled cocktail glass

IGUANA

½ oz. vodka
½ oz. tequila
¼ oz. Kahlúa
1½ oz. sour mix

1. Fill mixing glass with ice
2. Add vodka, tequila, Kahlúa and sour mix
3. Shake
4. Strain into a chilled cocktail glass
5. Garnish with a lime slice

IL MAGNIFICO

1 oz. Tuaca
1 oz. curaçao
1 oz. cream

1. In a blender with 3 oz. cracked ice, add Tuaca, curaçao and cream
2. Blend at low speed for a few seconds, until smooth
3. Pour into a chilled cocktail glass

IMPERIAL FIZZ

1 oz. bourbon
½ oz. lemon juice
½ tsp. sugar
chilled champagne

1. Fill mixing glass with ice
2. Add bourbon, lemon juice and sugar
3. Shake
4. Strain into a chilled champagne glass
5. Fill with chilled champagne

IN & OUT LEMONTINI

splash of limoncello
3 oz. vodka

1. Pour a splash of limoncello into a frozen cocktail glass
2. Swirl the liqueur around in the glass until all surfaces are coated
3. Shake the vodka in a cocktail shaker filled with ice
4. Throw away any excess limoncello in the glass
5. Strain the shaken vodka into the coated cocktail glass
6. Garnish with a lemon twist

INCOME TAX

1 oz. gin
1 tsp. dry vermouth
1 tsp. sweet vermouth
½ oz. orange juice
2–3 dashes Angostura
bitters

1. Fill mixing glass with ice
2. Add gin, dry vermouth, sweet vermouth, orange juice and bitters
3. Shake
4. Strain into a rocks glass filled with ice

INDIAN SUMMER (SHOOTER)

1 oz. vodka
1 oz. Kahlúa
2 oz. pineapple juice

(WILL FILL TWO 2-OZ. SHOT GLASSES)

1. Fill mixing glass with ice
2. Add vodka, Kahlúa and pineapple juice
3. Shake
4. Pour into shot glasses

INK STREET

1½ oz. blended whiskey
¾ oz. orange juice
¾ oz. lemon juice

1. Fill mixing glass with ice
2. Add blended whiskey, orange juice and lemon juice
3. Shake
4. Strain into a chilled cocktail glass
5. Garnish with an orange slice

THE INTERNATIONAL

1½ oz. cognac
1 tsp. vodka
2 tsp. anisette
2 tsp. Cointreau (any triple sec may be substituted)

1. Fill mixing glass with ice
2. Add cognac, vodka, anisette and Cointreau
3. Shake
4. Strain into a chilled cocktail glass

INTERNATIONAL STINGER

1½ oz. Metaxa
½ oz. Galliano

1. Fill a rocks glass with ice
2. Pour in Metaxa and Galliano
3. Stir

INTERPLANETARY PUNCH

24 oz. light rum
4 oz. dark rum
8 oz. peppermint schnapps
1 qt. mango nectar
12 oz. cream
1 qt. orange juice
8 mint sprigs
1 fresh mango, cut into
  pieces
1 small orange, thinly sliced

1. Combine light rum, dark rum,
   peppermint schnapps, mango
   nectar, cream and orange juice
   in a large punch bowl
2. Stir well
3. Add a block of ice
4. Float mint sprigs, mango
   chunks and orange slices
   on top
5. For best results, refrigerate for
   one hour before serving

INVISIBLE MAN

2 oz. gin
½ oz. brandy
½ oz. triple sec
2 dashes orange juice
ginger ale

1. Fill a highball glass with ice
2. Add gin, brandy, triple sec and
   orange juice
3. Fill with ginger ale
4. Stir

IRA COCKTAIL

1½ oz. Jameson Irish
  whiskey
1 oz. Baileys Original Irish
  Cream

1. Fill a rocks glass with ice
2. Add Jameson whiskey and
   Baileys
3. Stir

IRISH

1½ oz. Irish whiskey 2 dashes curaçao 2 dashes Pernod dash maraschino liqueur	1. Fill mixing glass with ice 2. Add Irish whiskey, curaçao, Pernod and maraschino liqueur 3. Stir 4. Strain into a chilled cocktail glass 5. Garnish with a lemon twist

IRISH CAR BOMB

½ shot Baileys Original Irish Cream ½ shot Jameson Irish whiskey ¾ pint Guinness Stout	1. Pour the Baileys Irish Cream into a shot glass, followed by the Jameson Irish whiskey. 2. Next, pour your Guinness into a beer mug; let the foam settle 3. Drop the Baileys/Jameson shot glass into the Guinness 4. Drink fast

IRISH COFFEE

1½ oz. Irish whiskey hot coffee	1. Pour Irish whiskey into a coffee mug 2. Fill with hot coffee 3. Top with whipped cream, if desired

IRISH COW

4½ oz. Baileys Original Irish Cream 4½ oz. milk	1. Combine Baileys and milk in a small saucepan 2. Warm at a low heat 3. Pour into a mug 4. Sprinkle nutmeg on top, if desired

IRISH FIX

2 oz. Irish whiskey
½ oz. Irish Mist
1 oz. pineapple juice
½ oz. lemon juice
½ tsp. sugar syrup

1. Fill mixing glass with ice
2. Add Irish whiskey, Irish Mist, pineapple juice, lemon juice and sugar syrup
3. Shake
4. Strain into a rocks glass filled with ice
5. Garnish with a lemon slice

IRISH SPRING

1 oz. Irish whiskey
½ oz. peach brandy
1 oz. orange juice
1 oz. sour mix

1. Fill a Collins glass with ice
2. Add Irish whiskey, peach brandy, orange juice and sour mix
3. Stir well
4. Garnish with a cherry and an orange slice

IRISH WHISKEY AND SODA

1½ oz. Irish whiskey
6 oz. club soda

1. Fill a highball glass with ice
2. Add Irish whiskey and club soda
3. Stir gently

IRISH WHISKEY COCKTAIL

2 oz. Irish whiskey
½ tsp. triple sec
½ tsp. anis
¼ tsp. maraschino liqueur
dash Angostura bitters

1. Fill mixing glass with ice
2. Add Irish whiskey, triple sec, anis, maraschino and bitters
3. Shake
4. Strain into a chilled cocktail glass
5. Garnish with an olive

ISRAELI COFFEE

2 oz. Sabra liqueur
hot coffee

1. Pour Sabra into a coffee mug
2. Fill with hot coffee
3. Top with whipped cream, if desired

ITALIAN ASSASSIN

1 oz. amaretto
1 oz. Jack Daniel's

1. Mix amaretto and Jack Daniel's together with crushed ice in a glass
2. Garnish with mint leaves

ITALIAN COFFEE

1½ oz. Galliano
hot coffee

1. Pour Galliano into a coffee mug
2. Fill with hot coffee
3. Top with whipped cream, if desired

ITALIAN DELIGHT

1 oz. amaretto
½ oz. orange juice
1½ oz. cream

1. Fill mixing glass with ice
2. Add amaretto, orange juice and cream
3. Shake
4. Strain into a chilled cocktail glass
5. Garnish with a cherry

ITALIAN STALLION

1½ oz. bourbon
½ oz. sweet vermouth
½ oz. Campari
1–2 dashes Angostura
  bitters

1. Fill mixing glass with ice
2. Add bourbon, sweet vermouth, Campari and bitters
3. Stir
4. Strain into a chilled cocktail glass
5. Garnish with a lemon twist

ITALIAN STINGER

1½ oz. brandy
½ oz. Galliano

1. Fill mixing glass with ice
2. Add brandy and Galliano
3. Stir
4. Strain into a rocks glass filled with ice

ITALIAN SURFER

1 oz. Malibu
1 oz. amaretto
½ oz. pineapple juice
½ oz. cranberry juice

1. Fill mixing glass with ice
2. Add Malibu, amaretto, pineapple juice and cranberry juice
3. Shake
4. Strain into a rocks glass

IXTAPA

2 oz. Kahlúa
¾ oz. tequila

1. Fill mixing glass with ice
2. Add Kahlúa and tequila
3. Stir
4. Strain into a chilled cocktail glass

J

JACK-IN-THE-BOX

1½ oz. applejack
1 oz. pineapple juice
1½ tsp. lemon juice
3 dashes Angostura bitters

1. Fill mixing glass with ice
2. Add applejack, pineapple juice, lemon juice and bitters
3. Shake
4. Strain into a chilled cocktail glass

JACK ROSE

1½ oz. applejack
¾ oz. sour mix
½ oz. grenadine

1. Fill mixing glass with ice
2. Add applejack, sour mix and grenadine
3. Shake
4. Strain into a sour glass
5. Add ice

JACK WITHERS

¾ oz. gin
¾ oz. dry vermouth
¾ oz. sweet vermouth

1. Fill mixing glass with ice
2. Add gin, dry vermouth, sweet vermouth and orange juice

½ oz. orange juice

3. Stir
4. Strain into a chilled cocktail glass

JADE

1½ oz. gold rum
½ oz. lime juice
½ tsp. green crème de menthe
1 tsp. sugar syrup
½ tsp. curaçao

1. Fill mixing glass with ice
2. Add gold rum, lime juice, green crème de menthe, sugar syrup and curaçao
3. Shake
4. Strain into a rocks glass filled with ice
5. Garnish with a lime slice

JAMAICA COOLER

2¼ oz. dark rum
1 tsp. superfine granulated sugar
½ oz. lemon juice
2 dashes orange bitters
7-Up

1. In a goblet or large wineglass, dissolve the sugar in the dark rum
2. Add lemon juice and bitters
3. Add 4 or 5 ice cubes
4. Fill with 7-Up
5. Stir

JAMAICA GINGER

2 oz. dark rum
¾ oz. grenadine
3 dashes curaçao
3 dashes maraschino liqueur
dash Angostura bitters

1. Fill mixing glass with ice
2. Add dark rum, grenadine, curaçao, maraschino liqueur and bitters
3. Shake
4. Strain into a chilled cocktail glass

JAMAICAN

1 oz. Jamaican rum	1. Fill mixing glass with ice
1 oz. Kahlúa	2. Add rum, Kahlúa, lime juice
1 oz. lime juice	and bitters
dash Angostura bitters	3. Shake
7-Up	4. Strain into a Collins glass
	5. Add ice
	6. Top with 7-Up

JAMAICAN COFFEE

(see Calypso)

JAMAICAN HOP

1 oz. coffee liqueur	1. Fill mixing glass with ice
1 oz. light cream	2. Add coffee liqueur, light cream
1 oz. crème de cacao	and crème de cacao
	3. Shake well
	4. Strain into a cocktail glass

JAMAICAN MILK SHAKE

2 oz. bourbon	1. Fill blender with 3 oz. cracked
1½ oz. Jamaican rum	ice
(dark)	2. Add bourbon, Jamaican rum
1½ oz. milk or cream	and milk or cream
	3. Blend at low speed, until
	smooth
	4. Pour into a rocks glass

JAMAICAN WIND

1½ oz. Myers's dark rum
½ oz. Kahlúa

1. Fill a rocks glass with ice
2. Add Myers's rum, then Kahlúa
3. Stir

JANET STANDARD

----

2 oz. brandy
dash Angostura bitters
1 tsp. orgeat syrup

1. Put one ice cube in the bottom of a chilled cocktail glass
2. Add brandy, bitters and orgeat syrup
3. Stir
4. Garnish with a twist of lemon

JAPANESE FIZZ

----

2 oz. blended whiskey
¾ oz. port
½ oz. lemon juice
1 tsp. sugar
club soda

1. Fill mixing glass with ice
2. Add whiskey, port, lemon juice and sugar
3. Shake
4. Pour into a chilled highball glass
5. Add ice
6. Fill with club soda
7. Garnish with an orange slice

JAVA COOLER

----

1 oz. gin
½ oz. lime juice
3 dashes bitters
tonic water

1. Fill a highball glass with ice
2. Add gin, lime juice and bitters
3. Stir
4. Fill with tonic water
5. Stir again

JAWBREAKER (SHOOTER)

1 oz. cinnamon schnapps ½ oz. Tabasco sauce	Pour cinnamon schnapps and Tabasco into a shot glass

JELL-O SHOOTS (SHOOTER)

cherry Jell-O brand gelatin 1 cup boiling water 1 cup vodka or lime Jell-O brand gelatin 1 cup boiling water 1 cup tequila 3–4 oz. lime juice	1. In a bowl, add liquor and boiling water to gelatin 2. Stir until gelatin has dissolved 3. Chill to set 4. Serve in paper soufflé cups

JELLY BEAN

1 oz. anisette 1 oz. blackberry brandy	1. Pour anisette and blackberry brandy into a cordial glass or a rocks glass 2. Stir 3. Add ice, if desired

JELLY DONUT MARTINI

1 shot vodka 1 shot raspberry liqueur 1 shot dark chocolate liqueur ½ cup coconut milk 2 fresh raspberries	1. Combine ingredients in a shaker with ice 2. Mix and strain into a chilled martini glass 3. Shave some chocolate on top, drop in 2 fresh raspberries

JEWEL

1 oz. gin
1 oz. sweet vermouth
1 tbsp. green Chartreuse
2 dashes orange bitters

1. Fill mixing glass with ice
2. Add gin, sweet vermouth, green Chartreuse and orange bitters
3. Shake
4. Strain into a rocks glass filled with ice

JOBURG

1½ oz. light rum
1½ oz. Dubonnet
3 dashes orange bitters

1. Fill mixing glass with ice
2. Add rum, Dubonnet and orange bitters
3. Stir
4. Strain into a chilled cocktail glass
5. Garnish with a lemon twist

JOCKEY CLUB

1½ oz. gin
½ oz. lemon juice
¼ tsp. white crème de cacao
dash of Angostura bitters

1. Fill mixing glass with ice
2. Add gin, lemon juice, white crème de cacao and bitters
3. Shake
4. Strain into a chilled cocktail glass

JOE COLLINS

1½ oz. scotch
3 oz. sour mix
1 oz. club soda

1. Fill mixing glass with ice
2. Add scotch and sour mix
3. Shake
4. Strain into a Collins glass
5. Add ice

6. Top with club soda
7. Garnish with a cherry and an orange slice

JOHN COLLINS

2 oz. blended whiskey
3 oz. sour mix
1 oz. club soda

1. Fill mixing glass with ice
2. Add whiskey and sour mix
3. Shake
4. Strain into a Collins glass
5. Add ice
6. Top with club soda
7. Garnish with a cherry and an orange slice

JOHNNIE'S COCKTAIL

2 oz. sloe gin
¾ oz. Cointreau
1 tsp. anisette

1. Fill mixing glass with ice
2. Add sloe gin, Cointreau and anisette
3. Stir
4. Strain into a chilled cocktail glass

JOLLY RANCHER (SHOOTER)

¾ oz. vodka
¼ oz. Midori melon liqueur
¼ oz. peach schnapps
splash cranberry juice

1. Fill mixing glass with ice
2. Add vodka, Midori, peach schnapps and cranberry juice
3. Shake
4. Strain into a shot glass

JOLLY ROGER

1 oz. dark rum
1 oz. banana liqueur
2 oz. lemon juice

1. Fill mixing glass with ice
2. Add rum, banana liqueur and lemon juice
3. Shake
4. Strain into a goblet or large wineglass
5. Add ice

JUDGE, JR.

1 oz. gin
1 oz. light rum
¾ oz. lemon juice
dash grenadine

1. Fill mixing glass with ice
2. Add gin, rum, lemon juice and grenadine
3. Shake
4. Strain into a chilled cocktail glass

JUNGLE JIM

1 oz. vodka
1 oz. banana liqueur
1 oz. milk or cream

1. Fill mixing glass with ice
2. Add vodka, banana liqueur and milk or cream
3. Shake
4. Strain into a rocks glass
5. Add ice, if desired

JUNIPER BLEND

1 oz. cherry brandy
1 oz. gin
1 tsp. dry vermouth

1. Fill mixing glass with ice
2. Add cherry brandy, gin and dry vermouth
3. Shake
4. Strain into a chilled cocktail glass

JUPITER COCKTAIL

1½ oz. gin
½ oz. dry vermouth
1 tsp. crème de violette
1 tsp. orange juice

1. Fill mixing glass with ice
2. Add gin, dry vermouth, crème de violette and orange juice
3. Shake
4. Strain into a chilled cocktail glass

K

KAHLÚA EGG CREAM

1 oz. Kahlúa	1. Fill a rocks glass with ice
2 oz. milk	2. Add Kahlúa
club soda	3. Add milk
	4. Top with club soda
	5. Stir

KAHLÚA TOREADOR

2 oz. brandy	1. Fill mixing glass with ice
1 oz. Kahlúa	2. Add brandy, Kahlúa and egg white
½ egg white	3. Shake
	4. Strain into a rocks glass filled with ice

KAMIKAZE

1 oz. vodka	1. Fill mixing glass with ice
1 oz. triple sec	2. Add vodka, triple sec and lime juice
1 oz. lime juice	3. Shake
	4. Strain into a rocks glass filled with ice

KAMIKAZE (SHOOTER)

----

    2 oz. vodka
    ½ oz. triple sec
    ¼ oz. Rose's lime juice

    (MAKES ABOUT 2 SHOTS)

1. Fill mixing glass with ice
2. Add vodka, triple sec and lime juice
3. Shake
4. Strain into shot glasses

KANGAROO

    1½ oz. vodka
    1 oz. dry vermouth

1. Fill mixing glass with cracked ice
2. Add vodka and dry vermouth
3. Stir
4. Strain into a chilled cocktail glass

KAPPA COLADA

----

    1 oz. brandy
    1 oz. cream of coconut
    2 oz. pineapple juice syrup

1. Fill mixing glass with ice
2. Add brandy, cream of coconut and pineapple syrup
3. Shake
4. Strain into a Collins glass
5. Add ice
6. Garnish with a cherry and an orange slice

(*Note:* 3 oz. piña colada mix may be substituted for cream of coconut and pineapple syrup.)

KCB

    1½ oz. gin
    2 tsp. kirschwasser
    3 drops apricot brandy

1. Fill mixing glass with ice
2. Add gin, kirschwasser, apricot brandy and lemon juice

3 drops lemon juice

3. Shake
4. Strain into a chilled cocktail glass

KENTUCKY COCKTAIL

2 oz. bourbon
1 oz. pineapple juice

1. Fill mixing glass with ice
2. Add bourbon and pineapple juice
3. Shake
4. Strain into a chilled cocktail glass

KENTUCKY COFFEE

1½ oz. Kentucky bourbon
hot coffee

1. Pour Kentucky bourbon into a coffee mug
2. Fill with hot coffee
3. Top with whipped cream, if desired

KENTUCKY COLONEL

1½ oz. bourbon
½ oz. Bénédictine

1. Fill mixing glass with ice
2. Add bourbon and Bénédictine
3. Shake
4. Strain into a rocks glass
5. Add ice
6. Garnish with a twist of lemon

KENTUCKY COOLER

1½ oz. bourbon
½ oz. rum
¼ oz. orange juice
¼ oz. lemon juice

1. Fill mixing glass with ice
2. Add bourbon, rum, orange juice, lemon juice and grenadine

dash grenadine

3. Shake
4. Strain into a chilled cocktail glass

KENTUCKY HAYRIDE

1 oz. whiskey
1 egg white
dash cream
½ oz. grenadine
club soda

1. Fill mixing glass with ice
2. Add whiskey, egg white, cream and grenadine
3. Shake
4. Strain into a highball glass
5. Fill with club soda; cream will slowly rise to top

KENTUCKY ORANGE BLOSSOM

1½ oz. bourbon
½ oz. triple sec
1 oz. orange juice

1. Fill mixing glass with ice
2. Add bourbon, triple sec and orange juice
3. Shake
4. Strain into a rocks glass filled with ice
5. Garnish with a twist of lemon

KERRY COOLER

2 oz. Irish whiskey
1½ oz. sherry
1 oz. orgeat syrup
1½ oz. lemon juice
1 oz. club soda

1. Fill mixing glass with ice
2. Add Irish whiskey, sherry, orgeat syrup and lemon juice
3. Shake
4. Strain into a highball glass
5. Add ice
6. Top with club soda
7. Garnish with a slice of lemon

KIALOA

1 oz. Kahlúa 1 oz. cream ½ oz. Mount Gay rum	1. Fill mixing glass with ice 2. Add Kahlúa, cream and Mount Gay rum 3. Strain into a rocks glass 4. Add ice

KILLER KOOL-AID

1½ oz. vodka ½ oz. peach schnapps ½ oz. amaretto 3 oz. cranberry juice cocktail	1. Fill a highball glass with ice 2. Layer ingredients 3. Do not stir

KING ALPHONSE

2 oz. Kahlúa 1 oz. cream	1. Pour Kahlúa into a cordial glass 2. Float cream on top

KINGDOM COME

¾ oz. gin 1½ oz. dry vermouth 1 tsp. white crème de menthe 1 tbsp. grapefruit juice	1. Fill shaker glass with ice 2. Add gin, dry vermouth, white crème de menthe and grapefruit juice 3. Shake 4. Strain into a rocks glass filled with about 4 oz. crushed ice

KING'S PEG

2½ oz. cognac
chilled brut champagne

1. Put several ice cubes into a wineglass
2. Add cognac
3. Fill with chilled champagne

KINGSTON

1½ oz. Jamaican rum
1 oz. gin
½ oz. lemon juice
½ oz. sugar syrup

1. Fill mixing glass with ice
2. Add Jamaican rum, gin, lemon juice and sugar syrup
3. Shake
4. Strain into a chilled cocktail glass

KIOKI COFFEE

¾ oz. brandy
¾ oz. Kahlúa
hot coffee

1. Pour brandy and Kahlúa into a coffee mug
2. Fill with hot coffee
3. Top with whipped cream, if desired

KIR

white wine
crème de cassis

1. Fill wineglass ¾ with chilled white wine
2. Add a few drops of crème de cassis
3. Garnish with a twist of lemon

(*Note:* Depending on the size of the wineglass, exact number of ounces may vary. In general, the proportion is 7 parts wine to 1 part crème de cassis.)

KIR ROYALE

chilled champagne
Framboise (crème de cassis
    may be substituted)

1. Fill wineglass ¾ with chilled champagne
2. Add a few drops of Framboise or crème de cassis
3. Garnish with a twist of lemon

(*Note:* Depending on the size of the wineglass, exact number of ounces may vary. In general, the proportion is 7 parts champagne to 1 part Framboise or crème de cassis.)

THE KISS

1½ oz. vodka
½ oz. chocolate liqueur
¼ oz. cherry liqueur
¾ oz. heavy cream

1. Fill mixing glass with ice
2. Add vodka, chocolate liqueur, cherry liqueur and cream
3. Shake
4. Strain into a chilled cocktail glass

KISS IN THE DARK

¾ oz. gin
¾ oz. cherry brandy
¼ oz. dry vermouth

1. Fill mixing glass with ice
2. Add gin, cherry brandy and dry vermouth
3. Shake
4. Strain into a chilled cocktail glass

KISS ME QUICK

2 oz. Pernod
1 tsp. Cointreau

1. Fill a rocks glass with ice
2. Add Pernod, Cointreau and bitters

          2–3 dashes Angostura
             bitters
          1 oz. club soda

3. Stir
4. Top with club soda

KISS THE BOYS GOODBYE

          1 oz. sloe gin
          1 oz. brandy
          ¼ oz. lemon juice
          ½ egg white

1. Fill mixing glass with ice
2. Add sloe gin, brandy, lemon
   juice and egg white
3. Shake
4. Strain into a chilled cocktail glass

KLONDIKE COOLER

          1½ oz. blended whiskey
          2 tbsp. orange rind
          2–3 oz. fresh orange juice
          ginger ale

1. Fill a highball glass with ice
2. Add whiskey, orange rind and
   orange juice
3. Stir
4. Top with ginger ale

KNICKERBOCKER

          2 oz. gin
          ½ oz. dry vermouth
          1 tsp. sweet vermouth

1. Fill mixing glass with ice
2. Add gin, dry vermouth and
   sweet vermouth.
3. Shake
4. Strain into a chilled cocktail glass

KNOCKOUT

          ¾ oz. Southern Comfort
          ¾ oz. apricot brandy
          ¾ oz. sloe gin
          ¾ oz. orange juice

1. Fill a rocks glass with ice
2. Add Southern Comfort, apricot
   brandy, sloe gin and orange juice
3. Stir well

KREMLIN COCKTAIL

1 oz. vodka
1 oz. white crème de cacao
1 oz. cream

1. Fill mixing glass with ice
2. Add vodka, white crème de cacao and cream
3. Shake
4. Strain into a rocks glass filled with ice

KRETCHMA

1 oz. vodka
1 oz. white crème de cacao
1 tsp. lemon juice
3 drops grenadine

1. Fill mixing glass with ice
2. Add vodka, white crème de cacao, lemon juice and grenadine
3. Shake
4. Strain into a rocks glass filled with ice

KYOTO

1½ oz. gin
½ oz. dry vermouth
½ oz. apricot brandy
½ oz. triple sec

1. Fill mixing glass with ice
2. Add gin, dry vermouth, apricot brandy and triple sec
3. Shake
4. Strain into a rocks glass filled with ice
5. Garnish with a cherry

LADIES

2 oz. Canadian whiskey 2 dashes Pernod 2 dashes Angostura bitters 2 dashes anisette	1. Fill mixing glass with ice 2. Add Canadian whiskey, Pernod, bitters and anisette 3. Shake 4. Strain into a chilled cocktail glass

LADY BE GOOD

1½ oz. brandy
¾ oz. white crème de
   menthe
¾ oz. sweet vermouth
	1. Fill mixing glass with ice
	2. Add brandy, white crème de
	   menthe and sweet vermouth
	3. Shake
	4. Strain into a chilled cocktail glass

LADYFINGER

1½ oz. gin
¾ oz. kirschwasser
¾ oz. cherry brandy
	1. Fill mixing glass with ice
	2. Add gin, kirschwasser and
	   cherry brandy
	3. Shake
	4. Strain into a chilled cocktail
	   glass

LAGER 'N' LIME

beer (preferably draft)
½ oz. Rose's lime juice

1. Pour cold beer into a beer glass or a beer mug
2. Add Rose's lime juice

LA JOLLA

1½ oz. brandy
½ oz. banana liqueur
1 tsp. orange juice
2 tsp. lemon juice

1. Fill mixing glass with ice
2. Add brandy, banana liqueur, orange juice and lemon juice
3. Shake
4. Strain into a chilled cocktail glass

LALLAH ROOKH

1½ oz. light rum
¾ oz. cognac
2 tsp. vanilla extract
1 tsp. sugar syrup
whipped cream

1. Fill mixing glass with cracked ice
2. Add light rum, cognac, vanilla extract and sugar syrup
3. Shake
4. Pour into a goblet or large wineglass
5. Top with whipped cream

LAMPLIGHTER

1½ oz. Dewar's White Label blended scotch
½ oz. Laird's applejack
½ oz. Sapling Vermont maple liqueur
½ oz. Galliano
½ oz. lemon juice

1. Combine the scotch, applejack, maple liqueur, Galliano, and lemon juice in a mixing glass
2. Shake with ice and strain into a chilled coupe
3. Garnish with a lemon twist

LASKY

¾ oz. gin
¾ oz. Swedish Punsch
1 tbsp. grape juice

1. Fill mixing glass with ice
2. Add gin, Swedish Punsch and grape juice
3. Shake
4. Strain into a rocks glass filled with ice

LAST ROUND

1 oz. gin
1 oz. dry vermouth
2 dashes brandy
2 dashes Pernod

1. Fill mixing glass with ice
2. Add gin, dry vermouth, brandy and Pernod
3. Shake
4. Strain into a chilled cocktail glass

THE LAURA

1½ oz. bourbon
1 oz. sweet vermouth
½ oz. dry vermouth
½ oz. Campari
½ oz. Galliano

1. Fill mixing glass with ice
2. Add bourbon, sweet vermouth, dry vermouth, Campari and Galliano
3. Shake
4. Strain into a chilled cocktail glass
5. Garnish with a cherry

LAVA LAMP MARTINI

splash raspberry liqueur
splash honey
3 oz. vodka

1. Mix raspberry liqueur and honey in a shot glass
2. Fill mixing glass with ice
3. Add vodka

4. Shake
5. Strain into a martini glass
6. Spoon in raspberry liqueur and honey mixture

LAWHILL

1½ oz. blended whiskey
¼ oz. dry vermouth
2 tsp. orange juice
3 drops Pernod
3 drops maraschino liqueur
3 dashes Angostura bitters

1. Fill mixing glass with ice
2. Add blended whiskey, dry vermouth, orange juice, Pernod, maraschino and bitters
3. Shake
4. Strain into a rocks glass filled with ice

LEAP FROG

1½ oz. gin
½ oz. lemon juice
ginger ale

1. Fill a highball glass with ice
2. Add gin and lemon juice
3. Stir
4. Fill with ginger ale

LEAP YEAR

1½ oz. gin
½ oz. Grand Marnier
½ oz. sweet vermouth
1 tsp. lemon juice

1. Fill mixing glass with ice
2. Add gin, Grand Marnier, sweet vermouth and lemon juice
3. Stir
4. Strain into a chilled cocktail glass

LEAVE IT TO ME

1 oz. gin	1. Fill mixing glass with ice
½ oz. apricot brandy	2. Add gin, apricot brandy, dry vermouth, lemon juice and grenadine
½ oz. dry vermouth	3. Shake
3 dashes lemon juice	4. Strain into a chilled cocktail glass
3 dashes grenadine	

LECTRIC LEMONADE

½ oz. vodka	1. Fill mixing glass with ice
½ oz. gin	2. Add vodka, gin, light rum, triple sec, tequila and sour mix
½ oz. light rum	3. Shake
½ oz. triple sec	4. Pour into a Collins glass
½ oz. tequila	5. Top with 7-Up
2–3 oz. sour mix	
7-Up	

LEMONADE (MODERN)

1½ oz. sloe gin	1. Fill mixing glass with ice
1½ oz. sherry	2. Add sloe gin, sherry, lemon juice and sugar syrup
2 oz. lemon juice	3. Shake
1 oz. sugar syrup	4. Pour into a highball glass
club soda	5. Top with club soda
	6. Garnish with a slice of lemon

LEMON DROP (SHOOTER)

½ oz. tequila, chilled	1. Coat the inside of a shot glass with sugar (use a lemon slice to moisten the glass first)
½ oz. vodka, chilled	2. Pour in tequila and vodka (preferably premium brands)

LEPRECHAUN

| 2 oz. Irish whiskey
tonic water | 1. Fill a rocks glass with ice
2. Add Irish whiskey
3. Fill with tonic water
4. Stir
5. Garnish with a twist of lemon |

LEPRECHAUN'S LIBATION*

| 1 oz. green crème de menthe
2½ oz. Old Bushmills Irish whiskey | 1. Fill blender with 3½ oz. cracked ice
2. Add green crème de menthe and Old Bushmills Irish whiskey
3. Blend
4. Pour into a goblet or large wineglass |

LIBERTY COCKTAIL

| 1½ oz. apple brandy
¾ oz. light rum
¼ tsp. sugar syrup | 1. Fill mixing glass with ice
2. Add apple brandy, light rum and sugar syrup
3. Stir
4. Strain into a chilled cocktail glass |

LIEBFRAUMILCH

| 1 oz. white crème de cacao
1 oz. cream
½ oz. lime juice | 1. Fill mixing glass with ice
2. Add white crème de cacao, cream and lime juice |

---

* Courtesy of Beach Grill, Westminster, Colorado.

3. Shake
4. Strain into a chilled cocktail glass

LILLET NOYAUX

1½ oz. Lillet
½ oz. gin
1 tsp. crème de noyaux

1. Fill mixing glass with ice
2. Add Lillet, gin and crème de noyaux
3. Shake
4. Strain into a chilled cocktail glass
5. Garnish with a twist of orange

LIMBO

2 oz. light rum
½ oz. banana liqueur
1 oz. orange juice

1. Fill mixing glass with ice
2. Add light rum, banana liqueur and orange juice
3. Shake
4. Strain into a chilled cocktail glass

LIME RICKEY

1½ oz. gin
½ oz. lime juice
club soda

1. Fill a highball glass with ice
2. Add gin, then lime juice
3. Fill with club soda
4. Stir gently
5. Garnish with a slice of lime

LINSTEAD

1½ oz. blended whiskey	1. Fill mixing glass with ice
1½ oz. pineapple juice	2. Add blended whiskey, pineapple
3 drops Pernod	juice, Pernod, lemon juice and
4–5 drops lemon juice	bitters
3 dashes Angostura bitters	3. Shake
	4. Strain into a rocks glass filled
	with ice
	5. Garnish with a twist of lemon

LION TAMER (SHOOTER)

¾ oz. Southern Comfort	1. Fill mixing glass with ice
¼ oz. lime juice	2. Add Southern Comfort and lime
	juice
	3. Stir
	4. Strain into a chilled shot glass

LITTLE DEVIL

1 oz. gin	1. Fill mixing glass with ice
1 oz. gold rum	2. Add gin, gold rum, triple sec
½ oz. triple sec	and lemon juice
½ oz. lemon juice	3. Stir
	4. Strain into a chilled cocktail glass

LITTLE PRINCESS

1½ oz. light rum	1. Fill mixing glass with ice
1½ oz. sweet vermouth	2. Add light rum and sweet
	vermouth
	3. Shake
	4. Strain into a rocks glass filled
	with ice

LITTLE PURPLE MEN

1 oz. sambuca
1 oz. Chambord

Pour sambuca and Chambord into a brandy snifter

(*Note:* It has been reported that after consuming two of these drinks you'll start seeing little purple men.)

LIVE BAIT'S BLUE BIJOU*

1¼ oz. light rum
1 oz. blue curaçao
3 oz. orange juice
3 oz. pineapple juice
3–4 drops Rose's lime juice

1. In blender, combine light rum, blue curaçao, orange juice, pineapple juice and Rose's lime juice with 3 oz. cracked ice
2. Blend until well mixed
3. Pour into a goblet or Collins glass
4. Garnish with a pineapple chunk

LOCH LOMOND

1½ oz. scotch
½ oz. sugar syrup
several dashes Angostura bitters

1. Fill mixing glass with ice
2. Add scotch, sugar syrup and bitters
3. Shake
4. Strain into a rocks glass filled with ice

LOLITA

1½ oz. tequila
¼ oz. lime juice
1 tsp. honey

1. Fill mixing glass with ice
2. Add tequila, lime juice, honey and bitters

---

* Courtesy of Live Bait, New York City.

3–4 dashes Angostura bitters	3. Shake 4. Strain into a rocks glass filled with ice

LOLLIPOP

¾ oz. Cointreau ¾ oz. kirschwasser 1 tbsp. green Chartreuse 2–3 drops maraschino liqueur	1. Fill mixing glass with ice 2. Add Cointreau, kirschwasser, green Chartreuse and maraschino liqueur 3. Shake 4. Strain into a rocks glass filled with ice

LONDON

1½ oz. gin 2 dashes Pernod 2 dashes orange bitters 1 tsp. powdered sugar	1. Fill mixing glass with ice 2. Add gin, Pernod, orange bitters and powdered sugar 3. Shake 4. Strain into a chilled cocktail glass

LONDON SPECIAL

1 sugar cube 2 dashes Angostura bitters chilled champagne	1. In a chilled champagne glass, place a large twist of orange, sugar cube and bitters 2. Fill with chilled champagne 3. Stir

LONE TREE

¾ oz. gin
¾ oz. dry vermouth
¾ oz. sweet vermouth
3 dashes orange bitters

1. Fill mixing glass with ice
2. Add gin, dry vermouth, sweet vermouth and orange bitters
3. Stir
4. Strain into a chilled cocktail glass
5. Garnish with an olive

LONG BEACH ICE TEA

½ oz. vodka
½ oz. gin
½ oz. rum
½ oz. triple sec
½ oz. tequila
1 oz. sour mix
cranberry juice cocktail

1. Fill mixing glass with ice
2. Add vodka, gin, rum, triple sec, tequila and sour mix
3. Shake
4. Pour into a Collins glass
5. Add more ice, if necessary
6. Top with cranberry juice
7. Garnish with a lemon slice

LONG HOT NIGHT

2 oz. bourbon
3 oz. pineapple juice
3 oz. cranberry juice cocktail

1. Place 4 or 5 ice cubes in a highball glass
2. Pour in bourbon
3. Stir
4. Add pineapple juice and cranberry juice
5. Stir again

LONG ISLAND ICE TEA

½ oz. vodka
½ oz. gin
½ oz. rum

1. Fill mixing glass with ice
2. Add vodka, gin, rum, triple sec, tequila and sour mix

½ oz. triple sec
½ oz. tequila
1 oz. sour mix
cola

3. Shake
4. Pour into a Collins glass
5. Add more ice, if necessary
6. Top with cola
7. Garnish with a lemon slice

LOOK OUT BELOW

1½ oz. 151-proof rum
2 tsp. lime juice
1 tsp. grenadine

1. Fill mixing glass with ice
2. Add 151-proof rum, lime juice and grenadine
3. Shake
4. Strain into a rocks glass filled with ice

LORD RODNEY

1½ oz. blended whiskey
¾ oz. dark rum
1 tsp. coconut syrup
3–4 drops white crème de cacao

1. Fill mixing glass with ice
2. Add blended whiskey, dark rum, coconut syrup and crème de cacao
3. Shake
4. Strain into a chilled cocktail glass

LOS ANGELES COCKTAIL

4 oz. blended whiskey
1 oz. lemon juice
2 oz. sugar syrup
4 dashes sweet vermouth
1 egg

(THIS RECIPE SERVES TWO)

1. Fill mixing glass with cracked ice
2. Add blended whiskey, lemon juice, sugar syrup, sweet vermouth and egg
3. Shake
4. Pour into two chilled rocks glasses

LOUD-HAILER

¾ oz. gin
¾ oz. dry vermouth
dash of Cointreau
1 tsp. grenadine
1 oz. orange juice

1. Fill mixing glass with ice
2. Add gin, dry vermouth, Cointreau, grenadine and orange juice
3. Shake
4. Strain into a chilled cocktail glass

LOUDSPEAKER

1 oz. brandy
1 oz. gin
1 tsp. Cointreau
2 tsp. lemon juice

1. Fill mixing glass with ice
2. Add brandy, gin, Cointreau and lemon juice
3. Stir
4. Strain into a chilled cocktail glass

LOUISIANA LULLABY

1½ oz. dark rum
2 tsp. Dubonnet
3 drops Grand Marnier

1. Fill mixing glass with ice
2. Add dark rum, Dubonnet and Grand Marnier
3. Shake
4. Strain into a chilled cocktail glass
5. Garnish with a twist of lemon

LOVE

2 oz. sloe gin
1 egg white
½ oz. lemon juice
several drops raspberry syrup

1. Fill mixing glass with ice
2. Add sloe gin, egg white, lemon juice and raspberry syrup
3. Shake
4. Strain into a chilled cocktail glass

LOVER'S DELIGHT

¾ oz. Cointreau
¾ oz. Forbidden Fruit
¾ oz. brandy

1. Fill mixing glass with ice
2. Add Cointreau, Forbidden Fruit and brandy
3. Shake
4. Strain into a rocks glass filled with ice

LUBE JOB

1 oz. Baileys Original Irish Cream
1 oz. vodka

1. Fill a rocks glass with ice
2. Add Baileys and vodka
3. Stir

LUGGER

1 oz. brandy
1 oz. apple brandy
1 oz. apricot brandy

1. Fill mixing glass with ice
2. Add brandy, apple brandy and apricot brandy
3. Shake
4. Strain into a chilled cocktail glass

LYNCHBURG LEMONADE

¾ oz. Jack Daniel's
¾ oz. triple sec
3 oz. sour mix
splash 7-Up

1. Fill mixing glass with ice
2. Add Jack Daniel's, triple sec, sour mix and 7-Up
3. Shake
4. Strain into a highball glass filled with ice
5. Garnish with a lemon wedge

MADEIRA COCKTAIL

1½ oz. blended whiskey
1½ oz. madeira
1 tsp. grenadine
dash lemon juice

1. Fill mixing glass with cracked ice
2. Add blended whiskey, madeira, grenadine and lemon juice
3. Shake
4. Pour into a rocks glass
5. Garnish with a slice of orange

MADRAS

1½ oz. vodka
2 oz. cranberry juice
2 oz. orange juice

1. Fill a highball glass with ice
2. Add vodka
3. Fill with cranberry juice and orange juice
4. Stir

MAFIA'S KISS

1 oz. amaretto
1 oz. Southern Comfort
1 oz. sour mix

1. Mix ingredients
2. Pour over ice

MAGPIE

----

1 oz. melon liqueur (Midori)
1 oz. vodka
½ oz. white crème de cacao
1 oz. cream

1. Fill mixing glass with ice
2. Add melon liqueur, vodka, white crème de cacao and cream
3. Shake
4. Strain into a rocks glass filled with ice

MAH-JONGG

----

1 oz. gin
½ oz. dark rum
½ oz. Cointreau

1. Fill mixing glass with ice
2. Add gin, dark rum and Cointreau
3. Shake
4. Strain into a chilled cocktail glass

MAIDEN'S BLUSH

----

1 oz. gin
4 dashes curaçao
4 dashes grenadine
2 dashes lemon juice

1. Fill mixing glass with ice
2. Add gin, curaçao, grenadine and lemon juice
3. Shake
4. Strain into a chilled cocktail glass

MAIDEN'S PRAYER

----

1 oz. gin
1 oz. triple sec
2 tbsp. lemon juice
½ tsp. orange juice

1. Fill mixing glass with ice
2. Add gin, triple sec, lemon juice and orange juice
3. Stir
4. Strain into a chilled cocktail glass

MAINBRACE

1½ oz. gin
¾ oz. triple sec
1 tbsp. grape juice

1. Fill mixing glass with ice
2. Add gin, triple sec and grape juice
3. Shake
4. Strain into a chilled cocktail glass

MAI TAI

1 oz. light rum
½ oz. orgeat syrup
½ oz. triple sec
1½ oz. sour mix

1. Fill mixing glass with ice
2. Add light rum, orgeat syrup, triple sec and sour mix
3. Shake
4. Strain into a Collins glass filled with ice
5. Garnish with a cherry and an orange slice

MALIBU MONSOON*

1½ oz. Bacardi light rum
¾ oz. Malibu liqueur
splash Grand Marnier
1 oz. pineapple juice
splash cranberry juice cocktail
a few drops grenadine

1. Fill mixing glass with ice
2. Add Bacardi light rum, Malibu liqueur, Grand Marnier, pineapple juice and cranberry juice
3. Shake
4. Pour into a large wineglass or goblet
5. Add a few drops of grenadine
6. Garnish with a cherry and a slice of orange

---

* Courtesy of Michael Benz at Ciaobella, New York City.

MALIBU WAVE

1 oz. tequila
½ oz. triple sec
1 tsp. blue curaçao
1½ oz. sour mix

1. Fill mixing glass with ice
2. Add tequila, triple sec, blue curaçao and sour mix
3. Shake
4. Strain into a chilled cocktail glass
5. Garnish with a lime slice

MAMIE TAYLOR

3 oz. scotch
½ oz. lime juice
ginger ale

1. Fill a Collins glass with ice
2. Add scotch and lime juice
3. Stir
4. Fill with ginger ale
5. Stir again
6. Garnish with a slice of lemon

MANDARINE COLADA*

1½ oz. light rum
1 oz. Mandarine Napoléon liqueur
2 oz. pineapple juice
1 oz. cream of coconut
2 orange slices

1. Fill blender with 3 oz. ice, light rum, Mandarine Napoléon liqueur, pineapple juice, cream of coconut and 1 orange slice
2. Blend until smooth
3. Pour into a 16-oz. soda glass
4. Garnish with other orange slice

MANGO MARGARITA

1½ oz. tequila
½ oz. triple sec
1 oz. sour mix

1. Fill mixing glass with ice
2. Add tequila, triple sec, sour mix and mango juice

---

* Courtesy of Sugar Reef, New York City.

1 oz. mango juice	3. Shake
	4. Sugar the rim of a chilled cocktail glass, if desired
	5. Strain into a chilled cocktail glass

MANHASSET

1½ oz. blended whiskey	1. Fill mixing glass with ice
½ oz. lemon juice	2. Add whiskey, lemon juice, dry vermouth and sweet vermouth
1 tsp. dry vermouth	3. Shake
1 tsp. sweet vermouth	4. Strain into a rocks glass filled with ice
	5. Garnish with a twist of lemon

MANHATTAN

1½ oz. blended whiskey	1. Fill mixing glass with ice
½ oz. sweet vermouth	2. Add whiskey and sweet vermouth
	3. Stir
	4. Strain into a chilled cocktail glass
	5. Garnish with a cherry

(*Note:* If serving "on the rocks," stir in a rocks glass filled with ice, garnish and serve.)

MANHATTAN (DRY)

1½ oz. blended whiskey	1. Fill mixing glass with ice
¼ oz. dry vermouth	2. Add whiskey and dry vermouth
	3. Stir

4. Strain into a chilled cocktail glass
5. Garnish with an olive

(*Note:* If serving "on the rocks," stir in a rocks glass filled with ice, garnish and serve.)

MANHATTAN (PERFECT)

1½ oz. blended whiskey
⅛ oz. dry vermouth
⅛ oz. sweet vermouth

1. Fill mixing glass with ice
2. Add whiskey, dry vermouth and sweet vermouth
3. Stir
4. Strain into a chilled cocktail glass
5. Garnish with a twist of lemon

(*Note:* If serving "on the rocks," stir in a rocks glass filled with ice, garnish and serve.)

MANHATTAN SOUTH

1 oz. gin
½ oz. dry vermouth
½ oz. Southern Comfort
dash Angostura bitters

1. Fill mixing glass with ice
2. Add gin, dry vermouth, Southern Comfort and bitters
3. Stir
4. Strain into a chilled cocktail glass

MAPLE LEAF

1 oz. Canadian whiskey
¼ oz. lemon juice
1 tsp. maple syrup

1. Fill mixing glass with ice
2. Add Canadian whiskey, lemon juice and maple syrup
3. Shake
4. Strain into a chilled cocktail glass

MARCONI WIRELESS

1½ oz. apple brandy
½ oz. sweet vermouth
2 dashes orange bitters

1. Fill mixing glass with ice
2. Add apple brandy, sweet vermouth and orange bitters
3. Shake
4. Strain into a chilled cocktail glass

MARGARITA

1½ oz. tequila
½ oz. triple sec
1½ oz. sour mix
several dashes lime juice

1. Fill mixing glass with ice
2. Add tequila, triple sec, sour mix and lime juice
3. Shake
4. Strain into a chilled cocktail glass or a rocks glass filled with ice
5. Garnish with a slice of lime

(*Note:* If drink is requested "with salt," frost the rim of the glass with salt before pouring in drink. To do so, moisten the rim of the glass with a wedge of lime, and dip into a plate of salt.)

MARGARITA, MY HONEY

1½ oz. Cuervo Especial gold tequila
¾ oz. Cointreau
juice of ½ lime
juice of ½ lemon
2 drops honey
drop orange juice

1. Fill mixing glass with ice
2. Add Cuervo gold, Cointreau, lime juice, lemon juice, honey and orange juice
3. Shake well
4. Salt the rim of a chilled cocktail glass, if desired
5. Strain drink into chilled cocktail glass
6. Garnish with a lime slice

MARLON BRANDO

1½ oz. scotch
½ oz. amaretto
cream

1. Fill a rocks glass with ice
2. Add scotch and amaretto
3. Float cream on top

MARMALADE

1½ oz. curaçao
tonic water

1. Fill a highball glass with ice
2. Add curaçao
3. Fill with tonic water
4. Stir
5. Garnish with a slice of orange

MARTINEZ

2 oz. gin (preferably Old
   Tom)
3 oz. dry vermouth
3–4 drops maraschino
   liqueur
3–4 drops Angostura bitters

1. Fill mixing glass with ice
2. Add gin, dry vermouth,
   maraschino liqueur and bitters
3. Shake
4. Strain into a rocks glass filled
   with ice

MARTINI

1½ oz. gin
dash (approx. ⅛ oz.) dry
   vermouth

1. Fill mixing glass with ice
2. Add gin and dry vermouth
3. Stir
4. Strain into a martini glass
5. Garnish with an olive

(*Note:* If serving "on the rocks," stir
in a rocks glass filled with ice,
garnish and serve.)

MARTINI (DRY)

1½ oz. gin
drop (approx. ⅒ oz.) dry
    vermouth

1. Fill mixing glass with ice
2. Add gin and dry vermouth
3. Stir
4. Strain into a martini glass
5. Garnish with an olive

(*Note:* If serving "on the rocks," stir in a rocks glass filled with ice, garnish and serve.)

MARTINI (VERY DRY)

1½ oz. gin
approx. ⅟₁₂ oz. dry vermouth

1. Fill mixing glass with ice
2. Add dry vermouth (In actuality, almost no dry vermouth is used. Let vermouth barely touch side of mixing glass)
3. Add gin
4. Stir
5. Strain into a martini glass
6. Garnish with an olive

(*Note:* If serving "on the rocks," stir in a rocks glass filled with ice, garnish and serve.)

MARTINI (EXTREMELY DRY)

---

2 oz. gin

Follow directions for other martini recipes. No vermouth is used. This translates to "gin straight up" or "gin on the rocks."

MARY GARDEN

1½ oz. Dubonnet
¾ oz. dry vermouth

1. Fill mixing glass with ice
2. Add Dubonnet and dry vermouth
3. Shake
4. Strain into a rocks glass filled with ice

MARY PICKFORD

1½ oz. light rum
½ oz. pineapple juice
3 dashes grenadine

1. Fill mixing glass with ice
2. Add light rum, pineapple juice and grenadine
3. Shake
4. Strain into a chilled cocktail glass

MASHED OLD-FASHIONED

1 maraschino cherry
1 piece orange
1 cube sugar
2 dashes bitters
dash club soda
1 oz. bourbon

1. In a rocks glass, place cherry, piece of orange, sugar cube, bitters and club soda
2. Mash with muddler or with the back of a spoon
3. Fill the glass with ice
4. Add bourbon
5. Garnish with a cherry and an orange slice

MATADOR

1 oz. tequila
1½ oz. pineapple juice
½ oz. lime juice

1. Fill mixing glass with ice
2. Add tequila, pineapple juice and lime juice

3. Shake
4. Strain into a chilled cocktail glass

MAURICE

1 oz. gin
½ oz. sweet vermouth
½ oz. dry vermouth
½ oz. orange juice
dash Angostura bitters

1. Fill mixing glass with ice
2. Add gin, sweet vermouth, dry vermouth, orange juice and bitters
3. Shake
4. Strain into a chilled cocktail glass

MAXIM

1½ oz. gin
1 oz. dry vermouth
dash white crème de cacao

1. Fill mixing glass with ice
2. Add gin, dry vermouth and white crème de cacao
3. Shake
4. Strain into a chilled cocktail glass

MAY BLOSSOM FIZZ

1½ oz. Swedish Punsch
1½ oz. lemon juice
1 tsp. grenadine
club soda

1. Fill mixing glass with ice
2. Add Swedish Punsch, lemon juice and grenadine
3. Shake
4. Strain into a highball glass
5. Add ice
6. Top with club soda

McCLELLAND

2 oz. sloe gin 1 oz. curaçao 3 dashes orange bitters	1. Fill mixing glass with ice 2. Add sloe gin, curaçao and orange bitters 3. Shake 4. Strain into a chilled cocktail glass

MELON BALL

1 oz. vodka ½ oz. Midori melon liqueur 5 oz. orange juice	1. Fill a highball glass with ice 2. Add vodka and Midori 3. Fill with orange juice 4. Stir

MELON BALL SUNRISE

1 oz. vodka ½ oz. Midori melon liqueur orange juice grenadine	1. Fill a highball glass with ice 2. Pour in vodka and Midori 3. Fill with orange juice 4. Stir 5. Pour in a drop of grenadine over the back of a spoon, allowing it to rise from the bottom

MELON COCKTAIL

2 oz. gin 3 drops lemon juice 3 drops maraschino liqueur	1. Fill mixing glass with ice 2. Add gin, lemon juice and maraschino liqueur 3. Shake 4. Strain into a chilled cocktail glass

MELON COLADA

1½ oz. light rum
½ oz. Midori (or other melon liqueur)
1 oz. cream of coconut
3 oz. pineapple juice
splash cream
½ oz. dark rum (optional)

1. Fill blender with 3 oz. crushed ice, light rum, Midori, cream of coconut, pineapple juice, cream and dark rum (if desired)
2. Blend at medium speed for approximately 15 seconds, until smooth
3. Pour into a goblet or a large wineglass
4. Garnish with a pineapple slice or spear

MELTDOWN (SHOOTER)

1 oz. Stolichnaya (chilled)
½ oz. peach schnapps

1. Pour chilled Stolichnaya into a shot glass
2. Top with peach schnapps

MEMPHIS BELLE COCKTAIL

1½ oz. brandy
¾ oz. Southern Comfort
½ oz. lemon juice
3-4 dashes orange bitters

1. Fill mixing glass with ice
2. Add brandy, Southern Comfort, lemon juice and orange bitters
3. Shake
4. Strain into a chilled cocktail glass

MERRY WIDOW

1½ oz. cherry brandy
1½ oz. maraschino liqueur

1. Fill mixing glass with ice
2. Add cherry brandy and maraschino liqueur
3. Shake
4. Strain into a chilled cocktail glass

MEXICAN COFFEE

½ oz. tequila
½ oz. Kahlúa
hot coffee

1. Pour tequila and Kahlúa into a coffee mug
2. Fill with hot coffee
3. Top with whipped cream, if desired

MEXICAN FLAG (SHOOTER)

½ oz. sloe gin
½ oz. vodka
½ oz. Midori melon liqueur

1. Pour sloe gin into a shot glass
2. Float vodka on top, and then float Midori on top of vodka

MEXICAN MISSILE (SHOOTER)*

¾ oz. tequila
¾ oz. green Chartreuse
dash Tabasco

1. Combine tequila and green Chartreuse in a shot glass
2. Add dash of Tabasco to season

MEXICANO

2 oz. light rum
2 tsp. orange juice
2 tsp. kümmel
3–4 dashes Angostura bitters

1. Fill mixing glass with ice
2. Add light rum, orange juice, kümmel and bitters
3. Shake
4. Strain into a rocks glass filled with ice

---

* Courtesy of Soapy Smith's Eagle Bar, Denver, Colorado.

MIAMI BEACH

1½ oz. scotch
1½ oz. dry vermouth
1 oz. grapefruit juice

1. Fill mixing glass with ice
2. Add scotch, dry vermouth and grapefruit juice
3. Stir
4. Strain into a chilled cocktail glass

MIDNIGHT SUN

2½ oz. vodka
½ oz. grenadine

1. In a mixing glass, combine 3 or 4 ice cubes, vodka and grenadine
2. Stir
3. Strain into a chilled cocktail glass

MIDORI MELON BALL DROP

sugar
2 oz. Midori Melon Liqueur
1 oz. citrus vodka
½ oz. elderflower liqueur
juice of ½ lemon

1. Rim a chilled cocktail glass with sugar
2. Pour the liquids into a cocktail shaker filled with ice
3. Shake well
4. Strain into the prepared glass
5. Garnish with a melon ball

MIDORI SOUR

2 oz. Midori (or other melon liqueur)
1 oz. lemon juice
1 tsp. sugar syrup

1. Fill mixing glass with ice
2. Add Midori, lemon juice and sugar syrup
3. Shake
4. Strain into a chilled sour glass filled with ice

MILLIONAIRE

1½ oz. bourbon
½ oz. Pernod
2–3 dashes curaçao
2–3 dashes grenadine
½ egg white

1. Fill mixing glass with ice
2. Add bourbon, Pernod, curaçao, grenadine and egg white
3. Shake
4. Strain into a chilled cocktail glass

MILLIONAIRE'S COFFEE

½ oz. Kahlúa
½ oz. Baileys Original Irish Cream
½ oz. Grand Marnier
½ oz. Frangelico
hot coffee

1. Pour Kahlúa, Baileys, Grand Marnier and Frangelico into a coffee mug or a hot drink glass
2. Fill with hot coffee
3. Top with whipped cream

MIMOSA

3 oz. orange juice
3 oz. chilled champagne
dash Cointreau or triple sec (optional)

1. Pour orange juice into a large, chilled wineglass
2. Fill with chilled champagne
3. Top with Cointreau or triple sec (if desired)
4. Stir gently

(*Note:* The proportion of orange juice to champagne may be changed to suit personal taste.)

MIND ERASER

¾ oz. Kahlúa
1¼ oz. vodka
1 oz. tonic water

1. Fill a rocks glass with ice
2. Add Kahlúa and vodka
3. Top with tonic
4. Stir lightly
5. Drink through a straw in one shot

MINT COOLER

2 oz. scotch
3 dashes white crème de menthe
club soda

1. Fill a Collins glass with ice
2. Add scotch and white crème de menthe
3. Stir
4. Fill with club soda
5. Stir gently

MINT JULEP

2 oz. bourbon
6 mint leaves
½ oz. sugar syrup

1. In a Collins glass, place the 6 mint leaves and sugar syrup
2. Mash leaves
3. Add 1 oz. of the bourbon
4. Fill glass with crushed ice
5. Add the rest of the bourbon
6. Stir well
7. Garnish with a mint sprig

MISSION ACCOMPLISHED (SHOOTER)

2 oz. vodka
½ oz. triple sec
¼ oz. Rose's lime juice
dash of grenadine

(MAKES ABOUT 2 SHOTS)

1. Fill mixing glass with ice
2. Add vodka, triple sec, lime juice and grenadine
3. Shake
4. Strain into shot glasses

MISSISSIPPI MULE

1½ oz. gin
1 tsp. crème de cassis
1 tsp. lemon juice

1. Fill mixing glass with ice
2. Add gin, crème de cassis and lemon juice
3. Shake
4. Strain into a rocks glass with ice

MOCHA MINT

1 oz. Kahlúa
1 oz. white crème de
menthe
1 oz. white crème de cacao

1. Fill mixing glass with ice
2. Add Kahlúa, white crème de
menthe and white crème de
cacao
3. Shake
4. Strain into a chilled cocktail
glass

MOCKINGBIRD

1½ oz. tequila
2 tsp. white crème de
menthe
1 oz. lime juice

1. Fill mixing glass with ice
2. Add tequila, white crème de
menthe and lime juice
3. Shake
4. Strain into a chilled cocktail
glass

MODERN (1)

1½ oz. sloe gin
¾ oz. scotch
2–3 drops Pernod
2–3 drops grenadine
2 dashes orange bitters

1. Fill mixing glass with some ice
2. Add sloe gin, scotch, Pernod,
grenadine and bitters
3. Shake
4. Pour into a rocks glass

MODERN (2)

3 oz. scotch
3 dashes dark rum
3 dashes Pernod
3 dashes lemon juice
3 dashes orange bitters

1. Fill mixing glass with some ice
2. Add scotch, dark rum, Pernod,
lemon juice and bitters
3. Shake
4. Pour into a rocks glass
5. Garnish with a cherry

MOJITO

mint leaves (approx. 8
  sprigs)
1 tbsp. sugar syrup (cooled)
1 lime
2½ oz. light rum
club soda

1. Put the mint leaves and cooled sugar syrup into a highball glass
2. Using a spoon, mash mint leaves with sugar syrup for about 20–30 seconds
3. Cut the lime in half and remove the seeds
4. Squeeze the juice from both halves into the glass
5. Add one-half of the lime to the glass
6. Pour in rum
7. Stir
8. Add ice
9. Top off with club soda
10. Garnish with a sprig of mint

MOJITO SMOOTHIE

1 oz. rum
1 tsp. pure vanilla extract
½–1 cup water
1 lime
½ medium banana
1 cup fresh mint leaves
1 cup spinach
1 serving of your favorite
  protein powder

1. Place liquids in blender first; heaviest ingredients in blender last
2. Add more or less water or ice to achieve desired consistency

MOLL

1 oz. gin
1 oz. sloe gin
1 oz. dry vermouth

1. Fill mixing glass with ice
2. Add gin, sloe gin, dry vermouth, orange bitters and sugar

dash orange bitters
½ tsp. sugar

3. Shake
4. Pour into a chilled cocktail glass

MONKEY WRENCH

3 oz. light rum
4 oz. grapefruit juice

1. Fill a highball glass with ice
2. Pour in light rum and grapefruit juice
3. Stir

MONTANA

1½ oz. brandy
2 tsp. dry vermouth
2 tsp. port

1. Fill a rocks glass with ice
2. Add brandy, dry vermouth and port
3. Stir

MONTE CARLO

1½ oz. rye whiskey
½ oz. Bénédictine
3–4 dashes Angostura bitters

1. Fill mixing glass with ice
2. Add rye, Bénédictine and bitters
3. Shake
4. Pour into a chilled cocktail glass

MONTMARTRE COCKTAIL

1½ oz. gin
½ oz. sweet vermouth
½ oz. triple sec

1. Fill mixing glass with ice
2. Add gin, sweet vermouth and triple sec
3. Shake
4. Pour into a rocks glass filled with ice

MONTREAL CLUB BOUNCER

1½ oz. gin
1½ oz. Pernod

1. Fill a rocks glass with ice
2. Add gin and Pernod
3. Stir

MOONLIGHT

2½ oz. apple brandy
3 tsp. lemon juice
2 tsp. sugar syrup
club soda

1. Fill mixing glass with ice
2. Add apple brandy, lemon juice and sugar syrup
3. Shake
4. Pour into a rocks glass filled with ice
5. Top with club soda
6. Garnish with a slice of lemon

MOONSHINE COCKTAIL

½ oz. white Dubonnet
dash Pernod
½ oz. brandy
½ oz. peach brandy

1. Fill mixing glass with ice
2. Add Dubonnet, Pernod, brandy and peach brandy
3. Shake
4. Strain into a chilled cocktail glass

MORNING

1 oz. brandy
1 oz. dry vermouth
3 drops Pernod
3 drops curaçao
3 drops maraschino liqueur
2 dashes orange bitters

1. Fill mixing glass with ice
2. Add brandy, dry vermouth, Pernod, curaçao, maraschino liqueur and orange bitters
3. Shake
4. Strain into a rocks glass filled with ice
5. Garnish with a cherry

MORNING BECOMES ELECTRIC

2 oz. dry vermouth
1 oz. brandy
2 tsp. port
dash curaçao

1. Fill mixing glass with ice
2. Add dry vermouth, brandy, port and curaçao
3. Stir well
4. Strain into a chilled cocktail glass

MORNING GLORY

1 oz. scotch
1 oz. brandy
3 drops curaçao
dash Pernod
2 dashes Angostura bitters
½ tsp. sugar syrup
club soda

1. Fill mixing glass with ice
2. Add scotch, brandy, curaçao, Pernod, bitters and sugar syrup
3. Shake
4. Strain into a Collins glass filled with ice
5. Top with club soda
6. Stir with a wet bar spoon coated with powdered sugar

MOSCOW MIMOSA

3 oz. chilled champagne
3 oz. chilled orange juice
½ oz. vodka

1. Pour champagne, orange juice and vodka into a wineglass
2. Stir gently

MOSCOW MULE

¾ oz. lime juice
1½ oz. vodka
ginger ale

1. Half fill a Collins glass with ice
2. Add lime juice and a slice of lime
3. Pour in the vodka
4. Top with ginger ale
5. Stir

MOTHER SHERMAN

1½ oz. apricot brandy
1 oz. orange juice
3–4 dashes orange bitters

1. Fill mixing glass with ice
2. Add apricot brandy, orange juice and orange bitters
3. Shake
4. Strain into a rocks glass filled with ice

MOULIN ROUGE

1½ oz. sloe gin
½ oz. sweet vermouth
3 dashes Angostura bitters

1. Fill mixing glass with ice
2. Add sloe gin, sweet vermouth and bitters
3. Shake
4. Strain into a chilled cocktail glass

MOUNTAIN RED PUNCH

3 bottles chilled red wine (preferably California wine)
4½ oz. amaretto
4½ oz. brandy
4½ oz. cherry-flavored brandy
16 oz. ginger ale

1. Pour red wine, amaretto, brandy and cherry-flavored brandy over a block of ice in a large punch bowl
2. Place in refrigerator for one hour
3. When ready to serve, pour in ginger ale
4. Stir lightly
5. Garnish with toasted almonds, chopped julienne style

MOUNT FUJI

1½ oz. gin
½ oz. lemon juice
½ oz. heavy cream
1 tsp. pineapple juice
1 egg white
3 dashes cherry brandy

1. Fill mixing glass with ice
2. Add gin, lemon juice, heavy cream, pineapple juice, egg white and cherry brandy
3. Shake
4. Strain into a rocks glass filled with ice

MUDSLIDE

1 oz. vodka
1 oz. Kahlúa
1 oz. Baileys Original Irish Cream

1. Fill mixing glass with ice
2. Add vodka, Kahlúa and Baileys
3. Shake
4. Strain into a chilled cocktail glass

MULE'S HIND LEG

½ oz. gin
½ oz. apple brandy
2 tsp. Bénédictine
2 tsp. apricot brandy
2 tsp. maple syrup (or to taste)

1. Fill mixing glass with ice
2. Add gin, apple brandy, Bénédictine, apricot brandy and maple syrup
3. Shake
4. Strain into a rocks glass filled with ice

N

NAPOLI

1 oz. Campari
1 oz. vodka
½ oz. dry vermouth
¼ oz. sweet vermouth
club soda

1. Fill a Collins glass with ice
2. Add Campari, vodka, dry vermouth and sweet vermouth
3. Stir well
4. Fill with club soda
5. Garnish with a twist of orange

NARRAGANSETT

1½ oz. bourbon
1 oz. sweet vermouth
dash anisette

1. Fill a rocks glass with ice
2. Add bourbon, sweet vermouth and anisette
3. Stir
4. Garnish with a twist of lemon

NAVY GROG

½ oz. light rum
½ oz. dark rum
¼ oz. Falernum
½ oz. guava nectar
½ oz. pineapple juice

1. Fill mixing glass with ice
2. Add all ingredients
3. Shake
4. Pour into a chilled highball glass or a chilled double rocks glass

½ oz. orange juice
1 oz. sour mix

5. Garnish with a lime slice and a sprig of mint (optional)

(*Note:* This drink may also be prepared in an electric blender.)

NEGRONI

1 oz. gin
1 oz. Campari
1 oz. sweet vermouth

1. Fill mixing glass with ice
2. Add gin, Campari and sweet vermouth
3. Stir
4. Strain into a chilled cocktail glass
5. Garnish with a twist of lemon

NEGRONI COOLER

1½ oz. Campari
1½ oz. sweet vermouth
½ oz. gin
club soda

1. Fill mixing glass with ice
2. Add Campari, sweet vermouth and gin
3. Shake
4. Strain into a highball glass filled with ice
5. Top with club soda
6. Garnish with a twist of lemon

NETHERLAND

1 oz. brandy
1 oz. triple sec
dash orange bitters

1. Fill mixing glass with ice
2. Add brandy, triple sec and orange bitters
3. Shake
4. Strain into a rocks glass filled with ice

NEVINS

1½ oz. bourbon
2 tsp. grapefruit juice
1 tsp. lemon juice
1 tsp. apricot brandy
3 dashes Angostura bitters

1. Fill mixing glass with ice
2. Add bourbon, grapefruit juice, lemon juice, apricot brandy and bitters
3. Shake
4. Strain into a highball glass filled with ice

NEWBURY

1 oz. gin
1 oz. sweet vermouth
3 dashes curaçao

1. Fill mixing glass with ice
2. Add gin, sweet vermouth and curaçao
3. Stir
4. Strain into a chilled cocktail glass
5. Garnish with a twist of lemon and a twist of orange

NEW ORLEANS

1½ oz. bourbon
½ oz. Pernod
3–4 dashes Angostura bitters
dash orange bitters
dash anisette
½ tsp. sugar syrup, or to taste

1. Fill mixing glass with cracked ice
2. Add bourbon, Pernod, Angostura bitters, orange bitters, anisette and sugar syrup
3. Shake
4. Pour into a chilled rocks glass
5. Garnish with a twist of lemon

NEWTON'S SPECIAL

2 oz. brandy
¾ oz. Cointreau

1. Fill mixing glass with ice
2. Add brandy, Cointreau and bitters

dash Angostura bitters

3. Stir
4. Strain into a chilled cocktail glass

NEW WORLD

1½ oz. blended whiskey
½ oz. lime juice
1 tsp. grenadine

1. Fill mixing glass with ice
2. Add blended whiskey, lime juice and grenadine
3. Shake
4. Pour into a chilled rocks glass
5. Garnish with a twist of lime

NEW YORK COCKTAIL

1½ oz. whiskey
½ tsp. powdered sugar
½ oz. lime juice
dash grenadine

1. Fill mixing glass with cracked ice
2. Add whiskey, powdered sugar, lime juice and grenadine
3. Shake
4. Pour into a chilled cocktail glass
5. Garnish with a twist of orange

NIGHT CAP

¾ oz. brandy
¾ oz. curaçao
¾ oz. anisette
1 egg yolk

1. Fill mixing glass with ice
2. Add brandy, curaçao, anisette and egg yolk
3. Shake
4. Pour into a chilled cocktail glass

NIGHTINGALE

1 oz. banana liqueur
½ oz. curaçao
1 oz. cream
½ egg white

1. Fill mixing glass with ice
2. Add banana liqueur, curaçao, cream and egg white
3. Shake
4. Pour into a chilled cocktail glass

NINETEEN

2 oz. dry vermouth
½ oz. gin
½ oz. kirschwasser
dash Pernod
4 dashes sugar syrup

1. Fill mixing glass with ice
2. Add dry vermouth, gin, kirschwasser, Pernod and sugar syrup
3. Stir well
4. Strain into a chilled cocktail glass

NINETEEN PICK-ME-UP

1½ oz. Pernod
¾ oz. gin
3–4 dashes sugar syrup
3–4 dashes Angostura bitters
3–4 dashes orange bitters
club soda

1. Fill mixing glass with ice
2. Add Pernod, gin, sugar syrup, Angostura bitters and orange bitters
3. Shake
4. Pour into a chilled highball glass
5. Fill with club soda

NINJA TURTLE

1½ oz. Tanqueray gin
½ oz. blue curaçao
orange juice

1. Fill a highball glass with ice
2. Add gin and blue curaçao
3. Fill with orange juice
4. Stir

NINOTCHKA

1½ oz. vodka
1 tsp. lemon juice
2 tsp. white crème de cacao

1. Fill mixing glass with ice
2. Add vodka, lemon juice and white crème de cacao
3. Shake
4. Pour into a chilled cocktail glass

NOCTURNAL

2 oz. bourbon
1 oz. dark crème de cacao
½ oz. cream

1. Fill mixing glass with ice
2. Add bourbon, dark crème de cacao and cream
3. Shake
4. Strain into a rocks glass filled with 2 oz. crushed ice

NUTTY COLADA

2 oz. amaretto
1 oz. gold rum
1½ oz. cream of coconut
2 oz. pineapple juice

1. Fill blender with 3 oz. cracked ice
2. Add amaretto, gold rum, cream of coconut and pineapple juice
3. Blend at low speed for approximately 10–15 seconds, or until smooth
4. Pour into a chilled Collins glass
5. Garnish with a slice of pineapple

NUTTY IRISHMAN

½ oz. Frangelico
½ oz. Irish whiskey
2 oz. cream

1. Fill mixing glass with ice
2. Add Frangelico, Irish whiskey and cream
3. Shake
4. Strain into a rocks glass filled with ice

NUTTY IRISHMAN (SHOOTER)

½ oz. Frangelico ½ oz. Baileys Original Irish Cream	Layer Frangelico and Baileys in a shot glass

NUTTY STINGER

1½ oz. amaretto 1 oz. white crème de menthe	1. Fill mixing glass with ice 2. Add amaretto and white crème de menthe 3. Shake 4. Strain into a chilled cocktail glass

ODD McINTYRE

1 oz. brandy
1 oz. triple sec
1 oz. Lillet
½ oz. lemon juice

1. Fill mixing glass with ice
2. Add brandy, triple sec, Lillet and lemon juice
3. Shake
4. Strain into a chilled cocktail glass

ODÉON CASINO

3 oz. peach juice
3 oz. chilled champagne
dash peach schnapps
(optional)

1. Pour peach juice into a large chilled wineglass
2. Fill with chilled champagne
3. Top with peach schnapps (if desired)
4. Stir gently

(*Note:* The proportion of peach juice to champagne may be changed to suit personal taste.)

OH, HENRY!

1½ oz. blended whiskey	1. Fill a rocks glass with ice
¼ oz. Bénédictine	2. Add blended whiskey, Bénédictine and ginger ale
3 oz. ginger ale	3. Stir
	4. Garnish with a slice of lemon

OIL SLICK*

1 oz. vodka	1. Fill a small rocks glass with ice
1 oz. white crème de cacao	2. Layer vodka, white crème de cacao and milk
1 oz. milk	3. Float dark rum on top
float of dark rum	

OLD ETONIAN

1 oz. gin	1. Fill mixing glass with ice
1 oz. Lillet	2. Add gin, Lillet, crème de noyaux and orange bitters
2 dashes crème de noyaux	3. Stir
2 dashes orange bitters	4. Strain into a chilled cocktail glass

OLD-FASHIONED

¼ oz. simple syrup (or one sugar cube, if preferred)	1. In an old-fashioned glass, add the syrup, bitters and orange peel
2 dashes Angostura bitters	2. Use a muddler to gently press the orange peel to release the citrus oils
orange peel	3. Add the whiskey and stir
2 oz. bourbon or rye whiskey	4. Add ice cubes and stir again

---

* Courtesy of The Cowgirl Hall of Fame, New York City.

OLD PALE

1 oz. peppermint schnapps
1½ oz. vodka
1 tsp. strawberry liqueur

1. In a mixing glass, combine several ice cubes with peppermint schnapps, vodka and strawberry liqueur
2. Stir
3. Pour into a chilled cocktail glass

OLYMPIC

¾ oz. brandy
¾ oz. curaçao
½ oz. orange juice

1. Fill mixing glass with ice
2. Add brandy, curaçao and orange juice
3. Shake
4. Strain into a rocks glass filled with ice

OOM PAUL

1 oz. apple brandy
1 oz. Dubonnet
3 dashes Angostura bitters

1. Fill mixing glass with ice
2. Add apple brandy, Dubonnet and bitters
3. Shake
4. Strain into a rocks glass filled with ice

OPENING

2 oz. whiskey
1 oz. sweet vermouth
1 tsp. grenadine

1. Fill mixing glass with ice
2. Add whiskey, sweet vermouth and grenadine
3. Stir
4. Strain into a chilled cocktail glass

OPERA (1)

1½ oz. gin
½ oz. Dubonnet
½ oz. cherry liqueur

1. Fill mixing glass with ice
2. Add gin, Dubonnet and cherry liqueur
3. Stir
4. Strain into a chilled cocktail glass
5. Garnish with a twist of orange

OPERA (2)

¾ oz. gin
¾ oz. Dubonnet
¾ oz. Grand Marnier
½ oz. orange juice

1. Fill mixing glass with ice
2. Add gin, Dubonnet, Grand Marnier and orange juice
3. Shake
4. Strain into a chilled cocktail glass

ORANGE BLOOM

1 oz. gin
½ oz. sweet vermouth
½ oz. Cointreau

1. Fill mixing glass with ice
2. Add gin, sweet vermouth and Cointreau
3. Stir
4. Strain into a chilled cocktail glass
5. Garnish with a cherry

ORANGE BLOSSOM

1 oz. gin
½ oz. sugar syrup (triple sec may be substituted)
1½ oz. orange juice

1. Fill mixing glass with ice
2. Add gin, sugar syrup (or triple sec) and orange juice
3. Shake

306

4. Strain into a chilled cocktail glass

(*Note:* If desired, frost rim of cocktail glass with sugar before pouring drink into it.)

ORANGE BUCK

1½ oz. gin
1 oz. orange juice
1 tbsp. lime juice
ginger ale

1. Fill mixing glass with ice
2. Add gin, orange juice and lime juice
3. Shake
4. Strain into a highball glass filled with ice
5. Top with ginger ale

ORANGE COMFORT

1½ oz. Southern Comfort
2 tsp. anisette
1 tbsp. orange juice
2 tsp. lemon juice

1. Fill mixing glass with ice
2. Add Southern Comfort, anisette, orange juice and lemon juice
3. Shake
4. Strain into a chilled rocks glass
5. Garnish with a slice of orange

ORANGE FIZZ

2½ oz. gin
1½ oz. orange juice
½ oz. lemon juice
2 tsp. triple sec
1 tsp. sugar
2 dashes orange bitters
club soda

1. Fill mixing glass with ice
2. Add gin, orange juice, lemon juice, triple sec, sugar and orange bitters
3. Shake
4. Strain into a highball glass filled with ice

5. Top with club soda
6. Garnish with a slice of orange

ORANGE GIMLET

1½ oz. gin
1 oz. Lillet
2 dashes orange bitters

1. Fill mixing glass with ice
2. Add gin, Lillet and orange bitters
3. Shake
4. Strain into a chilled cocktail glass

ORANGE OASIS

1½ oz. gin
½ oz. cherry brandy
4 oz. orange juice
ginger ale

1. Fill a highball glass with ice
2. Add gin, cherry brandy and orange juice
3. Stir
4. Top with ginger ale

ORGASM

½ oz. white crème de cacao
½ oz. amaretto
½ oz. triple sec
½ oz. vodka
1 oz. cream

1. Fill mixing glass with ice
2. Add white crème de cacao, amaretto, triple sec, vodka and cream
3. Shake
4. Strain into a rocks glass filled with ice

ORIENTAL

1 oz. rye whiskey
¼ oz. sweet vermouth
¼ oz. Cointreau

1. Fill mixing glass with ice
2. Add rye, sweet vermouth, Cointreau and lime juice

½ oz. lime juice

3. Shake
4. Strain into a chilled cocktail glass

OSTEND FIZZ

1 oz. kirschwasser
1 oz. crème de cassis
club soda

1. Fill a highball glass with ice
2. Add kirschwasser and crème de cassis
3. Stir
4. Fill with club soda
5. Garnish with a twist of lemon

OUT OF THE BLUE

¼ oz. Absolut vodka
¼ oz. blueberry schnapps
¼ oz. blue curaçao
splash sour mix
¼ oz. club soda

1. Fill mixing glass with ice
2. Add Absolut vodka, blueberry schnapps, blue curaçao and sour mix
3. Shake
4. Pour into a rocks glass
5. Top with club soda

OXBEND

1 oz. Southern Comfort
½ oz. tequila
6 oz. orange juice
dash of grenadine

1. Fill a highball glass with ice
2. Add Southern Comfort, tequila, orange juice and grenadine
3. Stir

PACIFIC PACIFIER

1 oz. Cointreau	1. Fill mixing glass with ice
½ oz. banana liqueur	2. Add Cointreau, banana liqueur
½ oz. cream	and cream
	3. Shake
	4. Strain into a rocks glass filled
	with ice

PADDY COCKTAIL

1½ oz. Irish whiskey	1. Fill mixing glass with ice
¾ oz. sweet vermouth	2. Add Irish whiskey, sweet
3 dashes Angostura bitters	vermouth and bitters
	3. Shake
	4. Strain into a chilled cocktail
	glass

PAGO PAGO

1½ oz. gold rum	1. Fill mixing glass with ice
½ oz. pineapple juice	2. Add gold rum, pineapple juice,
½ oz. lime juice	lime juice, green Chartreuse and
2–3 drops green Chartreuse	white crème de cacao

2–3 drops white crème de
cacao

3. Shake
4. Strain into a rocks glass filled
   with ice

PAISLEY MARTINI

2 oz. gin
1 tsp. dry vermouth
½ tsp. scotch

1. Fill mixing glass with ice
2. Add gin, dry vermouth and scotch
3. Shake
4. Strain into a rocks glass filled
   with ice

PALL MALL

¾ oz. gin
¾ oz. dry vermouth
¾ oz. sweet vermouth
1 tsp. white crème de menthe
dash orange bitters

1. Fill a rocks glass with ice
2. Add all ingredients
3. Stir

PALMETTO

1½ oz. light rum
½ oz. sweet vermouth
2 dashes orange bitters

1. Fill a rocks glass with ice
2. Add light rum, sweet vermouth
   and orange bitters
3. Stir
4. Garnish with a twist of lemon

PALOMA

2 oz. Partida Blanco Tequila
1 pinch salt
½ lime
grapefruit soda

1. Fill a highball glass with ice
   and add the tequila and salt
2. Squeeze the lime half into the
   glass and drop into the drink
3. Fill with grapefruit soda

PANAMA

1 oz. Myers's dark rum
½ oz. white crème de cacao
½ oz. cream

1. Fill mixing glass with ice
2. Add Myers's rum, crème de cacao and cream
3. Shake
4. Strain into a rocks glass filled with ice
5. Sprinkle nutmeg on top

PANCHO VILLA

1 oz. light rum
1 oz. gin
½ oz. apricot brandy
1 tsp. cherry brandy
1 tsp. pineapple juice

1. Fill mixing glass with ice
2. Add light rum, gin, apricot brandy, cherry brandy and pineapple juice
3. Shake
4. Strain into a rocks glass filled with ice

PANCHO VILLA (SHOOTER)*

½ oz. crème de almond
½ oz. Cuervo white tequila
½ oz. 151-proof rum

1. Layer crème de almond and tequila in a shot glass
2. Top with float of 151-proof rum

PANDA BEAR

1 oz. amaretto
½ oz. white crème de cacao
½ oz. dark crème de cacao
5 oz. vanilla ice cream
¼ oz. chocolate syrup
2–3 dashes vanilla extract

1. Fill blender with amaretto, both crèmes de cacao, vanilla ice cream, chocolate syrup and vanilla extract
2. Blend until smooth
3. Pour into a chilled goblet

* Courtesy of Soapy Smith's Eagle Bar, Denver, Colorado.

PANTHER

1½ oz. tequila
½ oz. sour mix

1. Fill mixing glass with ice
2. Add tequila and sour mix
3. Shake
4. Strain into a rocks glass filled with ice

PANTOMIME

1½ oz. dry vermouth
3 drops orgeat syrup
3 drops grenadine
1 egg white

1. Fill mixing glass with ice
2. Add dry vermouth, orgeat syrup, grenadine and egg white
3. Shake
4. Strain into a chilled cocktail glass

PAPACITO

1 part Hornitos Añejo tequila
½ part tawny port
¼ part orange liqueur
1 dash orange bitters

1. Stir ingredients briskly, and strain into a shot glass
2. Bite into an orange wedge and imbibe

PARADISE

1 oz. gin
1 oz. apricot brandy
1 oz. orange juice

1. Fill mixing glass with ice
2. Add gin, apricot brandy and orange juice
3. Stir
4. Strain into a chilled cocktail glass

PARALYZER

1 oz. tequila
½ oz. white crème de cacao
1 oz. Kahlúa
whipped cream

1. Fill mixing glass with ice
2. Add tequila, crème de cacao and Kahlúa
3. Shake
4. Strain into a rocks glass
5. Add whipped cream to top

PARISIAN

¾ oz. gin
¾ oz. dry vermouth
¾ oz. crème de cassis

1. Fill mixing glass with ice
2. Add gin, dry vermouth and crème de cassis
3. Shake
4. Strain into a chilled cocktail glass

PARISIAN BLONDE

1 oz. light rum
1 oz. curaçao
1 oz. heavy cream
½ tsp. powdered sugar

1. Fill mixing glass with ice
2. Add light rum, curaçao, heavy cream and powdered sugar
3. Shake
4. Strain into a chilled cocktail glass

PARK AVENUE

2 oz. gin
½ oz. sweet vermouth
1 oz. pineapple juice
2–3 drops curaçao

1. Fill mixing glass with ice
2. Add gin, sweet vermouth, pineapple juice and curaçao
3. Shake
4. Strain into a chilled cocktail glass

PAVAROTTI

1½ oz. amaretto	1. Fill mixing glass with ice
½ oz. brandy	2. Add amaretto, brandy and white
½ oz. white crème de cacao	crème de cacao
	3. Shake
	4. Strain into a rocks glass filled with ice

PEACH ALEXANDER

½ peach, pared, pitted and chopped	1. Combine peach, half-and-half, peach schnapps, white crème de cacao and 3 oz. crushed ice in a blender
1½ oz. half-and-half	
1 oz. peach schnapps	2. Blend until smooth
½ oz. white crème de cacao	3. Pour into an 8-oz. glass
	4. Garnish with a slice of fresh peach

PEACH-BASIL SANGRIA

¾ cup sugar	1. In a saucepan, combine the sugar, basil leaves, half of the peach nectar and the lemon juice
1 cup fresh basil leaves, loosely packed	
3½ cups peach nectar	2. Bring to a simmer, crushing the basil leaves with the back of a spoon to release their flavor
¼ cup fresh lemon juice	
1 bottle white wine such as a Pinot Grigio (750 ml)	3. Simmer basil mixture just long enough to melt the sugar, then remove from the heat and allow to cool
	4. Strain the basil mixture into a pitcher filled with ice cubes
	5. Pour in the wine and the remaining peach nectar
	6. Stir briefly and serve

PEACH BLOW FIZZ

2 oz. gin
1 oz. lemon juice
1 oz. heavy cream
1 tsp. sugar syrup
2 tsp. strawberry liqueur
club soda

1. Fill mixing glass with ice
2. Add gin, lemon juice, heavy cream, sugar syrup and strawberry liqueur
3. Shake
4. Strain into a sour glass
5. Add ice
6. Fill with club soda
7. Garnish with a strawberry

PEACH BUCK

1¼ oz. vodka
½ oz. peach brandy
½ oz. lemon juice
ginger ale

1. Fill mixing glass with cracked ice
2. Add vodka, peach brandy and lemon juice
3. Shake
4. Pour into a highball glass
5. Fill with ginger ale

PEACH COCONUT FLIP

1 peach, pared and pitted
1½ oz. light rum
2 oz. coconut cream
2 oz. milk

1. Fill blender with 3 oz. crushed ice, peach, light rum, coconut cream and milk
2. Blend until smooth
3. Pour into a goblet
4. Garnish with a slice of fresh peach

PEACH TREAT

1 oz. peach brandy
2 oz. orange juice
chilled champagne

1. Fill mixing glass with ice
2. Add peach brandy and orange juice

3. Shake
4. Strain into a Collins glass filled with ice
5. Fill with champagne
6. Garnish with a peach slice

PEACH VELVET

1½ oz. peach brandy
½ oz. white crème de cacao
½ oz. heavy cream

1. Fill blender with 4 oz. cracked ice
2. Add peach brandy, white crème de cacao and heavy cream
3. Blend at medium speed for 10 seconds, or until smooth
4. Pour into a rocks glass
5. Garnish with a slice of fresh peach

PEACHY KEEN FREEZE

1½ oz. amaretto
2 oz. heavy cream or half-and-half
1 tbsp. sugar
½ fresh peach, pared

1. Combine amaretto, cream, sugar and peach with 3 oz. crushed ice in a blender
2. Blend until smooth
3. Pour into a goblet

PEANUT BUTTER AND JELLY (SHOOTER)

¾ oz. Frangelico
¾ oz. Chambord

1. Fill mixing glass with ice
2. Add Frangelico and Chambord
3. Shake
4. Strain into a shot glass

PEARL HARBOR

1 oz. vodka
½ oz. Midori melon liqueur
pineapple juice

1. Fill a highball glass with ice
2. Add vodka and Midori
3. Fill with pineapple juice
4. Stir

PEAR TEQUILA SUPREME

1½ oz. white tequila
1 oz. triple sec
¼ cup undiluted frozen
   limeade concentrate
¾ cup fresh pear (Bartlett),
   pared, cored and diced
½ egg white

(MAKES 2 SERVINGS)

1. In a blender, combine tequila,
   triple sec, limeade, pear and
   egg white
2. Blend until smooth
3. Pour into goblets

PEGU CLUB

1½ oz. gin
¾ oz. orange curaçao
1 tsp. lime juice
dash Angostura bitters
dash orange bitters

1. Fill mixing glass with ice
2. Add gin, orange curaçao, lime
   juice, Angostura bitters and
   orange bitters
3. Shake
4. Strain into a chilled cocktail glass

PENDENNIS COCKTAIL

1½ oz. gin
1 tbsp. apricot brandy
½ oz. lime juice
2 dashes Peychaud's bitters

1. Fill mixing glass with ice
2. Add gin, apricot brandy, lime
   juice and bitters
3. Shake
4. Strain into a chilled cocktail glass

PENSACOLA

1½ oz. light rum
½ oz. guava nectar
½ oz. orange juice
½ oz. lemon juice

1. Fill blender with 3 oz. cracked ice
2. Add light rum, guava nectar, orange juice and lemon juice
3. Blend at medium speed for 10–15 seconds, or until smooth
4. Pour into large wineglass

PEPPAR MARTINI

2 oz. Absolut Peppar vodka
½ oz. dry vermouth (or to taste)

1. Fill mixing glass with ice
2. Add Absolut Peppar and dry vermouth
3. Stir
4. Strain into a chilled martini glass or a rocks glass filled with ice
5. Garnish with a jalapeño pepper

PEPPERMINT PATTY

½ oz. peppermint schnapps
½ oz. dark crème de cacao
1 oz. cream

1. Fill a rocks glass with ice
2. Add peppermint schnapps and dark crème de cacao
3. Add cream
4. Stir

PEPPERMINT STINGER

1½ oz. brandy
1 oz. peppermint schnapps

1. Fill blender with 4 oz. cracked ice
2. Add brandy and peppermint schnapps

3. Blend at low speed for 5
   seconds, or until smooth
4. Pour into a rocks glass

PERFECT MANHATTAN

See Manhattan (perfect)

PERFECT ROB ROY

See Rob Roy (perfect)

PERNOD COCKTAIL

2 oz. Pernod
½ oz. water
3 dashes sugar syrup
3 dashes Angostura bitters

1. Fill mixing glass with ice
2. Add Pernod, water, sugar syrup
   and bitters
3. Shake
4. Strain into a chilled cocktail glass

PERNOD FLIP

1 oz. Pernod
½ oz. Cointreau
½ oz. lemon juice
1½ tsp. sugar syrup
1 egg

1. Fill mixing glass with ice
2. Add Pernod, Cointreau, lemon
   juice, sugar syrup and egg
3. Shake
4. Strain into a rocks glass filled
   with ice

PERNOD FRAPPE

1½ oz. Pernod
½ oz. anisette

1. Fill mixing glass with ice
2. Add Pernod, anisette and bitters

| 3 dashes Angostura bitters | 3. Shake |
| | 4. Strain into a chilled cocktail glass |

PHILADELPHIA SCOTCHMAN

1 oz. apple brandy	1. Fill mixing glass with ice
1 oz. port	2. Add apple brandy, port and orange juice
1 oz. orange juice	3. Shake
club soda	4. Strain into a highball glass filled with ice
	5. Fill with club soda

PHOEBE SNOW

1½ oz. brandy	1. Fill mixing glass with ice
1½ oz. Dubonnet	2. Add brandy, Dubonnet and Pernod
3 drops Pernod	3. Shake
	4. Strain into a rocks glass filled with ice

PICON

1 oz. Amer Picon	1. Fill mixing glass with ice
1 oz. dry vermouth	2. Add Amer Picon and dry vermouth
	3. Shake
	4. Strain into a chilled cocktail glass

PICON FIZZ

1½ oz. Amer Picon 1 tbsp. grenadine club soda 2 tbsp. cognac	1. Pour Amer Picon and grenadine into a highball glass 2. Add 4 or 5 ice cubes 3. Stir 4. Fill with chilled club soda 5. Float cognac on top

PICON ORANGE

1½ oz. Amer Picon 1½ oz. orange juice club soda	1. Fill mixing glass with ice 2. Add Amer Picon and orange juice 3. Shake 4. Strain into a rocks glass filled with ice 5. Fill with club soda

PICON SOUR

1½ oz. Amer Picon 1½ oz. sour mix ½ tsp. sugar (if desired)	1. Fill mixing glass with ice 2. Add Amer Picon, sour mix and sugar (if desired) 3. Shake 4. Strain into a chilled sour glass filled with ice

PILOT BOAT

1½ oz. dark rum 1 oz. banana liqueur 2 oz. fresh lime juice or fresh lemon juice	1. Fill mixing glass with ice 2. Add dark rum, banana liqueur and fresh lime or lemon juice 3. Shake 4. Strain into a chilled cocktail glass

PIMM'S CUP

1½ oz. Pimm's No. 1
1 lemon slice
7-Up

1. Fill a highball glass with ice
2. Pour in Pimm's
3. Add lemon slice
4. Fill with 7-Up
5. Garnish with a slice of cucumber

PIÑA

1½ oz. tequila
3 oz. pineapple juice
1 oz. lime juice
1 tsp. sugar syrup

1. Fill mixing glass with ice
2. Add tequila, pineapple juice, lime juice and sugar syrup
3. Shake
4. Strain into a rocks glass filled with ice

PIÑA COLADA

1½ oz. light rum
1 oz. cream of coconut
2 oz. canned pineapple chunks
2 oz. pineapple juice
splash of cream

1. In a blender, combine light rum, cream of coconut, canned pineapple chunks, cream and 3 oz. crushed ice
2. Blend at medium speed for 10–15 seconds, or until smooth
3. Pour into a goblet or a large wineglass
4. Garnish with a cherry and an orange slice or a pineapple spear

PIÑATA

1 oz. tequila
1 tbsp. banana liqueur
1 oz. lime juice

1. Fill mixing glass with ice
2. Add tequila, banana liqueur and lime juice

3. Shake
4. Strain into a rocks glass filled
   with ice

PINEAPPLE BOMBER

1 oz. Captain Morgan rum	1. Fill mixing glass with ice
1 oz. Southern Comfort	2. Add Captain Morgan rum,
½ oz. amaretto	Southern Comfort, amaretto
3 oz. pineapple juice	and pineapple juice
	3. Shake
	4. Pour into a Collins glass filled
	with ice

PINEAPPLE BOMBER (SHOOTER)

¾ oz. Captain Morgan rum	1. Fill mixing glass with ice
¾ oz. Southern Comfort	2. Add Captain Morgan rum,
½ oz. amaretto	Southern Comfort, amaretto
1 oz. pineapple juice	and pineapple juice
	3. Stir well
(MAKES 2 SHOTS)	4. Strain into shot glasses

PINEAPPLE FRANCINE

½ oz. light rum	1. Fill blender with 3 oz. ice
½ oz. apricot brandy	2. Add light rum, apricot brandy,
1 oz. pineapple juice	pineapple juice, cream and
1 oz. cream	pineapple
1 oz. canned pineapple	3. Blend for 10–15 seconds, or
chunks, crushed	until smooth
	4. Pour into a goblet or a large
	wineglass

PINEAPPLE GIMLET

1½ oz. gin
½ oz. Rose's lime juice
pineapple juice

1. Fill a rocks glass with ice
2. Add gin and lime juice
3. Stir well
4. Top with pineapple juice

PINEAPPLE VODKA

premium vodka
fresh pineapple slices

1. Fill a large clean jar with fresh pineapple
2. Add a premium vodka
3. Cover and let stand for 3 days, turning the jar several times daily
4. Remove most of the fruit and refrigerate
5. Serve the vodka over ice in a wineglass or rocks glass

PINE TREE

1 oz. triple sec
lemonade (from a mix)

1. Fill a highball glass with crushed ice
2. Add triple sec
3. Fill with lemonade
4. Stir
5. Garnish with a mint leaf

PINK ALMOND

1 oz. blended whiskey
½ oz. crème de noyaux
½ oz. amaretto
½ oz. kirschwasser
½ oz. lemon juice

1. Fill mixing glass with ice
2. Add blended whiskey, crème de noyaux, amaretto, kirschwasser and lemon juice
3. Shake

4. Pour into a chilled sour glass
5. Garnish with a slice of lemon

PINK AND TAN*

1½ oz. Malibu coconut rum diet cola (with Nutrasweet)	**1.** Fill a highball glass with ice **2.** Add Malibu **3.** Fill with diet cola **4.** Stir

PINK GIN

2 oz. gin 2 dashes Angostura bitters	**1.** Fill mixing glass with ice **2.** Add gin and bitters **3.** Stir **4.** Strain into a rocks glass filled with ice

PINK LADY

1 oz. gin ½ oz. grenadine 1½ oz. cream	**1.** Fill mixing glass with ice **2.** Add gin, grenadine and cream **3.** Shake **4.** Strain into a chilled cocktail glass

PINK LEMONADE

1½ oz. vodka 1 oz. cranberry juice cocktail 2 oz. sour mix	**1.** Fill mixing glass with ice **2.** Add vodka, cranberry juice and sour mix **3.** Shake

* Courtesy of Michael Salatto, New York City.

7-Up

4. Pour into a highball glass or a Collins glass
5. Top with 7-Up
6. Garnish with a slice of lemon

PINK LEMONADE (FROZEN)

1½ oz. Stoli Citros
1 tbsp. sugar
juice of ½ lemon
splash of grenadine

1. Blend all ingredients with ice
2. Garnish with a lemon slice or a pretty and edible flower, such as an apple blossom gardenia or hollyhock

PINK LEMONADE (SHOOTER)

1 oz. vodka
1 oz. cranberry juice cocktail
1 oz. sour mix

(MAKES 2 SHOTS)

1. Fill mixing glass with ice
2. Add vodka, cranberry juice and sour mix
3. Shake
4. Strain into shot glasses

PINK PANTHER

¾ oz. gin
¾ oz. dry vermouth
½ oz. crème de cassis
½ oz. orange juice
1 egg white

1. Fill mixing glass with ice
2. Add gin, dry vermouth, crème de cassis, orange juice and egg white
3. Shake
4. Strain into a chilled cocktail glass

PINK PUSSYCAT

1½ oz. gin
¾ oz. grenadine
1 egg white

1. Fill mixing glass with ice
2. Add gin, grenadine and egg white
3. Shake well
4. Strain into a chilled cocktail glass

PINK ROSE

1½ oz. gin
1 tsp. lemon juice
1 tsp. heavy cream
1 egg white
3-4 dashes grenadine

1. Fill mixing glass with ice
2. Add gin, lemon juice, heavy cream, egg white and grenadine
3. Shake
4. Strain into a chilled cocktail glass

PINK SQUIRREL

½ oz. white crème de cacao
½ oz. crème de noyaux
2 oz. cream

1. Fill mixing glass with ice
2. Add white crème de cacao, crème de noyaux and cream
3. Shake
4. Strain into a chilled cocktail glass

PINK VERANDA

1 oz. gold rum
½ oz. dark rum
1½ oz. cranberry juice
½ oz. lime juice
1 tsp. sugar
½ egg white

1. Fill mixing glass with ice
2. Add gold rum, dark rum, cranberry juice, lime juice, sugar and egg white
3. Shake
4. Pour into a rocks glass

PINK WHISKERS

1 oz. apricot brandy ½ oz. dry vermouth 1 oz. orange juice 1 tsp. grenadine 3 dashes white crème de menthe 1 oz. port	1. Fill mixing glass with ice 2. Add apricot brandy, dry vermouth, orange juice, grenadine and white crème de menthe 3. Shake 4. Strain into a rocks glass filled with ice 5. Float port on top

PIRATE COCKTAIL

1½ oz. Jamaican rum ½ oz. sweet vermouth 2 dashes Angostura bitters	1. Fill mixing glass with ice 2. Add rum, sweet vermouth and bitters 3. Shake 4. Strain into a large glass 5. Add ice

PISCO PUNCH

3 oz. brandy 1 tsp. lime juice 1 tsp. pineapple juice 2 or 3 pineapple cubes cold water	1. Pour brandy, lime juice, pineapple juice and pineapple cubes into a brandy snifter 2. Fill with cold water 3. Stir

PISCO SOUR

2 oz. brandy (Pisco) 1½ oz. sour mix 1 tsp. lime juice ½ egg white 2 dashes Angostura bitters	1. Fill mixing glass with ice 2. Add brandy, sour mix, lime juice and egg white 3. Shake 4. Strain into a sour glass

5. Add ice
6. Top with Angostura bitters

PLANTER'S PUNCH (1)

1½–2 oz. Myers's dark rum
3 oz. orange juice
juice of ½ lemon or lime
1 tsp. superfine granulated
    sugar
dash grenadine

1. Fill mixing glass with cracked
   ice
2. Add Myers's rum, orange juice,
   lemon or lime juice, sugar and
   grenadine
3. Shake
4. Pour into chilled Collins glass
5. Garnish with cherry and an
   orange slice

PLANTER'S PUNCH (2)

1¼ oz. dark rum
½ oz. Rose's lime juice
¼ oz. grenadine
4 oz. orange juice

1. Fill mixing glass with ice
2. Add dark rum, lime juice,
   grenadine and orange juice
3. Shake
4. Strain into a highball glass
   filled with ice
5. Garnish with an orange slice
   and cherry pick

PLAZA

1 oz. gin
1 oz. dry vermouth
1 oz. sweet vermouth
1 tbsp. pineapple juice

1. Fill mixing glass with ice
2. Add gin, dry vermouth, sweet
   vermouth and pineapple juice
3. Shake
4. Strain into a chilled cocktail
   glass

POINSETTIA

4 oz. chilled champagne
2 oz. cranberry juice
cocktail

1. Pour chilled champagne into a champagne flute or tulip glass
2. Add cranberry juice

POKER

1½ oz. gold rum
1½ oz. dry vermouth

1. Fill mixing glass with ice
2. Add gold rum and dry vermouth
3. Shake
4. Strain into a chilled cocktail glass

POLLYANNA

1½ oz. gin
2 tsp. sweet vermouth
2 tsp. grenadine

1. Fill mixing glass with ice
2. Add gin, sweet vermouth and grenadine
3. Shake
4. Strain into a rocks glass filled with ice
5. Garnish with a slice of pineapple and a slice of orange

POLLY'S SPECIAL

1½ oz. scotch
½ oz. triple sec
½ oz. grapefruit juice

1. Fill mixing glass with ice
2. Add scotch, triple sec and grapefruit juice
3. Shake
4. Strain into a rocks glass filled with ice

POLO

1½ oz. gin
2 tsp. orange juice
2 tsp. grapefruit juice

1. Fill a rocks glass with ice
2. Add gin, orange juice and grapefruit juice
3. Stir

POLYNESIAN COCKTAIL

1½ oz. vodka
¾ oz. cherry brandy
3 tbsp. lime juice

1. Frost the rim of a cocktail glass with powdered sugar
2. Fill mixing glass with ice
3. Add vodka, cherry brandy and lime juice
4. Shake
5. Strain into chilled cocktail glass

POLYNESIAN PUNCH

12 oz. light rum
12 oz. dark rum
6 oz. cream of coconut
8 oz. sloe gin
4 oz. peppermint schnapps
½ oz. grenadine
1 qt. plus 1 pt. unsweetened pineapple juice
8 oz. lemon juice
8 oz. chilled club soda

1. Pour light rum, dark rum, cream of coconut, sloe gin, peppermint schnapps, grenadine, pineapple juice and lemon juice into a punch bowl over a block of ice
2. Stir
3. Garnish with thin slices of fresh pineapple and orange
4. Refrigerate for 1 hour
5. When ready to serve, add club soda and stir gently

POMEGRANATE FIZZ

1¼ cups demi-sec sparkling
   wine, chilled
⅔ cup pomegranate juice,
   chilled
1 tbsp. fresh lime juice

MAKES TWO SERVINGS

1. Combine ingredients
2. Garnish with lime wedges
   (optional)

POMEGRANATE MARGARITAS

1 can frozen limeade
   concentrate, thawed
2 cups water
3½ cups gold tequila
2 cups pomegranate juice
1 cup triple sec
5 limes
1 cup fresh pomegranate
   seeds (from 1
   pomegranate)

1. In a large pitcher, combine
   limeade and water until well
   blended
2. Stir in tequila, pomegranate
   juice and triple sec
3. Cut each lime crosswise into
   ¼-inch wheels; cut a slit in each
   wheel, from center to edge
4. To serve, place ice cubes and a
   few pomegranate seeds in each
   glass; place a lime wheel on rim

POOP DECK

1 oz. blackberry brandy
½ oz. port
½ oz. brandy

1. Fill mixing glass with ice
2. Add blackberry brandy, port
   and brandy
3. Shake
4. Strain into a chilled cocktail glass

POPPY COCKTAIL

1½ oz. gin
¾ oz. white crème de cacao

1. Fill mixing glass with ice
2. Add gin and white crème de
   cacao

3. Shake
4. Strain into a chilled cocktail glass

POPSICLE

1 oz. amaretto	1. Fill a highball glass with ice
orange juice	2. Add amaretto
cream	3. Fill glass half with orange juice, half with cream
	4. Stir well

PORT ANTONIO

1 oz. gold rum	1. Fill mixing glass with ice
½ oz. dark rum	2. Add gold rum, dark rum, lime juice, Tia Maria and Falernum
½ oz. lime juice	3. Shake
½ oz. Tia Maria	4. Strain into a highball glass
1 tsp. Falernum	5. Fill with ice
	6. Garnish with a slice of lime

PORT SANGAREE

½ tsp. powdered sugar	1. In a sour glass, dissolve powdered sugar in water
1 oz. water	2. Fill with ice cubes
2 oz. port	3. Pour in port
club soda	4. Fill with club soda
1 tbsp. brandy (optional)	5. Top with brandy (if desired)

PORT WINE COCKTAIL

2½ oz. port	1. Fill mixing glass with ice
½ tsp. brandy	2. Add port and brandy

3. Stir
4. Strain into a chilled cocktail glass

POUSSE-CAFÉ (1)

⅓ oz. banana liqueur
½ oz. cherry brandy
⅓ oz. cognac

1. Pour banana liqueur into a liqueur glass
2. Float the cherry brandy on top
3. Float the cognac on top of that

POUSSE-CAFÉ (2)

½ oz. green crème de menthe
½ oz. Galliano
½ oz. blackberry liqueur

1. Pour green crème de menthe into a liqueur glass
2. Float the Galliano on top
3. Float the blackberry liqueur on top of that

PRADO

1½ oz. tequila
½ oz. cherry liqueur
¾ oz. lime juice
½ egg white
1 tsp. grenadine

1. Fill mixing glass with cracked ice
2. Add tequila, cherry liqueur, lime juice, egg white and grenadine
3. Shake
4. Pour into a sour glass
5. Garnish with a cherry

PRAIRIE FIRE (SHOOTER)

1½ oz. Cuervo gold tequila, chilled
dash of Tabasco sauce

1. Fill shot glass with chilled Cuervo gold tequila
2. Add a dash of Tabasco

PREAKNESS

1½ oz. blended whiskey
¼ oz. Bénédictine
¼ oz. sweet vermouth
dash Angostura bitters

1. Fill mixing glass with ice
2. Add blended whiskey, Bénédictine, sweet vermouth and bitters
3. Shake
4. Strain into a chilled cocktail glass

PRESBYTERIAN

1 oz. whiskey
club soda
ginger ale

1. Fill a highball glass with ice
2. Add whiskey
3. Fill glass half with club soda, half with ginger ale
4. Stir well
5. Garnish with a twist of lemon

PRESIDENTE

1½ oz. light rum
½ oz. dry vermouth
1 tbsp. curaçao
dash grenadine

1. Fill mixing glass with ice
2. Add light rum, dry vermouth, curaçao and grenadine
3. Shake
4. Strain into a chilled cocktail glass
5. Garnish with a twist of lemon

PRINCE

1½ oz. blended whiskey
2 dashes orange bitters
3 drops white crème de menthe

1. Fill mixing glass with ice
2. Add blended whiskey and orange bitters
3. Shake

4. Strain into a rocks glass filled with ice
5. Top with a few drops of white crème de menthe

PRINCE EDWARD

1½ oz. scotch
½ oz. Lillet
1 tbsp. Drambuie

1. Fill mixing glass with ice
2. Add scotch, Lillet and Drambuie
3. Shake
4. Strain into a rocks glass filled with ice
5. Garnish with a slice of orange

PRINCE OF WALES

1 oz. madeira
1 oz. brandy
3–4 drops curaçao
2 dashes Angostura bitters
chilled champagne

1. Fill mixing glass with ice
2. Add madeira, brandy, curaçao and bitters
3. Shake
4. Strain into a chilled champagne glass
5. Fill with champagne
6. Garnish with a slice of orange

PRINCESS MARY'S PRIDE

1½ oz. apple brandy
2 tbsp. Dubonnet (rouge)
1 tbsp. dry vermouth

1. Fill mixing glass with ice
2. Add apple brandy, Dubonnet and dry vermouth
3. Shake
4. Strain into a rocks glass filled with ice

PRINCE'S SMILE

1 oz. gin
½ oz. apricot brandy
½ oz. apple brandy
dash lemon juice

1. Fill mixing glass with ice
2. Add gin, apricot brandy, apple brandy and lemon juice
3. Shake
4. Strain into a chilled cocktail glass

PRINCETON

1½ oz. gin
¾ oz. port
3–4 dashes orange bitters

1. Fill mixing glass with ice
2. Add gin, port and orange bitters
3. Shake
4. Strain into a chilled cocktail glass
5. Garnish with a twist of lemon

PROHIBITION

1 oz. gin
1 oz. Lillet
2 dashes orange juice
dash apricot brandy

1. Fill mixing glass with ice
2. Add gin, Lillet, orange juice and apricot brandy
3. Shake
4. Strain into a chilled cocktail glass
5. Garnish with a twist of lemon

PUMPKIN PIE MARTINI

½ oz. Stoli Vanil (vanilla vodka)
1 oz. pumpkin spice liqueur
½ oz. Kahlúa
½ oz. butterscotch schnapps
½ oz. half-and-half
graham crackers, crushed

1. Add all liquids in a shaker filled with ice
2. Shake and strain into large martini glass rimmed with crushed graham crackers
3. Garnish with a cinnamon stick

PUNT E MES NEGRONI

½ oz. gin
½ oz. Punt e Mes
½ oz. sweet vermouth

1. Fill mixing glass with ice
2. Add gin, Punt e Mes and sweet vermouth
3. Shake
4. Strain into a chilled cocktail glass
5. Garnish with a twist of orange

(*Note:* This drink may also be made with vodka instead of gin.)

PURPLE HAZE (SHOOTER)

½ oz. sambuca
½ oz. Chambord

1. Pour sambuca into a shot glass
2. Slowly add Chambord

THE PURPLE HOOTER SHOOTER*

3 oz. Absolut vodka
1 oz. Rose's lime juice
dash Chambord (for color)

(MAKES APPROXIMATELY 2 SHOTS)

1. Fill mixing glass with ice
2. Add Absolut, lime juice and Chambord
3. Stir
4. Strain into shot glasses

PURPLE PASSION

1½ oz. vodka
grape juice

1. Fill a highball glass with ice
2. Add vodka
3. Fill with grape juice
4. Stir

---

* Originated by Coleen Patrick, New York City.

PURPLE PEOPLE EATER

½ oz. vodka
½ oz. gin
¾ oz. rum
½ oz. tequila
½ oz. triple sec
½ oz. blue curaçao
sour mix
7-Up
dash grenadine

1. Fill a highball glass with ice
2. Add vodka, gin, rum, tequila, triple sec and blue curaçao
3. Top with sour mix
4. Fill with 7-Up
5. Add grenadine for color

QUAKER

1 oz. brandy	1. Fill mixing glass with ice
¾ oz. light rum	2. Add brandy, light rum, lemon
½ oz. lemon juice	juice and raspberry syrup
½ oz. raspberry syrup	3. Shake
	4. Strain into a chilled cocktail glass
	5. Garnish with a twist of lemon

QUARTER DECK

1½ oz. light rum	1. Fill mixing glass with ice
1 tbsp. sherry	2. Add light rum, sherry and lime
1 tsp. lime juice	juice
	3. Shake
	4. Strain into a rocks glass filled
	with ice

QUEBEC COCKTAIL

1½ oz. Canadian whiskey	1. Fill mixing glass with ice
½ oz. Amer Picon	2. Add whiskey, Amer Picon, dry
½ oz. dry vermouth	vermouth and cherry liqueur

½ oz. cherry liqueur

3. Shake
4. Strain into a chilled cocktail glass

QUEEN

several pineapple chunks
1½ oz. gin
¾ oz. sweet vermouth

1. In a mixing glass, muddle the pineapple chunks
2. Add ice, gin and sweet vermouth
3. Stir well
4. Strain into a rocks glass filled with ice

QUEEN ELIZABETH

1½ oz. gin
½ oz. Cointreau
½ oz. lemon juice
1 tsp. Pernod

1. Fill mixing glass with ice
2. Add gin, Cointreau, lemon juice and Pernod
3. Stir well
4. Strain into a chilled cocktail glass

QUEEN ELIZABETH WINE COCKTAIL

1½ oz. Bénédictine
¾ oz. dry vermouth
¾ oz. lemon juice

1. Fill mixing glass with ice
2. Add Bénédictine, dry vermouth and lemon juice
3. Stir well
4. Strain into a chilled cocktail glass

QUELLE VIE

1½ oz. brandy ¾ oz. kümmel	1. Fill mixing glass with ice 2. Add brandy and kümmel 3. Stir 4. Strain into a chilled cocktail glass

QUICKIE

1 oz. bourbon 1 oz. light rum ¼ oz. triple sec	1. Fill mixing glass with ice 2. Add bourbon, light rum and triple sec 3. Stir well 4. Strain into a chilled cocktail glass

RACQUET CLUB

1½ oz. gin
¾ oz. dry vermouth
dash orange bitters

1. Fill mixing glass with ice
2. Add gin, dry vermouth and
   orange bitters
3. Stir
4. Strain into a chilled cocktail glass

RAINBOW POUSSE-CAFÉ

½ oz. dark crème de cacao
½ oz. crème de violette
½ oz. yellow Chartreuse
½ oz. maraschino liqueur
½ oz. Bénédictine
½ oz. green Chartreuse
½ oz. cognac

1. Pour dark crème de cacao into
   pousse-café glass
2. Float each of the other
   ingredients, one on top of the
   other, in the order indicated

RAMOS FIZZ

1 oz. gin
½ oz. cream
1½ oz. sour mix

1. Fill mixing glass with ice
2. Add gin, cream, sour mix,
   orange juice and egg white

344

2 dashes orange juice
1 egg white
club soda

3. Shake
4. Strain into a chilled Collins glass
5. Fill with club soda

RAMOS GIN FIZZ

1½ oz. gin (such as Taaka or Tanqueray)
1 tsp. simple syrup
2 oz. half-and-half
1 egg white
⅛ tsp. vanilla extract
½ oz. orange flower water
1 oz. lemon-lime soda

1. In bottom part of cocktail shaker, combine the first 6 ingredients (except soda)
2. Blend with stick or immersion blender for 30 seconds
3. Partly fill highball or old-fashioned glass with 3 or 4 large ice cubes
4. Pour in drink
5. Top with soda
6. Garnish with orange wedge

RASPBERRY SMASH

1 oz. Absolut vodka
½ oz. Chambord
2 oz. pineapple juice

1. Fill mixing glass with ice
2. Add Absolut, Chambord and pineapple juice
3. Shake
4. Strain into a rocks glass filled with ice

RASPBERRY CHOCOLATE MARTINI

¼ cup mint-infused simple syrup, plus more for rim
3 chocolate cookies, finely crushed, such as Nabisco Famous Chocolate Wafers
10 raspberries

1. Fill a shallow dish with enough simple syrup to just cover the bottom
2. Place crushed cookies into another shallow dish
3. Invert a martini glass into simple syrup

¼ cup vodka
2 tablespoons cranberry
juice

and then immediately into crushed cookies to coat the rim of the glass
4. Place raspberries in a cocktail shaker; crush with a muddler
5. Add simple syrup and muddle again
6. Add vodka and cranberry juice; fill shaker with ice cubes
7. Shake well until chilled
8. Strain into prepared martini glass
9. Serve immediately

RASPBERRY VODKA

1 liter premium vodka
2 cups sugar
1 lb. fresh raspberries

1. In a container, combine vodka, sugar and raspberries
2. Cover tightly
3. Store container in a cool, dark place for approximately 8 weeks (every week or so, open container and stir mixture)
4. Using a sieve, strain mixture into a glass jar
5. Refrigerate or store in freezer
6. Serve straight up or on the rocks

RATTLESNAKE

1½ oz. blended whiskey
1 tsp. lemon juice
1 tsp. sugar
1 egg white

1. Fill mixing glass with ice
2. Add blended whiskey, lemon juice, sugar, egg white and Pernod

¼ tsp. Pernod

3. Shake
4. Strain into a rocks glass filled with ice

RED APPLE

1 oz. 100-proof vodka
1 oz. apple juice
½ oz. lemon juice
3–4 dashes grenadine
1–2 dashes orange bitters
   (optional)

1. Fill mixing glass with ice
2. Add vodka, apple juice, lemon juice, grenadine and orange bitters
3. Shake
4. Strain into a rocks glass filled with ice

RED BARON

2 oz. gin
½ oz. sour mix
½ oz. orange juice
dash grenadine

1. Fill mixing glass with ice
2. Add gin, sour mix, orange juice and grenadine
3. Shake
4. Strain into a chilled cocktail glass

RED CLOUD

1½ oz. gin
½ oz. apricot liqueur
½ oz. lemon juice
3 dashes grenadine
2 dashes Angostura bitters

1. Fill mixing glass with ice
2. Add gin, apricot liqueur, lemon juice, grenadine and bitters
3. Shake
4. Strain into a rocks glass filled with ice

RED DEVIL

½ oz. sloe gin
½ oz. vodka
½ oz. Southern Comfort
½ oz. triple sec
½ oz. banana liqueur
2 tbsp. Rose's lime juice
2 oz. orange juice

1. Fill mixing glass with ice
2. Add all ingredients
3. Shake well
4. Pour into a Collins glass

RED LION COCKTAIL

1 oz. gin
1 oz. Grand Marnier
½ oz. orange juice
½ oz. lemon juice

1. Fill mixing glass with ice
2. Add gin, Grand Marnier, orange juice and lemon juice
3. Shake
4. Strain into a chilled cocktail glass

RED SNAPPER

1 oz. gin
Bloody Mary mix (packaged or from scratch—see Bloody Mary)

1. Fill a highball glass with ice
2. Add gin
3. Fill with Bloody Mary mix
4. Stir well
5. Garnish with lime slice or celery stalk

REFORM

1½ oz. dry sherry
¾ oz. dry vermouth
dash orange bitters

1. Fill mixing glass with ice
2. Add dry sherry, dry vermouth and orange bitters
3. Strain into a chilled cocktail glass

RENAISSANCE COCKTAIL

1½ oz. gin
½ oz. dry sherry
1 tbsp. cream

1. Fill mixing glass with ice
2. Add gin, dry sherry and cream
3. Shake
4. Strain into a chilled cocktail glass
5. Garnish with a sprinkle of nutmeg

RENDEZVOUS

1½ oz. gin
½ oz. kirschwasser
½ oz. Campari

1. Fill mixing glass with ice
2. Add gin, kirschwasser and Campari
3. Shake
4. Strain into a chilled cocktail glass
5. Garnish with a lemon twist

RESOLUTE

1½ oz. gin
1 tbsp. apricot brandy
½ oz. lemon juice

1. Fill mixing glass with ice
2. Add gin, apricot brandy and lemon juice
3. Shake
4. Strain into a rocks glass filled with ice

RHETT BUTLER

1 oz. Southern Comfort
½ oz. lime juice
½ oz. lemon juice
1 tsp. curaçao
½ tsp. sugar

1. Fill mixing glass with ice
2. Add Southern Comfort, lime juice, lemon juice, curaçao and sugar
3. Shake
4. Strain into a rocks glass filled with ice

RHUBARB FIX

1½ oz. gin
1 oz. manzanilla sherry
¾ oz. rhubarb syrup
juice from ½ lemon

1. Add all the ingredients to a shaker and fill with ice
2. Shake, and strain into a rocks glass filled with crushed ice
3. Garnish with a mint sprig

TO MAKE RHUBARB SYRUP

2 quarts (64 oz.) water
8 cups sugar
4 cups rhubarb, roughly chopped

1. Add all the ingredients to a saucepan and cook over low heat, stirring until the sugar dissolves
2. Cook for 5 minutes more, turn off the heat and let cool completely
3. Strain and store in the refrigerator for up to a month

RICKEY

1½ oz. liquor (of choice)
club soda

1. Fill a highball glass with ice
2. Add liquor
3. Fill with club soda
4. Garnish with a twist of lime

ROASTED TOASTED ALMOND

¾ oz. vodka
¾ oz. Kahlúa
¾ oz. amaretto
¾ oz. cream

1. Fill mixing glass with ice
2. Add vodka, Kahlúa, amaretto and cream
3. Shake
4. Strain into a chilled cocktail glass

ROB ROY

¼ oz. sweet vermouth
1½ oz. scotch

1. Fill a rocks glass with ice
2. Pour in sweet vermouth, then scotch
3. Stir
4. Garnish with a cherry

(*Note:* If serving "straight up," mix scotch and vermouth in a mixing glass and strain into a martini glass.)

ROB ROY (DRY)

¼ oz. dry vermouth
1½ oz. scotch

1. Fill a rocks glass with ice
2. Pour in dry vermouth, then scotch
3. Stir
4. Garnish with an olive

(*Note:* If serving "straight up," mix scotch and vermouth in a mixing glass and strain into a martini glass.)

ROB ROY (PERFECT)

⅛ oz. dry vermouth
⅛ oz. sweet vermouth
1½ oz. scotch

1. Fill a rocks glass with ice
2. Pour in dry vermouth and sweet vermouth, then scotch
3. Stir
4. Garnish with a twist of lemon

(*Note:* If serving "straight up," mix scotch and vermouths in a mixing glass and strain into a martini glass.)

ROBSON

1½ oz. Jamaican rum
1 tbsp. orange juice
1 tsp. grenadine
1 tsp. lemon juice

1. Fill mixing glass with ice
2. Add Jamaican rum, orange juice, grenadine and lemon juice
3. Shake
4. Strain into a rocks glass filled with ice

ROCKAWAY BEACH

1½ oz. light rum
½ oz. dark rum
½ oz. tequila
1 oz. orange juice
½ oz. pineapple juice
½ oz. cranberry juice cocktail
1 tsp. crème de noyaux

1. Fill mixing glass with 4 oz. cracked ice
2. Add light rum, dark rum, tequila, orange juice, pineapple juice, cranberry juice and crème de noyaux
3. Shake
4. Strain into a chilled Collins glass
5. Add ice
6. Garnish with a cherry

ROCK LOBSTER (SHOOTER)

⅓ oz. Baileys Original Irish Cream
⅓ oz. amaretto
⅓ oz. white crème de cacao

Layer Baileys, amaretto and white crème de cacao in a shot glass

ROCKY GREEN DRAGON

1½ oz. gin
½ oz. green Chartreuse
½ oz. cognac

1. Fill mixing glass with ice
2. Add gin, green Chartreuse and cognac

3. Shake
4. Strain into a rocks glass filled with ice

ROLLS-ROYCE

1½ oz. gin	1. Fill mixing glass with ice
½ oz. dry vermouth	2. Add gin, dry vermouth, sweet
½ oz. sweet vermouth	vermouth and Bénédictine
3–4 dashes Bénédictine	3. Stir
	4. Strain into a chilled cocktail glass

ROMAN STINGER

1½ oz. brandy	1. Fill mixing glass with ice
¾ oz. sambuca	2. Add brandy, sambuca and white
¾ oz white crème de menthe	crème de menthe
	3. Shake
	4. Strain into a chilled cocktail glass

ROSE HALL

1½ oz. Jamaican rum	1. Fill mixing glass with ice
½ oz. banana liqueur	2. Add rum, banana liqueur,
1 oz. orange juice	orange juice and lime juice
1 tsp. Rose's lime juice	3. Shake
	4. Strain into a chilled cocktail glass
	5. Garnish with a slice of lime

ROSY RUM COSMO

1½ oz. Bacardi Limón Rum	1. Pour the rum, triple sec, lime
½ oz. triple sec orange liqueur	juice and cranberry juice into a cocktail shaker with ice

1 tbsp. lime juice
½ tbsp. cranberry juice

2. Shake well
3. Strain into chilled cocktail glass
4. Garnish with a mint leaf

ROUFFY PARTY PUNCH COOLER

1 liter vodka
1 6-oz. can frozen lemonade concentrate, defrosted
1 6-oz. can frozen orange juice concentrate, defrosted
1 cup water
7-Up

1. In a large bowl, combine vodka, frozen juice concentrates and water
2. Stir well
3. Place in freezer until frozen
4. When ready to serve, use an ice-cream scooper to shave off some of the concoction into highball glasses
5. Fill with 7-Up

ROYAL FIZZ

1 oz. gin
2 oz. sour mix
1 egg
club soda

1. Fill mixing glass with ice
2. Add gin, sour mix and egg
3. Shake
4. Strain into a chilled Collins glass
5. Fill with club soda

ROYAL GIN FIZZ

2 oz. gin
½ oz. Grand Marnier
1 oz. sour mix
1 egg
club soda

1. Fill mixing glass with ice
2. Add gin, Grand Marnier, sour mix and egg
3. Shake
4. Strain into a chilled sour glass
5. Fill with club soda
6. Garnish with a slice of lemon

ROYAL PEACH FREEZE

1½ oz. champagne
2 oz. peach schnapps
2 oz. orange juice
½ oz. Rose's lime juice

1. In blender, combine champagne, peach schnapps, orange juice and Rose's lime juice with 3 oz. crushed ice
2. Blend until smooth
3. Pour into a goblet

ROYAL SCREW

2 oz. cognac
2 oz. orange juice, chilled
champagne

1. Pour cognac into a champagne glass
2. Add orange juice
3. Stir gently
4. Fill with champagne

ROYAL SMILE

1½ oz. gin
1 oz. grenadine
3–4 drops lemon juice

1. Fill mixing glass with ice
2. Add gin, grenadine and lemon juice
3. Shake
4. Strain into a chilled cocktail glass

RUBY FIZZ

2 oz. sloe gin
½ oz. lemon juice
1 tsp. sugar
1 tsp. grenadine
1 egg white
club soda

1. Fill mixing glass with ice
2. Add sloe gin, lemon juice, sugar, grenadine and egg white
3. Shake
4. Strain into a chilled highball glass
5. Add ice
6. Fill with club soda

RUM AND ORANGE JUICE

1½ oz. rum (usually dark rum)
orange juice

1. Fill a highball glass with ice
2. Add rum
3. Fill with orange juice
4. Stir

RUM AND TONIC

1½ oz. rum (light or dark, depending on taste)
tonic water

1. Fill a highball glass with ice
2. Add rum
3. Fill with tonic water
4. Stir
5. Garnish with a slice of lime (optional)

RUM COLLINS

2 oz. light rum
1 tsp. sugar syrup
½ oz. lime juice
club soda

1. Fill a Collins glass with ice
2. Add light rum, sugar syrup and lime juice
3. Stir well
4. Fill with club soda
5. Garnish with a slice of lime

RUM CURAÇAO COOLER

1½ oz. dark rum
1½ oz. curaçao
½ oz. lime juice
club soda

1. Fill mixing glass with ice
2. Add dark rum, curaçao and lime juice
3. Shake
4. Strain into a highball glass filled with ice
5. Fill with club soda
6. Garnish with a slice of orange

RUM NUT

1 oz. rum ½ oz. Kahlúa cream of coconut	1. Fill mixing glass with ice 2. Add rum, Kahlúa and cream of coconut 3. Pour into a highball glass with ice

RUM RICKEY

1½ oz. light rum ½ oz. lime juice 1 tsp. sugar syrup (optional) club soda	1. Fill mixing glass with ice 2. Add light rum and lime juice (and sugar syrup, if desired) 3. Shake 4. Strain into a Collins glass filled with ice 5. Fill with club soda 6. Garnish with a wedge of lime

RUM RUNNER

1 cup ice 1 oz. dark rum ½ oz. blackberry brandy ½ oz. banana liqueur ½ oz. grenadine 2 oz. sour mix ¼ oz. rum (151 proof)	1. In a blender, put 1 cup ice 2. Add dark rum, blackberry brandy, banana liqueur, grenadine and sour mix 3. Blend until thick 4. Pour into a margarita glass 5. Float 151-proof rum on top 6. Garnish with a cherry

RUM SOUR

2 oz. light rum (dark rum may be used instead) 1 tsp. lime juice 1 oz. sour mix dash orange juice	1. Fill mixing glass with ice 2. Add rum, lime juice, sour mix and orange juice 3. Shake 4. Strain into a sour glass

5. Fill with ice
6. Garnish with a cherry and an orange slice

RUPTURED DUCK

1 oz. banana liqueur
1 oz. creme de noyaux
1 oz. cream

1. Fill mixing glass with ice
2. Add banana liqueur, crème de noyaux and cream
3. Shake
4. Strain into a chilled cocktail glass

RUSSIAN

1 oz. gin
1 oz. vodka
1 oz. white crème de cacao

1. Fill mixing glass with ice
2. Add gin, vodka and white crème de cacao
3. Shake
4. Strain into a chilled cocktail glass

RUSSIAN BANANA

¾ oz. vodka
¾ oz. banana liqueur
¾ oz. dark crème de cacao
1 oz. cream

1. Fill mixing glass with ice
2. Add vodka, banana liqueur, dark crème de cacao and cream
3. Shake
4. Strain into a chilled cocktail glass

RUSSIAN BEAR

1 oz. vodka
1 oz. dark crème de cacao
1 oz. heavy cream

1. Fill mixing glass with ice
2. Add vodka, dark crème de cacao and heavy cream
3. Shake
4. Strain into a chilled cocktail glass

RUSSIAN COFFEE

¾ oz. vodka
¾ oz. coffee liqueur
¾ oz. heavy cream

1. Fill blender with 3 oz. cracked ice
2. Add vodka, coffee liqueur and heavy cream
3. Blend for 5 seconds, or until smooth
4. Pour into a cocktail glass

RUSSIAN QUAALUDE

⅓ oz. Frangelico
⅓ oz. Baileys Original Irish Cream
⅓ oz. vodka

1. Layer Frangelico, Baileys and vodka in a rocks glass without ice

RUSSIAN ROSE

2 oz. vodka
2 tbsp. grenadine
dash orange bitters

1. Fill mixing glass with ice
2. Add vodka, grenadine and orange bitters
3. Shake
4. Strain into a chilled cocktail glass

RUSSIAN TURKEY

2 oz. vodka
2 oz. cranberry juice cocktail

1. Fill a rocks glass with ice
2. Add vodka and cranberry juice
3. Stir

RUSTY NAIL

2 oz. scotch
1 oz. Drambuie

1. Fill a rocks glass with ice
2. Add scotch and Drambuie
3. Stir

S

ST. PATRICK'S DAY MOCHA JAVA*

¾ oz. Baileys Original Irish Cream	1. Pour Baileys and Kahlúa into a mug
¾ oz. Kahlúa	2. Fill with hot coffee
hot coffee	3. Top with whipped cream
whipped cream	

SAKETINI

2½ oz. gin	1. Fill mixing glass with ice
½ oz. sake	2. Add gin and sake
	3. Stir
	4. Strain into a chilled cocktail glass or a rocks glass filled with ice
	5. Garnish with a twist of lemon

SALTY DOG

1½ oz. vodka	1. Salt the rim of a highball glass
grapefruit juice	2. Fill with ice
	3. Add vodka
	4. Fill with grapefruit juice
	5. Stir

---

* Courtesy of Carrow's, Santa Barbara, California.

SAMBUCA-GIN SHAKE

2 oz. gin
½ oz. sambuca
1 egg white
½ oz. cream

1. Half-fill mixing glass with crushed ice
2. Add gin, sambuca, egg white and cream
3. Shake
4. Pour into a rocks glass

SANCTUARY

1½ oz. Dubonnet (rouge)
¾ oz. Amer Picon
¾ oz. Cointreau

1. Fill mixing glass with ice
2. Add Dubonnet, Amer Picon and Cointreau
3. Shake
4. Strain into a rocks glass filled with ice

SAN FRANCISCO

¾ oz. sloe gin
½ oz. dry vermouth
½ oz. sweet vermouth
dash Angostura bitters
dash orange bitters

1. Fill mixing glass with ice
2. Add sloe gin, dry vermouth, sweet vermouth, Angostura bitters and orange bitters
3. Shake
4. Strain into a rocks glass filled with ice
5. Garnish with a cherry

SANGRIA

1 bottle dry red wine
1 oz. brandy (optional)
1 oz. triple sec or curaçao (optional)

1. In a large pitcher, combine red wine, brandy, triple sec, sugar and fruit
2. Refrigerate overnight

1 tbsp. sugar or to taste
club soda, very cold
orange slices
lime slices
lemon slice
several pineapple chunks

(For a white sangria, substitute
white wine for red wine.)

3. When ready to serve, add club
   soda and more sugar (if desired)
4. Stir

SANGRIA ESPECIALE

2 bottles red wine
1 bottle champagne
4 oz. gin
4 oz. cognac
sugar, to taste
juice of 2 oranges
juice of 2 lemons

1. Add all ingredients to a punch
   bowl
2. Stir
3. Add ice
4. Garnish with slices of oranges
   and lemons

SANGRIA SHABBABE

1 tbsp. sugar
1 tbsp. lemon juice
2 oz. red wine
1 oz. white wine
1 oz. orange juice
7-Up
fresh orange and lemon
   slices

1. In a bottle or large wineglass,
   dissolve sugar in lemon juice
2. Fill the bottle or glass with ice
3. Pour in red wine, white wine
   and orange juice
4. Stir well
5. Fill with 7-Up
6. Garnish with orange and lemon
   slices

SAN JUAN

1½ oz. Puerto Rican rum
1 oz. grapefruit juice
1 oz. lime juice
½ oz. cream of coconut
2–3 dashes 151-proof rum

1. In a blender, combine 3 oz. crushed ice, Puerto Rican rum, grapefruit juice, lime juice and cream of coconut
2. Blend for 10 seconds at medium speed, or until smooth
3. Pour into a goblet or large wineglass
4. Top with 151–proof rum

SAN SEBASTIAN

1 oz. gin
1½ tsp. light rum
1½ tsp. triple sec
1 tbsp. grapefruit juice
1 tbsp. lemon juice

1. Fill mixing glass with ice
2. Add gin, light rum, triple sec, grapefruit juice and lemon juice
3. Shake
4. Strain into a chilled cocktail glass

SAPPHIRE MARTINI*

¼ oz. Chambraise
1½ oz. Bombay Sapphire gin

1. Fill mixing glass with ice
2. Add Chambraise and Bombay Sapphire gin
3. Stir
4. Strain into a chilled cocktail glass or a rocks glass filled with ice
5. Garnish with a fresh strawberry

---

* Courtesy of Oscar Taylor's, Phoenix, Arizona.

SARATOGA

2 oz. brandy	1. Fill mixing glass with ice
1 oz. crushed pineapple	2. Add brandy, crushed pineapple, maraschino liqueur and bitters
2 dashes maraschino liqueur	3. Shake
2 dashes Angostura bitters	4. Strain into a chilled cocktail glass

SAUCY SUE

2 oz. apple brandy	1. Fill mixing glass with ice
½ tsp. apricot brandy	2. Add apple brandy, apricot brandy and Pernod
½ tsp. Pernod	3. Stir
	4. Strain into a chilled cocktail glass

SAVE THE PLANET

1 oz. vodka	1. Fill shaker glass with ice
1 oz. Midori melon liqueur	2. Add vodka, Midori and blue curaçao
½ oz. blue curaçao	3. Shake
1–2 dashes green Chartreuse	4. Strain into a chilled cocktail glass
	5. Float green Chartreuse on top

SAVOY HOTEL

½ oz. white crème de cacao	Slowly layer ingredients, beginning with white crème de cacao, into a pony glass
½ oz. Bénédictine	
½ oz. brandy	

SAVOY SPRINGTIME*

| ¼ oz. gin
¼ oz. Cointreau
¼ oz. fresh orange juice
chilled champagne | 1. Pour gin, Cointreau and orange juice into a champagne glass
2. Fill with chilled champagne
3. Stir very gently |

SAVOY TANGO

| 1½ oz. apple brandy
1 oz. sloe gin | 1. Fill mixing glass with ice
2. Add apple brandy and sloe gin
3. Stir
4. Strain into a chilled cocktail glass |

SAZERAC

| 2 oz. bourbon
1 tsp. superfine granulated sugar
2 dashes Angostura bitters
3 dashes Pernod | 1. Pour bourbon into a mixing glass
2. Add sugar and bitters
3. Stir until sugar is dissolved
4. Put Pernod into a rocks glass
5. Strain mixture into rocks glass
6. Fill with ice |

SCARLETT O'HARA

| 1½ oz. Southern Comfort
cranberry juice cocktail (grenadine may be substituted) | 1. Fill a highball glass with ice
2. Add Southern Comfort
3. Fill with cranberry juice |

---

* From the Savoy Hotel, London, England.

SCOOBY SNACKS

¾ oz. vodka
¾ oz. Midori melon liqueur
¾ oz. Malibu
1 oz. pineapple juice
½ oz. cream

1. Fill mixing glass with ice
2. Add vodka, Midori, Malibu, pineapple juice and cream
3. Shake
4. Strain into a rocks glass filled with ice

SCORPION

2 oz. light rum
1 oz. brandy
2 oz. orange juice
½ oz. lemon juice
½ oz. crème de noyaux

1. Fill blender with 3 oz. crushed ice, light rum, brandy, orange juice, lemon juice and crème de noyaux
2. Blend until smooth
3. Pour into a highball glass
4. Garnish with a slice of orange

SCOTCH AND SODA

1½ oz. scotch
club soda

1. Fill a highball glass with ice
2. Add scotch
3. Fill with club soda
4. Stir gently

SCOTCH MIST

1½ oz. scotch

1. Fill a rocks glass with crushed ice
2. Add scotch
3. Garnish with a twist of lemon

SCOTCH STONE SOUR

1½ oz. Scotch whiskey
¾ oz. lemon juice
1 tsp. sugar
1½ oz. orange juice

1. Fill mixing glass with ice
2. Add scotch, lemon juice, sugar and orange juice
3. Shake
4. Strain into a sour glass or a rocks glass filled with ice
5. Garnish with a cherry and a slice of orange

SCOTTISH COFFEE

1½ oz. Drambuie
hot coffee
whipped cream

1. Pour Drambuie into a coffee mug
2. Fill with hot coffee
3. Top with whipped cream

SCREAMING ORGASM

½ oz. vodka
½ oz. Baileys Original Irish Cream
½ oz. amaretto
½ oz. Kahlúa

1. Fill mixing glass with ice
2. Add vodka, Baileys, amaretto and Kahlúa
3. Shake
4. Strain into a rocks glass filled with ice

SCREWDRIVER

1½ oz. vodka
orange juice

1. Fill a highball glass with ice
2. Add vodka
3. Fill with orange juice
4. Stir

SEA BREEZE

1½ oz. vodka
3 oz. cranberry juice cocktail
3 oz. grapefruit juice

1. Fill a highball glass with ice
2. Add vodka, cranberry juice and grapefruit juice
3. Stir

(*Note:* In general, people usually like a bit more cranberry juice than grapefruit juice, but it is purely a matter of taste.)

SELF-STARTER

1 oz. gin
½ oz. Lillet
1 tsp. apricot brandy
2–3 drops Pernod

1. Fill mixing glass with ice
2. Add gin, Lillet, apricot brandy and Pernod
3. Shake
4. Strain into a chilled cocktail glass

SEPARATOR (ALSO CALLED A DIRTY MOTHER)

1½ oz. brandy
¾ oz. Kahlúa

1. Fill a rocks glass with ice
2. Add brandy and Kahlúa
3. Stir

SEPTEMBER MORN

2½ oz. light rum
½ oz. lime juice
1 tsp. grenadine
1 egg white

1. Fill mixing glass with ice
2. Add light rum, lime juice, grenadine and egg white
3. Shake
4. Strain into a chilled highball glass

7 & 7

1½ oz. Seagram's 7 blended whiskey **7-Up**	1. Fill a highball glass with ice 2. Add Seagram's 7 3. Fill with 7-Up 4. Garnish with cherry and an orange slice (optional) or a twist of lemon (optional)

SEVENTH HEAVEN

1 oz. Seagram's 7 whiskey **¼ oz. amaretto** **orange juice**	1. Fill a highball glass with ice 2. Add Seagram's 7 and amaretto 3. Fill with orange juice 4. Stir

SEVILLA

1 oz. dark Jamaican rum **1 oz. sweet vermouth**	1. Fill mixing glass with ice 2. Add dark Jamaican rum and sweet vermouth 3. Shake 4. Strain into a rocks glass filled with ice 5. Garnish with a twist of orange

SEVILLE

1½ oz. gin **½ oz. fino sherry** **½ oz. lemon juice** **½ oz. orange juice** **2 tsp. sugar syrup**	1. Half-fill mixing glass with ice 2. Add gin, fino sherry, lemon juice, orange juice and sugar syrup 3. Shake 4. Pour into a rocks glass

SEX ON THE BEACH

¾ oz. peach schnapps	1. Fill a highball glass with ice
¾ oz. vodka	2. Add peach schnapps and vodka
¾ oz. pineapple juice (grapefruit juice may be substituted)	3. Fill with pineapple juice (or grapefruit juice) and cranberry juice
3 oz. cranberry juice cocktail	4. Stir

SEX ON THE BEACH (THE ORIGINAL)

1 oz. vodka	1. Fill mixing glass with ice
½ oz. Midori melon liqueur	2. Add vodka, Midori, Chambord, pineapple juice and cranberry juice
½ oz. Chambord (or other raspberry liqueur)	3. Shake
1½ oz. pineapple juice	4. Pour into a highball glass
1½ oz. cranberry juice cocktail	

(*Note:* This can also be made into a shooter. This recipe will yield approximately 3 shots. You may want to cut down on the juices a bit.)

SEX ON THE BEACH IN WINTER

¾ oz. peach schnapps	1. Fill blender with 3 oz. ice, peach schnapps, vodka, pineapple juice (or grapefruit juice), cranberry juice and cream of coconut
¾ oz. vodka	
3 oz. pineapple juice (grapefruit juice may be substituted)	2. Blend until smooth
3 oz. cranberry juice cocktail	3. Pour into a goblet or Collins glass
½ tsp. cream of coconut	

SHANDY

| cold beer
1 oz. 7-Up | 1. Fill beer mug with cold beer (preferably draft beer)
2. Top with 7-Up |

SHANGHAI

| 1½ oz. dark rum
1 oz. sambuca
½ oz. lemon juice
3 drops grenadine | 1. Fill mixing glass with ice
2. Add dark rum, sambuca, lemon juice and grenadine
3. Shake
4. Strain into a chilled cocktail glass |

SHARK BITE*

| 1½ oz. Myers's dark rum
3 oz. orange juice
½ oz. sour mix
¾ oz. grenadine | 1. Combine Myers's rum, orange juice, sour mix and grenadine with 3 oz. ice in a blender
2. Blend until smooth
3. Pour into a goblet
4. Add a couple of straws and watch the pinks separate |

SHARK'S TOOTH

| 1½ oz. dark Jamaican rum
½ oz. lime juice
½ oz. lemon juice
¼ oz. grenadine
club soda | 1. Fill mixing glass with ice
2. Add rum, lime juice, lemon juice and grenadine
3. Shake
4. Strain into a highball glass filled with ice
5. Fill with club soda |

* Courtesy of The Shark Bar, New York City.

SHARKY PUNCH

1½ oz. apple brandy ½ oz. rye whiskey 1 tsp. sugar syrup club soda	1. Fill mixing glass with ice 2. Add apple brandy, rye whiskey and sugar syrup 3. Shake 4. Strain into a rocks glass filled with ice 5. Fill with club soda

SHERRY COCKTAIL

2½ oz. cream sherry 1 dash Angostura bitters	1. Fill mixing glass with ice 2. Add cream sherry and bitters 3. Stir 4. Strain into a chilled cocktail glass

SHERRY EGGNOG

3 oz. sherry 1 egg 1 tsp. powdered sugar 1 cup milk	1. In a blender, combine 3 oz. crushed ice, sherry, egg, sugar and milk 2. Blend 3. Pour into a chilled goblet or Collins glass 4. Garnish with a pinch of nutmeg

SHERRY TWIST

3 oz. sherry 1 oz. brandy 1 oz. dry vermouth ½ oz. curaçao 2–3 dashes lemon juice	1. Fill mixing glass with ice 2. Add sherry, brandy, dry vermouth, curaçao and lemon juice 3. Shake 4. Strain into a chilled sour glass

5. Add ice, if desired
6. Garnish with a pinch of ground cinnamon

SHOTGUN WEDDING COCKTAIL

2 tsp. cherry liqueur
¾ oz. Dubonnet
¾ oz. gin
2 tsp. orange juice

1. Fill a shaker half full with ice cubes
2. Pour all ingredients into shaker and shake well
3. Strain drink into a cocktail glass and serve

SICILIAN KISS

1½ oz. Southern Comfort
½ oz. amaretto

1. Fill a rocks glass with ice
2. Add Southern Comfort and amaretto
3. Stir

SIDECAR

1½ oz. brandy
¾ oz. triple sec
¾ oz. sour mix

1. Fill mixing glass with ice
2. Add brandy, triple sec and sour mix
3. Shake
4. Strain into a chilled cocktail glass

SILK PANTIES (SHOOTER)

¾ oz. peach schnapps
¾ oz. sambuca

1. Fill mixing glass with ice
2. Add peach schnapps and sambuca

3. Stir
4. Strain into a shot glass

SILK STOCKINGS

2 oz. tequila
1 oz. white crème de cacao
2 oz. light cream
dash grenadine

1. Fill mixing glass with ice
2. Add tequila, white crème de cacao, light cream and grenadine
3. Shake
4. Strain into a chilled cocktail glass
5. Sprinkle with cinnamon

SILVER FIZZ

1 oz. gin
2 oz. sour mix
1 egg white
club soda

1. Fill mixing glass with ice
2. Add gin, sour mix and egg white
3. Shake
4. Strain into a chilled Collins glass
5. Fill with club soda

SILVER KING

1 oz. gin
1 oz. lemon juice
1 egg white
2–3 drops sugar syrup
2 dashes orange bitters

1. Fill mixing glass with ice
2. Add gin, lemon juice, egg white, sugar syrup and orange bitters
3. Shake
4. Strain into a highball glass
5. Fill with ice

SILVER NIPPLE

1½ oz. sambuca	1. Fill a rocks glass with ice
1 oz. vodka	2. Add sambuca and vodka
	3. Stir

SINGAPORE SLING

1 oz. gin	1. Fill mixing glass with ice
2 oz. sour mix	2. Add gin, sour mix and grenadine
½ oz. grenadine	3. Shake
club soda	4. Strain into a Collins glass filled with ice
1 dash cherry brandy	5. Fill with club soda
	6. Top with cherry brandy

SINK OR SWIM

1½ oz. brandy	1. Fill mixing glass with ice
½ oz. sweet vermouth	2. Add brandy, sweet vermouth and bitters
2–3 dashes Angostura bitters	3. Shake
	4. Strain into a rocks glass filled with ice

SIR WALTER

1½ oz. brandy	1. Fill mixing glass with ice
¾ oz. light rum	2. Add brandy, light rum, curaçao, grenadine and lime juice
1 tsp. curaçao	3. Shake
1 tsp. grenadine	4. Strain into a rocks glass filled with ice
1 tsp. lime juice	

SKIP AND GO NAKED

1 oz. gin	1. Fill a Collins glass with ice
2 oz. sour mix	2. Add gin and sour mix
beer	3. Fill with beer
	4. Stir

SLEDGEHAMMER

¾ oz. brandy	1. Fill mixing glass with ice
¾ oz. gold rum	2. Add brandy, gold rum, apple
¾ oz. apple brandy	brandy and Pernod
1 dash Pernod	3. Shake
	4. Strain into a chilled cocktail
	glass

SLEEPYHEAD

1 oz. brandy	1. Fill a rocks glass with ice
ginger ale	2. Add brandy
	3. Fill with ginger ale
	4. Garnish with orange zest and
	mint leaves

SLIMEBALL (SHOOTER)*

½ cup Midori melon liqueur	1. Add Midori and boiling water
1 cup boiling water	to lime Jell-O
lime Jell-O brand gelatin	2. Add vodka
½ cup vodka	3. Chill to set
	4. Serve in paper soufflé cups

---

* The Slimeball is a variation of the Jell-O Shot.

SLIPPERY NIPPLE

2 oz. sambuca
1½ oz. Baileys Original Irish
   Cream
drop grenadine

1. Pour sambuca into a cocktail glass
2. Float Baileys on top
3. Put a drop of grenadine right in the center

SLOE BRANDY

2 oz. brandy
½ oz. sloe gin
1 tsp. lemon juice

1. Fill mixing glass with ice
2. Add brandy, sloe gin and lemon juice
3. Shake
4. Strain into a chilled cocktail glass

SLOE COMFORTABLE SCREW

½ oz. vodka
½ oz. sloe gin
½ oz. Southern Comfort
orange juice

1. Fill a highball glass with ice
2. Add vodka, sloe gin and Southern Comfort
3. Fill with orange juice
4. Stir

SLOE GIN FIZZ

1 oz. sloe gin
2 oz. sour mix
club soda

1. Fill mixing glass with ice
2. Add sloe gin and sour mix
3. Shake
4. Strain into a chilled Collins glass
5. Fill with club soda
6. Garnish with a cherry

SLOE SCREW

¾ oz. vodka	1. Fill a highball glass with ice
¾ oz. sloe gin	2. Add vodka and sloe gin
orange juice	3. Fill with orange juice
	4. Stir

SLOE TEQUILA

2 oz. tequila	1. Fill mixing glass with ice
½ oz. sloe gin	2. Add tequila, sloe gin and lime juice
1 tsp. lime juice	3. Shake
	4. Strain into a chilled cocktail glass

SLOPPY JOE

½ oz. light rum	1. Fill mixing glass with ice
½ oz. dry vermouth	2. Add light rum, dry vermouth, lime juice, triple sec and grenadine
1 oz. lime juice	3. Shake
2–3 drops triple sec	4. Strain into a rocks glass filled with ice
2–3 drops grenadine	

SMITH AND KERNS

1½ oz. Kahlúa	1. Fill a highball glass with ice
1 oz. cream	2. Add Kahlúa and cream
club soda	3. Stir
	4. Fill with club soda
	5. Stir again, gently

SNACK BITE (SHOOTER)

| 2 oz. Canadian whiskey
1 oz. Rose's lime juice | 1. Pour whiskey and lime juice into a shot glass
2. Garnish with a lime wedge |

SNOWBALL

| 1 oz. gin
¼ oz. white crème de menthe
¼ oz. Pernod
¼ oz. crème d'Yvette
¼ oz. cream | 1. Fill mixing glass with ice
2. Add gin, white crème de menthe, Pernod, crème d'Yvette and cream
3. Shake
4. Strain into a chilled cocktail glass or champagne saucer |

SNOW CAP (SHOOTER)

| ½ oz. tequila
½ oz. Baileys Original Irish Cream | Layer tequila and Baileys in a shot glass |

SNOW SHOE (SHOOTER)

| 1½ oz. 101-proof Wild Turkey bourbon
½ oz. peppermint schnapps | 1. Fill a rocks glass with ice
2. Add Wild Turkey and peppermint schnapps
3. Stir |

SNUGGLER

| 1½ oz. peppermint schnapps
hot chocolate | 1. Pour peppermint schnapps into a mug
2. Fill with hot chocolate |

3. Top with whipped cream, if desired

S.O.B. SHOOTER (SHOOTER)

⅓ oz. Cointreau ⅓ oz. brandy ⅓ oz. 151-proof rum	Pour all ingredients into a shot glass

SOMBRERO

1½ oz. Kahlúa ½ oz. cream	1. Fill a rocks glass with ice 2. Add Kahlúa 3. Top with cream 4. Stir

SOUL KISS

1 oz. whiskey 1 oz. dry vermouth ½ oz. Dubonnet ¾ oz. orange juice	1. Fill mixing glass with ice 2. Add whiskey, dry vermouth, Dubonnet and orange juice 3. Stir 4. Strain into a rocks glass filled with ice

SOUR APPLE MARTINI

1½ oz. vodka 1 oz. sour apple schnapps ½ oz. sour mix ¼ oz. sugar syrup	1. Fill mixing glass with ice 2. Add vodka, sour apple schnapps, sour mix and sugar syrup 3. Shake 4. Strain into a chilled martini glass

5. Garnish with a thin green apple slice, lemon twist or cherry

SOUR GRAPES (SHOOTER)

2 oz. vodka
2 oz. Chambord
2 oz. sour mix

(MAKES ABOUT 4 SHOTS)

1. Fill mixing glass with ice
2. Add vodka, Chambord and sour mix
3. Shake
4. Strain into shot glasses

SOUTHERN BRIDE

1½ oz. gin
1 oz. grapefruit juice
1 dash maraschino liqueur

1. Fill mixing glass with ice
2. Add gin, grapefruit juice and maraschino liqueur
3. Shake
4. Strain into a chilled cocktail glass

SOUTHERN GIN

2½ oz. gin
2 dashes orange bitters
3–4 drops curaçao

1. Fill mixing glass with ice
2. Add gin, orange bitters and curaçao
3. Shake
4. Strain into a chilled cocktail glass

SOVIET COCKTAIL

1½ oz. vodka
½ oz. amontillado sherry
½ oz. dry vermouth

1. Fill mixing glass with ice
2. Add vodka, amontillado sherry and dry vermouth
3. Shake
4. Strain into a chilled cocktail glass

SPANISH COFFEE

¾ oz. brandy
¾ oz. Tia Maria
hot coffee

1. Pour brandy and Tia Maria into a coffee mug
2. Fill with hot coffee
3. Top with whipped cream, if desired

SPANISH MOSS

1½ oz. tequila
1 oz. coffee liqueur
3 drops green crème de menthe

1. Fill mixing glass with ice
2. Add tequila and coffee liqueur
3. Shake
4. Strain into a chilled cocktail glass
5. Add a few drops of green crème de menthe to top

SPANISH TOWN

1½ oz. light rum
2 dashes triple sec

1. Fill mixing glass with ice
2. Add light rum and triple sec
3. Stir
4. Strain into a chilled cocktail glass

SPARKLING PEAR COCKTAIL

1⅓ cups brut sparkling wine, chilled
⅔ cup pear liqueur

1. Combine wine and liqueur
2. Garnish with chilled pear slices, if desired

SPARKLING WINE JULEP

2 sprigs of mint
1 tbsp. sugar syrup
1½ oz. brandy
3 oz. chilled dry sparkling
wine

1. In a champagne glass, put 1
   sprig of mint and sugar syrup
2. Crush mint in sugar syrup
3. Fill glass with crushed ice
4. Add brandy
5. Fill with sparkling wine
6. Stir gently
7. Garnish with the other sprig of
   mint

SPARKLING WINE POLONAISE

1 tsp. blackberry liqueur
1 tsp. blackberry brandy
½ tsp. cognac
3 oz. chilled dry sparkling
wine

1. Moisten the rim of a chilled
   champagne glass with
   blackberry liqueur and
   sugar-frost the rim
2. Pour in blackberry brandy,
   cognac and sparkling wine
3. Stir very gently two or three times

SPECIAL ROUGH

1 oz. apple brandy
1 oz. brandy
dash Pernod

1. Fill mixing glass with ice
2. Add apple brandy, brandy and
   Pernod
3. Stir
4. Strain into a chilled cocktail glass

SPHINX

2 oz. gin
2 tsp. sweet vermouth
2 tsp. dry vermouth

1. Fill mixing glass with ice
2. Add gin, sweet vermouth and
   dry vermouth

3. Stir
4. Strain into a chilled cocktail glass
5. Garnish with a slice of lemon

SPICY HOT COCOA

4 cups whole milk
2 tbsp. unsweetened cocoa powder
2 tsp. vanilla extract
1 tsp. ground cinnamon
½ to 1 tsp. cayenne pepper
1 cup semisweet chocolate chips
4 cinnamon sticks for garnish

1. In a large heavy-bottomed saucepan, bring milk, cocoa powder, vanilla, cinnamon and cayenne pepper to a simmer over medium low heat
2. Simmer for 5 minutes until thoroughly warmed through
3. Add chocolate chips and whisk vigorously until smooth
4. Remove from heat and divide between four glasses
5. Serve with cinnamon sticks in each glass to be used as a stir stick
6. Add a splash of Kahlúa or chocolate liqueur to each serving (optional)

SPLASHY SIPPER

8 oz. Plymouth gin
4 oz. Lillet blanc
1 oz. simple syrup
1 oz. freshly squeezed lemon juice

1. In a shaker filled with ice, mix all ingredients and shake well
2. Pour into ice-filled Collins glasses
3. Garnish with a lemon wedge and serve

SPIKED JONES

½ cup milk
1 cup heavy cream
¼ cup whole coffee beans
2 oz. semisweet chocolate (61% Valrhona), chopped
2 tbsp. Kahlúa
1 tsp. confectioners' sugar
1 tbsp. dark chocolate–covered coffee beans, chopped

1. In a saucepan over medium heat, combine milk, ½ cup heavy cream, and whole coffee beans
2. Bring to a simmer, turn off heat, cover, and steep beans for 1 hour
3. Strain liquid and return to saucepan; discard beans
4. Bring the milk-and-cream mixture back to a simmer, add chocolate, and whisk until incorporated
5. Remove from heat; whisk in Kahlúa
6. Whip remaining ½ cup cream and the confectioners' sugar until soft peaks form
7. Divide the hot chocolate between two cups and garnish each portion with a dollop of the whipped cream and a sprinkling of chopped chocolate-covered coffee beans

STAR

1½ oz. apple brandy
1½ oz. sweet vermouth
2 dashes orange bitters

1. Fill mixing glass with ice
2. Add apple brandy, sweet vermouth and orange bitters
3. Shake
4. Strain into a chilled cocktail glass

STARS AND STRIPES

1 oz. grenadine 1 oz. heavy cream 1 oz. blue curaçao	1. Pour grenadine into a pousse-café glass 2. Float cream on top 3. Float blue curaçao on top of that

STINGER

1½ oz. brandy ½ oz. white crème de menthe	1. Fill mixing glass with ice 2. Add brandy and white crème de menthe 3. Stir 4. Strain into a chilled cocktail glass

STONE FENCE

3 oz. apple brandy 2 dashes Angostura bitters sweet apple cider	1. Fill a rocks glass with ice 2. Pour in apple brandy and bitters 3. Fill glass with chilled cider

STONE SOUR

1½ oz. bourbon ½ oz. lemon juice 1 tsp. white crème de menthe ½ tsp. sugar (or to taste) club soda	1. Fill a sour glass almost to the top with crushed ice 2. Pour in bourbon, lemon juice, white crème de menthe and sugar 3. Stir 4. Fill with club soda 5. Garnish with several sprigs of mint

STONEWALL

2 oz. apple cider
1 oz. Jamaican rum

1. Fill mixing glass with ice
2. Add apple cider and rum
3. Shake
4. Strain into a rocks glass filled with ice

STONY BROOK

1½ oz. blended whiskey
½ oz. triple sec
½ egg white
2–3 drops almond extract

1. Fill mixing glass with ice
2. Add blended whiskey, triple sec, egg white and almond extract
3. Shake
4. Strain into a rocks glass filled with ice
5. Garnish with a twist of lemon

STORMIN' GORMAN*

1½ oz. vodka
juice of ½ lemon
splash Cointreau
splash Mandarine Napoléon liqueur

1. Fill mixing glass with ice
2. Add vodka, lemon juice, Cointreau and Mandarine Napoléon liqueur
3. Shake
4. Strain into a chilled martini glass

STRAIGHT LAW

2½ oz. dry sherry
¼ oz. gin

1. Fill mixing glass with ice
2. Add dry sherry and gin

---

* Courtesy of Christine Gorman at Strings, Denver, Colorado.

3. Shake
4. Strain into a chilled cocktail glass
5. Garnish with a twist of lemon

STRAWBERRY-CRANBERRY FROST

2 oz. vodka
4 oz. sliced frozen strawberries, in syrup, partially thawed
4 oz. cranberry juice cocktail

1. Fill blender with vodka, frozen strawberries, cranberry juice and 3 oz. crushed ice
2. Blend until smooth
3. Pour into a large goblet
4. Garnish with a whole strawberry and a sprig of mint

STRAWBERRY DAIQUIRI (FROZEN)

2 oz. light rum
1½ oz. fresh lime juice
¾ oz. simple syrup

1. Blend the light rum, lime juice, and syrup with 1 cup ice until desired thickness
2. Pour into a chilled Collins glass
3. Garnish with a lime wedge

STRAWBERRY SHORTCAKE

2 scoops vanilla ice cream
1 oz. crème de noyaux
½ oz. crème de cacao
6 whole strawberries, stems removed
whipped cream
1 tsp. strawberry liqueur

1. Combine vanilla ice cream, crème de noyaux, crème de cacao and 5 of the 6 strawberries in a blender
2. Blend until smooth
3. Pour into a large goblet
4. Top with whipped cream
5. Drizzle strawberry liqueur on top
6. Garnish with the 6th strawberry

STREGA SOUR

1 oz. gin	1. Fill mixing glass with ice
½ oz. Strega	2. Add gin, Strega and sour mix
2 oz. sour mix	3. Shake
	4. Strain into a chilled cocktail glass

SUISESSE

1 oz. Pernod	1. Fill mixing glass with ice
1 oz. lemon juice	2. Add Pernod, lemon juice and egg white
1 egg white	3. Shake
club soda	4. Strain into a rocks glass filled with ice
	5. Top with club soda

SUMMER SHARE

1 oz. vodka	1. Fill mixing glass with ice
1 oz. light rum	2. Add vodka, light rum, tequila, orange juice, cranberry juice and apricot liqueur
½ oz. tequila	3. Shake
1 oz. orange juice	4. Strain into a chilled Collins glass
1 oz. cranberry juice cocktail	5. Add ice
1 dash apricot liqueur	6. Top with 7-Up
7-Up	7. Garnish with a slice of orange

SUNBEAM

1½ oz. Galliano	1. Fill a rocks glass with ice
½ oz. sweet vermouth	2. Add Galliano and sweet vermouth
	3. Stir

SUNBURN

1¼ oz. tequila
¾ oz. triple sec
4 oz. cranberry juice

1. Fill mixing glass with ice
2. Add tequila, triple sec and cranberry juice
3. Shake
4. Strain into a highball glass filled with ice
5. Garnish with a lime wedge

SUNDOWNER

2 oz. light rum
1 oz. lemon juice
3–4 dashes grenadine
tonic water

1. Fill mixing glass with ice
2. Add light rum, lemon juice and grenadine
3. Shake
4. Strain into a highball glass filled with ice
5. Fill with tonic water

SUPER COFFEE

¾ oz. brandy
¾ oz. Kahlúa
hot coffee

1. Pour brandy and Kahlúa into a coffee mug or hot drink glass
2. Fill with hot coffee
3. Top with whipped cream

SURFER ON ACID (SHOOTER)

1 oz. Jägermeister
1 oz. coconut rum
½ oz. pineapple juice
dash of grenadine

1. Fill mixing glass with ice
2. Add Jägermeister, coconut rum, pineapple juice and grenadine
3. Shake
4. Strain into a highball glass filled with ice or a shot glass

SWAMP WATER

2 oz. rum
¼ oz. blue curaçao
1 oz. orange juice
½ oz. lemon juice

1. Fill mixing glass with ice
2. Add rum, blue curaçao, orange juice and lemon juice
3. Shake
4. Strain into a rocks glass filled with ice

SWAYZE SWIZZLE*

1½ oz. dark rum
passion fruit juice
orange juice
cranberry juice cocktail

1. Fill a highball glass with ice
2. Add dark rum
3. Fill glass with equal parts passion fruit juice, orange juice and cranberry juice
4. Stir

SWEDISH LULLABY

1½ oz. Swedish Punch
1 oz. cherry liqueur
½ oz. lemon juice

1. Fill mixing glass with ice
2. Add Swedish Punch, cherry liqueur and lemon juice
3. Shake
4. Strain into a chilled cocktail glass

SWEET CREAM

1½ oz. Kahlúa
½ oz. Baileys Original Irish Cream

1. Pour Kahlúa into cordial glass or pousse-café
2. Float Baileys on top

---

* Courtesy of Mulholland Drive Cafe, New York City, which was owned by Patrick Swayze.

SWEETIE BABY

2 oz. amaretto
5 oz. vanilla ice cream
½ oz. milk (optional)

1. In a blender, combine amaretto, vanilla ice cream and milk
2. Blend at medium speed until smooth
3. Pour into a goblet or other large stemmed glass
4. Garnish with crushed almonds

SWEET INDEPENDENCE*

1 oz. marshmallow-infused vodka
1 oz. blue curaçao
maraschino cherry

1. Pour the marshmallow-infused vodka into a chilled martini glass
2. Drop in a maraschino cherry
3. Carefully layer the blue curaçao over the vodka to make three layers—red, white and blue

SWEET PATOOTIE

1 oz. gin
½ oz. triple sec
½ oz. orange juice

1. Fill mixing glass with ice
2. Add gin, triple sec and orange juice
3. Shake
4. Strain into a chilled cocktail glass

---

* Courtesy of Mixthatdrink.com.

SWEET TART COCKTAIL

2 oz. Hangar 1 citron
1 oz. limoncello
1 oz. simple syrup (dissolve
 one part sugar in one
 part boiling water; let
 cool)
8 raspberries
4 mint leaves
1 oz. lemon juice
1 cup ice

1. Blend everything until smooth
2. Add mint and raspberries for
 garnish

T

T.K.O. (SHOOTER)

⅓ oz. tequila
⅓ oz. Kahlúa
⅓ oz. ouzo

Layer tequila, Kahlúa and ouzo in
a shot glass

TAHITI CLUB

2 oz. gold rum
½ oz. lime juice
½ oz. lemon juice
½ oz. pineapple juice
2–3 dashes maraschino
liqueur

1. Fill mixing glass with cracked ice
2. Add gold rum, lime juice,
   lemon juice, pineapple juice and
   maraschino liqueur
3. Shake
4. Pour into a rocks glass
5. Garnish with a slice of orange

TANGO

1½ oz. gin
¼ oz. dry vermouth
¼ oz. sweet vermouth
¾ oz. orange juice
2–3 dashes curaçao

1. Fill mixing glass with cracked
   ice
2. Add gin, dry vermouth, sweet
   vermouth, orange juice and
   curaçao

3. Shake
4. Strain into a rocks glass filled with ice

TANTALUS

1 oz. brandy 1 oz. lemon juice ¼ oz. Forbidden Fruit	1. Fill mixing glass with ice 2. Add brandy, lemon juice and Forbidden Fruit 3. Shake 4. Strain into a rocks glass filled with ice

TAWNY RUSSIAN

1 oz. amaretto 1 oz. vodka	1. Fill a rocks glass with ice 2. Add amaretto and vodka 3. Stir

TEATINI

1¾ oz. vodka 1 oz. sweet iced tea ¼ oz. fresh lemon juice	1. Pour the ingredients into a cocktail shaker with ice cubes 2. Shake well 3. Strain into a chilled cocktail glass rimmed with sugar 4. Garnish with a lemon wedge

TEDDY BEAR (SHOOTER)

½ oz. root-beer schnapps ½ oz. vodka	Layer root-beer schnapps and vodka in a shot glass

TEMPTATION

2 oz. blended whiskey
¼ oz. triple sec
¼ oz. Pernod
¼ oz. Dubonnet

1. Fill mixing glass with ice
2. Add blended whiskey, triple sec, Pernod and Dubonnet
3. Shake
4. Strain into a chilled cocktail glass

TEMPTER COCKTAIL

1½ oz. port
1½ oz. apricot brandy

1. Fill mixing glass with ice
2. Add port and apricot brandy
3. Shake
4. Strain into a rocks glass filled with ice

TENNESSEE

2½ oz. rye whiskey
½ oz. maraschino liqueur
½ oz. lemon juice

1. Fill mixing glass with ice
2. Add rye, maraschino liqueur and lemon juice
3. Shake
4. Strain into a rocks glass filled with ice

TEQUILA COLLINS

1 oz. tequila
2 oz. sour mix
club soda

1. Fill a Collins glass with ice
2. Add tequila and sour mix
3. Stir
4. Fill with club soda
5. Stir
6. Garnish with a cherry

TEQUILA DAISY

1½ oz. tequila
2 tsp. lemon juice
¼ oz. raspberry syrup
club soda (optional)
dash Grand Marnier

1. Fill mixing glass with cracked ice
2. Add tequila, lemon juice and raspberry syrup
3. Shake
4. Pour into a highball glass
5. Fill with club soda (if desired)
6. Float Grand Marnier on top

TEQUILA GHOST

2 oz. tequila
1 oz. Pernod
½ oz. lemon juice

1. Fill mixing glass with ice
2. Add tequila, Pernod and lemon juice
3. Shake
4. Strain into a rocks glass filled with ice

TEQUILA GIMLET

1½ oz. tequila
1 oz. Rose's lime juice

1. Fill a rocks glass with ice
2. Add tequila and Rose's lime juice
3. Stir well
4. Garnish with a slice or wedge of lime

TEQUILA MANHATTAN

2 oz. tequila
1½ oz. sweet vermouth

1. Fill mixing glass with ice
2. Add tequila and sweet vermouth
3. Stir
4. Strain into a chilled cocktail glass or a rocks glass filled with ice

TEQUILA MARTINI

2 oz. tequila
½ oz. dry vermouth

1. Fill a rocks glass with ice
2. Add tequila and dry vermouth
3. Stir
4. Garnish with a twist of lemon or orange

TEQUILA OLD-FASHIONED

1 sugar cube
3–4 dashes Angostura bitters
1½ oz. gold tequila
2–3 oz. water
2–3 drops lime juice (optional)

1. Place sugar cube in a rocks glass
2. Add bitters and muddle until sugar is dissolved
3. Fill the glass with ice
4. Pour in tequila
5. Add water
6. Add lime juice (if desired)
7. Stir
8. Garnish with a twist of lemon

TEQUILA POPPER (SHOOTER)

1 oz. tequila
½ oz. 7-Up

1. Pour tequila into a shot glass
2. Fill with 7-Up
3. Place a napkin over the top of the glass and bang the glass down onto the table
4. Drink immediately

TEQUILA SCREWDRIVER

1½ oz. tequila
5 oz. orange juice

1. Fill a highball glass with ice
2. Add tequila
3. Fill with orange juice
4. Stir

TEQUILA SHOT (SHOOTER)

1½ oz. tequila (premium brand is recommended)
1 pinch salt
1 lemon or lime wedge

1. Fill a shot glass with tequila (chilled, if desired)
2. Put salt between thumb and index finger of left hand
3. While holding shot glass in the same hand, and the lemon or lime wedge in the other hand, lick the salt and quickly drink the shot of tequila
4. Suck the lemon or lime juice immediately afterward

TEQUILA SOUR

1½ oz. tequila
2–3 oz. sour mix

1. Fill mixing glass with ice
2. Add tequila and sour mix
3. Shake
4. Strain into a sour glass
5. Add ice

TEQUILA STINGER

1½ oz. gold tequila
¾ oz. white crème de menthe

1. Fill mixing glass with ice
2. Add gold tequila and white crème de menthe
3. Shake
4. Strain into a chilled cocktail glass

TEQUILA SUNRISE

1½ oz. tequila
2–3 dashes lime juice (optional)
orange juice

1. Fill a highball glass with ice
2. Add tequila (and lime juice, if desired)
3. Fill with orange juice

½ oz. grenadine

4. Stir
5. Pour grenadine down a spoon and let it rise from the bottom (do NOT stir)

TEQUILA SUNSET

1½ oz. tequila
2–3 dashes lime juice (optional)
orange juice
½ oz. blackberry brandy

1. Fill a highball glass with ice
2. Add tequila (and lime juice, if desired)
3. Fill with orange juice
4. Stir
5. Pour blackberry brandy down a spoon and let it rise from the bottom (do NOT stir)

TEQUINI

1½ oz. tequila
½ oz. dry vermouth
dash Angostura bitters (optional)

1. Fill mixing glass with ice
2. Add tequila, dry vermouth and bitters
3. Stir
4. Strain into a chilled cocktail glass or a rocks glass filled with ice

TEXAS TEA

1 oz. tequila
½ oz. vodka
½ oz. rum
½ oz. triple sec
1 oz. sour mix
cola

1. Fill mixing glass with ice
2. Add tequila, vodka, rum, triple sec and sour mix
3. Shake
4. Pour into a Collins glass
5. Add more ice, if necessary
6. Top with cola
7. Garnish with a lemon slice

THANKSGIVING COCKTAIL

1 oz. gin
1 oz. dry vermouth
1 oz. apricot brandy
½ tsp. lemon juice

1. Fill mixing glass with ice
2. Add gin, dry vermouth, apricot brandy and lemon juice
3. Shake
4. Strain into a rocks glass filled with ice
5. Garnish with a cherry

THIRD DEGREE

1½ oz. gin
½ oz. dry vermouth
½ tsp. Pernod

1. Fill mixing glass with ice
2. Add gin, dry vermouth and Pernod
3. Stir
4. Strain into a chilled cocktail glass

THIRD RAIL

1 oz. brandy
1 oz. apple brandy
1 oz. light rum
dash Pernod

1. Fill mixing glass with ice
2. Add brandy, apple brandy, light rum and Pernod
3. Shake
4. Strain into a chilled cocktail glass

THISTLE

1½ oz. Scotch whiskey
¾ oz. sweet vermouth
3–4 dashes Angostura bitters

1. Fill mixing glass with ice
2. Add Scotch whiskey, sweet vermouth and bitters
3. Shake
4. Strain into a chilled cocktail glass

THREE MILES

1 oz. brandy	1. Fill mixing glass with ice
½ oz. light rum	2. Add brandy, light rum, lemon
dash lemon juice	juice and grenadine
1 tsp. grenadine	3. Stir
	4. Strain into a chilled cocktail
	glass

THREE STRIPES

1 oz. gin	1. Fill mixing glass with ice
½ oz. dry vermouth	2. Add gin, dry vermouth and
½ oz. orange juice	orange juice
	3. Shake
	4. Strain into a chilled cocktail
	glass

THUNDER

2 oz. brandy	1. Fill mixing glass with ice
1 tsp. sugar syrup	2. Add brandy, sugar syrup, egg
1 egg yolk	yolk and cayenne pepper
pinch cayenne pepper	3. Shake
	4. Strain into a rocks glass filled
	with ice

TIDBIT

1 oz. gin	1. In blender, combine gin, vanilla
1 scoop vanilla ice cream	ice cream and dry sherry
2–3 drops dry sherry	2. Blend at low speed until smooth
	3. Pour into a highball glass

TIDY BOWL (SHOOTER)

1½ oz. vodka
1–2 drops blue curaçao
1 or 2 raisins

1. Combine vodka and blue curaçao with ice
2. Strain into a shot glass
3. Throw in 1 or 2 raisins

TIGER'S MILK

----

1 oz. Jamaican rum
1 oz. brandy
4 oz. heavy cream
¼ oz. sugar syrup

1. Fill mixing glass with ice
2. Add Jamaican rum, brandy, heavy cream and sugar syrup
3. Shake
4. Strain into a rocks glass filled with ice

TIGER TAIL

1½ oz. Pernod
dash curaçao
orange juice

1. Fill a highball glass with ice
2. Add Pernod and curaçao
3. Fill with orange juice
4. Stir
5. Garnish with a slice of lime

TIME BOMB

----

1 oz. tequila
3 oz. cranberry juice cocktail

1. Fill mixing glass with ice
2. Add tequila and cranberry juice
3. Stir
4. Strain into a sour glass
5. Add ice
6. Garnish with an orange peel

TIJUANA SUNRISE

1½ oz. tequila
2–3 dashes lime juice
(optional)
orange juice
½ oz. Angostura bitters

1. Fill a highball glass with ice
2. Add tequila (and lime juice, if desired)
3. Fill with orange juice
4. Stir
5. Pour bitters down a spoon and let it rise from the bottom (do NOT stir)

TINTON

2 oz. port
2 oz. apple brandy

1. Fill mixing glass with ice
2. Add port and apple brandy
3. Stir
4. Strain into a chilled cocktail glass

TINTORETTO

½ oz. pear puree
chilled champagne
dash pear brandy

1. Pour pear puree into a champagne glass
2. Fill with chilled champagne
3. Add dash of pear brandy

TIPPERARY

1 oz. Irish whiskey
1 oz. green Chartreuse
1 oz. sweet vermouth

1. Fill mixing glass with ice
2. Add Irish whiskey, green Chartreuse and sweet vermouth
3. Shake
4. Strain into a chilled cocktail glass

TIVOLI

1½ oz. bourbon ½ oz. aquavit ½ oz. sweet vermouth 3–4 drops Campari	1. Fill mixing glass with ice 2. Add bourbon, aquavit, sweet vermouth and Campari 3. Shake 4. Strain into a chilled cocktail glass

T.N.T.

1 oz. tequila tonic water	1. Fill a highball glass with ice 2. Add tequila 3. Fill with tonic water 4. Stir 5. Garnish with a slice of lime

TOASTED ALMOND

½ oz. Kahlúa ½ oz. amaretto 2 oz. cream	1. Fill mixing glass with ice 2. Add Kahlúa, amaretto and cream 3. Shake 4. Strain into a highball glass 5. Add ice

TOM AND JERRY

1 egg ½ oz. sugar syrup 1 oz. dark rum 1 oz. brandy hot milk or hot water	1. Separate the egg 2. Beat yolk and white separately 3. Fold together and combine with sugar syrup in a heat-proof mug 4. Slowly add dark rum and brandy 5. Beat mixture 6. Fill with hot milk or hot water 7. Garnish with ground nutmeg

TOM COLLINS

1 oz. gin
2 oz. sour mix
club soda

1. Fill a Collins glass with ice
2. Add gin and sour mix
3. Stir
4. Fill with club soda
5. Stir
6. Garnish with a cherry

TOOTSIE ROLL

1 oz. Sabra
1 oz. orange juice

1. Fill a rocks glass with ice
2. Add Sabra and orange juice
3. Stir

(*Note:* 1½ oz. Kahlúa may be substituted for Sabra.)

TOP SHELF MARGARITA

1½ oz. Cuervo gold tequila
½ oz. Grand Marnier
1 oz. sour mix
1 oz. lime juice

1. Fill mixing glass with ice
2. Add Cuervo, Grand Marnier, sour mix and lime juice
3. Shake
4. Strain into a chilled cocktail glass or a rocks glass filled with ice

TOREADOR

1½ oz. tequila
½ oz. white crème de cacao
½ oz. cream

1. Fill mixing glass with ice
2. Add tequila, white crème de cacao and cream
3. Shake
4. Strain into a chilled cocktail glass
5. Top with 1 tsp. whipped cream
6. Sprinkle with cocoa (if desired)

TORPEDO

1½ oz. apple brandy
¾ oz. brandy
1–2 dashes gin

1. Fill mixing glass with ice
2. Add apple brandy, brandy and gin
3. Shake
4. Strain into a chilled cocktail glass

TOVARICH

1½ oz. vodka
¾ oz. kümmel
1 tbsp. lime juice

1. Fill mixing glass with ice
2. Add vodka, kümmel and lime juice
3. Shake
4. Strain into a chilled cocktail glass

TRADE WINDS

2 oz. gold rum
½ oz. plum brandy
½ oz. lime juice
2 tsp. sugar syrup

1. Fill blender with 3 oz. ice, gold rum, plum brandy, lime juice and sugar syrup
2. Blend until smooth
3. Pour into a large wineglass

TRAFFIC LIGHT

⅓ oz. green crème de menthe
⅓ oz. crème de banana
⅓ oz. sloe gin

1. Pour green crème de menthe into a liqueur glass or a brandy snifter
2. Float crème de banana
3. Float sloe gin

TRILBY

1½ oz. bourbon
½ oz. sweet vermouth
2 dashes orange bitters

1. Fill mixing glass with ice
2. Add bourbon, sweet vermouth and orange bitters
3. Stir
4. Strain into a rocks glass filled with ice

TRINIDAD COCKTAIL

1 oz. light rum
1 tbsp. lime juice
1 tsp. sugar
2-3 dashes Angostura bitters

1. Fill mixing glass with ice
2. Add light rum, lime juice, sugar and bitters
3. Shake
4. Strain into a chilled cocktail glass

TRINITY COCKTAIL

¾ oz. dry vermouth
¾ oz. sweet vermouth
¾ oz. gin

1. Fill mixing glass with ice
2. Add dry vermouth, sweet vermouth and gin
3. Stir
4. Strain into a cocktail glass

TROIS RIVIERES

1½ oz. Canadian whiskey
¾ oz. Dubonnet
½ oz. triple sec

1. Fill mixing glass with ice
2. Add Canadian whiskey, Dubonnet and triple sec
3. Shake
4. Strain into a rocks glass filled with ice

TROLLEY

2 oz. bourbon
cranberry juice cocktail
pineapple juice

1. Fill a highball glass with ice
2. Add bourbon
3. Fill with equal parts cranberry juice and pineapple juice
4. Stir

TROPHY ROOM*

½ oz. Amaretto di Saronno
½ oz. Vandermint
½ oz. Myers's dark Jamaican rum
hot coffee
½ oz. Tia Maria

1. Pour amaretto, Vandermint and Myers's into a coffee mug
2. Fill with hot coffee
3. Top with whipped cream
4. Float Tia Maria on top

TROPICAL COCKTAIL

¾ oz. white crème de cacao
¾ oz. maraschino liqueur
¾ oz. dry vermouth
1 dash Angostura bitters

1. Fill mixing glass with ice
2. Add white crème de cacao, maraschino liqueur, dry vermouth and bitters
3. Stir
4. Strain into a chilled cocktail glass

TROPICAL GRAPEFRUIT SPLASH

½–1 cup water
11 oz. vodka
1 serving of a favorite protein powder
22 cups spinach

1. Place liquids in blender first, adding heaviest foods last
2. Blend, adding more water or ice to reach desired consistency

---

* Courtesy of Hotel Park, Tucson, Arizona.

11 kiwis, peeled
11 cups grapefruit
11 cups pineapple

TRUFFLE MARTINI

3½ oz. cognac
splash lime juice
splash Grand Marnier
7 paper-thin slices of black
   truffle

1. Fill mixing glass with ice
2. Add cognac, lime juice, Grand Marnier and 2 slices of black truffle
3. Shake well
4. Strain into a chilled martini glass
5. Garnish with remaining 5 slices of black truffle

TUACA COCKTAIL

1 oz. vodka
1 oz. Tuaca
2 tbsp. lime juice

1. Fill mixing glass with ice
2. Add vodka, Tuaca and lime juice
3. Shake
4. Strain into a chilled cocktail glass

TULIP

¾ oz. sweet vermouth
¾ oz. apple brandy
1½ tsp. apricot brandy
1½ tsp. lemon juice

1. Fill mixing glass with ice
2. Add sweet vermouth, apple brandy, apricot brandy and lemon juice
3. Shake
4. Strain into a chilled cocktail glass

TUMBLEWEED

1 oz. white crème de cacao
1 oz. amaretto
2 oz. cream

1. In blender, combine white crème de cacao, amaretto and cream with 3 oz. crushed ice
2. Blend until smooth
3. Pour into a goblet or large wineglass

TURF

1 oz. gin
½ oz. dry vermouth
2 dashes anis
2 dashes maraschino liqueur
2 dashes Angostura bitters

1. Fill mixing glass with ice
2. Add gin, dry vermouth, anis, maraschino liqueur and bitters
3. Shake
4. Strain into a rocks glass filled with ice

TURKEY SHOOTER

¾ oz. 101-proof Wild Turkey bourbon
¼ oz. white crème de menthe

1. Pour Wild Turkey into a liqueur glass or brandy snifter
2. Float white crème de menthe

TUXEDO

2 oz. fino sherry
½ oz. anisette
3–4 dashes maraschino liqueur
3–4 dashes Angostura bitters

1. Fill mixing glass with ice
2. Add fino sherry, anisette, maraschino liqueur and bitters
3. Stir
4. Strain into a chilled cocktail glass

411

TWIN HILLS

1½ oz. blended whiskey
2 tsp. Bénédictine
1½ tsp. lemon juice
1½ tsp. lime juice
1 tsp. sugar syrup

1. Fill mixing glass with ice
2. Add blended whiskey, Bénédictine, lemon juice, lime juice and sugar syrup
3. Shake
4. Strain into a chilled cocktail glass
5. Garnish with a slice of lemon and a slice of lime

TWIN SIX

1 oz. gin
½ oz. sweet vermouth
2 tsp. grenadine
1 tbsp. orange juice
1 egg white

1. Fill mixing glass with ice
2. Add gin, sweet vermouth, grenadine, orange juice and egg white
3. Shake
4. Strain into a chilled cocktail glass

TWISTER

2 oz. vodka
½ oz. lime juice, freshly squeezed
7-Up

1. Fill a highball glass with ice
2. Add vodka and lime juice
3. Top with 7-Up
4. Stir gently

ULANDA

1½ oz. gin
¾ oz. Cointreau
2–3 drops Pernod

1. Fill mixing glass with ice
2. Add gin, Cointreau and Pernod
3. Shake
4. Strain into a rocks glass filled with ice

THE ULTIMATE MARGARITA

1½ oz. Sauza Conmemorativo tequila
¾ oz. Cointreau
1 oz. fresh lemon juice
½ oz. fresh lime juice
½ tsp. sugar

1. Fill mixing glass with ice
2. Add tequila, Cointreau, lemon juice, lime juice and sugar
3. Shake well
4. If desired, salt the rim of a large cocktail glass
5. Strain into glass
6. Garnish with a slice of lime

UNION JACK

1½ oz. gin
¼ oz. crème d'Yvette

1. Fill mixing glass with ice
2. Add gin and crème d'Yvette

3. Stir
4. Strain into a chilled cocktail glass

UNION LEAGUE

2 oz. gin
1 oz. port
2 dashes orange bitters

1. Fill a rocks glass with ice
2. Add gin, port and orange bitters
3. Stir
4. Garnish with a twist of orange

V

VALENCIA

2 oz. apricot brandy
1 oz. orange juice
2–3 dashes orange bitters
chilled champagne

1. Fill mixing glass with ice
2. Add apricot brandy, orange juice and orange bitters
3. Shake
4. Strain into a chilled goblet or tulip glass
5. Fill with chilled champagne

VANCOUVER COCKTAIL

2 oz. Canadian whiskey
1 oz. Dubonnet (rouge)
2 tbsp. lemon juice
½ egg white
½ tsp. maple syrup (sugar syrup may be substituted)
3–4 dashes Angostura bitters

1. Half-fill mixing glass with cracked ice
2. Add Canadian whiskey, Dubonnet, lemon juice, egg white, maple syrup and bitters
3. Shake
4. Pour into a large wineglass or large cocktail glass

VANDERBILT

1½ oz. brandy
¾ oz. cherry brandy
1 tsp. sugar syrup
2 dashes Angostura bitters

1. Fill mixing glass with ice
2. Add brandy, cherry brandy, sugar syrup and bitters
3. Stir
4. Strain into a chilled cocktail glass

VANILLA CREAMSICLE

1½ oz. vanilla schnapps
1½ oz. triple sec
1½ oz. crème de cacao
milk

1. Pour the three liqueurs into a hurricane glass
2. Pour in the milk
3. Stir and serve

VANITY FAIR COCKTAIL

1½ oz. apple brandy
½ oz. cherry brandy
½ oz. cherry liqueur
1 tsp. crème de noyaux

1. Fill mixing glass with 1–2 oz. cracked ice
2. Add apple brandy, cherry brandy and cherry liqueur
3. Shake
4. Pour into a cocktail glass
5. Float crème de noyaux on top

VELVET HAMMER

½ oz. white crème de cacao
½ oz. triple sec
2 oz. cream

1. Fill mixing glass with ice
2. Add white crème de cacao, triple sec and cream
3. Shake
4. Strain into a stemmed glass

VELVET KISS

1 oz. gin
½ oz. banana liqueur
½ oz. pineapple juice
1 oz. heavy cream

1. Fill mixing glass with ice
2. Add gin, banana liqueur, pineapple juice and heavy cream
3. Shake
4. Strain into a chilled cocktail glass

VENETIAN COFFEE

1 sugar cube
1 oz. brandy
hot coffee

1. Place sugar cube in a coffee mug
2. Pour in brandy
3. Fill with hot coffee
4. Top with whipped cream

VERMOUTH CASSIS

1 oz. sweet vermouth or dry vermouth (depending on taste)
1 oz. crème de cassis
club soda

1. Fill a highball glass with ice
2. Add vermouth and crème de cassis
3. Stir
4. Fill with club soda
5. Stir gently
6. Garnish with a twist of lemon

VERMOUTH FRAPPE

1½ oz. sweet vermouth
dash Angostura bitters

1. Fill mixing glass with shaved ice
2. Add sweet vermouth and bitters
3. Stir
4. Strain into a chilled cocktail glass

VERONA

1 oz. gin
1 oz. amaretto
½ oz. sweet vermouth
1–2 dashes lemon juice

1. Half-fill mixing glass with cracked ice
2. Add gin, amaretto, sweet vermouth and lemon juice
3. Shake
4. Pour into a rocks glass
5. Garnish with a slice of orange

VIA VENETO

1½ oz. brandy
½ oz. sambuca
½ oz. lemon juice
1½ tsp. sugar syrup
½ egg white

1. Fill mixing glass with ice
2. Add brandy, sambuca, lemon juice, sugar syrup and egg white
3. Shake
4. Strain into a rocks glass filled with ice

VICTOR

1 oz. gin
1 oz. brandy
½ oz. sweet vermouth

1. Fill mixing glass with ice
2. Add gin, brandy and sweet vermouth
3. Stir
4. Strain into a chilled cocktail glass

VICTORY

1½ oz. Pernod
¾ oz. grenadine
club soda

1. Fill mixing glass with ice
2. Add Pernod and grenadine
3. Shake
4. Strain into a highball glass filled with ice
5. Fill with club soda

VIKING

1½ oz. Swedish Punsch
1 oz. aquavit
1 oz. lime juice

1. Fill mixing glass with ice
2. Add Swedish Punsch, aquavit and lime juice
3. Shake
4. Strain into a rocks glass filled with ice

VIRGIN

1 oz. gin
½ oz. white crème de menthe
1 oz. Forbidden Fruit

1. Fill mixing glass with ice
2. Add gin, white crème de menthe and Forbidden Fruit
3. Shake
4. Strain into a rocks glass filled with ice

VODKA AND TONIC

1½ oz. vodka
5 oz. tonic water

1. Fill a highball glass with ice
2. Add vodka
3. Fill with tonic water
4. Stir
5. Garnish with a lime slice

VODKA COLLINS

1 oz. vodka
2 oz. sour mix
club soda

1. Fill a Collins glass with ice
2. Add vodka and sour mix
3. Stir
4. Fill with club soda
5. Stir
6. Garnish with a cherry

VODKA COOLER

1 oz. vodka
½ oz. sweet vermouth
7-Up

1. Fill mixing glass with ice
2. Add vodka and sweet vermouth
3. Shake
4. Strain into a Collins glass filled with ice
5. Fill with 7-Up

VODKA FIZZ

1 oz. vodka
2 oz. pineapple juice
1 tsp. lemon juice
1 tsp. powdered sugar
club soda

1. Fill mixing glass with ice
2. Add vodka, pineapple juice, lemon juice and sugar
3. Shake
4. Strain into a Collins glass
5. Add several ice cubes
6. Fill with club soda

VODKA GIBSON

2 oz. vodka
½ oz. dry vermouth

1. Fill mixing glass with ice
2. Add vodka and dry vermouth
3. Stir
4. Strain into a chilled martini glass or a rocks glass filled with ice
5. Garnish with a pearl onion

(*Note:* A Gibson is a martini with a pearl onion as garnish instead of an olive. As in a vodka martini, the drier the Gibson, the less vermouth is used in proportion to the vodka.)

420

VODKA GIMLET

1½ oz. vodka
½ oz. Rose's lime juice

1. Fill a rocks glass with ice
2. Add vodka and Rose's lime juice
3. Stir
4. Garnish with a lime slice

VODKA GRAND MARNIER COCKTAIL

1½ oz. vodka
½ oz. Grand Marnier
2 tbsp. lime juice

1. Fill mixing glass with ice
2. Add vodka, Grand Marnier and lime juice
3. Shake
4. Strain into a chilled cocktail glass
5. Garnish with a slice of orange or a twist of orange

VODKA GRASSHOPPER

1 oz. white crème de cacao
1 oz. green crème de menthe
½ oz. vodka

1. Fill mixing glass with ice
2. Add white crème de cacao, green crème de menthe and vodka
3. Shake
4. Strain into a chilled cocktail glass

VODKA MARTINI

1½ oz. vodka
dash (approx. ⅛ oz.) dry vermouth

1. Fill mixing glass with ice
2. Add vodka and dry vermouth
3. Stir
4. Strain into a chilled martini glass
5. Garnish with an olive

(*Note:* If serving "on the rocks," stir in a rocks glass filled with ice, garnish and serve.)

VODKA MARTINI (DRY)

1½ oz. vodka
drop (approx. ⅒ oz.) dry
   vermouth

1. Fill mixing glass with ice
2. Add vodka and dry vermouth
3. Stir
4. Strain into a chilled martini glass
5. Garnish with an olive

(*Note:* If serving "on the rocks," stir in a rocks glass filled with ice, garnish and serve.)

VODKA MARTINI (VERY DRY)

1½ oz. vodka
approx. ⅟₁₂ oz. dry vermouth

1. Fill mixing glass with ice
2. Add dry vermouth (In actuality, almost no dry vermouth is used. Let vermouth barely touch side of mixing glass.)
3. Add vodka
4. Stir
5. Strain into a chilled martini glass
6. Garnish with an olive

(*Note:* If serving "on the rocks," stir in a rocks glass filled with ice, garnish and serve.)

VODKA MARTINI (EXTREMELY DRY)

2 oz. vodka

Follow directions for other martini recipes. No vermouth is used. This translates to "vodka straight up" or "vodka on the rocks."

VODKA ON THE ROCKS

2 oz. premium imported
vodka

1. Fill a rocks glass with ice
2. Add vodka

(*Note:* Vodkas such as Absolut, Stolichnaya and Finlandia are extremely popular. To best enjoy the flavor, store the bottle of vodka in your freezer, allowing the alcohol to thicken. You may also serve it "straight up"—chilled, without ice.)

VODKA SAKETINI

2½ oz. vodka
½ oz. sake

1. Fill mixing glass with ice
2. Add vodka and sake
3. Stir
4. Strain into a chilled cocktail glass or a rocks glass filled with ice
5. Garnish with a twist of lemon

VODKA STINGER

1½ oz. vodka
½ oz. white crème de menthe

1. Fill mixing glass with ice
2. Add vodka and white crème de menthe
3. Stir
4. Strain into a chilled cocktail glass

VOLGA BOATMAN

1 oz. vodka
1 oz. cherry brandy
1 oz. orange juice

1. Fill mixing glass with ice
2. Add vodka, cherry brandy and orange juice
3. Stir
4. Strain into a chilled cocktail glass

WAGON WHEEL

1½ oz. cognac	1. Fill mixing glass with ice
2½ oz. Southern Comfort	2. Add cognac, Southern Comfort, lemon juice and grenadine
1 oz. lemon juice	
½ oz. grenadine	3. Shake
	4. Strain into a rocks glass filled with ice

WALDORF

1½ oz. bourbon	1. Fill mixing glass with ice
¾ oz. Pernod	2. Add bourbon, Pernod, sweet vermouth and bitters
½ oz. sweet vermouth	
dash Angostura bitters	3. Stir
	4. Strain into a chilled cocktail glass

WARDAY'S COCKTAIL

1 oz. gin	1. Fill mixing glass with ice
1 oz. sweet vermouth	2. Add gin, sweet vermouth, apple brandy and yellow Chartreuse
1 oz. apple brandy	
1 tsp. yellow Chartreuse	3. Shake

4. Strain into a chilled cocktail glass
5. Garnish with a cherry

WARD 8

1 oz. whiskey 2 oz. sour mix ¼ oz. grenadine	1. Fill mixing glass with ice 2. Add whiskey, sour mix and grenadine 3. Shake 4. Strain into a sour glass 5. Add ice, if necessary 6. Garnish with a cherry

WARSAW

1½ oz. vodka ½ oz. blackberry liqueur ½ oz. dry vermouth ¼ oz. lemon juice	1. Fill mixing glass with ice 2. Add vodka, blackberry liqueur, dry vermouth and lemon juice 3. Shake 4. Strain into a chilled cocktail glass

WASHINGTON

1½ oz. dry vermouth ¾ oz. brandy 2 dashes sugar syrup 2 dashes Angostura bitters	1. Fill mixing glass with ice 2. Add dry vermouth, brandy, sugar syrup and bitters 3. Stir 4. Strain into a chilled cocktail glass

WASHINGTON APPLE

1 oz. vodka
1 oz. apple schnapps
1 oz. cranberry juice

1. Fill mixing glass with ice
2. Add vodka, apple schnapps and cranberry juice
3. Shake
4. Strain into a chilled shot glass

WATERBURY

2 oz. cognac
½ oz. lemon juice
1 tsp. sugar syrup
½ egg white
2–3 dashes grenadine

1. Fill mixing glass with ice
2. Add cognac, lemon juice, sugar syrup, egg white and grenadine
3. Shake
4. Strain into a chilled cocktail glass

WATERMELON

¾ oz. vodka
¾ oz. Midori melon liqueur
3 oz. cranberry juice cocktail

1. Fill a highball glass with ice
2. Add vodka, Midori and cranberry juice
3. Stir

WEDDING BELLE

½ oz. gin
½ oz. Dubonnet
¼ oz. cherry-flavored brandy
¼ oz. orange juice

1. Fill mixing glass with ice
2. Add gin, Dubonnet, cherry-flavored brandy and orange juice
3. Shake
4. Strain into a rocks glass filled with ice

WEEKENDER

¾ oz. gin	1. Fill mixing glass with ice
¾ oz. dry vermouth	2. Add gin, dry vermouth, sweet vermouth, triple sec and Pernod
¾ oz. sweet vermouth	3. Shake
¾ oz. triple sec	4. Strain into a chilled cocktail glass
3 dashes Pernod	

WEEP NO MORE

1 oz. brandy	1. Fill mixing glass with ice
1 oz. Dubonnet	2. Add brandy, Dubonnet and lime juice
1 oz. lime juice	3. Shake
	4. Strain into a chilled cocktail glass

WEISSEN SOUR

2 oz. bourbon	1. Combine all ingredients and gently shake with ice cubes
¾ oz. fresh lemon juice	2. Strain over fresh ice cubes into a glass
¼ oz. simple syrup (1:1)	3. Garnish with a lemon twist
bar spoon of orange marmalade	
2 dashes orange bitters	
2 oz. white ale	

WEMBLEY

1½ oz. gin	1. Fill mixing glass with ice
¾ oz. dry vermouth	2. Add gin, dry vermouth and apple brandy
3 dashes apple brandy	3. Stir
	4. Strain into a chilled cocktail glass

WHICH WAY

1 oz. brandy
1 oz. Pernod
1 oz. anisette

1. Fill mixing glass with ice
2. Add brandy, Pernod and anisette
3. Shake
4. Strain into a chilled cocktail glass

WHIP

1½ oz. dry vermouth
1 oz. brandy
1 dash curaçao
2 drops Pernod

1. Fill mixing glass with ice
2. Add dry vermouth, brandy, curaçao and Pernod
3. Shake
4. Strain into a chilled cocktail glass

WHIPPET

2½ oz. blended whiskey
1 oz. peppermint schnapps
1 oz. white crème de cacao

1. Fill mixing glass with ice
2. Add blended whiskey, peppermint schnapps and white crème de cacao
3. Shake
4. Strain into a rocks glass filled with ice

WHIRLAWAY

1½ oz. bourbon
¾ oz. curaçao
2–3 dashes Angostura bitters
club soda

1. Half-fill mixing glass with cracked ice
2. Add bourbon, curaçao and bitters
3. Shake
4. Pour into a rocks glass
5. Fill with club soda

WHISKEY AND WATER

1½ oz. whiskey
water

1. Fill a highball glass with ice
2. Add whiskey
3. Fill with water
4. Stir

WHISKEY COLLINS

1 oz. whiskey
2 oz. sour mix
club soda

1. Fill a Collins glass with ice
2. Add whiskey and sour mix
3. Stir
4. Fill with club soda
5. Garnish with a cherry and an
   orange slice

WHISKEY DAISY

1½ oz. blended whiskey
2 tsp. lemon juice
¼ oz. raspberry syrup
club soda (optional)
dash yellow Chartreuse
   (Grand Marnier or curaçao
   may be substituted)

1. Fill mixing glass with cracked ice
2. Add blended whiskey, lemon
   juice and raspberry syrup
3. Shake
4. Pour into a highball glass
5. Fill with club soda (if desired)
6. Float Chartreuse (or Grand
   Marnier or curaçao) on top

WHISKEY FIX

2 oz. scotch whiskey
1 oz. lemon juice
1 tsp. powdered sugar

1. Fill a Collins glass with
   crushed ice
2. Add scotch, lemon juice and
   powdered sugar
3. Stir
4. Garnish with fresh fruits in
   season

WHISKEY HIGHBALL

1 oz. whiskey
club soda or ginger ale

1. Fill a highball glass with ice
2. Add whiskey
3. Fill with club soda or ginger ale
4. Stir gently

WHISKEY RICKEY

1½ oz. blended whiskey
½ oz. lime juice
1 tsp. sugar syrup
club soda

1. Fill a Collins glass with cracked ice
2. Add blended whiskey, lime juice and sugar syrup
3. Fill with club soda
4. Garnish with a slice of lime

WHISKEY SOUR

1 oz. whiskey
2 oz. sour mix

1. Fill mixing glass with ice
2. Add whiskey and sour mix
3. Shake
4. Strain into a sour glass
5. Garnish with a cherry

WHIST

1 oz. apple brandy
½ oz. dark rum
½ oz. sweet vermouth

1. Fill mixing glass with ice
2. Add apple brandy, dark rum and sweet vermouth
3. Shake
4. Strain into a chilled cocktail glass

WHITE BABY

----

1 oz. gin
1 oz. triple sec
1 oz. heavy cream

1. Fill mixing glass with ice
2. Add gin, triple sec and heavy cream
3. Shake
4. Strain into a chilled cocktail glass

WHITE BULL

----

1 oz. tequila
¾ oz. Kahlúa
cream

1. Fill a rocks glass with ice
2. Add tequila and Kahlúa
3. Top with cream
4. Stir

WHITE CARGO

2½ oz. gin
½ oz. maraschino liqueur
2 dashes dry white wine
1 scoop vanilla ice cream

1. In a blender, combine gin, maraschino liqueur, wine and vanilla ice cream
2. Blend until smooth
3. Pour into a goblet

WHITE ELEPHANT

½ oz. vodka
½ oz. white crème de cacao
2 oz. cream

1. Fill mixing glass with ice
2. Add vodka, white crème de cacao and cream
3. Shake
4. Strain into a chilled stemmed glass

WHITE GRAPE, TANGERINE AND SPARKLING WINE PUNCH

----

48 oz. unsweetened white
   grape juice, chilled
6 oz. frozen tangerine juice
   concentrate, thawed
8 oz. club soda
3 oz. brandy
2 oz. lemon juice
1 bottle (750 ml) sweet
   sparkling wine (e.g., Asti
   Spumante)
thin slices of tangerine

1. In a punch bowl, over a block of
   ice, combine white grape juice,
   tangerine concentrate, club
   soda, brandy and lemon juice
2. Mix
3. Cover punch bowl and
   refrigerate until cold
4. Just before serving, add the
   sparkling wine
5. Float thinly sliced tangerine
   on top

WHITE HEART

½ oz. sambuca
½ oz. white crème de cacao
2 oz. cream

1. Fill mixing glass with ice
2. Add sambuca, white crème de
   cacao and cream
3. Shake
4. Strain into a chilled stemmed
   glass

WHITE HEAT

----

1 oz. gin
½ oz. triple sec
½ oz. dry vermouth
1 oz. pineapple juice

1. Fill mixing glass with ice
2. Add gin, triple sec, dry
   vermouth and pineapple juice
3. Shake
4. Strain into a rocks glass filled
   with ice

WHITE LADY (1)

1½ oz. gin
3 oz. sour mix
1 oz. cream

1. Fill mixing glass with ice
2. Add gin, sour mix and cream
3. Shake
4. Strain into a sour glass
5. Fill with ice
6. Garnish with a cherry and an orange slice

WHITE LADY (2)

½ oz. vodka
½ oz. crème de cacao
2 oz. cream

1. Fill mixing glass with ice
2. Add vodka, crème de cacao and cream
3. Shake
4. Strain into a chilled cocktail glass

WHITE LILY

1 oz. gin
1 oz. light rum
1 oz. triple sec
2–3 drops Pernod

1. Fill mixing glass with ice
2. Add gin, light rum, triple sec and Pernod
3. Shake
4. Strain into a rocks glass filled with ice

WHITE LION

1½ oz. light rum
½ oz. lemon juice
1 tsp. sugar
½ tsp. grenadine
2 dashes Angostura bitters

1. Fill mixing glass with ice
2. Add light rum, lemon juice, sugar, grenadine and bitters
3. Shake
4. Strain into a chilled cocktail glass

WHITE MINT AND BRANDY FRAPPE

2 oz. white crème de menthe 1 oz. brandy	1. Fill a champagne glass with crushed ice 2. Pour in white crème de menthe and brandy

WHITE ROSE

1½ oz. gin ¾ oz. cherry liqueur 2 oz. orange juice 2 tbsp. lime juice 1 tsp. sugar ½ egg white	1. Fill mixing glass with ice 2. Add gin, cherry liqueur, orange juice, lime juice, sugar and egg white 3. Shake 4. Strain into a rocks glass filled with ice

WHITE RUSSIAN

1½ oz. vodka 1½ oz. Kahlúa cream	1. Fill a rocks glass with ice 2. Add vodka and Kahlúa 3. Float cream on top

WHITE SPIDER

2 oz. vodka 1 oz. white crème de menthe	1. Fill mixing glass with ice 2. Add vodka and white crème de menthe 3. Shake 4. Strain into a chilled cocktail glass

WHITE WINE SPRITZER

white wine
club soda

1. Half-fill a tulip glass or a Collins glass with ice
2. Fill the glass halfway with chilled white wine
3. Fill with club soda
4. Stir gently
5. Garnish with a twist of lemon

WHITE WINE SUPER SANGRIA

2 bottles dry white wine
½ cup Cointreau or triple sec
2 oz. brandy
1 cup orange juice
1 pint strawberries, hulled and quartered
1 lime, cut into thin slices
1 lemon, cut into thin slices
½ orange, cut into thin slices
1½ cups seedless green grapes
1½ cups seedless red grapes
1 oz. superfine granulated sugar
1½ cups club soda

1. Combine all ingredients (except club soda) in a large bowl
2. Refrigerate for several hours
3. When ready to serve, add club soda
4. Stir
5. Serve in large wineglasses

WHITE WING

2 oz. gin
1 oz. white crème de menthe

1. Fill mixing glass with ice
2. Add gin and white crème de menthe
3. Shake
4. Strain into a chilled cocktail glass

WHY NOT

1 oz. gin
1 oz. dry vermouth
½ oz. apricot brandy
dash lemon juice

1. Fill mixing glass with ice
2. Add gin, dry vermouth, apricot brandy and lemon juice
3. Shake
4. Strain into a chilled cocktail glass

WIDOW'S DREAM

2 oz. Bénédictine
1 oz. heavy cream
1 egg

1. Fill mixing glass with ice
2. Add Bénédictine, heavy cream and egg
3. Shake
4. Strain into a large chilled cocktail glass

WIDOW'S KISS

1 oz. apple brandy
½ oz. Bénédictine
½ oz. yellow Chartreuse
dash Angostura bitters

1. Fill mixing glass with ice
2. Add apple brandy, Bénédictine, yellow Chartreuse and bitters
3. Shake
4. Strain into a chilled cocktail glass

WILD FLING

1½ oz. DeKuyper WilderBerry schnapps
4 oz. pineapple juice
splash cranberry juice cocktail

1. Fill a highball glass with ice
2. Add WilderBerry schnapps
3. Fill with pineapple juice
4. Add a splash of cranberry juice
5. Stir

WILD IRISH ROSE

1½ oz. Irish whiskey
1½ tsp. grenadine
½ oz. lime juice
club soda

1. Fill a highball glass with ice
2. Add Irish whiskey, grenadine and lime juice
3. Stir well
4. Fill with club soda

WILL ROGERS

1½ oz. gin
½ oz. dry vermouth
dash triple sec
1 tbsp. orange juice

1. Fill mixing glass with ice
2. Add gin, dry vermouth, triple sec and orange juice
3. Shake
4. Strain into a chilled cocktail glass

WILSON COCKTAIL

2 oz. gin
2 dashes dry vermouth
1 tbsp. orange juice

1. Fill mixing glass with ice
2. Add gin, dry vermouth and orange juice
3. Stir well
4. Strain into a chilled cocktail glass
5. Garnish with a twist of orange

WINDEX

¾ oz. vodka
¾ oz. triple sec
¾ oz. blue curaçao
¾ oz. Rose's lime juice

1. Fill mixing glass with ice
2. Add vodka, triple sec, blue curaçao and lime juice
3. Shake
4. Strain into a rocks glass

WINE COOLER

burgundy or rosé wine
7-Up

1. Half-fill a tulip glass or a Collins glass with ice
2. Fill the glass halfway with wine
3. Fill with 7-Up
4. Stir gently
5. Garnish with a cherry

WOMBAT (SHOOTER)*

a mixing glass full of fresh watermelon, seeded (approximately 6 oz. fresh watermelon juice)
2 oz. dark rum
½ oz. strawberry liqueur
3 oz. orange juice
3 oz. pineapple juice

(MAKES ABOUT 4 SHOTS)

1. Pulverize fresh watermelon in a mixing glass and remove seeds
2. Combine with dark rum, strawberry liqueur, orange juice and pineapple juice
3. Shake well
4. Pour into shot glasses

WOO WOO

¾ oz. vodka
¾ oz. peach schnapps
3 oz. cranberry juice cocktail

1. Fill a highball glass with ice
2. Add vodka, peach schnapps and cranberry juice
3. Stir

WOO WOO (SHOOTER)

½ oz. vodka
½ oz. peach schnapps

1. Fill mixing glass with ice
2. Add vodka, peach schnapps and cranberry juice

---

* Courtesy of Bamboo Bernie's, New York City.

½ oz. cranberry juice
cocktail

3. Stir
4. Strain into a shot glass

WYOMING SWING COCKTAIL

1 oz. sweet vermouth
1 oz. dry vermouth
1 tsp. powdered sugar
2 oz. orange juice
(preferably freshly
squeezed)
½ tsp. sugar syrup, or to
taste

1. Half-fill mixing glass with
cracked ice
2. Add sweet vermouth, dry
vermouth, powdered sugar,
orange juice and sugar syrup
3. Shake
4. Pour into a highball glass
5. Add more ice, if necessary

XANGO

1½ oz. light rum	1. Fill mixing glass with ice
½ oz. triple sec	2. Add light rum, triple sec and
1 oz. grapefruit juice	grapefruit juice
	3. Shake
	4. Strain into a chilled cocktail glass

XANTHIA

¾ oz. gin	1. Fill mixing glass with ice
¾ oz. yellow Chartreuse	2. Add gin, yellow Chartreuse and
¾ oz. cherry-flavored brandy	cherry-flavored brandy
	3. Shake
	4. Strain into a rocks glass filled with ice

XERES COCKTAIL

| 2½ oz. dry sherry | 1. Fill mixing glass with ice |
| 1 dash orange bitters | 2. Add dry sherry and orange bitters |

3. Stir
4. Strain into a chilled cocktail glass

XYLOPHONE

----

1 oz. tequila
½ oz. white crème de cacao
½ oz. sugar syrup
1 oz. cream

1. Fill blender with 3 oz. crushed ice, tequila, crème de cacao, sugar syrup and cream
2. Blend until smooth
3. Pour into a goblet or large wineglass
4. Garnish with a cherry

XYZ

1½ oz. light rum
½ oz. triple sec
½ oz. lemon juice

1. Fill mixing glass with ice
2. Add light rum, triple sec and lemon juice
3. Shake
4. Strain into a chilled cocktail glass

YALE COCKTAIL

1½ oz. gin
½ oz. dry vermouth
3–4 dashes blue curaçao
dash Angostura bitters

1. Fill mixing glass with ice
2. Add gin, dry vermouth, blue curaçao and bitters
3. Stir
4. Strain into a chilled cocktail glass

A YARD OF FLANNEL

1 qt. ale
4 oz. gold rum
3 oz. superfine granulated sugar
4 eggs
½ tsp. grated nutmeg
½ tsp. ground cinnamon

1. Warm (don't boil) ale in a large saucepan over low heat
2. In a separate bowl, combine rum, sugar, eggs, nutmeg and cinnamon
3. Beat well
4. Pour mixture into a heat-resistant pitcher
5. Add ale slowly, stirring constantly
6. Stir until mixture is creamy
7. Pour into warmed mugs

YASHMAK

1½ oz. rye whiskey
¾ oz. dry vermouth
½ oz. Pernod
3–4 dashes Angostura bitters
½ tsp. sugar syrup, or to taste

1. Half-fill mixing glass with cracked ice
2. Add rye, dry vermouth, Pernod, bitters and sugar syrup
3. Shake
4. Pour into a highball glass

YELLOWBIRD

¾ oz. white crème de cacao
¾ oz. vodka
¾ oz. orange juice
¾ oz. cream
½ oz. Galliano

1. Fill mixing glass with ice
2. Add white crème de cacao, vodka, orange juice, cream and Galliano
3. Shake
4. Strain into a chilled champagne glass

YELLOW FEVER

1½ oz. vodka
5–6 oz. lemonade

1. Fill a highball glass with ice
2. Add vodka
3. Fill with lemonade
4. Stir
5. Garnish with a slice of lemon

YELLOW PARROT

1 oz. apricot brandy
1 oz. Pernod
¾ oz. yellow Chartreuse

1. Fill mixing glass with ice
2. Add apricot brandy, Pernod and yellow Chartreuse
3. Shake
4. Strain into a rocks glass filled with ice

YELLOW RATTLER

1 oz. dry vermouth
1 oz. sweet vermouth
1 oz. gin
3 oz. orange juice
(preferably freshly
squeezed)

1. Fill mixing glass with ice
2. Add dry vermouth, sweet
   vermouth, gin and orange
   juice
3. Shake
4. Strain into a chilled goblet

YELLOW STRAWBERRY

1 oz. light rum
½ oz. banana liqueur
4 oz. frozen strawberries,
thawed
1 oz. sour mix

1. Fill blender with 3 oz. ice, light
   rum, banana liqueur, frozen
   strawberries and sour mix
2. Blend
3. Pour into a goblet
4. Garnish with a banana slice

YODEL

1½ oz. Fernet Branca
1½ oz. orange juice
club soda

1. Fill a rocks glass with ice
2. Add Fernet Branca and orange
   juice
3. Stir
4. Fill with club soda

YORK SPECIAL

2½ oz. dry vermouth
½ oz. maraschino liqueur
3–4 dashes orange bitters

1. Fill mixing glass with ice
2. Add dry vermouth, maraschino
   liqueur and orange bitters
3. Stir
4. Strain into a chilled cocktail
   glass

Z

ZAMBOANGA HUMMER

½ oz. gold rum
½ oz. gin
½ oz. brandy
½ oz. curaçao or triple sec
2 oz. orange juice
2 oz. pineapple juice
½ oz. lemon juice
1 tsp. brown sugar

1. Fill mixing glass with 3 oz. ice
2. Add all ingredients
3. Shake well
4. Strain into a Collins glass filled with ice

ZANZIBAR

2½ oz. dry vermouth
1 oz. gin
½ oz. lemon juice
1 tsp. sugar syrup
2–3 dashes orange bitters

1. Fill mixing glass with ice
2. Add dry vermouth, gin, lemon juice, sugar syrup and orange bitters
3. Shake
4. Strain into a chilled sour glass
5. Add ice, if desired
6. Garnish with a twist of lemon

ZIPPERHEAD

1 oz. Chambord 1 oz. vodka 1 oz. 7-Up	1. Fill a rocks glass with ice 2. Add Chambord, vodka and 7-Up 3. Suck shot through a thick straw

ZOMBIE

1 oz. light rum
½ oz. crème de noyaux
½ oz. triple sec
1½ oz. sour mix
1½ oz. orange juice
½ oz. 151-proof rum
	1. Fill mixing glass with ice
	2. Add light rum, crème de
	    noyaux, triple sec, sour mix
	    and orange juice
	3. Strain into a Collins glass filled
	    with ice
	4. Top with 151-proof rum
	5. Garnish with a cherry

ZOOM

1½ oz. brandy ¼ oz. honey ½ oz. cream	1. Fill mixing glass with ice 2. Add brandy, honey and cream 3. Shake well 4. Strain into a chilled cocktail glass

NONALCOHOLIC DRINK RECIPES

BANANA MILK SHAKE

1 medium-sized ripe banana, peeled ½ pt. milk 1 tsp. honey	1. Combine banana, milk and honey in a blender 2. Blend well 3. Pour into a rocks glass 4. Add ice

BLACK COW

2 scoops vanilla ice cream root beer	1. Put ice cream into a Collins glass 2. Fill with cold root beer 3. Stir

CAFÉ MOCHA

4 oz. strong hot black coffee 4 oz. hot chocolate whipped cream	1. Combine black coffee and hot chocolate in a large mug 2. Top with whipped cream 3. Sprinkle cinnamon and/or nutmeg on top

CAFÉ VIENNOISE

8 oz. strong cold black coffee 1 oz. heavy cream 1 tsp. chocolate syrup several dashes cinnamon powder	1. In blender, combine coffee, heavy cream, chocolate syrup and cinnamon 2. Blend until smooth 3. Pour into a goblet or large wineglass 4. Sprinkle nutmeg on top, if desired

CENTER COURT

½ lb. strawberries, stems
   removed
½ pt. sweet cream
2 tsp. powdered sugar
½ tsp. powdered ginger
club soda

1. Combine strawberries, sweet
cream, sugar and ginger in a
blender
2. Blend well
3. Pour into a pitcher
4. Add club soda and ice cubes
5. Stir

CHOCOLATE ALMOND SHAKE

1 oz. chocolate syrup
1 oz. almond syrup
4 oz. cream

1. In a blender, combine chocolate
syrup, almond syrup, cream and
3 oz. crushed ice
2. Blend until smooth
3. Pour into a goblet or large
wineglass

COLA FLOAT

2 scoops vanilla ice cream
cola

1. Put ice cream in a Collins glass
2. Fill with cola
3. Stir

CRANBERRY COOLER

2 oz. cranberry juice
   cocktail
½ oz. lime juice
club soda or ginger ale

1. Fill mixing glass with ice
2. Add cranberry juice and lime
juice
3. Shake
4. Strain into a rocks glass filled
with ice
5. Fill with club soda or ginger ale

CRANBERRY-GRAPE DRINK

3 oz. cranberry juice
cocktail
3 oz. grape juice

1. Fill a highball glass with ice
2. Add cranberry juice and grape juice
3. Stir

CRANBERRY SPARKLER

3 oz. cranberry juice
cocktail
3 oz. club soda

1. Fill a highball glass with ice
2. Add cranberry juice and club soda
3. Stir gently

CRANBERRY SPLASH

5 oz. club soda
1 oz. cranberry juice
cocktail

1. Fill a highball glass with ice
2. Add club soda
3. Top with cranberry juice
4. Garnish with a slice of lemon and a slice of lime (optional)

DRY GRAPE VINE

2 oz. grape juice
1 oz. lemon juice
1 dash grenadine

1. Fill mixing glass with ice
2. Add grape juice, lemon juice and grenadine
3. Shake
4. Strain into a chilled cocktail glass

EASTER EGG HATCH*

3½ oz. frozen vanilla yogurt 2 oz. orange juice 1 tbsp. sugar syrup	1. In blender, combine frozen yogurt, orange juice, sugar syrup and 3½ oz. crushed ice 2. Blend 3. Pour into a goblet

EGG CREAM

1–1½ oz. chocolate syrup cold milk seltzer	1. Pour chocolate syrup into a highball glass 2. Fill glass approximately ⅔ with milk 3. Top with seltzer 4. Stir

FRUIT JUICE

2 oz. pineapple juice 2 oz. orange juice 2 oz. grapefruit juice 2 oz. cranberry juice cocktail	1. Combine all juices in a highball glass or Collins glass 2. Stir well

FRUIT JUICE COOLER

1½ oz. pineapple juice 1½ oz. orange juice 1½ oz. grapefruit juice 1½ oz. cranberry juice 2 oz. club soda or ginger ale	1. Combine all juices in a highball glass or Collins glass 2. Stir well 3. Top with club soda or ginger ale

---

* Courtesy of Beach Grill, Westminster, Colorado.

GINGER ALE AND BITTERS

6 oz. ginger ale
2–3 dashes Angostura
  bitters

1. Fill highball glass with ice
2. Add ginger ale and bitters
3. Stir

GRAPE CRUSH

3 oz. grape juice
1 oz. cranberry juice
  cocktail
1 oz. sour mix
7-Up

1. Fill a highball glass with
   crushed ice
2. Add grape juice, cranberry
   juice and sour mix
3. Stir well
4. Top with 7-Up

LEMONADE

1½ oz. freshly squeezed
  lemon juice
2 tsp. superfine granulated
  sugar, or to taste
distilled or springwater

1. Pour lemon juice into a Collins
   glass
2. Add sugar
3. Dissolve sugar
4. Fill with ice
5. Fill with water
6. Stir

LEMONADE FIZZ

1 oz. lemon juice
2 tsp. powdered sugar
club soda

1. Combine lemon juice and sugar
   in a Collins glass
2. Stir until sugar is dissolved
3. Fill glass with ice cubes
4. Fill with club soda

LIMEADE

1½ oz. freshly squeezed lime juice 3–4 tsp. sugar distilled or springwater	1. Pour lime juice into a Collins glass 2. Add sugar 3. Dissolve sugar 4. Fill with ice 5. Fill with water 6. Stir

LIME COLA

½ oz. freshly squeezed lime juice cola	1. Fill a Collins glass with ice 2. Pour in lime juice 3. Fill with cola 4. Stir

LIME COOLER

1 tbsp. lime juice tonic water	1. Fill a Collins glass with ice 2. Add lime juice 3. Fill with tonic water 4. Garnish with a slice of lime

LIME RICKEY

1 oz. Rose's lime juice club soda dash of grenadine	1. Fill a highball glass with ice 2. Pour in lime juice 3. Fill with club soda 4. Stir 5. Add grenadine 6. Stir again

MALTED (CHOCOLATE)

- -

2 scoops chocolate ice
cream
1 cup milk
2 oz. chocolate syrup
2 tbsp. malt powder

1. Combine chocolate ice cream,
   milk, chocolate syrup and malt
   powder in a blender
2. Blend until smooth
3. Pour into a goblet or other large
   glass

NO-GIN FIZZ

- -

4 oz. lemon juice
1 oz. lime juice
1 tbsp. confectioners' sugar
club soda

1. Fill a Collins glass with ice
2. Add lemon juice, lime juice and
   sugar
3. Stir until sugar is dissolved
4. Fill with club soda
5. Garnish with a lime wedge

OLD-TIME STRAWBERRY MILK SHAKE

- -

4 oz. fresh strawberries,
stems removed
8 oz. cold milk
1 tbsp. honey (sugar may be
substituted)

1. Fill blender with several ice
   cubes, fresh strawberries, cold
   milk and honey or sugar
2. Blend until smooth
3. Pour into a goblet or large
   wineglass

ORANGE AID

- -

6 oz. orange juice
1 tbsp. sugar syrup
club soda

1. Fill a Collins glass with ice
2. Add orange juice and sugar syrup
3. Stir well
4. Fill with club soda
5. Garnish with a slice of orange

ORANGE AND TONIC

5 oz. orange juice
tonic water

1. Fill a Collins glass with ice
2. Add orange juice
3. Fill with tonic water
4. Stir gently

ORANGE FIZZ

5 oz. orange juice
1 oz. sour mix
club soda

1. Fill a Collins glass with ice
2. Add orange juice and sour mix
3. Top with club soda

ORANGE 'N' BITTERS

orange juice
2–3 dashes Angostura bitters

1. Fill a highball glass with ice
2. Add orange juice and bitters
3. Stir

ORANGE SPARKLER

3 oz. orange juice
3 oz. club soda

1. Fill a highball glass with ice
2. Add orange juice and club soda
3. Stir gently

PASSION FRUIT SPRITZER

4 oz. passion fruit juice
club soda

1. Pour passion fruit juice over several ice cubes in a tulip glass
2. Fill with club soda
3. Garnish with a wedge of lime

PINEAPPLE-CRANBERRY JUICE PUNCH

2 qts. chilled unsweetened
   pineapple juice
2 qts. cranberry juice cocktail
16 oz. club soda
16 oz. ginger ale

1. Combine all ingredients in a large punch bowl, over a block of ice
2. Stir
3. Garnish with pineapple slices

PINEAPPLE MILK SHAKE

3 oz. pineapple juice
3 or 4 pineapple cubes
4 oz. cold milk
1 tbsp. honey (sugar may be
   substituted)

1. Fill blender with several ice cubes, pineapple juice, pineapple, cold milk and honey or sugar
2. Blend until smooth
3. Pour into a goblet or large wineglass

PRAIRIE OYSTER

1 egg
1 dash Tabasco
salt and pepper to taste

1. Combine all ingredients in a glass
2. Stir well
3. Drink down in one gulp

(*Note:* This drink is reputed to be a cure for hangovers.)

RAINBOW SHERBET PUNCH

8 oz. orange juice
8 oz. pineapple juice
8 oz. Hawaiian Punch
1 bottle club soda
1 bottle ginger ale
1 qt. rainbow sherbet

1. Combine juices in a punch bowl over ice
2. Before serving, add sodas and scoops of rainbow sherbet

459

RASPBERRY CRANBERRY PUNCH

12-oz. can frozen raspberry
    cranberry juice cocktail
    concentrate, thawed
36 oz. (3 cans) water
1 liter 7-Up
raspberry sherbet

1. Combine all ingredients (except sherbet) in a large punch bowl
2. Add ice
3. Serve in rocks glasses or punch glasses
4. Add a scoop of raspberry sherbet to each serving

RASPBERRY SELTZER

1 tsp. raspberry syrup
seltzer or club soda

1. Pour raspberry syrup into a tall glass
2. Fill with cold seltzer
3. Add ice, if necessary

ROSE'S RUBY HEART

5 or 6 fresh strawberries
cream
1 oz. sour mix

1. In blender, combine strawberries, cream and sour mix with 3 oz. crushed ice
2. Blend until smooth
3. Pour into a goblet

SAFE SEX ON THE BEACH

1 oz. peach nectar
3 oz. pineapple juice (or
    grapefruit juice)
3 oz. orange juice

1. Pour peach nectar, pineapple juice (or grapefruit juice) and orange juice into a highball glass with several ice cubes
2. Stir

SHIRLEY TEMPLE

1 dash grenadine
ginger ale

1. Fill a Collins glass with ice
2. Add grenadine
3. Fill with ginger ale
4. Decorate with a cherry and an orange slice

SOBER SPRITZER

3 oz. white grape juice
club soda

1. Fill wineglass with several ice cubes
2. Add 3 oz. grape juice
3. Fill with club soda
4. Garnish with a twist of lemon

SOBER THOUGHTS

3 oz. orange juice
3 oz. fresh lime juice
1 tbsp. grenadine
tonic water

1. Fill a highball glass with ice
2. Add orange juice, lime juice and grenadine
3. Stir well
4. Fill with tonic water

SODA AND BITTERS

5 oz. club soda
2–3 dashes Angostura bitters

1. Fill a highball glass with ice
2. Fill with club soda
3. Add bitters
4. Stir

SUMMER COOLER

¼ lb. strawberries, stems removed
½ cup plain yogurt
1 cup milk
sugar or honey, to taste

1. Combine strawberries, yogurt, milk and sugar or honey in a blender
2. Blend well
3. Fill rocks glasses with ice cubes and pour in mixture
4. Garnish with strawberry slices

SWAMP WATER

3 oz. root beer
3 oz. orange soda

1. Fill a highball glass with ice
2. Add equal amounts of root beer and orange soda
3. Stir

TEQUILA SUNSET

2 oz. orange juice
1 tbsp. grenadine

1. Fill a rocks glass with ice
2. Pour in orange juice
3. Slowly add grenadine, by pouring over the back of a spoon; let it rise from bottom of the glass

TROPICAL FRUIT PUNCH

4 46-oz. cans pineapple juice
2 6-oz. cans orange juice concentrate
2 6-oz. cans lemonade concentrate
8 oz. fresh lime juice
8 oz. grenadine

1. Pour all ingredients over a block of ice in a punch bowl
2. Stir
3. Garnish with lime slices and fresh sprigs of mint

VERY LEMON LEMONADE

2 oz. sour mix
club soda
7-Up

1. Fill a Collins glass with ice
2. Add sour mix
3. Fill with equal parts club soda and 7-Up
4. Stir gently

VIRGIN MADRAS

3 oz. cranberry juice cocktail
3 oz. orange juice

1. Fill a highball glass with ice
2. Add cranberry juice and orange juice
3. Stir

VIRGIN MARGARITA

1½ oz. sour mix
½ oz. Rose's lime juice
½ oz. orange juice

1. Fill mixing glass with ice
2. Add sour mix, lime juice and orange juice
3. Shake
4. Strain into a chilled cocktail glass or a rocks glass filled with ice

VIRGIN MARY

4 oz. tomato juice
½ oz. lemon juice
3 drops Tabasco sauce
3 drops Worcestershire sauce
pinch celery salt
pinch pepper
dab horseradish (squeeze out liquid)

1. Combine tomato juice, lemon juice and seasonings (to taste) in a well-chilled shaker
2. Shake
3. Pour into an oversized wineglass or a chilled Collins glass
4. Garnish with a lime slice or a celery stalk

VIRGIN PIÑA COLADA

1 oz. pineapple juice
3 or 4 pineapple chunks
(optional)
1 oz. cream of coconut
1 tsp. orange juice
1 tbsp. cream

1. Combine pineapple juice,
   pineapple chunks, cream of
   coconut, orange juice and
   cream with 3 oz. ice in a
   blender
2. Blend until smooth
3. Pour into a goblet or large
   wineglass
4. Garnish with a cherry and an
   orange slice

VIRGIN SEA BREEZE

3 oz. grapefruit juice
3 oz. cranberry juice
cocktail

1. Pour grapefruit juice and
   cranberry juice into a highball
   glass filled with ice
2. Stir

YOGURT SUPREME

1 oz. lemon juice
1 oz. orange juice
1½ oz. milk
1½ oz. plain yogurt
½ tsp. honey

1. Combine lemon juice, orange
   juice, milk, yogurt and honey in
   a blender
2. Blend well
3. Pour into a goblet and add ice

INDEX BY INGREDIENTS

(NA = NONALCOHOLIC)

Amaretto Drinks

Absolut Royalty Cocktail, 78
Alabama Slammer
  (shooter), 82
Almond Cocktail, 85
Almond Joy, 85
Amaretto and Cream, 86
Amaretto Coffee (Italian Coffee),
  86, 238
Amaretto Mist, 86
Amaretto Sour, 86
Blind Melon, 114
Bocci Ball, 120
Brain Eraser, 123
Café Zurich, 133
Chocolate-Covered Cherry
  (shooter), 144
Climax, 147
Cream Soda, 156
Dr. Pepper, 167
Dominican Coco
  Loco, 167
Electric Kool-Aid, 175
Ferrari, 182
Filby, 184
Foxy Lady, 190
French Connection, 191
Godchild, 205

Godfather, 205
Hammerhead, 218
Homecoming, 222
Italian Assassin, 238
Italian Delight, 238
Italian Surfer, 239
Killer Kool-Aid, 253
Mafia's Kiss, 272
Marlon Brando, 279
Mountain Red Punch, 294
Nutty Colada, 301
Nutty Stinger, 302
Orgasm, 308
Panda Bear, 312
Pavarotti, 315
Peachy Keen Freeze, 317
Pineapple Bomber
  (shooter), 324
Pink Almond, 325
Popsicle, 334
Roasted Toasted Almond, 350
Rock Lobster (shooter), 352
Screaming Orgasm, 367
Seventh Heaven, 369
Sicilian Kiss, 373
Sweetie Baby, 392
Tawny Russian, 395

Toasted Almond, 405
Trophy Room, 409

Tumbleweed, 411
Verona, 418

Aperol

Cranberry Spice Cocktail, 155

Amer Picon

Amer Picon Cocktail, 88
Picon, 321
Picon Fizz, 322
Picon Orange, 322

Picon Sour, 322
Quebec Cocktail, 341
Sanctuary, 361

Anise and Anisette Drinks

Blanche, 113
Café Zurich, 133
Dream Cocktail, 169
Eye-Opener, 178
Good and Plenty, 209
International, The 234
Irish Whiskey Cocktail, 237
Jelly Bean, 244
Johnnie's Cocktail, 246

Ladies, 258
Narragansett, 296
New Orleans, 298
Night Cap, 299
Orange Comfort, 307
Turf, 411
Tuxedo, 411
Which Way, 429

Apple Brandy/Apple Liqueur

A.J., 81
Angel Face, 88
Ante, 89
Applecar, 90
Apple Ginger Punch, 91
Apple Grog, 91
Apple Jacques, 92
Apple Pie, 92

Bentley, 107
Bolero, 120
Deauville Cocktail, 163
Dempsey, 163
Depth Bomb, 164
Empire, 176
Froot Loop, 193
Grand Apple, 211

Honeymoon, 223
Ichbien, 232
Jack-in-the-Box, 240
Jack Rose, 240
Lamplighter, 259
Liberty Cocktail, 263
Lugger, 271
Marconi Wireless, 278
Moonlight, 292
Mule's Hind Leg, 295
Oom Paul, 305
Philadelphia Scotchman, 321
Princess Mary's Pride, 337
Prince's Smile, 338
Saucy Sue, 364

Savoy Tango, 365
Sharky Punch, 372
Sledgehammer, 376
Special Rough, 383
Star, 385
Third Rail, 401
Tinton, 404
Torpedo, 407
Tulip, 410
Vanity Fair Cocktail, 416
Warday's Cocktail, 425
Washington Apple, 427
Wembley, 428
Whist, 431
Widow's Kiss, 437

Apricot Brandy/Apricot Liqueur Drinks

After Dinner, 81
Angel Face, 88
Apple Pie, 92
Apricot, 92
Apricot Fizz, 93
Apricot Sour, 93
Atlantic Breeze, 95
Aviation, 97
Barnum, 103
Black Witch, 113
Bronx Cheer, 127
Claridge, 147
Costa del Sol, 154
Cruise Control, 157
Czarina, 159
Darb, 161
Empire, 176
English Rose, 177
Everything But, 178
Fairbanks, 180
Father Sherman, 182
Favorite, 182
Festival, 183
Flamingo, 185

Frankenjack Cocktail, 190
Gasper, 198
Golden Dawn, 206
Golden Daze, 207
Golden Slipper, 209
Gradeal Special, 210
Hop Toad, 224
Ice Palace, 231
KCB, 250
Knockout, 256
Kyoto, 257
Leave It to Me, 262
Lugger, 271
Mother Sherman, 294
Mule's Hind Leg, 295
Nevins, 298
Pancho Villa, 312
Paradise, 313
Pendennis Cocktail, 318
Pineapple Francine, 324
Pink Whiskers, 329
Prince's Smile, 338
Prohibition, 338
Red Cloud, 347

Resolute, 349
Saucy Sue, 364
Self-Starter, 368
Summer Share, 389
Tempter Cocktail, 396

Thanksgiving Cocktail, 401
Tulip, 410
Valencia, 415
Why Not, 437
Yellow Parrot, 444

Aquavit Drinks

Aalborg Sour, 77
Alliance, 85
Danish Mary, 161
Fjord, 185

Great Dane, 213
Tivoli, 405
Viking, 419

Baileys Original Irish Cream Drinks

After Eight (shooter), 81
After Five (shooter), 81
B-52, 98
B-53 (shooter), 98
Baileys and Coffee, 99
Beam Me Up, Scotty
    (shooter), 104
Brain, 123
Brain Tumor, 124
Buttery Nipple (shooter), 130
Café Theatre, 133
Cerebral Hemorrhage, 139
Death By Chocolate, 162
E.T. (shooter), 177
Homecoming, 222

IRA Cocktail, 235
Irish Car Bomb, 236
Irish Cow, 236
Lube Job, 271
Millionaire's Coffee, 287
Mudslide, 295
Nutty Irishman, 302
Rock Lobster (shooter), 352
Russian Quaalude, 359
St. Patrick's Day Mocha
    Java, 360
Screaming Orgasm, 367
Slippery Nipple, 377
Snow Cap (shooter), 379
Sweet Cream, 391

Banana Liqueur/Creme de Banana Drinks

Banana Banshee, 100
Banana Boat, 100
Banana Daiquiri (Frozen), 100
Banana Mama, 101
Banana Moo, 101

Banana Split, 101
Banana Tree, 102
Beam Me Up, Scotty, 104
Boardwalk Breezer, 119
Bubble Gum (shooter), 128

Café Foster, 132
Capri, 137
Chiquita Cocktail, 144
Chocolate Banana
    Banshee, 144
Climax, 147
Dutch Velvet, 172
Georgia Peach Fizz, 199
Hawaiian Eye, 220
Jolly Roger, 247
Jungle Jim, 247
La Jolla, 259
Limbo, 264

Nightingale, 300
Pacific Pacifier, 310
Pilot Boat, 322
Piñata, 323
Pousse-Café (1), 335
Red Devil, 348
Rose Hall, 353
Rum Runner, 357
Ruptured Duck, 358
Russian Banana, 358
Traffic Light, 407
Velvet Kiss, 417
Yellow Strawberry, 445

Beer and Ale Drinks

Beer Buster, 105
Black Velvet, 113
Boilermaker, 120
Dr. Pepper, 167
Foxtail, 189
Ginger Shandy, 203

Irish Car Bomb, 236
Lager 'N' Lime, 259
Shandy, 371
Skip and Go Naked, 376
Weissen Sour, 428
A Yard of Flannel, 443

Bénédictine Drinks

Aunt Jemima, 96
B & B, 98
Bobby Burns, 119
Honeymoon, 223
Honolulu Lulu, 223
Hoot Mon, 224
Kentucky
    Colonel, 251
Oh, Henry!, 304

Preakness, 336
Queen Elizabeth Wine
    Cocktail, 342
Rainbow Pousse-Café, 344
Rolls-Royce, 353
Savoy Hotel, 364
Twin Hills, 412
Widow's Dream, 437
Widow's Kiss, 437

Blackberry Brandy/Liqueur Drinks

Allegheny, 84
Blackberry Demitasse, 109

Black Martini, 112
Cadiz, 131

Chi-Chi, 143
Dark Eyes, 162
Down the Hatch, 168
Jelly Bean, 244
Poop Deck, 333

Pousse-Café (2), 335
Rum Runner, 357
Sparkling Wine Polonaise, 383
Tequila Sunset, 400
Warsaw, 426

Blueberry Schnapps

Out of the Blue, 309

Bourbon Drinks

Admiral Cocktail, 79
Allegheny, 84
Americana, 87
Artillery Punch, 94
Blizzard, 114
Blue Denim, 117
Bourbon Daisy, 122
Bourbon Old-Fashioned, 122
Bourbon Sour, 122
Bourbon Street, 123
Brown, 127
Buffalo Sweat
    (shooter), 128
Fiji Fizz, 183
Forester, 188
Frozen Mint
    Julep, 196
Geisha, 199
Ground Zero, 216
Hawaiian Eye, 220
Hot Toddy, 228
Huntress Cocktail, 229
Imperial Fizz, 233
Italian Stallion, 239
Jamaican Milk
    Shake, 242
Kentucky Cocktail, 251
Kentucky Coffee, 251

Kentucky Colonel, 251
Kentucky Cooler, 251
Kentucky Orange
    Blossom, 252
Laura, The 260
Long Hot
    Night, 268
Mashed Old-Fashioned, 281
Millionaire, 287
Mint Julep, 288
Narragansett, 296
Nevins, 298
New Orleans, 298
Nocturnal, 301
Old-Fashioned, 304
Quickie, 343
Sazerac, 365
Sink or Swim, 375
Snow Shoe
    (shooter), 379
Stone Sour, 386
Tivoli, 405
Trilby, 408
Trolley, 409
Turkey Shooter, 411
Waldorf, 425
Weissen Sour, 428
Whirlaway, 429

Adrienne's Dream, 79
Alabama, 82
American Beauty, 87
Andalusia, 88
April Shower, 93
Artillery Punch, 94
Aunt Jemima, 96
B & B, 98
Bermuda Highball, 108
Betsy Ross, 108
Between the Sheets, 108
Blackberry Demitasse, 109
Black-Eyed Susan, 110
Black Lady, 111
Bombay, 120
Booster, 121
Brandy Alexander, 124
Brandy Cobbler, 124
Brandy Eggnog, 124
Brandy Gump, 125
Brandy Ice, 125
Brandy Manhattan, 125
Brandy Milk Punch, 126
Brandy Old-Fashioned, 126
Breakfast Eggnog, 127
Café Bonaparte, 132
California Lemonade, 135
Carroll Cocktail, 138
Champagne-Maraschino
    Punch, 140
Chicago, 143
City Slicker, 146
Classic, 147
Coffee Keokee, 150
Cold Deck, 151
Cold Weather Punch, 151
Cricket, 157
Deauville Cocktail, 163
Delmonico, 163
Depth Bomb, 164
Diana, 165

Dirty Mother (Separator),
    166, 368
Dirty White Mother, 167
Dream, 169
Dream Cocktail, 169
East India Cocktail, 173
Fantasio, 181
Father Sherman, 182
Fish House Punch, 185
Fjord, 185
Florida Punch, 187
Fogcutter, 187
Foxhound, 189
French Connection, 191
Froupe, 194
Gazette, 198
Georgia Peach Fizz, 199
Green Hornet, 215
Green Room, 215
Grenadier, 215
Harvard, 219
Hoopla, 224
Invisible Man, 235
Italian Stinger, 239
Janet Standard, 243
Kahlúa Toreador, 249
Kappa Colada, 250
Kioki Coffee, 254
Kiss the Boys Goodbye, 256
Lady Be Good, 258
La Jolla, 259
Last Round, 260
Loudspeaker, 270
Lover's Delight, 271
Lugger, 271
Memphis Belle Cocktail, 284
Montana, 291
Moonshine Cocktail, 292
Morning, 292
Morning Becomes Electric, 293
Morning Glory, 293

Mountain Red Punch, 294
Netherland, 297
Newton's Special, 298
Night Cap, 299
Odd McIntyre, 303
Olympic, 305
Pavarotti, 315
Phoebe Snow, 321
Pisco Punch, 329
Pisco Sour, 329
Poop Deck, 333
Port Sangaree, 334
Port Wine Cocktail, 334
Prince of Wales, 337
Quaker, 341
Quelle Vie, 343
Roman Stinger, 353
Sangria, 361
Saratoga, 364
Savoy Hotel, 364
Scorpion, 366
Separator (Dirty Mother),
    166, 368
Sherry Twist, 372
Sidecar, 373
Sir Walter, 375
Sledgehammer, 376
Sleepyhead, 376

Sloe Brandy, 377
S.O.B. Shooter (shooter), 380
Spanish Coffee, 382
Sparkling Wine Julep, 383
Special Rough, 383
Stinger, 386
Stone Fence, 386
Super Coffee, 390
Tantalus, 395
Third Rail, 401
Three Miles, 402
Thunder, 402
Tiger's Milk, 403
Tom and Jerry, 405
Torpedo, 407
Vanderbilt, 416
Venetian Coffee, 417
Via Veneto, 418
Victor, 418
Washington, 426
Weep No More, 428
Which Way, 429
Whip, 429
White Grape, Tangerine and
    Sparkling Wine Punch, 433
White Wine Super Sangria, 436
Zamboanga Hummer, 446
Zoom, 447

Butterscotch Schnapps

Buttery Nipple (shooter), 130   Pumpkin Pie Martini, 338

Campari Drinks

Alfredo, 84
Americano, 87
Bitter Bikini, 109
Campari and Soda, 136
Campobello, 136

Dubonnet Negroni, 170
Filby, 184
Genoa, 199
Italian Stallion, 239
Laura, The 260

Napoli, 296
Negroni, 297
Negroni Cooler, 297

Rendezvous, 349
Tivoli, 405

Canadian Whiskey

Bent Nail, 108
Canada Cocktail, 136
Ladies, 258
Maple Leaf, 277

Quebec Cocktail, 341
Trois Rivieres, 408
Vancouver Cocktail, 415

Caramel Liqueur Drinks

Caramel Nut, 138

Chambord Drinks

Absolut Royalty Cocktail, 78
Absolut Santo, 78
Chambord Daiquiri, 140
Chambord Royale Spritzer, 140
Club Med, 148
French Summer, The 192
Grape Crush, 212
Grateful Dead, 213
Little Purple Men, 266

Peanut Butter and Jelly
    (shooter), 317
Purple Hooter Shooter, The 339
Purple Haze (shooter), 339
Raspberry Smash, 345
Sex on the Beach (the original),
    370
Sour Grapes (shooter), 381
Zipperhead, 447

Chambraise

Sapphire Martini, 363

Champagne and Sparkling Wine Drinks

Alto Parlarle, 86
Americana, 87

Bellini, 105
Bellini Punch, 106

Black Velvet, 113
Chambord Royale Spritzer, 140
Champagne Cocktail, 140
Champagne-Maraschino
    Punch, 140
Champagne Punch, 141
Champagne Sherbet Punch, 141
Chicago, 143
Concorde, 152
Death in the Afternoon, 162
Diamond Fizz, 165
Eve, 177
French Lift, 191
French 75, 191
Frobisher, 193
Frozen Bikini, 194
Imperial Fizz, 233
King's Peg, 254
Kir Royale, 255

London Special, 267
Mimosa, 287
Moscow Mimosa, 293
Odéon Casino, 303
Poinsettia, 331
Pomegranate Fizz, 333
Prince of Wales, 337
Royal Peach Freeze, 355
Royal Screw, 355
Sangria Especiale, 362
Savoy Springtime, 365
Sparkling Pear Cocktail, 382
Sparkling Wine Julep, 383
Sparkling Wine Polonaise, 383
Tintoretto, 404
Valencia, 415
White Grape, Tangerine
    and Sparkling Wine
    Punch, 433

Chartreuse Drinks

Alaska, 83
April Shower, 93
Cat's Eye, 139
French Green Dragon, 191
Golden Slipper, 209
Green Lizard (shooter), 215
Jewel, 245
Lollipop, 267
Mexican Missile (shooter), 285
Pago Pago, 310

Rainbow Pousse-Café, 344
Rocky Green Dragon, 352
Save the Planet, 364
Tipperary, 404
Warday's Cocktail, 425
Whiskey Daisy, 430
Widow's Kiss, 437
Xanthia, 441
Yellow Parrot, 444

Cherry Brandy

Banana Split, 101
Blood and Sand, 114
Electric Kool-Aid, 175
Froot Loop, 193
Great Dane, 213

Hudson Bay, 228
Hunter's Cocktail, 229
Juniper Blend, 247
Kiss in the Dark, 255
Ladyfinger, 258

Orange Oasis, 308
Vanderbilt, 416
Vanity Fair Cocktail, 416

Volga Boatman, 424
Wedding Belle, 427
Xanthia, 441

Cherry/Maraschino Liqueur Drinks

Apple Ginger Punch, 91
Aviation, 97
Banana Split, 101
Blood and Sand, 114
Casablanca, 138
Champagne-Maraschino
    Punch, 140
Champagne Punch, 141
Cherry Cola, 142
Cherry Daiquiri (frozen), 142
Classic, 147
Diplomat, 166
Dubonnet Fizz, 170
Fiji Fizz, 183
Forester, 188
French Rose, 191
Ginger Breeze, 202
Huntress Cocktail, 229
Kiss, The 255
Merry Widow, 284
Mountain Red Punch, 294
Mount Fuji, 295

Opera (1), 306
Pancho Villa (shooter), 312
Polynesian Cocktail, 332
Pousse-Café (1), 335
Prado, 335
Quebec Cocktail, 341
Rainbow Pousse-Café, 344
Saratoga, 364
Shotgun Wedding
    Cocktail, 373
Singapore Sling, 375
Southern Bride, 381
Swedish Lullaby, 391
Tahiti Club, 394
Tennessee, 394
Tropical Cocktail, 409
Turf, 411
Tuxedo, 411
Vanity Fair Cocktail, 416
White Cargo, 432
White Rose, 435
York Special, 445

Chocolate Liqueur

Jelly Donut Martini, 244
Kiss, The 255

Spicy Hot Cocoa, 384

Chocolate Mint Liqueur

Dutch Velvet, 172

Coffee Drinks

Amaretto Coffee (Italian Coffee), 86, 238
Baileys and Coffee, 99
Café Bonaparte, 132
Café Foster, 132
Café Marnier, 132
Café Mocha (NA), 451
Café Theatre, 133
Café Viennoise (NA), 451
Café Zurich, 133
Calypso (Jamaican Coffee), 135
Cappuccino Mocha, 137
Charro, 141
Coffee Cooler, 150
Coffee Frappe, 150
Coffee Keokee, 150
Dutch Coffee, 171
Hot Coconut Coffee, 225
Irish Coffee, 236
Israeli Coffee, 238
Italian Coffee (Amaretto Coffee), 86, 238
Jamaican Coffee (Calypso), 135
Kentucky Coffee, 251
Kioki Coffee, 254
Mexican Coffee, 285
Millionaire's Coffee, 287
St. Patrick's Day Mocha Java, 360
Scottish Coffee, 367
Spanish Coffee, 382
Trophy Room, 409
Venetian Coffee, 417

Coffee Liqueur

Russian Coffee, 359

Spanish Moss, 382

Cognac Drinks

Alabazam, 82
Café Zurich, 133
Concorde, 152
Eggnog (standard recipe), 174
Eve, 177
Fish House Punch, 185
French Green Dragon, 191
French 75, 191
Grand Apple, 211
International, The 234
King's Peg, 254
Lallah Rookh, 259
Picon Fizz, 322
Pousse-Café (1), 335
Rainbow Pousse-Café, 344
Rocky Green Dragon, 352
Royal Screw, 355
Sangria Especiale, 362
Sparkling Wine Polonaise, 383
Truffle Martini, 410
Wagon Wheel, 425
Waterbury, 427

Cointreau Drinks

Alto Parlarle, 86
Barbarella, 103
Blanche, 113
Chiquita Cocktail, 144
Claret Cup, 146
Claridge, 147
Classic, 147
Cruise Control, 157
Derby Special, 164
Dream Cocktail, 169
Fans, 181
Fine and Dandy, 184
Happy Feller (shooter), The 218
Hoopla, 224
International, The 234
Johnnie's Cocktail, 246
Kiss Me Quick, 255
Lollipop, 267

Loud-Hailer, 270
Loudspeaker, 270
Lover's Delight, 271
Mah-Jongg, 273
Margarita, My Honey, 278
Newton's Special, 298
Orange Bloom, 306
Oriental, 308
Pacific Pacifier, 310
Pernod Flip, 320
Queen Elizabeth, 342
Sanctuary, 361
Savoy Springtime, 365
S.O.B. Shooter (shooter), 380
Stormin' Gorman, 387
Ulanda, 413
Ultimate Margarita, The 413
White Wine Super Sangria, 436

Cranberry Liqueur Drinks

Cape Grape, 137

Cream and Milk Drinks

Alexander, 83
Alexander's Sister's Cocktail, 84
Almond Joy, 85
Amaretto and Cream, 86
Angel's Kiss, 88
Angel's Tit, 89
Banana Banshee, 100
Banana Daiquiri (frozen), 100
Banana Moo, 101
Banana Milk Shake (NA), 451
Banana Split, 101
Barbary Coast, 103
Bee-Stung Lips, 105

Belmont, 106
Blue Carnation, 116
Brandy Alexander, 124
Brandy Eggnog, 124
Brandy Milk Punch, 126
Breakfast Eggnog, 127
Brown Bomber, 128
Cadiz, 131
Café Bonaparte, 132
California Stripper, 135
Cappuccino Mocha, 137
Capri, 137
Center Court (NA), 452

Charro, 141
Chiquita Cocktail, 144
Chocolate Almond Shake
    (NA), 452
Chocolate Banana Banshee, 144
Chocolate Rum, 145
Climax, 147
Coffee Alexander, 149
Coffee Cooler, 150
Coffee Frappe, 150
Continental, 153
Cream Supreme, 156
Cricket, 157
Cupid's Kiss, 158
Dirty White Mother, 167
Dominican Coco Loco, 167
Dutch Velvet, 172
Easter Egg Cocktail, 173
Egg Cream (NA), 454
Eggnog (standard recipe), 174
Everglades Special, 178
Festival, 183
Foxy Lady, 190
Frostbite, 193
Frozen Fruit Daiquiri, 194
Gentle Bull, 199
Girl Scout Cookie, 203
Godchild, 205
Golden Cadillac, 206
Golden Dream, 206
Grasshopper, 213
Hawaiian Eye, 220
Henry Morgan's Grog, 221
High Jamaican Wind, 221
Huntress Cocktail, 230
Iceball, 231
Ichbien, 232
Il Magnifico, 233
Interplanetary Punch, 235
Irish Cow, 236
Italian Delight, 238
Jamaican Milk Shake, 242
Jungle Jim, 247
Kahlúa Egg Cream, 249

Kentucky Hayride, 252
Kialoa, 253
King Alphonse, 253
Kiss, The 255
Kremlin Cocktail, 257
Liebfraumilch, 263
Magpie, 273
Marlon Brando, 279
Mount Fuji, 295
Nightingale, 300
Nocturnal, 301
Nutty Irishman, 302
Oil Slick, 304
Old-Time Strawberry Milk Shake
    (NA), 457
Orgasm, 308
Pacific Pacifier, 310
Panama, 312
Parisian Blonde, 314
Peach Alexander, 315
Peach Blow Fizz, 316
Peach Coconut Flip, 316
Peach Velvet, 317
Peachy Keen Freeze, 317
Peppermint Patty, 319
Pineapple Francine, 324
Pineapple Milk Shake (NA), 459
Pink Lady, 326
Pink Rose, 328
Pink Squirrel, 328
Popsicle, 334
Ramos Fizz, 344
Ramos Gin Fizz, 345
Renaissance Cocktail, 349
Roasted Toasted Almond, 350
Rose's Ruby Heart (NA), 460
Ruptured Duck, 358
Russian Banana, 358
Russian Bear, 358
Russian Coffee, 359
Sambuca-Gin Shake, 361
Scooby Snacks, 366
Sherry Eggnog, 372
Silk Stockings, 374

Smith and Kerns, 378
Snowball, 379
Sombrero, 380
Spicy Hot Cocoa, 384
Spiked Jones, 385
Stars and Stripes, 386
Summer Cooler (NA), 462
Sweetie Baby, 392
Tiger's Milk, 403
Toasted Almond, 405
Tom and Jerry, 405
Toreador, 406
Tumbleweed, 411
Vanilla Creamsicle, 416

Velvet Hammer, 416
Velvet Kiss, 417
White Baby, 432
White Bull, 432
White Elephant, 432
White Heart, 433
White Lady (1), 434
White Lady (2), 434
White Russian, 435
Widow's Dream, 437
Xylophone, 442
Yellowbird, 444
Yogurt Supreme (NA), 464
Zoom, 447

Crème de Almond

Hawaiian Punch (shooter), 220

Pancho Villa (shooter), 312

Crème de Cacao Drinks

Adrienne's Dream, 79
Alexander, 83
Almond Joy, 85
Angel's Kiss, 88
Angel's Tit, 89
Après Ski, 92
Aunt Jemima, 96
Azteca, 97
Banana Banshee, 100
Banana Split, 101
Banana Tree, 102
Barbary Coast, 103
Blanche, 113
Blue Carnation, 116
Brandy Alexander, 124
Brandy Ice, 125
Brown Bomber, 128
Café Theatre, 133
Cappuccino Mocha, 137

Capri, 137
Caramel Nut, 138
Chocolate Banana Banshee, 144
Chocolate-Covered Cherry
    (shooter), 144
Chocolate Martini, 145
Chocolate Rum, 145
Climax, 147
Coffee Alexander, 149
Cream Supreme, 156
Creamy Mimi, 157
Cricket, 157
Cupid's Kiss, 158
Death by Chocolate, 162
Easter Egg Cocktail, 173
Everglades Special, 178
Eye-Opener, 178
Fantasio, 181
Festival, 183

'57 Chevy with a White License Plate, 183
Fox River, 189
Foxy Lady, 190
Frostbite, 193
Golden Cadillac, 206
Golden Dream, 207
Golden Gate, 207
Grand Occasion, 211
Grasshopper, 213
Hot Peppermint Patty, 226
Jockey Club, 245
Kremlin Cocktail, 257
Kretchma, 257
Liebfraumilch, 263
Lord Rodney, 269
Magpie, 273
Maxim, 282
Mocha Mint, 289
Ninotchka, 301
Nocturnal, 301
Oil Slick, 304
Orgasm, 308
Pago Pago, 310
Panama, 312
Panda Bear, 312

Paralyzer, 314
Pavarotti, 315
Peach Alexander, 315
Peach Velvet, 317
Peppermint Patty, 319
Pink Squirrel, 328
Poppy Cocktail, 333
Rainbow Pousse-Café, 344
Rock Lobster (shooter), 352
Russian, 358
Russian Banana, 358
Russian Bear, 358
Savoy Hotel, 364
Silk Stockings, 374
Toreador, 406
Tropical Cocktail, 409
Tumbleweed, 411
Vanilla Creamsicle, 416
Velvet Hammer, 416
Vodka Grasshopper, 421
Whippet, 429
White Elephant, 432
White Heart, 433
White Lady (2), 434
Xylophone, 442
Yellowbird, 444

Crème de Cassis

Black-Cherry Rum Punch, 110
Claret Cup, 146
El Diablo, 175
Gin Cassis, 201
Kir, 254
Kir Royale, 255

Mississippi Mule, 288
Ostend Fizz, 309
Parisian, 314
Pink Panther, 327
Vermouth Cassis, 417

Crème de Menthe Drinks

After Eight (shooter), 81
Alexander's Sister's Cocktail, 84

American Beauty, 87
Anti-Freeze (shooter), 90

Around the World, 94
Black-Eyed Susan, 110
Caruso, 138
Chocolate Rum, 145
Cricket, 157
Diana, 165
Emerald Isle Cooler, 176
Fallen Angel, 181
Flying Grasshopper, 187
Grasshopper, 213
Grass Is Greener, 213
Green Fire, 214
Green Hornet, 215
Hot Peppermint Patty, 226
Houston Hurricane, 228
Iceball, 231
Jade, 241
Kingdom Come, 253
Lady Be Good, 258
Leprechaun's Libation, 263
Mint Cooler, 288

Mocha Mint, 289
Mockingbird, 289
Nutty Stinger, 302
Pall Mall, 311
Pink Whiskers, 329
Pousse-Café (2), 335
Prince, 336
Roman Stinger, 353
Snowball, 379
Spanish Moss, 382
Stinger, 386
Stone Sour, 386
Tequila Stinger, 399
Traffic Light, 407
Turkey Shooter, 411
Virgin, 419
Vodka Grasshopper, 421
Vodka Stinger, 423
White Spider, 435
White Wing, 436

Crème de Noyaux Drinks

Banana Split, 101
Cupid's Kiss, 158
Fern Gully, 182
Lillet Noyaux, 264
Old Etonian, 304
Pink Almond, 325

Rockaway Beach, 352
Ruptured Duck, 358
Scorpion, 366
Strawberry Shortcake, 388
Vanity Fair Cocktail, 416
Zombie, 447

Crème de Violette Drinks (Crème d'Yvette)

Jupiter Cocktail, 248
Rainbow Pousse-Café, 344

Snowball, 379
Union Jack, 413

Curaçao Drinks

After Dinner, 81
Alabama, 82

Alabazam, 82
Azteca, 97

Betsy Ross, 108
Big Blue Sky, 109
Blue Bayou, 116
Blue Carnation, 116
Blue Denim, 117
Blue Hawaiian, 117
Blue Margarita, 117
Blue Moon, 118
Blue Shark, 118
Bombay, 120
Booster, 121
Breakfast Eggnog, 127
Chicago, 143
City Slicker, 146
Coronado, 154
Diamond Head, 165
Drawbridge, 169
Dream, 169
Easter Egg
    Cocktail, 173
El Presidente
    Eduardo, 176
Eve, 177
Fair and Warmer, 180
Fare-Thee-Well, 181
Frostbite, 193
Gloom Chaser, 204
Go-Go Juice, 206
Golden Margarita, 208
Gorilla Punch, 210
Grapeshot, 212
Green Eye-Opener, 214
Green Room, 215
Hammerhead, 218
Harper's Ferry, 219
Hawaiian Orange
    Blossom, 220
Hula-Hula, 229
Ichbien, 232
Il Magnifico, 233
Irish, 236
Jade, 241
Jamaica Ginger, 241
Live Bait's Blue Bijou, 266

Maiden's Blush, 273
Malibu Wave, 275
Marmalade, 279
McClelland, 283
Millionaire, 287
Morning, 292
Morning Becomes
    Electric, 293
Morning Glory, 293
Newbury, 298
Night Cap, 299
Nightingale, 300
Ninja Turtle, 300
Olympic, 305
Out of the
    Blue, 309
Parisian Blonde, 314
Park Avenue, 314
Pegu Club, 318
Presidente, 336
Prince of Wales, 337
Purple People
    Eater, 340
Rhett Butler, 349
Rum Curaçao
    Cooler, 356
Save the Planet, 364
Sherry Twist, 372
Sir Walter, 375
Southern Gin, 381
Stars and Stripes, 386
Swamp Water, 391
Sweet Independence, 392
Tango, 394
Tidy Bowl
    (shooter), 403
Tiger Tail, 403
Whip, 429
Whirlaway, 429
Whiskey Daisy, 430
Windex, 438
Yale Cocktail, 443
Zamboanga
    Hummer, 446

Drambuie Drinks

Bent Nail, 108
Butterscotch Collins, 129
Dundee, 171

Prince Edward, 337
Rusty Nail, 359
Scottish Coffee, 367

Dry Vermouth Drinks

Addington, 79
Admiral Cocktail, 79
Algonquin, 84
Allegheny, 84
Alliance, 85
Almond Cocktail, 85
American Beauty, 87
Assassino, 95
Bamboo Cocktail, 100
Beadlestone Cocktail, 104
Beauty Spot Cocktail, 104
Bermuda Highball, 108
Bitter Bikini, 109
Blue Denim, 117
Blue Martini, 118
Blue Moon, 118
Bobby Burns, 119
Bombay, 120
Brown, 127
B.V.D., 130
Caruso, 138
Cat's Eye, 139
Cinzano, 145
Claridge, 147
Czarina, 159
Darb, 161
Davis, 162
Delmonico, 163
Diplomat, 166
Douglas, 168
Duchess, 171
El Presidente Eduardo, 176
English Rose, 177
Fairbanks, 180

Fantasio, 181
Favorite, 182
Ferrari, 182
Fifty-Fifty, 183
Filby, 184
Frankenjack Cocktail, 190
Gibson, 200
Glasgow, 204
Golf, 209
Grand Slam, 211
Green Room, 215
Habanero Martini, 217
Harper's Ferry, 219
Havana Club, 219
Hoffman House, 222
Income Tax, 234
Jack Withers, 240
Juniper Blend, 247
Jupiter Cocktail, 248
Kangaroo, 250
Kingdom Come, 253
Kiss in the Dark, 255
Knickerbocker, 256
Kyoto, 257
Last Round, 260
Laura, The 260
Lawhill, 261
Leave It to Me, 262
Lone Tree, 268
Loud-Hailer, 270
Manhasset, 276
Manhattan (dry), 276
Manhattan (perfect), 277
Manhattan South, 277

Martinez, 279
Martini, 279
Martini (dry), 280
Martini (very dry), 280
Mary Garden, 281
Maurice, 282
Maxim, 282
Miami Beach, 286
Moll, 290
Montana, 291
Morning, 292
Morning Becomes Electric, 293
Napoli, 296
Nineteen, 300
Paisley Martini, 311
Pall Mall, 311
Palmetto, 311
Pantomime, 313
Parisian, 314
Peppar Martini, 319
Picon, 321
Pink Panther, 327
Pink Whiskers, 329
Plaza, 330
Poker, 331
Presidente, 336
Princess Mary's Pride, 337
Quebec Cocktail, 341
Queen Elizabeth Wine
    Cocktail, 342
Racquet Club, 344
Reform, 348
Rob Roy (dry), 351
Rob Roy (perfect), 351
Rolls-Royce, 353

San Francisco, 361
Sherry Twist, 372
Sloppy Joe, 378
Soul Kiss, 380
Soviet Cocktail, 380
Sphinx, 383
Tango, 394
Tequila Martini, 398
Tequini, 400
Thanksgiving Cocktail, 401
Third Degree, 401
Three Stripes, 402
Trinity Cocktail, 408
Tropical Cocktail, 409
Turf, 411
Vermouth Cassis, 417
Vodka Gibson, 420
Vodka Martini, 421
Vodka Martini (dry), 422
Vodka Martini (very dry), 422
Warsaw, 426
Washington, 426
Weekender, 428
Wembley, 428
Whip, 429
White Heat, 433
Why Not, 437
Will Rogers, 438
Wilson Cocktail, 438
Wyoming Swing Cocktail, 440
Yale Cocktail, 443
Yashmak, 444
Yellow Rattler, 445
York Special, 445
Zanzibar, 446

Dubonnet Drinks

Ante, 89
Bentley, 107
Dandy, 161
Dubonnet Cocktail, 170

Dubonnet Fizz, 170
Dubonnet Manhattan, 170
Dubonnet Negroni, 170
Joburg, 245

Louisiana Lullaby, 270
Mary Garden, 281
Moonshine Cocktail, 292
Oom Paul, 305
Opera (1), 306
Opera (2), 306
Phoebe Snow, 321
Princess Mary's Pride, 337
Sanctuary, 361

Shotgun Wedding
Cocktail, 373
Soul Kiss, 380
Temptation, 396
Trois Rivieres, 408
Vancouver Cocktail, 415
Wedding Belle, 427
Weep No More, 428
Zamboanga Hummer, 446

Elderflower Liqueur

Goose in Spring, 210

Midori Melon Ball Drop, 286

Fernet Branca

Yodel, 445

Forbidden Fruit

Lover's Delight, 271
Tantalus, 395

Virgin, 419

Framboise

Happy Feller (shooter), The 218

Kir Royale, 255

Frangelico Drinks

Baby Ruth (shooter), 99
Café Theatre, 133
Candy Bar (shooter), 136
El Salvador, 176
Friar Tuck, 192
Millionaire's Coffee, 287

Nutty Irishman, 301
Nutty Irishman
(shooter), 302
Peanut Butter and Jelly
(shooter), 317
Russian Quaalude, 359

Galliano Drinks

Alabama Slammer, 82
Atlantic Breeze, 95
Banana Tree, 102
California Root Beer, 135
Freddy Fudpucker, 190
Golden Cadillac, 206
Golden Dream, 207
Harbor Light, 218
Harvey Wallbanger, 219
Ice Palace, 231

International
    Stinger, 235
Italian Coffee, 238
Italian Stinger, 239
Lamplighter, 259
Laura, The 260
Pousse-Café
    (2), 335
Sunbeam, 389
Yellowbird, 444

Gin Drinks

Abbey Cocktail (1), 77
Abbey Cocktail (2), 77
Alaska, 83
Albermarle, 83
Alexander, 83
Alexander's Sister's
    Cocktail, 84
Alfredo, 84
Alliance, 85
Almond Cocktail, 85
Angel Face, 88
Aperitivo Cocktail, 90
Apricot, 92
Around the World, 94
Artillery, 94
Artillery Punch, 94
Aviation, 97
Barbary Coast, 103
Barnum, 103
Beauty Spot Cocktail, 104
Belmont, 106
Bennet, 107
Bermuda Highball, 108
Black Martini, 112
Blue Martini, 118
Blue Moon, 118
Bucks Fizz, 128

Bulldog, 129
B.V.D., 130
California Ice
    Tea, 134
California Lemonade, 135
Campobello, 136
Caruso, 138
Claridge, 147
Coco-Loco, 148
Coronado, 154
Costa del Sol, 154
Damn-the-Weather, 160
Delmonico, 163
Dempsey, 163
Depth Charge, 164
Diamond Fizz, 165
Diamond Head, 165
Dirty Martini, 166
Dodge Special, 167
Douglas, 168
Dubonnet Cocktail, 170
Dubonnet Fizz, 170
Dubonnet Negroni, 170
Dundee, 171
Earthquake, 173
Eclipse, 174
Empire, 176

English Rose, 177
Everything But, 178
Fairbanks, 180
Fallen Angel, 181
Favorite, 182
Fifty-Fifty, 183
Filby, 184
Fine and Dandy, 184
Flamingo, 185
Florida, 186
Fogcutter, 187
Foggy Day, 188
Fog Horn, 188
Frankenjack Cocktail, 190
French Rose, 191
Frobisher, 193
Froth Blower, 193
Gasper, 198
Gibson, 200
Gimlet, 200
Gin Alexander, 200
Gin and Soda, 201
Gin and Tonic, 201
Gin Cassis, 201
Gin Daiquiri, 201
Gin Daisy, 202
Gin Fizz, 202
Gin Rickey, 203
Gin Sour, 203
Go-Go Juice, 206
Golden Dawn, 206
Golden Daze, 207
Golden Fizz, 207
Golden Gate, 207
Golf, 209
Gradeal Special, 210
Grape Vine, 212
Great Secret, 214
Green Fire, 214
Harlem Cocktail, 218
Hawaiian Cocktail, 220
Hawaiian Orange
    Blossom, 220
Hoffman House, 222

Hollywood Tea, 222
Honolulu Lulu, 223
Hotel Georgia, 226
Houston Hurricane, 228
Hudson Bay, 228
Hula-Hula, 229
Huntington Special, 229
Iceball, 231
Ideal, 232
Income Tax, 234
Invisible Man, 235
Jack Withers, 240
Java Cooler, 243
Jewel, 245
Jockey Club, 245
Judge, Jr., 247
Juniper Blend, 247
Jupiter Cocktail, 248
KCB, 250
Kingdom Come, 253
Kingston, 254
Kiss in the Dark, 255
Knickerbocker, 256
Kyoto, 257
Ladyfinger, 258
Lasky, 260
Last Round, 260
Leap Frog, 261
Leap Year, 261
Leave It to Me, 262
Lectric Lemonade, 262
Lillet Noyaux, 264
Lime Rickey, 264
Little Devil, 265
London, 267
Lone Tree, 268
Long Beach Ice Tea, 268
Long Island Ice Tea, 268
Loud-Hailer, 270
Loudspeaker, 270
Mah-Jongg, 273
Maiden's Blush, 273
Maiden's Prayer, 273
Mainbrace, 274

Manhattan South, 277
Martinez, 279
Martini, 279
Martini (dry), 280
Martini (very dry), 280
Martini (extremely dry), 280
Maurice, 282
Maxim, 282
Melon Cocktail, 283
Mississippi Mule, 288
Moll, 290
Montmartre Cocktail, 291
Montreal Club
    Bouncer, 292
Mount Fuji, 295
Mule's Hind Leg, 295
Negroni, 297
Negroni Cooler, 297
Newbury, 298
Nineteen, 300
Nineteen Pick-Me-Up, 300
Ninja Turtle, 300
Old Etonian, 304
Opera (1), 306
Opera (2), 306
Orange Bloom, 306
Orange Blossom, 306
Orange Buck, 307
Orange Fizz, 307
Orange Gimlet, 308
Orange Oasis, 308
Paisley Martini, 311
Pall Mall, 311
Pancho Villa
    (shooter), 312
Paradise, 313
Parisian, 314
Park Avenue, 314
Peach Blow Fizz, 316
Pegu Club, 318
Pendennis Cocktail, 318
Pineapple Gimlet, 325
Pink Gin, 326
Pink Lady, 326

Pink Panther, 327
Pink Pussycat, 328
Pink Rose, 328
Plaza, 330
Pollyanna, 331
Polo, 332
Poppy Cocktail, 333
Prince's Smile, 338
Princeton, 338
Prohibition, 338
Punt e Mes Negroni, 339
Purple People
    Eater, 340
Queen, 342
Queen Elizabeth, 342
Racquet Club, 344
Ramos Fizz, 344
Ramos Gin Fizz, 345
Red Baron, 347
Red Cloud, 347
Red Lion Cocktail, 348
Red Snapper, 348
Renaissance Cocktail, 349
Rendezvous, 349
Resolute, 349
Rhubarb Fix, 350
Rocky Green Dragon, 352
Rolls-Royce, 353
Royal Fizz, 354
Royal Gin Fizz, 354
Royal Smile, 355
Russian, 358
Saketini, 360
Sambuca-Gin
    Shake, 361
Sangria Especiale, 362
San Sebastian, 363
Sapphire Martini, 363
Savoy Springtime, 365
Self-Starter, 368
Seville, 369
Shotgun Wedding
    Cocktail, 373
Silver Fizz, 374

Silver King, 374
Singapore
    Sling, 375
Skip and Go
    Naked, 376
Snowball, 379
Southern Bride, 381
Southern Gin, 381
Sphinx, 383
Splashy Sipper, 384
Straight Law, 387
Strega Sour, 389
Sweet Patootie, 392
Tango, 394
Thanksgiving
    Cocktail, 401
Third Degree, 401
Three Stripes, 402
Tidbit, 402
Tom Collins, 406
Tropedo, 407
Trinity Cocktail, 408
Turf, 411
Twin Six, 412
Ulanda, 413

Union Jack, 413
Union League, 414
Velvet Kiss, 417
Verona, 418
Victor, 418
Virgin, 419
Warday's Cocktail, 425
Wedding Belle, 427
Weekender, 428
Wembley, 428
White Baby, 432
White Cargo, 432
White Heat, 433
White Lady (1), 434
White Lily, 434
White Rose, 435
White Wing, 436
Why Not, 437
Will Rogers, 438
Wilson Cocktail, 438
Xanthia, 441
Yale Cocktail, 443
Yellow Rattler, 445
Zamboanga Hummer, 446
Zanzibar, 446

Grand Marnier Drinks

B-52, 98
B-53 (shooter), 98
Black-Eyed Susan, 110
Black Lady, 111
Café Marnier, 132
Costa del Sol, 154
Czar, 158
Express, 178
Gloom Chaser, 204
Grand Apple, 211
Grand Occasion, 211
High Roller, 222
Leap Year, 261
Louisiana Lullaby, 270

Malibu Monsoon, 274
Millionaire's
    Coffee, 287
Opera (2), 306
Red Lion
    Cocktail, 348
Royal Gin Fizz, 354
Tequila Daisy, 397
Top Shelf
    Margarita, 406
Truffle Martini, 410
Vodka Grand Marnier
    Cocktail, 421
Whiskey Daisy, 430

Hard Cider

Cranberry Spice Cocktail, 155

Ice Cream Drinks

Banana Tree, 102
Black Cow (NA), 451
Brandy Ice, 125
Caramel Nut, 138
Chocolate Black Russian, 144
Coco-Toastie, 149
Coffee Cooler, 150
Coffee Frappe, 150

Cola Float (NA), 452
Death by Chocolate, 162
Emerald Isle Cooler, 176
Panda Bear, 312
Strawberry Shortcake, 388
Sweetie Baby, 392
Tidbit, 402
White Cargo, 432

Irish Mist

Irish Fix, 237

Irish Whiskey

Black Manhattan, 111
Eclipse, 174
IRA Cocktail, 235
Irish, 236
Irish Car Bomb, 236
Irish Coffee, 236
Irish Fix, 237
Irish Spring, 237
Irish Whiskey and Soda, 237

Irish Whiskey Cocktail, 237
Kerry Cooler, 252
Leprechaun, 263
Leprechaun's
    Libation, 263
Nutty Irishman, 301
Paddy Cocktail, 310
Tipperary, 404
Wild Irish Rose, 438

Kahlúa Drinks

After Eight (shooter), 81
After five (shooter), 81
Après Ski (shooter), 92

Azteca, 97
B-52, 98
B-53 (shooter), 98

Beam Me Up, Scotty
(shooter), 104
Black Lady, 111
Black Licorice, 111
Black Magic, 111
Black Russian, 112
Blow Job (shooter), 116
Brain, 123
Brain Eraser, 123
Brave Bull, 127
California Root Beer, 135
Cappuccino Mocha, 137
Cerebral Hemorrhage, 139
Chocolate Banana Banshee, 144
Chocolate-Black Russian, 144
Chocolate-Covered Cherry
(shooter), 144
Cocoa-Colada, 148
Coffee Alexander, 149
Coffee Cooler, 150
Coffee Keokee, 150
Colorado Bulldog, 151
Deep Throat (shooter), 163
Dirty Mother (Separator),
166, 368
Dirty White Mother, 167
Everglades Special, 178
Gentle Bull, 199
Girl Scout Cookie, 203
Godmother, 206
Ground Zero, 216
Hawaiian Eye, 220
High Jamaican Wind, 221
Iguana, 232
Indian Summer (shooter), 234

Ixtapa, 239
Jamaican, 242
Jamaican Wind, 243
Kahlúa Egg Cream, 249
Kahlúa Toreador, 249
Kialoa, 253
King Alphonse, 253
Kioki Coffee, 254
Mexican Coffee, 285
Millionaire's Coffee, 287
Mind Eraser, 287
Mocha Mint, 289
Mudslide, 295
Paralyzer, 314
Pumpkin Pie
Martini, 338
Roasted Toasted
Almond, 350
Rum Nut, 357
St. Patrick's Day Mocha
Java, 360
Screaming Orgasm, 367
Separator (Dirty Mother),
166, 368
Slippery Nipple, 377
Smith and Kerns, 378
Sombrero, 380
Spicy Hot Cocoa, 384
Spiked Jones, 385
Sweet Cream, 391
T.K.O. (shooter), 394
Toasted Almond, 405
Tootsie Roll, 406
White Bull, 432
White Russian, 435

Kirsch

Apple Ginger Punch, 91
Bent Nail, 108
Cherry Daiquiri, 142
Coronado, 154

Florida, 186
KCB, 250
Ladyfinger, 258
Lollipop, 267

Nineteen, 300
Ostend Fizz, 309

Pink Almond, 325
Rendezvous, 349

Kümmel Drinks

Foxhound, 189
Green Fire, 214
Mexicano, 285

Quelle Vie, 343
Tovarich, 407

Lillet Drinks

Apple Jacques, 92
Country Club Cooler, 154
Cranberry Spice Cocktail, 155
Depth Charge, 164
Great Secret, 214
Hoopla, 224
Lillet Noyaux, 264

Odd McIntyre, 303
Old Etonian, 304
Orange Gimlet, 308
Prince Edward, 337
Prohibition, 338
Self-Starter, 368
Splashy Slipper, 384

Limoncello

In & Out Lemontini, 233

Sweet Tart Cocktail, 393

Madeira

Madeira Cocktail, 272

Prince of Wales, 337

Malibu

Cheap Man's Piña
    Colada, 142
Coconut Cola, 149
Coco-Toastie, 149
Hot Coconut Coffee, 225

Italian Surfer, 239
Malibu Monsoon, 274
Pink and
    Tan, 326
Scooby Snacks, 366

Mandarine Napoléon Liqueur

Mandarine Colada, 275

Stormin' Gorman, 387

Maple Liqueur

Lamplighter, 259

Metaxa

Harbor Light, 218

International Stinger, 235

Midori Drinks

Blind Melon, 114
Electric Kool-Aid, 175
E.T. (shooter), 177
Jolly Rancher (shooter), 246
Magpie, 273
Melon Ball, 283
Melon Ball Sunrise, 283
Melon Colada, 284
Mexican Flag (shooter), 285

Midori Melon Ball Drop, 286
Midori Sour, 286
Pearl Harbor, 318
Save the Planet, 364
Scooby Snacks, 366
Sex on the Beach
 (original), 370
Slimeball (shooter), 376
Watermelon, 427

Orange Liqueur

Papacito, 313

Rosy Rum Cosmo, 353

Ouzo

Coffee Frappe, 150
Good and Plenty, 209

T.K.O.
 (shooter), 394

Peach Brandy/Peach Liqueur Drinks

Brain, 123
Brandy Cobbler, 124
Bubble Gum
    (shooter), 128
Cooler by the Lake, 153
Fish House Punch, 185
Fuzzy Fruit, 197
Fuzzy Navel, 197
Georgia Peach
    Fizz, 199
Irish Spring, 237
Meltdown (shooter), 284

Moonshine
    Cocktail, 292
Peach Buck, 316
Peach Treat, 316
Peach Velvet, 317
Sex on the Beach, 370
Sex on the Beach in
    Winter, 370
Silk Panties
    (shooter), 373
Woo Woo, 439
Woo Woo (shooter), 439

Peach Schnapps

Absolut Royalty
    Cocktail, 78
Brain, 123
Cerebral Hemorrhage, 139
Down Under
    Snowball, 169
Frozen Bikini, 194
Fuzzy Fruit, 197
Fuzzy Martini, 197
Glamour Girl
    Martini, 204

Hairy Navel, 217
Halley's Comfort, 217
Jolly Rancher
    (shooter), 246
Killer Kool-Aid, 253
Meltdown (shooter), 284
Peach Alexander, 315
Royal Peach Freeze, 355
Sex on the Beach, 370
Sex on the Beach in
    Winter, 370

Peanut Liqueur

Brown Bomber, 128

Pear Brandy/Pear Liqueur Drinks

Sparkling Pear
    Cocktail, 382

Tintoretto, 404

Peppermint Schnapps

Adrienne's Dream, 79
Adult Hot Chocolate, 80
After Five (shooter), 81
Après Ski, 92
Cold Deck, 151
Girl Scout Cookie, 203
Ground Zero, 216
Hot Pants, 226
Hot Peppermint Patty, 226

Hot Shots (shooter), 227
Interplanetary Punch, 235
Old Pale, 305
Peppermint Patty, 319
Polynesian Punch, 332
Snow Shoe
    (shooter), 379
Snuggler, 379
Whippet, 429

Pernod Drinks

Bombay, 120
City Slicker, 146
Death in the
    Afternoon, 162
Depth Charge, 164
Duchess, 171
Earthquake, 173
Eve, 177
Foggy Day, 188
Hawaiian Eye, 220
Henry Morgan's
    Grog, 221
Iceberg, The 231
Irish, 236
Kiss Me Quick, 255
Ladies, 258
Last Round, 260
Lawhill, 261
Linstead, 265
London, 267
Millionaire, 287
Modern (1), 289
Modern (2), 289
Montreal Club
    Bouncer, 292
Moonshine Cocktail, 292
Morning, 292

Morning Glory, 293
New Orleans, 298
Nineteen, 300
Nineteen Pick-Me-Up, 300
Pernod Cocktail, 320
Pernod Flip, 320
Pernod Frappe, 320
Phoebe Snow, 321
Queen Elizabeth, 342
Rattlesnake, 346
Saucy Sue, 364
Sazerac, 365
Self-Starter, 368
Sledgehammer, 376
Snowball, 379
Special Rough, 383
Suisesse, 389
Temptation, 396
Tequila Ghost, 397
Third Degree, 401
Third Rail, 401
Tiger Tail, 403
Ulanda, 413
Victory, 418
Waldorf, 425
Weekender, 428
Which Way, 429

Whip, 429
White Lily, 434

Yashmak, 444
Yellow Parrot, 444

Peter Heering

Black-Cherry Rum Punch, 110

Great Dane, 213

Pimms

Pimms Cup, 393

Plum Brandy

Trade Winds, 407

Pomegranate Liqueur

Blushing Lady, 119

Port Wine Drinks

Affinity Cocktail, 80
Betsy Ross, 108
Claret Cup, 146
Japanese Fizz, 243
Montana, 291
Morning Becomes
    Electric, 293
Papacito, 313

Philadelphia Scotchman, 321
Poop Deck, 333
Port Sangaree, 334
Port Wine Cocktail, 334
Princeton, 338
Tempter Cocktail, 396
Tinton, 404
Union League, 414

Punt e Mes

Punt e Mes Negroni, 339

Raspberry Liqueur

Black Martini, 112
Jelly Donut Martini, 244

Lava Lamp Martini, 260
Sex on the Beach (original), 370

Raspberry Schnapps

California Stripper, 135

Root-Beer Schnapps

Teddy Bear (shooter), 395

Rum Drinks

Acapulco, 78
Andalusia, 88
Apple Daiquiri, 90
Apple Grog, 91
Apple Pie, 92
Arawak Punch, 94
Artillery Punch, 94
Astronaut, 95
Atlantic Breeze, 95
Aubade, 96
Aunt Agatha, 96
Azteca, 97
Bacardi, 99
Bahama Mama, 99
Banana Daiquiri (frozen), 100
Banana Mama, 101
Barbados Bowl, 102
Barbary Coast, 103
Bee's Knees, 105
Bee-Stung Lips, 105
Between the Sheets, 108
Big Blue Sky, 108
Black-Cherry Rum Punch, 110

Black Witch, 113
Bloody Rum Punch, 116
Blue Hawaiian, 117
Boardwalk Breezer, 119
Bolero, 120
Boston Rum Punch, 121
Brass Monkey, 126
B.V.D., 130
Café Foster, 132
Caipirinha, 133
California Ice Tea, 134
Calypso (Jamaican Coffee), 135
Casablanca, 138
Chambord Daiquiri, 140
Champagne Punch, 141
Cherry Bomb (Fireworks), 142
Cherry Cola, 142
Cherry Daiquiri, 142
Chi-Chi, 143
Chinese Cocktail, 143
Chocolate Rum, 145
Cocoa-Colada, 148
Coco-Loco, 148

Coco-Toastie, 149
Cold Weather Punch, 151
Columbia Cocktail, 152
Continental, 153
Cruise Control, 157
Cuba Libre (Rum and Coke), 158
Cuban Cooler, 158
Daiquiri, 160
Davis, 162
Derby Special, 164
Dr. Pepper, 167
Dominican Coco Loco, 167
Down Under Snowball, 169
Dunlop, 171
East India Cocktail, 173
Eggnog (standard), 174
El Presidente Eduardo, 176
El Salvador, 176
Everglades Special, 178
Eye-Opener, 178
Fair and Warmer, 180
Fern Gully, 182
Fiji Fizz, 183
Fish House Punch, 185
Flim Flam, 186
Florida Punch, 187
Fogcutter, 187
Fox Trot, 189
Frozen Daiquiri, 194
Frozen Fruit
    Daiquiri, 194
Frozen Mint Daiquiri, 196
Fuzzy Mother, 197
Gaugin, 198
Gin Daiquiri, 201
Ginger Breeze, 202
Go-Go Juice, 206
Golden Gate, 207
Gradeal Special, 210
Grand Occasion, 211
Grapefruit Highball, 212
Grass Is Greener, 213
Grateful Dead, 213
Green Lizard (shooter), 215

Grog, 216
Hammerhead, 218
Havana Club, 219
Henry Morgan's
    Grog, 221
High Jamaican Wind, 221
Hollywood Tea, 222
Honey Bee, 223
Hop Toad, 224
Hot Buttered Rum, 225
Hot Rum, 227
Hot Rum Toddy, 227
Hudson Bay, 228
Hurricane, 230
Ice Palace, 231
Interplanetary Punch, 235
Jade, 241
Jamaica Cooler, 241
Jamaica Ginger, 241
Jamaican, 242
Jamaican Milk Shake, 242
Jamaican Wind, 243
Joburg, 245
Jolly Roger, 247
Judge, Jr., 247
Kentucky Cooler, 251
Kialoa, 253
Kingston, 254
Lallah Rookh, 259
Lectric Lemonade, 262
Liberty Cocktail, 263
Limbo, 264
Little Devil, 265
Little Princess, 265
Live Bait's Blue
    Bijou, 266
Long Beach Ice Tea, 268
Long Island Ice Tea, 268
Look Out Below, 269
Lord Rodney, 269
Louisiana Lullaby, 270
Mah-Jongg, 273
Mai Tai, 274
Malibu Monsoon, 274

Mandarine Colada, 275
Mary Pickford, 281
Melon Colada, 284
Mexicano, 285
Modern (2), 289
Mojito, 290
Mojito Smoothie, 290
Monkey Wrench, 291
Navy Grog, 296
Nutty Colada, 301
Oil Slick, 304
Pago Pago, 310
Palmetto, 311
Panama, 312
Pancho Villa, 312
Pancho Villa (shooter), 312
Parisian Blonde, 314
Peach Coconut Flip, 316
Pensacola, 319
Pilot Boat, 322
Piña Colada, 323
Pineapple Bomber, 324
Pineapple Bomber (shooter), 324
Pineapple Francine, 324
Pink Veranda, 328
Pirate Cocktail, 329
Planter's Punch, 330
Poker, 331
Polynesian Punch, 332
Port Antonio, 334
Presidente, 336
Purple People Eater, 340
Quaker, 341
Quarter Deck, 341
Quickie, 343
Robson, 352
Rockaway Beach, 352
Rose Hall, 353
Rosy Rum Cosmo, 353
Rum and Orange Juice, 356
Rum and Tonic, 356
Rum Collins, 356
Rum Curaçao Cooler, 356
Rum Nut, 357

Rum Rickey, 357
Rum Runner, 357
Rum Sour, 357
San Juan, 363
San Sebastian, 363
Scorpion, 366
September Morn, 368
Sevilla, 369
Shanghai, 371
Shark Bite, 371
Shark's Tooth, 371
Sir Walter, 375
Sledgehammer, 376
Sloppy Joe, 378
S.O.B. Shooter
    (shooter), 380
Spanish Town, 382
Stonewall, 387
Strawberry Daiquiri
    (frozen), 388
Summer Share, 389
Sundowner, 390
Surfer on Acid (shooter), 390
Swamp Water, 391
Swayze Swizzle, 391
Tahiti Club, 394
Texas Tea, 400
Third Rail, 401
Three Miles, 402
Tiger's Milk, 403
Tom and Jerry, 405
Trade Winds, 407
Trinidad Cocktail, 408
Trophy Room, 409
Whist, 431
White Lily, 434
White Lion, 434
Wombat (shooter), 439
Xango, 441
XYZ, 442
A Yard of Flannel, 443
Yellow Strawberry, 445
Zamboanga Hummer, 446
Zombie, 447

Sabra Drinks

Israeli Coffee, 238   Tootsie Roll, 406

Sake

Geisha, 199   Vodka Saketini, 423
Saketini, 360

Sambuca Drinks

Aperitivo Cocktail, 90   Roman Stinger, 353
Assassino, 95   Sambuca-Gin Shake, 361
Barbarella, 103   Shanghai, 371
Black Licorice, 111   Silk Panties (shooter), 373
Bootleg, 121   Silver Nipple, 375
Iceball, 231   Slippery Nipple, 377
Little Purple Men, 266   Via Veneto, 418
Purple Haze (shooter), 339   White Heart, 433

Scotch Drinks

Affinity Cocktail, 80   Loch Lomond, 266
Barbary Coast, 103   Mamie Taylor, 275
Barn Door, 103   Marlon Brando, 279
Beadlestone Cocktail, 104   Miami Beach, 286
Blood and Sand, 114   Mint Cooler, 288
Bobby Burns, 119   Modern (1), 289
Butterscotch Collins, 129   Modern (2), 289
Dundee, 171   Morning Glory, 293
Fans, 181   Paisley Martini, 311
Flying Scot, 187   Polly's Special, 331
Glasgow, 204   Prince Edward, 337
Godfather, 205   Rob Roy, 351
Highland Fling, 221   Rob Roy (dry), 351
Hoot Mon, 224   Rob Roy (perfect), 351
Joe Collins, 245   Rusty Nail, 359
Lamplighter, 259   Scotch and Soda, 366

Scotch Mist, 366
Scotch Stone Sour, 367

Thistle, 401
Whiskey Fix, 430

Sherry Drinks

Adonis, 79
Affinity Cocktail, 80
Andalusia, 88
Bamboo Cocktail, 100
Belmont Breeze, 107
Cadiz, 131
Cold Weather Punch, 151
Dunlop, 171
Fino, 184
Kerry Cooler, 252
Lemonade (modern), 262
Quarter Deck, 341

Reform, 348
Renaissance Cocktail, 349
Rhubarb Fix, 350
Seville, 369
Sherry Cocktail, 372
Sherry Eggnog, 372
Sherry Twist, 372
Soviet Cocktail, 381
Straight Law, 387
Tidbit, 402
Tuxedo, 411
Xeres Cocktail, 441

Sloe Gin Drinks

Alabama Slammer, 82
Alabama Slammer (shooter), 82
Black Hawk, 110
Blackthorn, 112
Eclipse, 174
Johnnie's Cocktail, 246
Kiss the Boys Goodbye, 256
Knockout, 256
Lemonade (modern), 262
Love, 270
McClelland, 283
Mexican Flag (shooter), 285
Modern (1), 289

Moll, 290
Moulin Rouge, 294
Polynesian Punch, 332
Red Devil, 348
Ruby Fizz, 355
San Francisco, 361
Savoy Tango, 365
Sloe Brandy, 377
Sloe Comfortable Screw, 377
Sloe Gin Fizz, 377
Sloe Screw, 378
Sloe Tequila, 378
Traffic Light, 407

Southern Comfort Drinks

Alabama Slammer, 82
Alabama Slammer (shooter), 82

Blind Melon, 114
Bootleg, 121

Bourbon Daisy, 122
Electric Kool-Aid, 175
Halley's Comfort, 217
Hammerhead, 218
Harper's Ferry, 219
Hawaiian Punch (shooter), 220
Knockout, 256
Lion Tamer (shooter), 265
Mafia's Kiss, 272
Manhattan South, 277
Memphis Belle Cocktail, 284

Orange Comfort, 307
Oxbend, 309
Pineapple Bomber, 324
Pineapple Bomber
    (shooter), 324
Red Devil, 348
Rhett Butler, 349
Scarlett O'Hara, 365
Sicilian Kiss, 373
Sloe Comfortable Screw, 377
Wagon Wheel, 425

Strawberry Liqueur Drinks

Affair, 80
Brain Tumor, 124
Brassy Blonde, 126
Old Pale, 305

Peach Blow
    Fizz, 316
Strawberry Shortcake, 388
Wombat (shooter), 439

Strega Drinks

Strega Sour, 389

Swedish Punsch Drinks

Doctor, 167
Grand Slam, 211
Hundred Percent, 229
Lasky, 260

May Blossom
    Fizz, 282
Swedish Lullaby, 391
Viking, 419

Sweet Vermouth Drinks

Abbey Cocktail (2), 77
Addington, 79
Adonis, 79
Americano, 87

Apple Pie, 92
Artillery, 94
Beauty Spot Cocktail, 104
Black Manhattan, 111

Blackthorn, 112
Blood and Sand, 114
Bobby Burns, 119
Bolero, 120
Bombay, 120
Brandy Manhattan, 125
Campobello, 136
Carroll Cocktail, 138
Cold Deck, 151
Creamy Mimi, 157
Damn-the-Weather, 160
Delmonico, 163
Diamond Head, 165
Diplomat, 166
Duchess, 171
Fair and Warmer, 180
Fino, 184
Flying Scot, 187
Froupe, 194
Gazette, 198
Grand Slam, 211
Harvard, 219
Highland Fling, 221
Hoot Mon, 224
Ideal, 232
Income Tax, 234
Italian Stallion, 239
Jack Withers, 240
Jewel, 245
Knickerbocker, 256
Lady Be Good, 258
Laura, The 260
Leap Year, 261
Little Princess, 265
Lone Tree, 268
Los Angeles Cocktail, 269
Manhasset, 276
Manhattan, 276
Manhattan (perfect), 277
Marconi Wireless, 278
Maurice, 282
Montmartre Cocktail, 291
Moulin Rouge, 294
Napoli, 296

Narragansett, 296
Negroni, 297
Negroni Cooler, 297
Newbury, 298
Orange Bloom, 306
Oriental, 308
Paddy Cocktail, 310
Pall Mall, 311
Park Avenue, 314
Pirate Cocktail, 329
Plaza, 330
Pollyanna, 331
Preakness, 336
Punt e Mes Negroni, 339
Queen, 342
Rob Roy, 351
Rob Roy (perfect), 351
Rolls-Royce, 353
San Francisco, 361
Sevilla, 369
Sink or Swim, 375
Sphinx, 383
Star, 385
Sunbeam, 389
Tango, 394
Tequila Manhattan, 397
Thistle, 401
Tipperary, 404
Tivoli, 405
Trilby, 408
Trinity Cocktail, 408
Tulip, 410
Twin Six, 412
Vermouth Cassis, 417
Vermouth Frappe, 417
Verona, 418
Victor, 418
Vodka Cooler, 420
Waldorf, 425
Warday's Cocktail, 425
Weekender, 428
Whist, 431
Wyoming Swing Cocktail, 440
Yellow Rattler, 445

Tequila Drinks

Acapulco, 78
Azteca, 97
Banana Boat, 100
Bloody Maria, 115
Blue Margarita, 117
Blue Shark, 118
Brave Bull, 127
California Ice Tea, 134
Charro, 141
Cherry Bomb (Fireworks), 142
Coco-Loco, 148
Combier Margarita, 152
Conchita, 152
Daisy, 160
Devil's Handshake, 165
Dorado, 168
El Cid, 175
El Diablo, 175
Freddy Fudpucker, 190
Frostbite, 193
Frozen Fruit Margarita, 195
Frozen Margarita, 195
Frozen Matador, 195
Fuzzy Mother, 197
Gentle Bull, 199
Go-Go Juice, 206
Golden Lemonade, 208
Golden Margarita, 208
Grapeshot, 212
Grateful Dead, 213
Habanero Martini, 217
Hollywood Tea, 222
Honeydew Margarita, 223
Hot Pants, 226
Iguana, 232
Ixtapa, 239
Jell-O Shoots (shooter), 244
Lectric Lemonade, 262
Lemon Drop (shooter), 262
Lolita, 266
Long Beach Ice Tea, 268
Long Island Ice Tea, 268

Malibu Wave, 275
Mango Margarita, 275
Margarita, 278
Margarita, My Honey, 278
Matador, 281
Mexican Coffee, 285
Mexican Missile (shooter), 285
Mockingbird, 289
Oxbend, 309
Paloma, 311
Pancho Villa (shooter), 312
Panther, 313
Papacito, 313
Paralyzer, 314
Pear Tequila Supreme, 318
Piña, 323
Piñata, 323
Pomegranate Margaritas, 333
Prado, 335
Prairie Fire (shooter), 335
Purple People Eater, 340
Rockaway Beach, 352
Silk Stockings, 374
Sloe Tequila, 378
Snow Cap (shooter), 379
Spanish Moss, 382
Summer Share, 389
Sunburn, 390
Tequila Collins, 396
Tequila Daisy, 397
Tequila Ghost, 397
Tequila Gimlet, 397
Tequila Manhattan, 397
Tequila Martini, 398
Tequila Old-Fashioned, 398
Tequila Popper (shooter), 398
Tequila Screwdriver, 398
Tequila Shot (shooter), 399
Tequila Sour, 399
Tequila Stinger, 399
Tequila Sunrise, 399
Tequila Sunset, 400

Tequini, 400
Texas Tea, 400
Tijuana Sunrise, 404
Time Bomb, 403
T.K.O. (shooter), 394
T.N.T., 405

Top Shelf Margarita, 406
Toreador, 406
Ultimate Margarita,
    The 413
White Bull, 432
Xylophone, 442

Tia Maria Drinks

Calypso (Jamaican Coffee), 135
Port Antonio, 334

Spanish Coffee, 382
Trophy Room, 409

Triple Sec Drinks

Acapulco, 78
Alabama Slammer, 82
Ante, 89
Applecar, 90
Barn Door, 103
Between the Sheets, 108
Bible Belt, 109
Bitter Bikini, 109
Bloody Rum Punch, 116
Cadiz, 131
California Ice Tea, 134
Canada Cocktail, 136
Casablanca, 138
Champagne Punch, 141
Chinese Cocktail, 143
Climax, 147
Combier Margarita, 152
Cosmopolitan, 154
Cream Supreme, 156
Creamy Mimi, 157
Damn-the-Weather, 160
Deauville Cocktail, 163
East India Cocktail, 173
Electric Kool-Aid, 175
Eye-Opener, 178
Flim Flam, 186

Florida, 186
Frankenjack Cocktail, 190
Frozen Bellini, 106
Frozen Fruit Margarita, 195
Frozen Margarita, 195
Golden Dream, 207
Grateful Dead, 213
Green-Eye-Opener, 214
Hawaiian Cocktail, 220
Hollywood Tea, 222
Honeydew Margarita, 223
Honeymoon, 223
Huntress Cocktail, 230
International, The 234
Invisible Man, 235
Irish Whiskey Cocktail, 237
Kamikaze, 249
Kamikaze (shooter), 250
Kentucky Orange Blossom, 252
Kyoto, 257
Lectric Lemonade, 262
Little Devil, 265
Long Beach Ice Tea, 268
Long Island Ice Tea, 268
Lynchburg Lemonade, 271
Mainbrace, 274

Mai Tai, 274
Malibu Wave, 275
Mango Margarita, 275
Margarita, 278
Mission Accomplished
  (shooter), 288
Montmartre Cocktail, 291
Netherland, 297
Odd McIntyre, 303
Orange Fizz, 307
Orgasm, 308
Pear Tequila Supreme, 318
Pine Tree, 325
Polly's Special, 331
Pomegranate Margaritas, 333
Purple People Eater, 340
Quickie, 343
Red Devil, 348
Rosy Rum Cosmo, 353
Sangria, 361
San Sebastian, 363
Sidecar, 373

Sloppy Joe, 378
Spanish Town, 382
Stony Brook, 387
Sunburn, 390
Sweet Patootie, 392
Temptation, 396
Texas Tea, 400
Trois Rivieres, 408
Vanilla Creamsicle, 416
Velvet Hammer, 416
Weekender, 428
White Baby, 432
White Heat, 433
White Lily, 434
White Wine Super
  Sangria, 436
Will Rogers, 438
Windex, 438
Xango, 441
XYZ, 442
Zamboanga Hummer, 446
Zombie, 447

Tuaca Drinks

Hot Apple Pie, 225
Il Magnifico, 233

Tuaca Cocktail, 410

Vandermint Drinks

Dutch Coffee, 171

Trophy Room, 409

Vodka Drinks

Absolut Royalty Cocktail, 78
Absolut Santo, 78
Anna's Banana, 89
Anti-Freeze (shooter), 90

Apple Eden, 91
Astronaut, 95
B-53 (shooter), 98
Baby Ruth (shooter), 99

Bay Breeze, 104
Beer Buster, 105
Black Magic, 111
Black Marble, 112
Black Martini, 112
Black Russian, 112
Blended Raspberry Cocktail, 113
Blind Melon, 114
Bloody Mary, 115
Blow Job (shooter), 116
Blue Bayou, 116
Blue Shark, 118
Blushing Lady, 119
Bottom Line, The 121
Brain Eraser, 123
Brass Monkey, 126
Bubble Gum (shooter), 128
Bull Frog, 129
Bull Shot, 129
Caesar, The 131
Cajun Bloody Mary, 134
California Driver, 134
California Ice Tea, 134
California Lemonade, 134
Candy Bar (shooter), 136
Cape Cod, 137
Cape Grape, 137
Chablis Cooler, 139
Cherry Bomb (Fireworks), 142
Chocolate Black Russian, 144
Chocolate Martini, 145
Clamdigger, 146
Climax, 147
Club Med, 148
Coffee Cooler, 150
Colorado Bulldog, 151
Cool Breeze, 153
Cosmopolitan, 154
Cranberry Pineapple Vodka
    Punch, 155
Cranberry Splash, 155
Cranberry Vodka, 156
Cranberry-Vodka Punch, 156
Creamy Mimi, 157

Czar, 158
Czarina, 159
Dark Eyes, 162
Death by Chocolate, 162
Deep Throat (shooter), 163
007 Cocktail, 168
Dubonnet Cocktail, 170
Egghead, 174
E.T. (shooter), 177
Express, 178
'57 Chevy with a White License
    Plate, 183
Flying Grasshopper, 187
Froot Loop, 193
Fuzzy Martini, 197
Genoa, 199
Godchild, 205
Godmother, 206
Go-Go Juice, 206
Golden Screw, 209
Goose in Spring, 210
Gorilla Punch, 210
Grape Crush, 212
Grateful Dead, 213
Green Dragon, 214
Green Eye-Opener, 214
Greyhound, 216
Ground Zero, 216
Gypsy, 216
Hairy Navel, 217
Happy Feller (shooter), The 218
Harvey Wallbanger, 219
Hawaiian Eye, 220
Hawaiian Punch (shooter), 220
High Roller, 222
Hollywood Tea, 222
Hot Shots (shooter), 227
Iceberg, The 231
Iguana, 232
In & Out Lemontini, 233
Indian Summer (shooter), 234
International, The 234
Jell-O Shoots (shooter), 244
Jelly Donut Martini, 244

Jolly Rancher (shooter), 246
Jungle Jim, 247
Kamikaze, 249
Kamikaze (shooter), 250
Kangaroo, 250
Killer Kool-Aid, 253
Kiss, The 255
Kremlin Cocktail, 257
Kretchma, 257
Lava Lamp Martini, 260
Lectric Lemonade, 262
Lemon Drop (shooter), 262
Long Beach Ice Tea, 268
Long Island Ice Tea, 268
Lube Job, 271
Madras, 272
Magpie, 273
Melon Ball, 283
Melon Ball Sunrise, 283
Meltdown (shooter), 284
Mexican Flag (shooter), 285
Midnight Sun, 286
Midori Melon Ball Drop, 286
Mind Eraser, 287
Mission Accomplished
    (shooter), 288
Moscow Mimosa, 293
Moscow Mule, 293
Mudslide, 295
Napoli, 296
Ninotchka, 301
Oil Slick, 304
Old Pale, 305
Orgasm, 308
Out of the Blue, 309
Peach Buck, 316
Pearl Harbor, 318
Peppar Martini, 319
Pineapple Vodka, 325
Pink Lemonade, 326
Pink Lemonade (frozen), 327
Pink Lemonade (shooter), 327
Polynesian Cocktail, 332
Pumpkin Pie Martini, 338

Punt e Mes Negroni, 339
Purple Hooter Shooter (shooter),
    The 339
Purple Passion, 339
Purple People Eater, 340
Raspberry Chocolate
    Martini, 345
Raspberry Smash, 345
Raspberry Vodka, 346
Red Apple, 347
Red Devil, 348
Roasted Toasted Almond, 350
Rouffy Party Punch Cooler, 354
Russian, 358
Russian Banana, 358
Russian Bear, 358
Russian Coffee, 358
Russian Quaalude, 358
Russian Rose, 358
Russian Turkey, 358
Salty Dog, 360
Save the Planet, 364
Scooby Snacks, 366
Screaming Orgasm, 367
Screwdriver, 367
Sea Breeze, 368
Sex on the Beach, 370
Sex on the Beach (original), 370
Sex on the Beach in Winter, 370
Silver Nipple, 375
Slimeball (shooter), 376
Sloe Comfortable Screw, 377
Sloe Screw, 378
Soviet Cocktail, 381
Stormin' Gorman, 387
Strawberry-Cranberry Frost, 388
Summer Share, 389
Sweet Independence, 392
Sweet Tart Cocktail, 393
Tawny Russian, 395
Teatini, 395
Teddy Bear (shooter), 395
Texas Tea, 400
Tidy Bowl (shooter), 403

Tovarich, 407
Tropical Grapefruit Splash, 409
Tuaca Cocktail, 410
Twister, 412
Vodka and Tonic, 419
Vodka Collins, 419
Vodka Cooler, 420
Vodka Fizz, 420
Vodka Gibson, 420
Vodka Gimlet, 421
Vodka Grand Marnier
   Cocktail, 421
Vodka Grasshopper, 421
Vodka Martini, 421
Vodka Martini (dry), 422
Vodka Martini (very dry), 422
Vodka Martini
   (extremely dry), 422

Vodka on the Rocks, 423
Vodka Saketini, 423
Vodka Stinger, 423
Volga Boatman, 424
Warsaw, 426
Washington Apple, 427
Watermelon, 427
White Elephant, 432
White Lady (2), 434
White Russian, 435
White Spider, 435
Windex, 438
Woo Woo, 439
Woo Woo
   (shooter), 439
Yellowbird, 444
Yellow Fever, 444
Zipperhead, 447

Whiskey Drinks

Algonquin, 84
Assassino, 95
Belmont Breeze, 107
Black Hawk, 110
Blinker, 114
Boilermaker, 120
Bootleg, 121
Brassy Blonde, 126
Cablegram, 131
Dandy, 161
De Rigueur, 164
Dinah Cocktail, 166
Down the Hatch, 168
Dubonnet Manhattan, 170
Emerald Isle Cooler, 176
Everything But, 178
Frisco Sour, 192
Gloom Lifter, 205
Henry Morgan's Grog, 221
Horse's Neck, 224
Hot Brick, 225

Houston Hurricane, 228
Hunter's Cocktail, 229
Ink Street, 234
Italian Assassin, 238
Japanese Fizz, 243
John Collins, 246
Kentucky Hayride, 252
Klondike Cooler, 256
Lawhill, 261
Linstead, 265
Lord Rodney, 269
Los Angeles Cocktail, 269
Lynchburg Lemonade, 271
Madeira Cocktail, 272
Manhasset, 276
Manhattan, 276
Manhattan (dry), 276
Manhattan (perfect), 277
New World, 299
New York Cocktail, 299
Oh, Henry!, 304

Old-Fashioned, 304
Pink Almond, 325
Preakness, 336
Presbyterian, 336
Prince, 336
Rattlesnake, 346
7 & 7, 369
Seventh Heaven, 369
Snack Bite (shooter), 379
Soul Kiss, 380
Stony Brook, 387
Temptation, 396

Tipperary, 404
Trois Rivieres, 408
Twin Hills, 412
Whippet, 429
Whiskey and
    Water, 430
Whiskey Collins, 430
Whiskey Daisy, 430
Whiskey Fix, 430
Whiskey Highball, 431
Whiskey Rickey, 431
Whiskey Sour, 431

Wilderberry Schnapps

Wild Fling, 437

Wine Drinks

Apple Ginger Punch, 91
Artillery Punch, 94
Bloody Rum Punch, 116
Chablis Cooler, 139
Champagne Sherbet Punch, 141
Claret Cup, 146
Cooler by the Lake, 153
Czar, 158
Drawbridge, 169
Frozen Bellini, 106
Glamour Girl Martini, 204

Glüwein, 205
Kir, 254
Mountain Red Punch, 294
Peach-Basil Sangria, 315
Sangria, 361
Sangria Especiale, 362
Sangria Shabbabe, 362
White Cargo, 432
White Wine Spritzer, 436
White Wine Super Sangria, 436
Wine Cooler, 439

INDEX BY TYPE

(NA = NONALCOHOLIC)
Blender Drinks

Banana Boat, 100
Banana Daiquiri (frozen), 100
Banana Mama, 101
Banana Milk Shake (NA), 451
Banana Split, 101
Banana Tree, 102
Batido Mango, 104
Big Blue Sky, 109
Blended Raspberry Cocktail, 113
Blue Bayou, 116
Blue Hawaiian, 117
Brandy Ice, 125
Café Viennoise (NA), 451
Caramel Nut, 138
Center Court (NA), 452
Chambord Daiquiri, 140
Cheap Man's Piña Colada, 142
Cherry Daiquiri, 142
Chocolate Almond Shake
    (NA), 452
Chocolate Black Russian, 144
Cocoa-Colada, 148
Coco-Toastie, 149
Coffee Frappe, 150
Death by Chocolate, 162
Derby Special, 164
Dominican Coco Loco, 167

Egghead, 174
Frozen Bellini, 106
Frozen Bikini, 194
Frozen Daiquiri, 194
Frozen Fruit Daiquiri, 194
Frozen Fruit Margarita, 195
Frozen Margarita, 195
Frozen Matador, 195
Frozen Mint Daiquiri, 196
Frozen Mint Julep, 196
Gaugin, 198
Hawaiian Eye, 220
Iceball, 231
Il Magnifico, 233
Jamaican Milk Shake, 242
Leprechaun's Libation, 263
Live Bait's Blue Bijou, 266
Mandarine Colada, 275
Melon Colada, 284
Mojito Smoothie, 290
Nutty Colada, 301
Old-Time Strawberry Milk Shake
    (NA), 457
Panda Bear, 312
Peach Alexander, 315
Peach Velvet, 317
Peachy Keen Freeze, 317

Pear Tequila Supreme, 318
Pensacola, 319
Peppermint Stinger, 319
Piña Colada, 323
Pineapple Francine, 324
Pineapple Milk Shake (NA), 459
Pink Lemonade (frozen), 327
Pomegranate Margaritas, 333
Ramos Gin Fizz, 345
Rose's Ruby Heart (NA), 460
Royal Peach Freeze, 355
Russian Coffee, 359
San Juan, 363
Scorpion, 366
Sex on the Beach in Winter, 370

Shark Bite, 371
Strawberry-Cranberry Frost, 388
Strawberry Daiquiri (frozen), 388
Strawberry Shortcake, 388
Summer Cooler (NA), 462
Sweetie Baby, 392
Sweet Tart Cocktail, 393
Tidbit, 402
Trade Winds, 407
Tropical Grapefruit Splash, 409
Tumbleweed, 411
White Cargo, 432
Xylophone, 442
Yellow Strawberry, 445
Yogurt Supreme (NA), 464

Cobblers

Brandy Cobbler, 124

Collins

Butterscotch
    Collins, 129
Joe Collins, 245
John Collins, 246

Rum Collins, 356
Tequila Collins, 396
Tom Collins, 406
Vodka Collins, 419

Coolers

Chablis Cooler, 139
Coffee Cooler, 150
Cooler by the Lake, 153
Country Club Cooler, 154
Cranberry Cooler (NA), 452
Cuban Cooler, 158
Emerald Isle Cooler, 176
Fruit Juice Cooler (NA), 454
Jamaica Cooler, 241

Java Cooler, 243
Kerry Cooler, 252
Klondike Cooler, 256
Lime Cooler (NA), 456
Mint Cooler, 288
Negroni Cooler, 297
Rouffy Party Punch
    Cooler, 354
Rum Curaçao Cooler, 356

Summer Cooler (NA), 462
Vodka Cooler, 420

Whiskey Collins, 430
Wine Cooler, 439

Daiquiris

Apple Daiquiri, 90
Banana Daiquiri (frozen), 100
Chambord Daiquiri (frozen), 140
Cherry Daiquiri (frozen), 142
Frozen Daiquiri, 194

Frozen Fruit Daiquiri, 194
Frozen Mint Daiquiri, 196
Gin Daiquiri, 201
Strawberry Daiquiri (frozen), 388

Exotic Drinks

Atlantic Breeze, 95
Bahama Mama, 99
Banana Mama, 101
Batido Mango, 104
Big Blue Sky, 109
Blue Hawaiian, 117
Blue Margarita, 117
Blushing Lady, 119
Boardwalk Breezer, 119
Cherry Bomb (Fireworks), 142
Club Med, 148
Coco-Loco, 148
Diamond Head, 165
Dominican Coco Loco, 167
Fogcutter, 187
Frozen Daiquiri, 194
Gorilla Punch, 210
Hawaiian Eye, 220
Ice Palace, 231

Kappa Colada, 250
Mai Tai, 274
Malibu Monsoon, 274
Mandarine Colada, 275
Melon Colada, 284
Peach Treat, 316
Piña Colada, 323
Planter's Punch, 330
Pomegranate Fizz, 333
Pomegranate Margaritas, 333
Scorpion, 366
Sex on the Beach in
    Winter, 370
Shark Bite, 371
Singapore Sling, 375
Tahiti Club, 394
Trade Winds, 407
Zamboanga Hummer, 446
Zombie, 447

Fizzes

Apricot Fizz, 93
Bucks Fizz, 128
Diamond Fizz, 165

Dubonnet Fizz, 170
Fiji Fizz, 183
Georgia Peach Fizz, 199

Gin Fizz, 202
Golden Fizz, 207
Imperial Fizz, 233
Japanese Fizz, 243
Lemonade Fizz
     (NA), 455
May Blossom Fizz, 282
No-Gin Fizz (NA), 457
Orange Fizz, 307
Orange Fizz (NA), 458
Ostend Fizz, 309

Peach Blow Fizz, 316
Picon Fizz, 322
Pomegranate Fizz, 333
Ramos Fizz, 344
Ramos Gin Fizz, 345
Royal Fizz, 354
Royal Gin Fizz, 354
Ruby Fizz, 355
Silver Fizz, 374
Sloe Gin Fizz, 377
Vodka Fizz, 420

Flip

Peach Coconut Flip, 316

Pernod Flip, 320

Frappes

Coffee Frappe, 150
Pernod Frappe, 320

Vermouth Frappe, 417

Frozen Drinks

Anna's Banana, 89
Banana Boat, 100
Banana Daiquiri, 100
Banana Mama, 101
Banana Milk Shake (NA), 451
Banana Split, 101
Banana Tree, 102
Big Blue Sky, 109
Blended Raspberry Cocktail, 113
Blizzard, 114
Blue Bayou, 116
Blue Hawaiian, 117
Brandy Ice, 125
Caramel Nut, 138
Center Court (NA), 452

Chambord Daiquiri, 140
Cheap Man's Piña Colada, 142
Cherry Daiquiri, 142
Chocolate Almond Shake
     (NA), 452
Chocolate Black Russian, 144
Cocoa-Colada, 148
Coco-Toastie, 149
Coffee Frappe, 150
Derby Special, 164
Dominican Coco Loco, 167
Frozen Bellini, 106
Frozen Bikini, 194
Frozen Fruit Daiquiri, 194
Frozen Fruit Margarita, 195

Frozen Margarita, 195
Frozen Matador, 195
Frozen Mint Daiquiri, 196
Frozen Mint Julep, 196
Gaugin, 198
Hawaiian Eye, 220
Il Magnifico, 233
Jamaican Milk Shake, 242
Leprechaun's Libation, 263
Live Bait's Blue Bijou, 266
Mandarine Colada, 275
Melon Colada, 284
Nutty Colada, 301
Old-Time Strawberry Milk Shake
    (NA), 457
Panda Bear, 312
Peach Alexander, 315
Peach Velvet, 317
Peachy Keen Freeze, 317
Pensacola, 319
Peppermint Stringer, 319
Piña Colada, 323

Pineapple Francine, 324
Pineapple Milk Shake (NA), 459
Pink Lemonade, 327
Rose's Ruby Heart (NA), 460
Royal Peach Freeze, 355
Russian Coffee, 359
San Juan, 363
Scorpion, 366
Sex on the Beach in Winter, 370
Shark Bite, 371
Strawberry-Cranberry Frost, 388
Strawberry Daiquiri, 388
Strawberry Shortcake, 388
Summer Cooler (NA), 462
Sweetie Baby, 392
Tidbit, 402
Trade Winds, 407
Tropical Grapefruit Splash, 409
Tumbleweed, 411
White Cargo, 432
Xylophone, 442
Yellow Strawberry, 445

Hot Drinks

Adult Hot Chocolate, 80
Amaretto Coffee (Italian Coffee),
    86, 238
Apple Grog, 91
Baileys and Coffee, 99
Blackberry Demitasse, 109
Café Bonaparte, 132
Café Foster, 132
Café Marnier, 132
Café Mocha (NA), 451
Café Theatre, 133
Café Viennoise (NA), 451
Café Zurich, 133
Calypso (Jamaican Coffee), 135
Cappuccino Mocha, 137
Coffee Keokee, 150
Dutch Coffee, 171

Glüwein, 205
Grog, 216
Hot Apple Pie, 225
Hot Brick, 225
Hot Buttered Rum, 225
Hot Coconut Coffee, 225
Hot Peppermint Patty, 226
Hot Rum, 227
Hot Rum Toddy, 227
Hot Toddy, 228
Irish Coffee, 236
Irish Cow, 236
Israeli Coffee, 238
Italian Coffee (Amaretto Coffee),
    86, 238
Jamaican Coffee (Calypso), 135
Kentucky Coffee, 251

Kioki Coffee, 254
Mexican Coffee, 285
Millionaire's Coffee, 287
St. Patrick's Day Mocha Java, 360
Scottish Coffee, 367
Snuggler, 379

Spanish Coffee, 382
Super Coffee, 390
Tom and Jerry, 405
Trophy Room, 409
Venetian Coffee, 417
A Yard of Flannel, 443

Margaritas

Combier Margarita, 152
Frozen Fruit Margarita, 195
Frozen Margarita, 195
Honeydew Margarita, 223
Mango Margarita, 275

Margarita, 278
Margarita, My Honey, 278
Pomegranate Margaritas, 333
Top Shelf Margarita, 406
Ultimate Margarita, The 413

Martini

Black Martini, 112
Blue Martini, 118
Chocolate Martini, 145
Cosmopolitan, 154
Dirty Martini, 166
Fuzzy Martini, 197
Glamour Girl Martini, 204
Habanero Martini, 217
Hennessey Martini, 221
Jelly Donut Martini, 244
Lava Lamp Martini, 260
Martini, 279

Martini (dry), 280
Martini (very dry), 280
Martini (extremely dry), 280
Pumpkin Pie Martini, 338
Raspberry Chocolate
    Martini, 345
Truffle Martini, 410
Vodka Martini, 421
Vodka Martini (dry), 422
Vodka Martini (very dry), 422
Vodka Martini
    (extremely dry), 422

Pousse-Cafés

Angel's Kiss, 88
Angel's Tit, 89
Aunt Jemima, 96
Easter Egg
    Cocktail, 173
Hot Brick, 225

King Alphonse, 253
Pousse-Café (1), 335
Pousse-Café (2), 335
Rainbow Pousse-Café, 344
Savoy Hotel, 364
Slippery Nipple, 377

Stars and Stripes, 386
Sweet Cream, 391

Sweet Independence, 392
Traffic Light, 407

Punches

Apple Ginger Punch, 91
Arawak Punch, 94
Artillery Punch, 94
Barbados Bowl, 102
Bellini Punch, 106
Black-Cherry Rum Punch, 110
Bloody Rum Punch, 116
Boston Rum Punch, 121
Brandy Milk Punch, 126
Breakfast Eggnog, 127
Champagne-Maraschino
    Punch, 140
Champagne Punch, 141
Champagne Sherbet
    Punch, 141
Claret Cup, 146
Cold Weather Punch, 151
Cranberry Pineapple Vodka
    Punch, 155
Cranberry-Vodka
    Punch, 156
Eggnog (standard), 174
Fish House Punch, 185
Florida Punch, 187

Gorilla Punch, 210
Interplanetary Punch, 235
Mountain Red Punch, 294
Pineapple-Cranberry Juice Punch
    (NA), 459
Pisco Punch, 329
Planter's Punch, 330
Polynesian Punch, 332
Rainbow Sherbet Punch
    (NA), 459
Raspberry Cranberry Punch
    (NA), 460
Rouffy Party Punch
    Cooler, 354
Sangria, 361
Sangria Especiale, 362
Sharky Punch, 372
Sherry Eggnog, 372
Tropical Fruit Punch
    (NA), 462
White Grape, Tangerine and
    Sparkling Wine Punch, 433
White Wine Super Sangria, 436
A Yard of Flannel, 443

Rickey

Gin Rickey, 203
Lime Rickey (NA), 456

Rum Rickey, 357
Whiskey Rickey, 431

Shandies

Ginger Shandies, 203

Shandy, 371

Shooters

After Eight, 81
After Five, 81
Alabama Slammer, 82
Anti-Freeze, 90
B-53, 98
Baby Ruth, 99
Beam Me Up, Scotty, 104
Blow Job, 116
Bubble Gum, 128
Buffalo Sweat, 128
Buttery Nipple, 130
Candy Bar, 136
Chocolate-Covered Cherry, 144
Deep Throat, 163
E.T., 177
Green Lizard, 215
Hawaiian Punch, 220
Hot Shots, 227
Indian Summer, 234
Jawbreaker, 244
Jell-O Shoots, 244
Jolly Rancher, 246
Kamikaze, 249
Lemon Drop, 262
Lion Tamer, 265
Meltdown, 284
Mexican Flag, 285
Mexican Missile, 285

Mission Accomplished, 288
Nutty Irishman, 302
Out of the Blue, 309
Pancho Villa, 312
Peanut Butter and Jelly, 317
Pineapple Bomber, 324
Pink Lemonade, 326
Prairie Fire, 335
Purple Haze, 339
Purple Hooter-Shooter,
    The 339
Rock Lobster (shooter), 352
Russian Quaalude, 359
Silk Panties, 373
Slimeball, 376
Snack Bite, 379
Snow Cap, 379
Snow Shoe, 379
S.O.B. Shooter, 380
Sour Grapes, 381
Surfer on Acid, 390
Teddy Bear, 395
Tequila Popper, 398
Tequila Shot, 399
Tidy Bowl, 403
T.K.O., 394
Wombat, 439
Woo Woo, 439

Sours

Aalborg Sour, 77
Amaretto Sour, 86
Apricot Sour, 93
Bourbon Sour, 122
Electric Kool Aid, 175
Frisco Sour, 192
Hollywood Tea, 222
Lynchbury Lemonade, 271
Mango Margarita, 275
Midori Sour, 286

Picon Sour, 322
Pisco Sour, 329
Purple People Eater, 340
Rum Sour, 357
Scotch Stone Sour, 367
Stone Sour, 386
Strega Sour, 389
Tequila Sour, 399
Weissen Sour, 428
Whiskey Sour, 431

INDEX OF LOW-CALORIE DRINKS

Abbey, 77
Addington, 79
Admiral Cocktail, 79
Adonis, 79
Americana, 87
Americano, 87
Andalusia, 88
April Shower, 93
B & B, 98
Bellini, 105
Blended Raspberry
    Cocktail, 113
Bloody Mary, 115
Bull Shot, 129
Campari and Soda, 136
Chablis Cooler, 139
Champagne Cocktail, 140
Coffee Drinks (if whipped
    cream is not used) See:
    Index by Ingredients
Cranberry Splash, 155
Cream Soda, 156
Dubonnet Cocktail, 170
Dubonnet Manhattan, 170
Frappes (provided that the
    liqueur used is under
    110 calories) See: Index
    by Type
French Summer, The 192
Gimlet, 200
Gin Rickey, 203

Good and Plenty, 209
Green Lizard (shooter), 215
Harbor Light, 218
Java Cooler, 243
Jelly Bean, 244
Kir, 254
Lemonade (modern), 262
Lion Tamer (shooter), 265
Manhattan (provided you use
    only 1½ oz. of liquor and
    no more than ½ oz.
    vermouth), 276
Martini (provided you use only
    1½ oz. of liquor and no
    more than ½ oz. of
    vermouth), 279
Mimosa, 287
Mint Julep, 288
Mojito Smoothie, 290
Picon, 321
Picon Orange, 322
Polo, 332
Port Sangaree, 334
Presbyterian, 336
Punt e Mes Negroni, 339
Rickey, 350
Rob Roy (provided you use only
    1½ oz. of liquor and no more
    than ½ oz. vermouth), 351
Scotch and Soda, 366
Shandy, 371

Sherry Cocktail, 372
Shooters (Most contain only 1½ oz. of liquid, so it is likely that the calorie count will be lower than a full cocktail or mixed drink.) See: Index by Type
Tequila Popper (shooter), 398
Tequila Sunset, 400

T.N.T., 405
Tropical Grapefruit Splash, 409
Turkey Shooter, 411
Virgin Mary (NA), 463
Whiskey and Water, 430
White Wine Spritzer, 436
Wine Cooler, 439
Xeres Cocktail, 441

GLOSSARY

Abisante a pale green, anise-flavored liqueur

Absinthe a redistilled alcohol containing wormwood

Advokaat an eggnog liqueur originally from Holland

Akvavit (aquavit) Scandinavian; made from rye with an infusion of caraway

Aperitif an alcoholic drink taken before a meal, or any of several wines and bitters, such as vermouth

Ale a beer similar to lager but with a more bitter taste

Amaretto an almond-flavored liqueur made from apricot pits; the original amaretto is Amaretto di Saronno, from Italy

Amer Picon a French aperitif, made from quinine, oranges and gentian

Anise; anisette licorice-flavored liqueur made from anise seeds

Apple brandy an apple liqueur, such as Calvados or applejack

Apricot liqueur a cordial made from apricot pits

Armagnac a high-quality brandy like cognac, but distilled only once and available in vintages

Banana liqueur (crème de banana) a sweet liqueur made from bananas

Beer an alcoholic beverage brewed from malted barley; flavored with hops after fermentation

Bénédictine an herb liqueur made from a secret formula by the Benedictine monks in France

Bitters a sweet to dry flavored drink made from aromatic plants, usually spirit-based; considered an aperitif

Blackberry liqueur a cordial made from blackberries

Blended whiskey a combination of different whiskeys that have been "married" in casks; more common than straight whiskey

Bourbon whiskey a brown liquor made from at least 51 percent corn and aged for at least two years in white oak casks

Brandy a single distillate or mixture of distillates obtained from wine or the fermented juice of fruit; some brandies have caramel added for color

Canadian whiskey a liquor made from corn, rye and barley; always blended and usually aged for six or more years in charred oak casks

Chambord a French liqueur made from small black raspberries

Chambraise a French liqueur made from wild strawberries

Chartreuse an herb-based cordial that comes in either yellow or green varieties; created by Carthusian monks in France in the early seventeenth century and made from a secret recipe

Chaser a mild drink, such as beer, taken after a hard liquor

Cherry Heering a Danish liqueur made from cherries

Cherry Marnier a French cherry liqueur with a hint of almond

Cocktail a chilled alcoholic drink made from a combination of liquors and flavoring ingredients; the term is used fairly broadly these days to describe most mixed drinks

Coffee liqueur a coffee-flavored drink

Cognac a fine brandy from the Cognac region of France

Cointreau a high-quality orange-flavored liqueur, made from the skins of curaçao oranges; the generic term is curaçao, which if redistilled clear is called triple sec

Collins a tall drink made with liquor (usually gin or vodka), sour mix and club soda; the Tom Collins, made with gin, is the most famous variety

Cooler a drink made with wine or another spirit and a carbonated mixer

Cordials sweetened spirits distilled from fruits, seeds, herbs and peels; the same as liqueurs

Cranberry liqueur a cranberry-flavored cordial

Cream of coconut a coconut syrup used in many exotic drinks, especially piña coladas

Crème liqueurs a group of liqueurs (cordials) with a high sugar content, resulting in a consistency similar to that of cream, e.g., crème de ananas (from pineapples), crème de cacao (dark or white—from cacao), crème de cassis (from black currants), crème de menthe (green or white—from mint) or crème de vanille (from vanilla beans)

Curaçao a delicate orange-flavored liqueur; comes in orange and blue

Drambuie a sweet liqueur with a Scotch malt whiskey base

Dubonnet a light, zesty aperitif from France

Falernum a fruity sweetener with a spicy, limey taste; available in liquor stores and specialty stores

Fix a sour drink, usually made with pineapple syrup and crushed ice

Fizz similar to a Collins, made with sour mix, sugar and club soda; sometimes an egg is used, as in the Ramos Fizz

Forbidden Fruit a drink of shaddock-infused brandy

Fortified wine a wine, such as port or sherry, with extra alcohol added to it

Fraises a strawberry liqueur with a high sugar content

Framboise a raspberry liqueur with a high alcohol content

Frangelico a hazelnut-flavored liqueur from Italy

Frappe a drink made by packing a glass with crushed ice and pouring the liqueur or liquor of your choice over it

Galliano (Liquore Galliano) a piquant golden Italian liqueur made from herbs and spices; most familiar as an ingredient of the Harvey Wallbanger

Garnish an ingredient used to decorate or top off a drink, such as fruit, olives or nutmeg

Gin a liquor distilled from juniper berries and other botanicals, such as herbs, seeds, berries and roots; English gin (the most common variety) is made from a base spirit of 75 percent corn, 15 percent barley malt and 10 percent other grains

Grand Marnier an orange-flavored, cognac-based liqueur from France

Grenadine a sweet red flavoring made from pomegranates

Highball a basic drink containing ice, 1½ to 2 ounces of liquor and 6 to 10 ounces of a mixer such as soda or juice

Irish cream liqueur a sweet, rich liqueur made from cream, Irish whiskey and sweetener; the original is Baileys Original Irish Cream

Irish Mist an Irish whiskey–based liqueur flavored with honey and orange

Irish whiskey a light-colored liquor made from malted and unmalted barley and heated in a kiln; the only whiskey that is distilled three times

Kahlúa a premium coffee-flavored liqueur from Mexico

Kirsch (kirschwasser) a liqueur distilled from black cherries

Kümmel a caraway-flavored brandy

Liqueur see Cordials

Liquor an alcoholic beverage most often distilled, rather than fermented

Lillet an aperitif wine from France; comes in red or white

Lowball (also called an old-fashioned) a type of drink served "on the rocks" in a rocks glass (also called an old-fashioned glass)

Malibu a coconut rum liqueur

Mandarine a tangerine-flavored, cognac-based liqueur

Maraschino technically a brandy, but usually considered a liqueur; cherry-and-almond flavored

Metaxa a sweetened Greek brandy

Midori a honeydew-flavored liqueur produced in Japan

Mixing glass part of the cocktail shaker set, used to mix drinks

Neat refers to any liquor (usually whiskey) served straight in a shot glass; can be taken with a chaser

"On the rocks" a term used to describe wine or spirits served over ice, usually in a rocks glass

Orgeat almond syrup

Ouzo an anise-flavored Greek aperitif

Parfait Amour a purple cordial made from citron

Passion fruit liqueur a liqueur from Hawaii, flavored with either peach or mango

Peach liqueur a brandy- or neutral spirit–based liqueur flavored with fresh and/or dried peaches

Pear liqueur a liqueur from pears, made in Hungary; one brand, Williams Pear Liqueur, has a whole pear in the bottle

Peanut Lolita a liqueur made from peanuts

Peppermint schnapps a light, minty liqueur

Pernod a licorice-flavored liqueur

Peter Heering a brand-name cherry liqueur from Denmark

Pineapple liqueur a liqueur made from pineapples, usually from Hawaii or the Caribbean

Pousse-Café a drink made by floating one ingredient on top of another in layers

Proof the alcoholic content of a spirit; determined in the United States by doubling the percentage of alcohol (an 80-proof liquor, for example, has a 40 percent alcohol content)

Punch a mixture of spirits, wines, flavorings, sweeteners and fruit, sometimes combined with carbonated beverages or other ingredients, usually made in a large bowl, but also in single-serving portions

Rickey a drink made with a spirit such as gin and lime juice, club soda and ice

Rock and Rye a liqueur made from rye whiskey and rock candy

Rum a liquor distilled from fermented sugar cane or molasses; lighter rums are distilled at a higher proof than darker rums; certain rums, especially Puerto Rican rums, are aged

Rye or American whiskey liquor made from at least 51 percent rye; aged in oak casks

Sabra an orange liqueur with a hint of chocolate; from Israel

Sambuca a well-known Italian licorice-flavored liqueur; often served with 3 coffee beans floating on top

Sangaree a chilled tall drink made using liquor, wine or beer; it is sweet and topped with nutmeg

Scotch whiskey a liquor made from grain and malt, distilled in copper coil stills and heated over peat; most scotch is blended, but many single-malt varieties are available; scotch sold in the United States must be aged for at least four years

Shooter whiskey or other spirit poured directly into the glass from the bottle; the term can also be used to describe a mixed drink that has been strained into a shot glass and is taken in one gulp

Slivovitz a brandy distilled from plums

Sloe gin a fruity liqueur made from sloe berries steeped in gin

Sour a tart drink served in a sour glass; made from a liquor or liqueur and sour mix (lemon, lime and sugar); whiskey sours are the best known

Sour mix (also called sweet and sour mix) a combination of lemon and lime juice and sugar; used in many mixed drinks, including sours, Collinses and fizzes; fresh juices can be used instead, or there are several commercial premixes on the market (see recipe for sour mix on p. 22)

Southern Comfort a high-proof liqueur made from bourbon, peach liqueur and fresh peaches

"Straight up" any spirit served chilled and without ice

Straight whiskey a whiskey made from one strain of barley malt

Strawberry liqueur a liqueur made from strawberries; imported versions are called Fraises or Fraise de Bois, which translates as "wild strawberries"

Strega a sweet Italian liqueur made from a variety of herbs and spices

Swedish Punsch a citrus-flavored liqueur with a rum base

Tequila a liquor distilled from the fermented sap of the mezcal plant; produced near the city of Tequila in Mexico; gold tequila is aged in oak casks for two to four years

Tia Maria a coffee-flavored liqueur from Jamaica

Toddy a mixture of sweetened spirits and hot water, usually with a lemon slice or peel and one or more spices; traditionally a hot drink, but there are also cold versions

Tonic a tall drink made with ice, spirits and tonic water

Tonic water a carbonated beverage flavored with quinine, lemon and lime

Triple sec an orange-flavored liqueur

Tuaca an Italian brandy-based liqueur with citrus flavors; sometimes called "milk brandy" since there is milk in it

Vandermint a Dutch chocolate-mint liqueur

Vermouth a dry or sweet aperitif wine, flavored with aromatic herbs

"Virgin" used to indicate mixed drinks made without alcohol (e.g., Virgin Piña Colada is made without rum)

Vodka a liquor distilled from a fermented mash of grain and distilled at high proof so it has little taste; it is not aged

Wild Turkey liqueur a bourbon-based liqueur that is lightly flavored with spices

Wine a beverage made from the fermented juice of grapes

Yukon Jack a Canadian whiskey–based liqueur, with citrus and herb flavors

Robyn M. Feller is a New York–based writer and editor. In her spare time she works as a professional mixologist. She is lots of fun at parties.

Laura Lifshitz is a blond, pint-sized, battery-operated tour de force of wit and neuroticism. A comedienne, writer, Columbia University graduate, and ex-MTV personality, Laura attended bartending school, but to her Jewish father's stern disapproval, never became the big, successful bartender he was dreaming she would be. He still harasses her for the money she spent on tuition. To read more of her rantings on drinks, sex, love, parenthood, and life, dash over to frommtvtomommy.com or follow her at facebook.com/lauralifshitzwriter and twitter.com/LauraLifshitz. She likes to make friends with strangers.